Coast & Mountains BC

Image © allcanadaphotos.com (Grouse Mountain)

Backroad Mapbooks

"The maps present a potpourri of helpful information for hunters, fishers, hikers - even Sunday drivers - essentially anyone who takes advantage of Canada's outdoor pastimes."

~ GeoBase Canada

"The Backroad Mapbooks document virtually all corners of B.C. and beyond, covering off on trails, lakes, logging roads and recreational sites, among other things."

~ Coquitlam Now

"I find them extraordinarily useful in navigating my way to finding my way around the backroads during our fly fishing expeditions."

~ Ralph Weller – Fishing Guide

www.backroadmapbooks.com

British Columbia
Total Area... 944 735 km²
Population...4 113 487
Capital...Victoria
Largest City...Vancouver
Highest Point...Mount Fairweather
4 663 meters (15 299 ft)
Tourism info...1.800.HELLO.BC
www.hellobc.com

I

Acknowledgements

Published by:

Backroad Mapbooks

Mussio Ventures Ltd.
#106- 1500 Hartley Ave,
Coquitlam, BC, V3K 7A1
Toll Free: 1-877-520-5670
E-mail: info@backroadmapbooks.com
www.backroadmapbooks.com

Backroad Mapbooks

DIRECTORS
Russell Mussio
Wesley Mussio
Penny Stainton-Mussio

ASSOCIATE DIRECTOR
Jason Marleau

VICE PRESIDENT
Chris Taylor

COVER DESIGN & LAYOUT
Farnaz Faghihi

COVER PHOTO
Allcanadaphotos.com
(Grouse Mountain)

CREATIVE CONTENT
Russell Mussio
Wesley Mussio

PROJECT MANAGER
Andrew Allen

PRODUCTION
Shaun Filipenko, Justin Quesnel,
Dale Tober, Jonathan Wang

SALES / MARKETING
Joshua Desnoyers
Chris Taylor

WRITER
Trent Ernst

Library and Archives Canada Cataloguing in Publication

Ernst, Trent
Vancouver, coast & mountains BC backroad mapbook [cartographic material] : outdoor recreation guide / [writer, Trent Ernst]. -- 2nd ed.

(Backroad mapbooks)
Cover title.
Includes index.
ISBN 978-1-897225-66-0

1. Recreation areas--British Columbia--Lower Mainland--Maps. 2. Recreation areas--British Columbia--Squamish-Lillooet--Maps. 3. Recreation areas--British Columbia--Fraser Valley--Maps. 4. Outdoor recreation--British Columbia--Lower Mainland--Guidebooks. 5. Outdoor recreation--British Columbia--Squamish-Lillooet- -Guidebooks. 6. Outdoor recreation--British Columbia--Fraser Valley--Guidebooks. 7. Lower Mainland (B.C.)--Maps. 8. Squamish-Lillooet (B.C.)--Maps. 9. Fraser Valley (B.C.)--Maps. 10. Lower Mainland (B.C.)--Guidebooks. 11. Squamish-Lillooet (B.C.)--Guidebooks. 12. Fraser Valley (B.C.)--Guidebooks. I. Title. II. Title: Vancouver, coast and mountains BC backroad mapbook. III. Series: Backroad mapbooks

G1172.S68E63E76 2010   796.509711'3   C2009-907489-3

Acknowledgement

This book could not have been compiled without the relentless effort of Trent Ernst. He headed the research and writing effort and did a fabulous job of digging up new recreational opportunities and describing them in a creative, yet appealing way. As his life gets busier, his wife, Colette, has started to help him with his research. Combined with the talented people at Mussio Ventures Ltd., Andrew Allen, Joshua Desnoyers, Farnaz Faghihi, Shaun Filipenko, Justin Quesnet, Chris Taylor, Dale Tober and Jonathan Wang we were able to produce the most comprehensive guidebook for a truly spectacular region of British Columbia.

Books like this are an exercise in research, not only by us, but by the many people who we can turn to for answers and information. Some are paid to know what they know (recreation officers, forest rangers, etc.), some, like us, are just passionate about the outdoors, and have spent their lives learning all they can about their neck of the woods. Some of the people whose knowledge we leaned upon for this update were:

To all the folks at Clubtread.com who offered corrections, comments and kind words, thank you.

Sea to Sky trail chairman Gordon McKeever answered our questions about the Sea to Sky trail, but he and the committee deserve commendations for picking up on the earlier ground-work on this stunning multi-day trail. Now if they could just extend it north to Bella Coola…

There were a number of people in various government offices who fielded questions from us, mostly about the state of Recreation Sites. Some of these included Teresa McMillen, Barry Miller and Edle Abels; Martin Holloway with BC Parks, and Debra Sneddon and Bill Shaw at the DFO for updates on fishing. We hassled many other people for answers to questions about which recreation sites, which trails and which parks are currently open, and which ones are closed, knowing that by next year, everything may change.

Thanks to Ray at Totally Awesome Adventures who helped us with snowmobiling info in the Sea to Sky area, Claudia Schwab at the Vancouver Kayak Club (who just published her own book, Whitewater in Southwest British Columbia) for feedback on paddling, Cam Kenny, Allison Macdonald at the Squamish Lillooet Regional District, and least we forget Murphy Shewchuk and his helpful Backroad articles and books. Check out Sonotek.com for more information.

These maps are a synthesis of a variety of sources, mostly Federal, Provincial and Municipal Government. We would like to express our gratitude to the helpful map providers GeoBase©, Canfor, Natural Resources Canada, Statistics Canada and BC's Ministry of Water, Land and Air Protection.

Finally we would like to thank Allison, Devon, Jasper, Madison, Nancy and Penny Mussio for their continued support of the Backroad Mapbook Series. As our family grows, it is becoming more and more challenging to break away from it all to explore our beautiful country.

Sincerely,

Russell and Wesley Mussio

Disclaimer

Mussio Ventures Ltd. does not warrant that the backroads, paddling routes and trails indicated in this Mapbook are passable nor does it claim that the Mapbook is completely accurate. Therefore, please be careful when using this or any source to plan and carry out your outdoor recreation activity.

Please note that traveling on logging roads, river routes and trails is inherently dangerous, and without limiting the generality of the foregoing, you may encounter poor road conditions, unexpected traffic, poor visibility, and low or no road/trail maintenance. Please use extreme caution when traveling logging roads and trails.

Please refer to the Fishing and Hunting Regulations for closures and restrictions. It is your responsibility to know when and where closures and restrictions apply.

Help Us Help You

A comprehensive resource such as Backroad Mapbooks for Vancouver, Coast & Mountains BC could not be put together without a great deal of help and support. Despite our best efforts to ensure that everything is accurate, errors do occur. If you see any errors or omissions, please continue to let us know.

All updates will be posted on our web site: www.backroadmapbooks.com

Please contact us at:
Mussio Ventures Ltd.
 #106- 1500 Hartley Ave,
Coquitlam, BC, V3K 7A1

Email: updates@backroadmapbooks.com
P: 604-521-6277 F: 604-521-6260
Toll Free 1-877-520-5670
www.backroadmapbooks.com

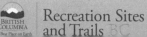

Vancouver, Coast & Mountains BC

Welcome to the second edition of the Vancouver, Coast and Mountains Backroad Mapbook. With this latest release our flagship Southwestern BC edition—just in time for the 2010 Olympics—we have made many small tweaks and a few bold changes to better meet the needs of outdoor adventurers exploring this expanding, dynamic area for both locals and visitors alike.

This book covers the southwest corner of beautiful British Columbia, Canada. Vancouver, Gibsons and Powell River frame the western edge of the area, while Hope, Manning Park, Boston Bar and Lillooet make up the eastern edge. Chilliwack, Maple Ridge, Squamish, Whistler and Gold Bridge are just a few of the prominent cities or towns. This dramatic area is highlighted by lush rainforests, spectacular coastal inlets and rivers surrounded by snow-capped mountains, with deep, dark lakes in the west. In areas closer to the coast, rugged mountains that literally rise out of the ocean floor dominate the area. Its natural beauty is second to none, a verdant landscape of looming mountains, wild rivers and fertile valleys. As you make your way inland, forests and eventually rangeland replace the coastal rainforest.

The Vancouver, Coast and Mountains region is an outdoor recreation paradise that will rival any recreational playground in the country. No matter the season, the breadth and variety of opportunities is amazing. It is an area where you can go ocean kayaking and alpine skiing in the same day. Anglers are just as active in the winter looking for steelhead as they are in the summer and fall chasing salmon. Trail enthusiasts can explore some amazing opportunities on foot, bike, ski or snowshoe, while kayakers can have as much fun on the wild rivers as they will exploring the endless coast. Of course, these are just a few examples of the many, many things to see and do in Southwestern BC.

The most obvious change for this new edition is the maps. In addition to the countless roads, trails and recreational additions, the new colouring is certainly creating a buzz among readers. We have taken this to new lengths to help define motorized and long distance trails, better classified the highways and paved roads and added a few more themes to aid the user.

The writing has also been expanded and updated. With the press towards the Olympics in 2010, many trails have been improved, expanded and otherwise changed. And we've added in a new section on hunting and expanded our backroads section to include popular attractions that don't easily fit into any of our other sections but are well worth a visit.

The Backroad Mapbook is much more than a set of maps; it is an explorer's guide and an armchair adventurer's delight. The maps and writing will let the latter dream of places not so far away and will allow the former to navigate to some of the most (and least) popular places in Southwestern BC. So sit back and enjoy what this guide has to offer.

History

The Backroad Mapbook idea came into existence when Wesley and Russell Mussio were out exploring. They had several books and a few maps to try to find their way through the maze of logging roads around southern BC. The brothers were getting very frustrated trying to find their way and eventually gave up. Not to be outdone, the two ambitious brothers started brainstorming. Eventually the Backroad Mapbook idea was born.

They published their first book in January 1994 and it quickly sold out. Rather than simply reprinting it, they listened to the feedback of customers and made several alterations that helped improve the book. This formula of continuing to make the product better continues today and has helped establish the Backroad Mapbook series as the top selling outdoor recreation guidebook series in the country. From the tiny beginnings in that Vancouver apartment with maps strewn all over the walls, to one of the most sought after outdoor products in the country, the Backroad Mapbook series has truly come a long way.

Russell & Wesley Mussio -
Founders of Backroad Mapbooks

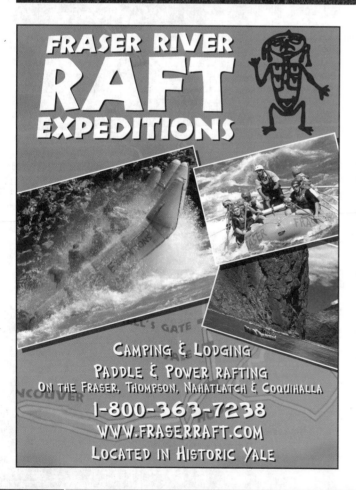
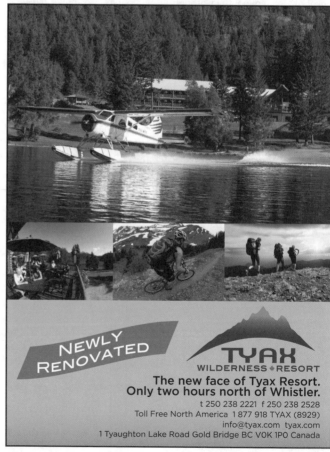

GET ANSWERS TO YOUR TRAVEL QUESTIONS!

- ❖ What to see
- ❖ What to do
- ❖ How to get there
- ❖ Transportation
- ❖ Accommodations
- ❖ Tours
- ❖ Attractions
- ❖ Special Events
- ❖ ...and more

BRITISH COLUMBIA
The Best Place on Earth

Abbotsford

Nestled in the shadow of majestic Mt. Baker, in the heart of the Fraser Valley, you will find Abbotsford, British Columbia, Canada. Visiting Abbotsford introduces you to an eclectic blend of modern urban style and friendly country living.
(Year Round)

Tourism Abbotsford
34561 Delair Rd
Abbotsford, BC, V2S 2E1
604-859-1701 Phone
888-332-2229 Toll-free

www.tourismabbotsford.ca

See Map 3

Chilliwack

Chilliwack is "The Great Outside". Pick up a copy of the Chilliwack Hiking Trails brochure. Features 26 hikes in the area. Great Fishing and Camping.

(Year Round)

Tourism Chilliwack
44150 Luckakuck Way
Chilliwack, BC, V2R 4A7
604-858-8121 Phone
800-567-9535 Toll-free

www.thegreatoutside.com

See Map 4

Delta

Delta is a gateway to the dynamic Vancouver area, by highway, ferry and air.
Your destination for eco-tourism: River Kayaking & Boat Tours, Millenium Trail , Watershed Park, Burns Bog, Reifel Bird Sanctuary & Boundary Bay.
(Year Round)

Delta Visitor Centre
6201 60th Ave
Delta, BC, V4K 4E2
604-946-4232 Phone
tourism@deltachamber.com

www.deltachamber.com

See Map 3

Hope

Experience Hope- Pick up your free 56 page Hope Visitor Guide & the Hope Trails brochure plus fishing, camping, rock hounding & gold panning information.

(Year Round)

Hope Visitor Centre & Museum Complex
919 Water Ave, Hope, BC, V0X 1L0
604-869-2021 Phone
866-HOPEVIC Toll-free

www.hope.ca or www.hopebc.ca

See Map 15

Maple Ridge - Pitt Meadows

The twin summits of Golden Ears Mountain rise majestically above Maple Ridge & Pitt Meadows, inviting you to explore our extraordinary combination of parks, trails, lakes, golf courses and cultural events. Just 40km east of Vancouver.
(Year Round)

Maple Ridge- Pitt Meadows Visitor Centre
12492 Harris Rd, Pitt Meadows, BC, V3Y 2J4
604-460-8300 Phone
877-465-8300 Toll-free

www.mapleridge-pittmeadows.com

See Map 2

Peace Arch

Courteous, knowledgeable staff provide detailed itinerary planning, accommodation reservations, transportation and attraction tickets and unique mementoes. A currency exchange is on site.

(Year Round)

British Columbia Visitor Centre
356 Hwy 99
Surrey, BC, V3S 9N7
1-800 HELLO BC ® Toll-free

www.hellobc.com

See Map 2

GET ANSWERS TO YOUR TRAVEL QUESTIONS!

- ❖ What to see
- ❖ What to do
- ❖ How to get there
- ❖ Transportation
- ❖ Accommodations
- ❖ Tours
- ❖ Attractions
- ❖ Special Events
- ❖ ...and more

Pemberton

Summer activities, golf, fishing, cycling, 2 Provincial Parks, winter sports, water sports, horseback riding, historic Museum, BMX & Stock Car Tracks, Airport

(Seasonal: May to September)

Pemberton Visitor Centre
Hwy 99 & Portage Rd
Pemberton, BC, V0N 2L0
604-894-6175 Phone
www.tourismpembertonbc.com

www.pembertonchamber.com

See Map 30

Powel River

Sunshine Coast adventures await: Hike the Sunshine Coast Trail, Paddle the Powell Forest Canoe Route or explore back country roads. Camp & fish all year.

(Year Round)

Powell River Visitor Centre
#111- 4871 Joyce Ave
Powel River, BC, V8A 5P4
604-485-4701 Phone
877-817-8669 Toll-free

www.discoverpowellriver.com

See Map 18

Squamish

Visit our Provincial Parks & explore our extensive trail system. Hike, bike, climb, windsurf or kite board. Visit the West Coast Railway Heritage Park & the BC Museum of Mining.

(Year Round)

Squamish Visitor Centre
#102- 38551 Loggers Ln
Squamish, BC, V8B 0H2
604-815-4994 Phone
866-333-2010 Toll-free

www.squamishchamber.com

See Map 22

Whistler

Located in the spectacular Coast Mountains of British Columbia, Whistler is Canada's premier, year-round destination for adventure.

(Year Round)

Whistler Visitor Centre
4230 Gateway Dr
Whistler, BC, V0N 1B4
604-935-3357 Phone
877-991-9988 Toll-free

www.whistler.com

See Map 29

YVR

Courteous, knowledgeable staff provide detailed itinerary planning, accommodation reservations, transportation and attraction tickets at visitor centres located in domestic and international arrivals areas.

(Year Round)

British Columbia Visitor Centre
3211 Grant McConachie Way
Richmond, BC, V7B 1Y2
1-800 HELLO BC ® Toll-free

www.hellobc.com

See Map 1

BRITISH COLUMBIA
The Best Place on Earth

Image © Karl-Heins Kern (Duffey Lake)

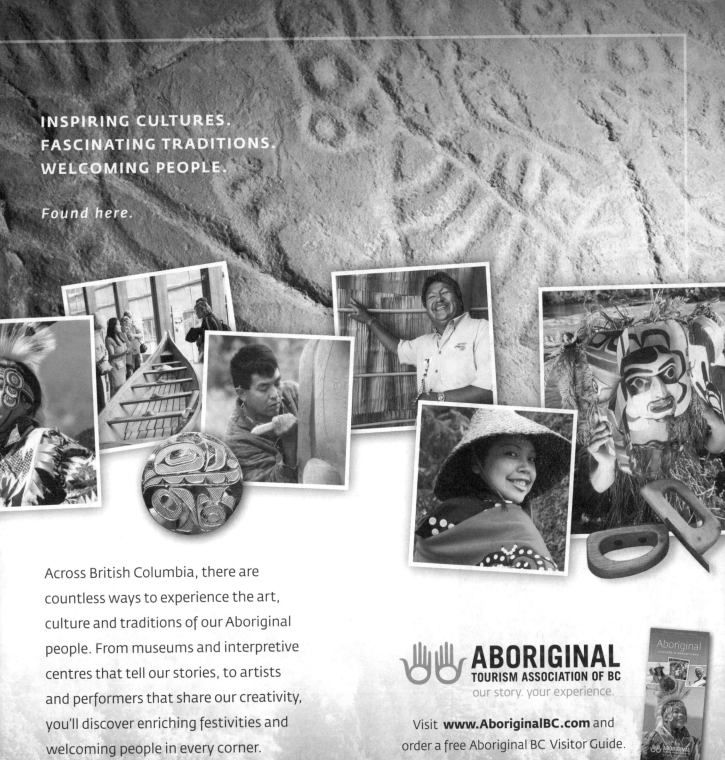

INSPIRING CULTURES.
FASCINATING TRADITIONS.
WELCOMING PEOPLE.

Found here.

Across British Columbia, there are countless ways to experience the art, culture and traditions of our Aboriginal people. From museums and interpretive centres that tell our stories, to artists and performers that share our creativity, you'll discover enriching festivities and welcoming people in every corner.

ABORIGINAL
TOURISM ASSOCIATION OF BC
our story. your experience.

Visit **www.AboriginalBC.com** and order a free Aboriginal BC Visitor Guide.

Legend

CANADA

Scale Bar

Scale 1:150 000 1 Centimetre = 1.5 Kilometres

1.5km   0km   3km   7.5km

Map Information

Map Projection:
Universal Transverse Mercator Zone 10

Map Datum:
North American Datum 1983 (NAD 83)

Elevation Bar:

over 2000m
1750m-2000m
1500-1750m
1250-1500m
1000-1250m
750-1000m
500-750m
250-500m
0-250m

Area Indicators:

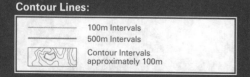

Provincial / National Park   City

Conservation / Natural Area   First Nations

Swamps   Glaciers

Water   Restricted Area

Contour Lines:

100m Intervals
500m Intervals
Contour Intervals approximately 100m

Line and Area Classifications:

Freeways	Trans Canada Trail
Highways	Long Distance Trail
Secondary Highways	Duo Sport Trails
Arterial Paved Roads	Snowmobile Trails
Rural Paved Roads	ATV Trails
Local Paved Roads	Developed Trail
Forest Service / Main Industry Roads	Routes (Undeveloped Trails)
Active Industry Roads (2wd)	Ferry Routes
Other Industry Roads (2wd / 4wd)	Lake / River Paddling Routes
Unclassified / 4wd Roads	Powerlines
Deactivated Roads	Pipelines
Railways	TFL - Tree Farm Licence A
WMU - Wildlife Management Zones	

Recreational Activities:

Anchorage	Hang-gliding
Boat Launch	Hiking
Beach	Horseback Riding
Campsite / Limited Facilities	Motorbiking / ATV
RV Campsite / Trailer Park	Paddling (canoe-kayak)
Campsite (back country / water access only)	Picnic Site
Canoe Access Put-in / Take-out	Portage
Cross Country Skiing / Back Country Ski Touring	Resort
Cycling	Rock Climbing
Diving	Snowmobiling
Downhill Skiing	Snowshoeing
Golf Course	Wildlife Viewing
	Windsurfing

Miscellaneous:

Airport / Airstrip	Marsh
Arrow / Location Pointer	Microwave Tower
BC Ferries	Mine Site (abandoned)
Beacon	Parking
Cabin / Chalet / Hut /	Pictograph
City, Town, Village Indicator	Point of Interest
Customs	Portage Distance
Deakin Equipment	Ranger Station
Ferries	Travel Information
Float Plane Landing	Valhalla Pure Outfitters
Gate	Viewpoint / Forestry Lookout (abandoned)
Highway: Trans Canada	Visitor Centre
Highway: Primary	Waterfalls
Highway Interchange	Wilderness Area / Wildlife Area / Wildlife Reserve
Lighthouse	Winery
Long Distance Trail	

Map Features

Recreational Features

You will find the maps mark points of interest, paddling routes, parks and conservation areas, trail systems and even wildlife viewing opportunities. **ATV, snowmobile trails** and **long distance trails** are highlighted with a background colour to aid users in tracking these systems. Hunters and anglers will also be happy to see that we have included the **Management Units** on the maps. The big green number notes the zones while the boundaries are marked with a faint green border. For a complete list of symbols and what they mean please refer to our Map Legend.

Road Features & Map Legend

By combining city and rural roads with current forestry and logging road maps our maps are designed for people wishing to get outdoors. However, they are very detailed and the myriad of current logging and industrial roads in addition to the various trail systems can be confusing. We provide a **map legend** at the start of each section of the maps to illustrate the region we cover as well as how to decipher the various grades of roads and symbols used on the maps.

Below are some more common features of our maps:

Roads & Trails

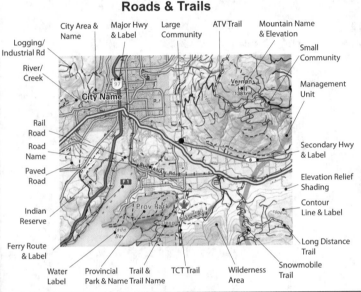

Recreational & Misc

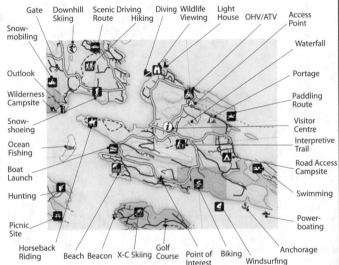

UTM Grid & Longitude and Latitude

A useful navigational feature on our maps is the small numbers provided around our map borders. These blue numbers represent UTM Grids and the black numbers represent Longitude and Latitude reference points. Although most GPS units are set to longitude and latitude, switching the unit to UTM (NAD 83) is both easier and more accurate for land-based travel. Since our maps provide UTM grid lines that are 10,000 metres apart (both east & north), users can accurately pinpoint the location of features by dividing the grid into 10 equal parts (both east & north). Counting the number of tics from the nearest coordinate value and multiplying by 1,000 will give you the UTM coordinate. Do this for both the Easting (the numbers along the top and bottom of the map border) and the Northing (the numbers along the side) and you will have an accurate GPS waypoint.

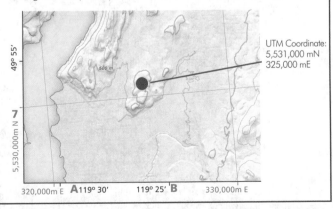

UTM Coordinate:
5,531,000 mN
325,000 mE

How to use the Scale Bar

To use the scale bar provided for each map, you can do one of the following things:

1) Use a piece of paper & mark the distance intervals from the scale bar. Then put that piece of paper on the map and measure the distance between two points. In example below the distance between "Adventure" & "Discovery" is 2 units or 3 kilometres.

2) Measure your distance with a piece of string, then place the string on the scale bar to find out the kilometres.

3) You can draw the approximate unit lines on the map itself (the green bars below) and then estimate the distance.

Note that all measurements are approximate.

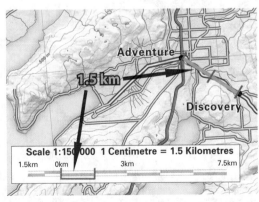

Scale 1:150,000 1 Centimetre = 1.5 Kilometres

1.5km   0km   3km   7.5km

Image © allcanadaphotos.com

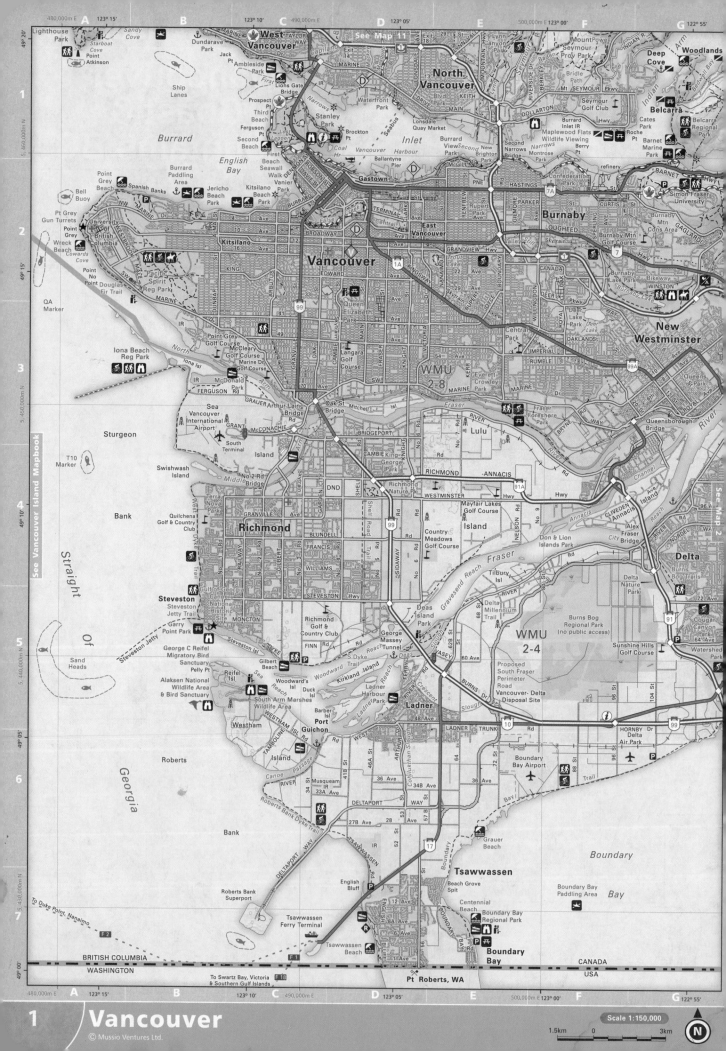

Vancouver

© Mussio Ventures Ltd.

Scale 1:150,000

1.5km   0   3km

1

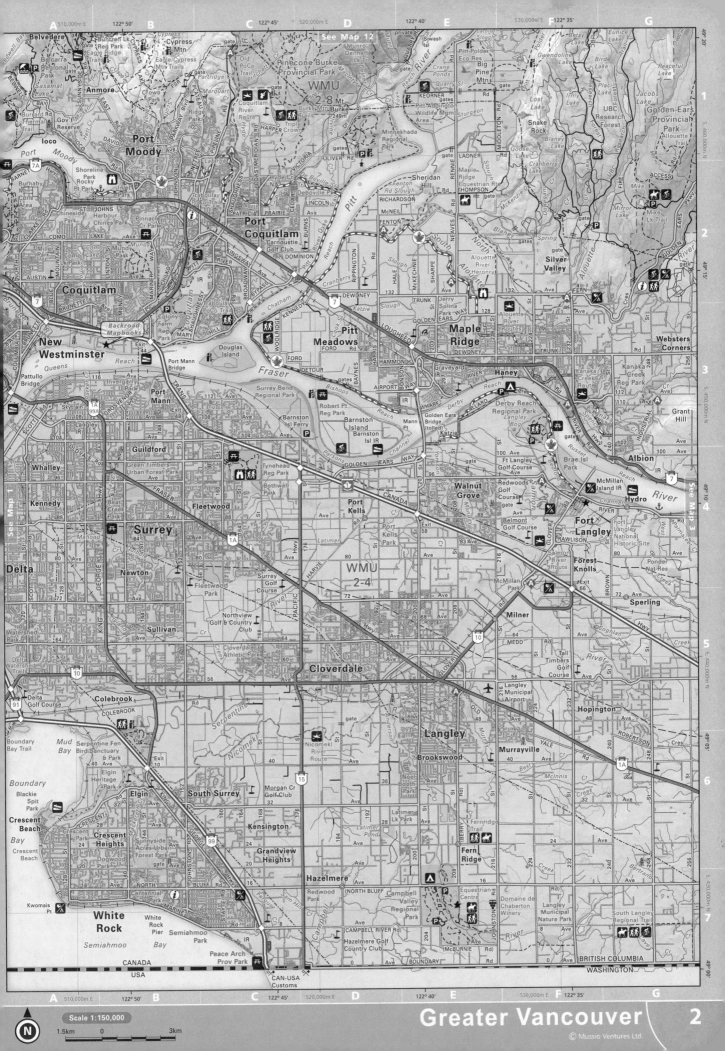

Scale 1:150,000

1.5km   0   3km

© Mussio Ventures Ltd.

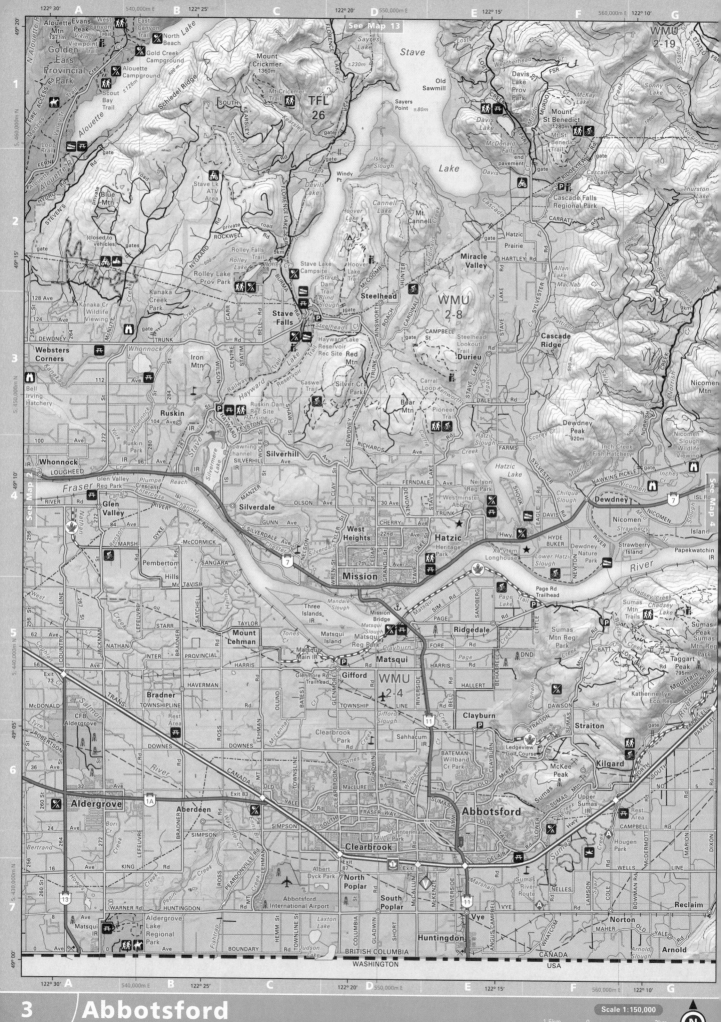

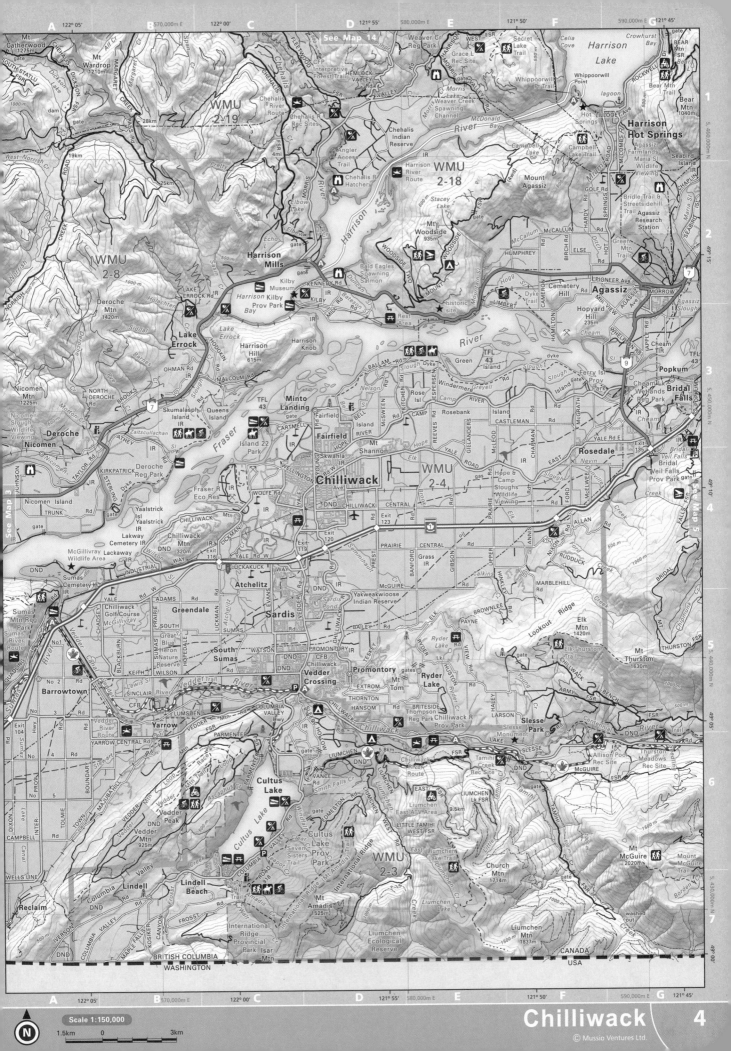

Chilliwack Lake

Scale 1:150,000

1.5km   0   3km

5

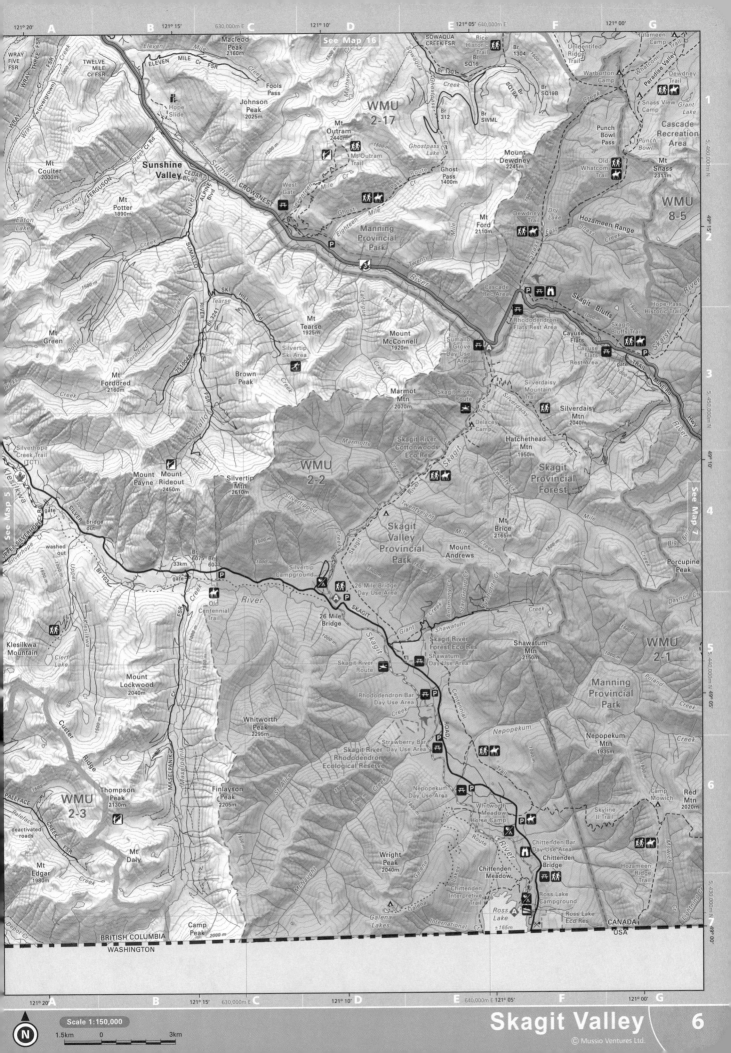

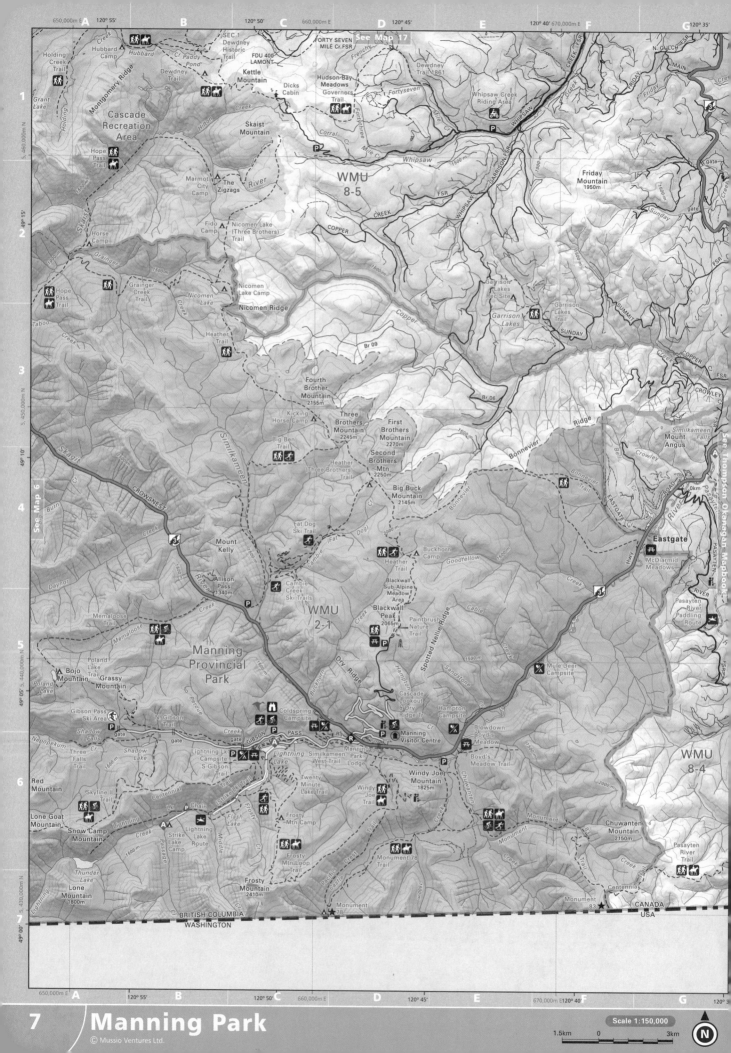

© Mussio Ventures Ltd.

Scale 1:150,000

1.5km 0 3km

N

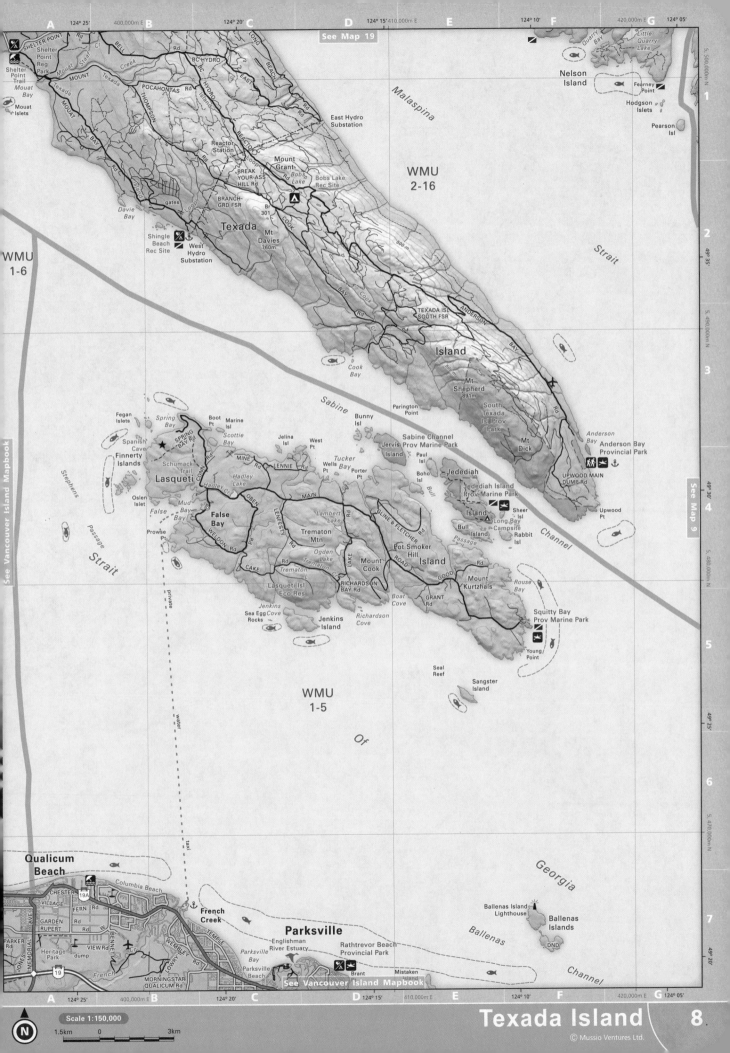

WMU
2-16

WMU
1-6

WMU
1-5

Texada

Island

Malaspina

Strait

Sabine

Channel

Strait

Of

Georgia

Channel

Lasqueti

Island

Nelson
Island

Little
Quarry
Lake

Quarry
Bay

Fearney
Point

Hodgson
Islets

Pearson
Isl

Shelter Point
Trail

SHELTER POINT

Shelter
Point Reg
Park

Mouat
Bay

Mouat
Islets

BELL

Cr

Rd

Rd

MOUAT

BAY

THOMPSON

POCAHONTAS

Rd

MOUNT

Texada

Staaf

Cr

BC HYDRO

Rd

BC
HYDRO

LONG

BEACH

EAST

Rd

Rd

Rd

East Hydro
Substation

Reactor
Station

REACTOR

Rd

LOOP

Mount
Grant

Bobs
Lake

Bobs Lake
Rec Site

BREAK
YOUR ASS
HILL Rd

BRANCH
GRD FSR

Br
301

COOK

Mt
Davies
760m

Davie Bay

gates

Texada

Island

Rd

Rd

Shingle
Beach
Rec Site

West
Hydro
Substation

BAY

Cook

Rd

Cr

Rd

500 m

TEXADA ISL
SOUTH FSR

ANDERSON

BAY

Cook Bay

Island

Mt
Shepherd
891m

South
Texada
Isl Prov
Park

Parington
Point

Rd

Anderson
Bay

Anderson Bay
Provincial Park

Mt
Dick

UPWOOD MAIN
DUMP Rd

Upwood
Pt

See Map 9

See Vancouver Island Mapbook

Fegan
Islets

Spring
Bay

Boot
Pt

Marine
Pt

Scottie
Bay

Jelina
Isl

West
Pt

Bunny
Isl

Sabine Channel
Jervis Prov Marine Park

Spanish
Cave

Finnerty
Islands

SPRING

BAY

Rd

MINE

Rd

Schumack
Trail

Hadley
Lake

LENNIE

Rd

Tucker
Bay

Wells
Pt

Porter
Pt

Jervis
Island

Paul Isl

Boho
Isl

Bull

Jedediah

Jedediah Island
Prov Marine Park

Island

Sheer
Isl

Long Bay
Campsite

Rabbit
Isl

Oslen
Islet

Stephens

Lasqueti

CONN

Hadley Cr

OBEN

MAIN

Lambert
Lake

Rd

Bull
Island

Passage

Bull
Passage

Mud
Bay

False
Bay

False
Bay

LENFESTY

WELDON Rd

Rd

Trematon
Mtn

Ogden
Lake

Trematon Cr

LAKE

Rd

GLINE & FLETCHER

Pot Smoker
Hill

ROAD

Island

Mount
Kurtzhals

Rouse
Bay

Prowse
Pt

Passage

Pt

CAKE

Rd

Trematon

Lasqueti Isl
Eco Res

RICHARDSON
BAY Rd

Mount
Cook

Boat
Cove

GOOD

GRANT
Rd

Rd

Squitty Bay
Prov Marine Park

Young
Point

Jenkins
Sea Egg Cove
Rocks

Jenkins
Island

Richardson
Cove

Seal
Reef

Sangster
Island

WMU
1-5

See Vancouver Island Mapbook

water

private

taxi

Qualicum
Beach

Columbia Beach

JONES

PARKER
Rd

MEMORIAL
AVE

Heritage
Park

CHESTER

VILLAGE

FERN
Rd

GARDEN

RUPERT

VIEW Rd

BENNETT

W

dump

French

Cr

MORNINGSTAR
QUALICUM Rd

WEMBLEY

LOWRY

TEMPLE

French
Creek

Parksville

Englishman
River Estuary

Parksville
Bay

Parksville
Beach

Brant

Rathtrevor Beach
Provincial Park

Mistaken
Island

Ballenas

Ballenas Island
Lighthouse

Ballenas
Islands

DND

See Vancouver Island Mapbook

19A

19

N

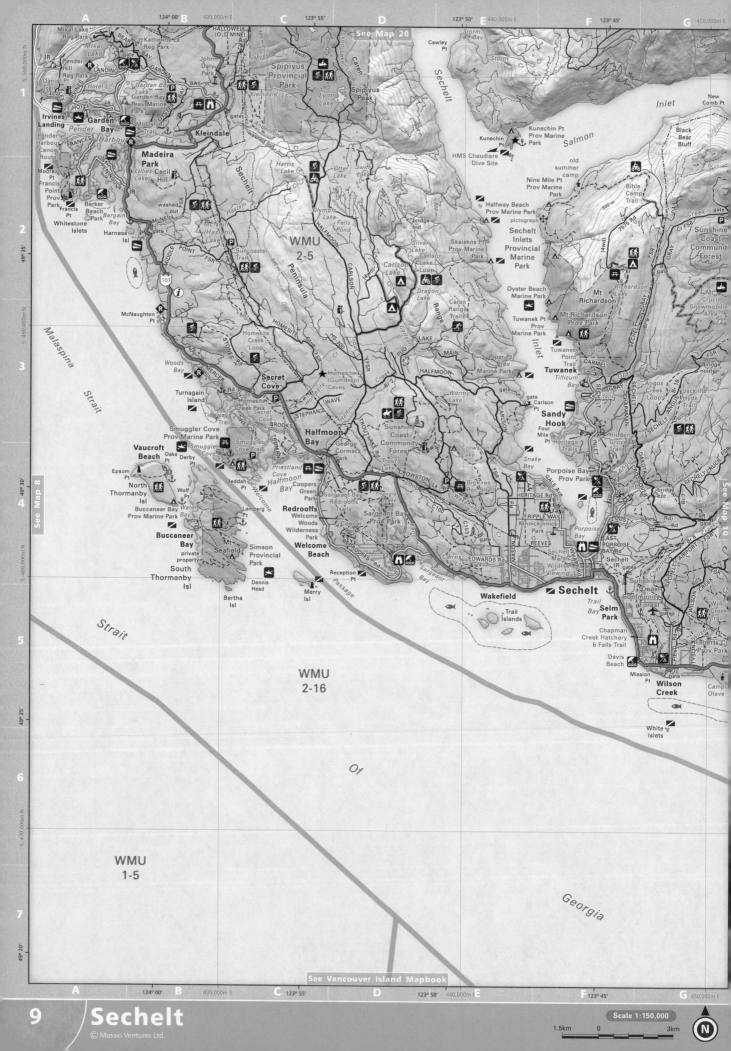

Scale 1:150,000

1.5km   0   3km

N

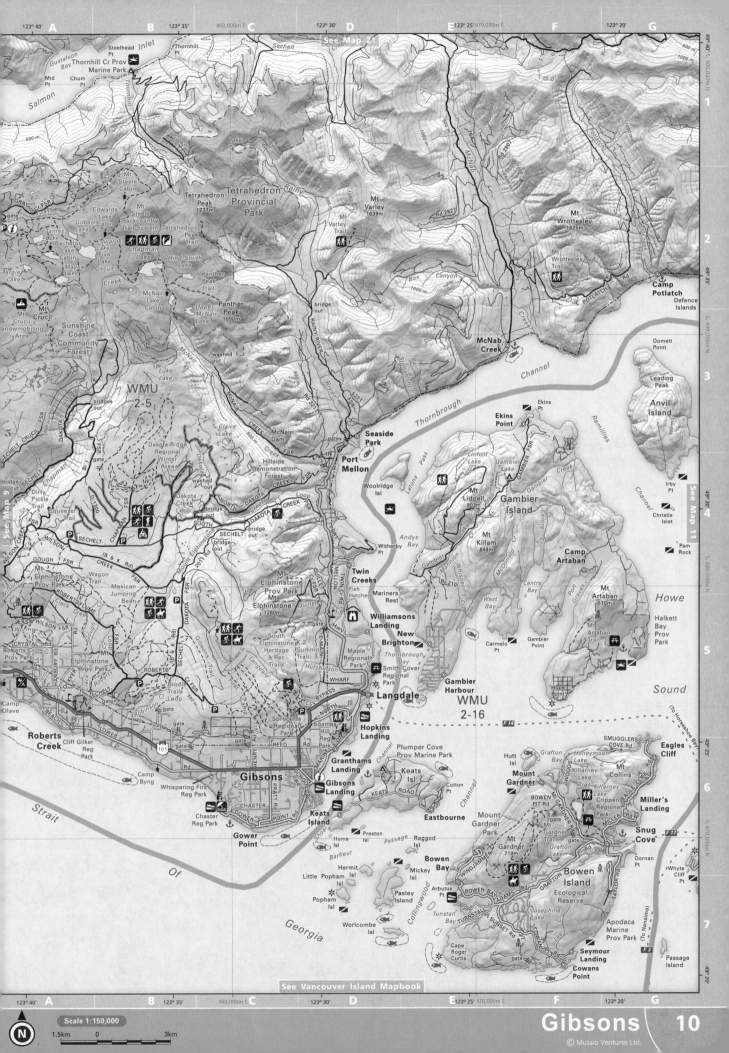

Gibsons

Scale 1:150,000

1.5km 0 3km

N

© Mussio Ventures Ltd.

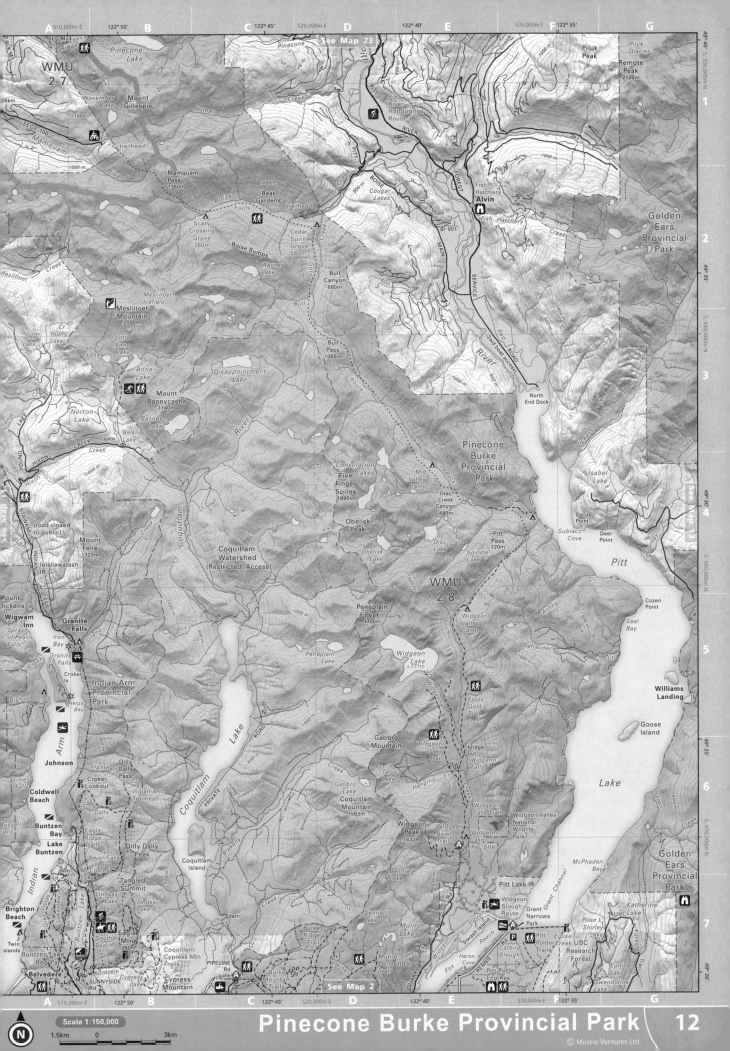

Pinecone Burke Provincial Park

Scale 1:150,000

1.5km 0 3km

© Mussio Ventures Ltd.

13 / Stave Lake

Scale 1:150,000

1.5km 0 3km

© Mussio Ventures Ltd.

Harrison Lake

14

Scale 1:150,000

1.5km   0   3km

N

© Mussio Ventures Ltd

Scale 1:150,000

1.5km   0   3km

N

Scale 1:150,000

1.5km 0 3km

N

Manning

Mount Spearing

Boulder Mountain

HBC Hope Bridge Trail 1849-1862

Otter Lake Prov Park

Mount Rabbitt

Mount Riddell

Tulameen Trail (TCT)

Coquihalla Lakes Snowmobile Trails

Murphy Lakes

Murphy Lakes West Rec Site

Grasshopper Mtn 1486m

Mount Britton

Olivine Mountain 1798m

Tulameen River Route

Mount Jackson

Hamilton Hill

Coalmont

Kettle Valley (TCT) Railway

Granite Creek Rec Site

Lodestone Snowmobile Trails

Lodestone Tanglewood Hill

China Ridge Ski Trails

WEST CHINA

Lodestone Lake Rec Site

Blakeburn

Tulameen River Route

Lodestone Mtn 1895m

NEWTON BLAKEBURN FSR

WMU 8-5

Dear Mtn 1951m

HBC Brigade Trail 1849-1862

Lodestone Snowmobile Trails

Dalby Meadows

One Mile IR

WMU 8-6

Wells Lake Rec Site

Whipsaw Cr Ecological Reserve

Dewdney Trail 1861

Whipsaw Creek Riding Area

Granite Mountain

Salt Lick Camp

Tulameen Camp

Cascade Recreation Area

Holding Creek Trail

Hubbard Camp

Dewdney Trail 1861

Mount Kennedy

Kennedy Lake

NORTH GULCH FSR

Princeto

© Mussin Ventures Ltd.

Scale 1:150,000

1.5km   0   3km

N

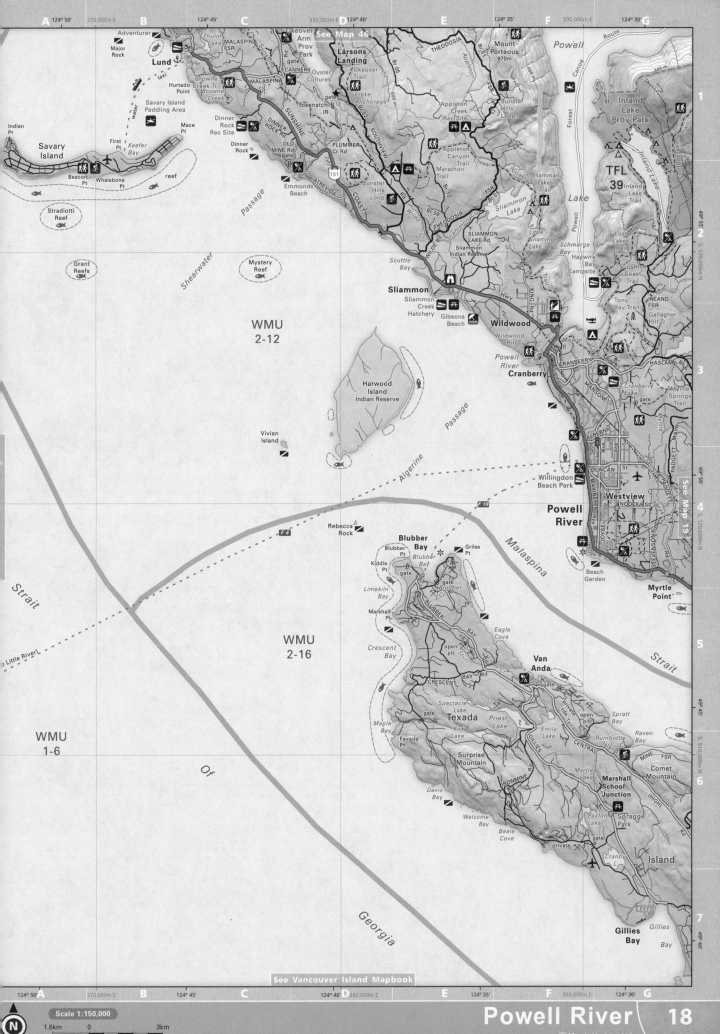

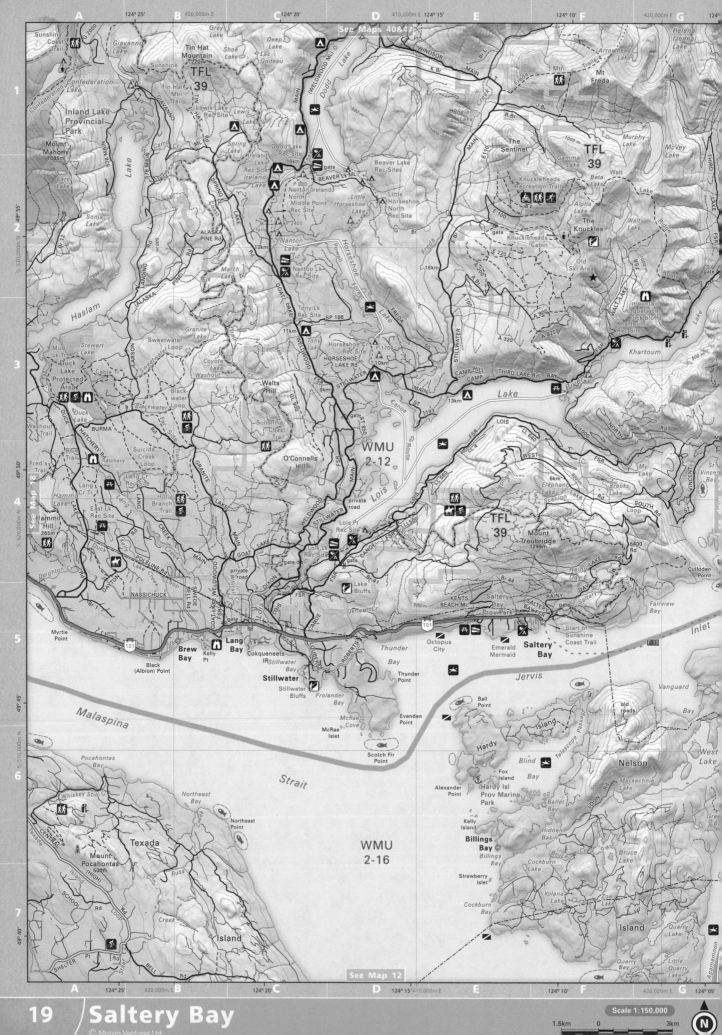

Scale 1:150,000

1.5km   0   3km

© Mussio Ventures Ltd.

Scale 1:150,000

© Mussio Ventures Ltd.

TFL 38

Tricouni Meadows Trail

Black Tusk Village

See Map 29

BLACK TUSK MICROWAVE ROAD

Empetrum Peak 1985m

Empetrum Ridge

Corrie Peak 2064m

Cheakamus Lake

The Black Tusk 2319m

Helm Trail

Helm Peak 2146m

Upper Helm Lakes

Cinder Cone 1901m

Corrie Ridge

Castle Towers

Mt Davidson 2516m

Chance Creek Snowmobile Area

WMU 2-6

Cheakamus Canyon (Sea to Sky) Trail

High Falls Creek Trail

Cloudburst Mtn

Black Tusk Trail

Packer Meadows

Taylor Meadows

Taylor Cr

Mimulus Lake

Gentian Peak 2197m

Gentian Pass

Castle Towers Mtn 2676m

Phyllis's Engine 2517m

Barrier Lake

Black Tusk Huts

Battleship Lakes Camp

Garibaldi

Price Bay

Sphinx Bay

Burton Hut

Gray Pass

check point

Butterfly Lake

Lewis Lake

Cheakamus Canyon

Mt Price 2052m Clinker Peak 1992m

Lake

Table Bay

Sentinel Bay

Sphinx Glacier

Isosceles Peak 2530m

Black Tusk Nature Conservancy Area

Lava Flow

Table Meadow

The Table 2021m

Sentinel Glacier Huts

Garibaldi Park Routes

Mt Luxor 2332m

WMU 2-9

Cheakamus River Route

Clinker Ridge

Culliton Creek Route

Old Growth Valley

Warren Glacier

Sentinel Glacier

Phoenix Glacier

Tutankhamen Peak 2163m

WMU 2-7

Swift Creek

Glacier Pikes 2145m

Garibaldi Provincial Park

Squamish River Route

Hut Lake Trails

Jack Webster Bridge

Tenderfoot Cr Hatchery

Brohm Ridge Snowmobile Area

Brohm Ridge Route

Mt Garibaldi 2678m

Garibaldi Park Routes

Bishop Glacier

Viking Ridge

Squamish IR

Paradise Valley

Brohm Lake

Brohm Line Bike Tr

Atwell Peak

Mamquam Lake

See Map 23

Evans Lake Camp

Cheekye

Brohm Lake Interpretive Trails

Cat Lake Rec Site

Cheekye R FSR

Alice Ridge Route

Diamond Head 2620m

Opal Cone 1736m

Pyramid Mtn 2113m

Tantalus Provincial Park

Alpha Mtn 2305m

Lake Lovely Water Trail

Lake Lovely Water Hut

Omega Mtn

Stump Lake

Alice Lake Prov Park

Watershed Reserve

The Gargoyles 1830m Columnar Peak

Lava Glacier

Rampart Ponds

Eanastick Meadows

Mt Pandareus

Mt Niobe 2010m

Red Tusk Route

Brackendale

Garibaldi Highlands Trails

Round Mtn

Elfin Lakes Hut

Elfin Lakes

Hiking Route

Mt Thyestes

Eagle Viewing

Powersmart Trails

Paul Ridge

Mt Conybeare

Brackendale Eagles Prov Park

Garibaldi Estates

Red Heather Day Shelter

16km

Diamond Head

WMU 2-5

Scott Lake

Mt Murchison

Monmouth Creek Trail

Mamquam Rd

Mamquam Route

Ring Cr N Rd

PARK Rd

Ring Creek

Br Skookum

Echo Lake

West-Coast Railway Heritage Park

Mamquam Spawning Channels

Crumpit Woods

12.7km

Mt Habrich 1700m

Smoke Bluffs

Squamish

Stawamus Chief Prov Park

BAY BASIN FSR

Mt Mulligan

Alpen Mtn 1705m

Squaw Trail

Stawamus Mt Mulligan Trail 1820m

Indian River

Woodfibre

Shannon Falls Prov Park

Stawamus Chief

Shannon Falls

WMU 2-8 Mt Habrich 1700m

See Map 11

CRAWFORD

Darrell Bay

Woodfibre Mill

Howe Sound

N

Scale 1:150,000
1.5km 0 3km

Squamish

22

© Mussio Ventures Ltd.

23 Garibaldi Provincial Park

Scale 1:150,000

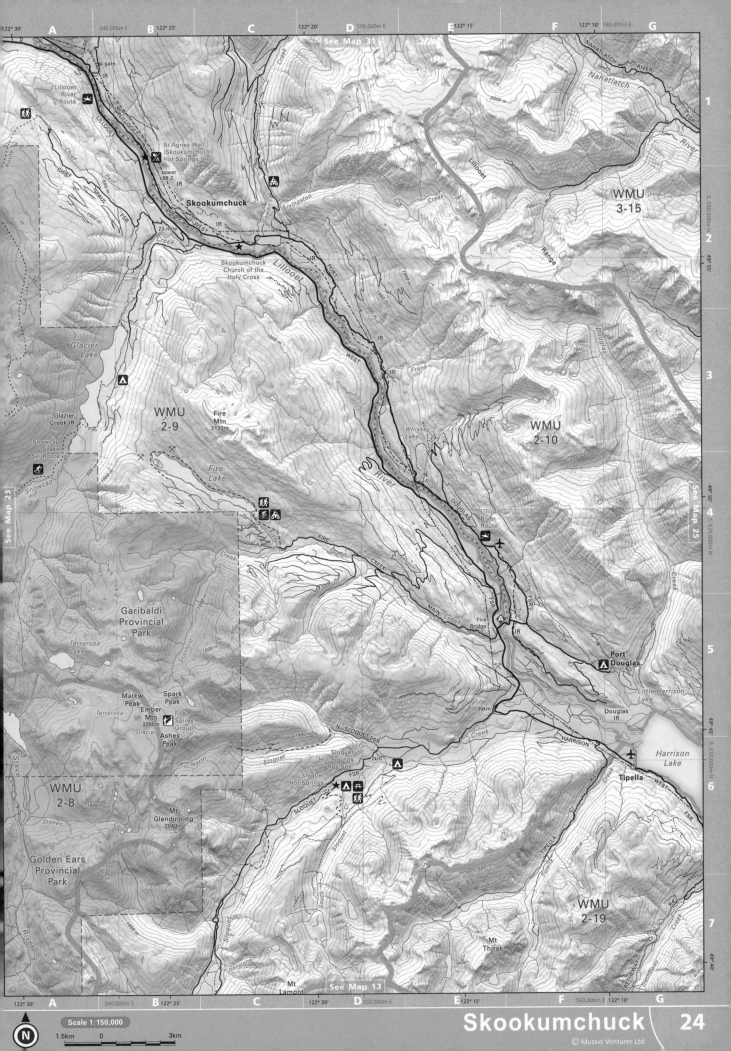

A 540,000m E B 122° 25' C 122° 20' D 550,000m E E 122° 15' F 122° 10' 560,000m E G

1
2
3
4
5
6
7

49° 55'
49° 50'
49° 45'

5,530,000m N
5,520,000m N
5,510,000m N

See Map 23
See Map 25
See Map 13

Lillooet River Route
gate
IR
Chief
Paul
FSR
CHIEF
STAUL
SRAUL
St Agnes Well (Skookumchuck) Hot Springs
tower 68.2
IR
Skookumchuck
23 mile
Creek
IR
WEST
IR
Glacier Lake
Glazier Creek IR
Snowcap Lake Ski Route
Snowcap
WMU 2-9
Fire Mtn 2120m
Fire Lake
Gowan
Livingston
Creek
PORT
WEST
Lillooet
Skookumchuck Church of the Holy Cross
IR
IR
Frank
Whiskey Lake
Douglas Range
WMU 3-15
WMU 2-10
River
Rush
DOUGLAS
Lillooet River Route
FSR
Garibaldi Provincial Park
Terrarosa Lake
Stanford
FIRE
CREEK
MAIN
Creek
Fire Bridge
IR
FSR
FSR
Trail
Port Douglas
Little Harrison Lake
Terrarosa
Matkw Peak
Spark Peak
Ember Mtn 2260m
Fire Spires Group
Ashes Peak
Glacier
N. SLOQUET FSR
Sloquet
North
Creek
35km
Douglas IR
HARRISON
WMU 2-8
Stave
River
Stoney
Cr
Mt Glendinning 2040m
Golden Ears Provincial Park
SLOQUET
Sloquet
Sloquet Hot Springs Rec Site
7km
Sloquet Hot Springs
South
Ironstone
HARRISON
WEST
Tipella
TIPELLA
Tipella
Cr
Harrison Lake
FSR
WMU 2-19
Mt Thirsk
Mt Lamont
TRETHEWAY
Trethway

122° 30'
122° 25'
122° 20'
122° 15'
122° 10'

A · 122° 05' · B · 570,000m E · 122° 00' · C · D · 121° 55' · 580,000m E · E · 121° 50' · F · G · 590,000m E · 121° 45'

Squakum & Salmon Beach Campsites

Nahatlatch Needle 1950m

Nahatlatch Lake Route

KOOKIPI SEVEN

Mehatl Creek Provincial Park

Nahatlatch Provincial Park

1

Mt Widdess 2240m

NAHATLATCH RIVER

River

See Map 26

Mehatl Falls Trail

48km bridge

Nahatlatch Watershed Protected Area

2

WMU 3-15

Whistlepig

Mt Whistlepig

KOOKIPI NINE FSR

3

Mt Mason

Liflooet

Creek

Hunger

Creek

KOOKIPI CREEK

4

WMU 2-10

Cairn Needle 2245m

Butter

Creek

Big

Big

SILVER

KOOKIPI FSR

Granite Falls

canyon

SHOVEL FSR

HORNET

Cr

SHOVEL Cr 2

SHOVEL Cr 4

SHOVEL Cr 3

1500 m

STOKKE

Range

Gold

Creek

Shovel

Spade

5

WMU 2-18

Purcell

Cr

CREEK

FSR

Creek

Snowshoe

Creek

6

Harrison

Penal Camp

Stokke

Mt Breakenridge 2385m

SILVER

MAIN

FSR

EAST

Clear Creek Hot Springs

HARRISON (4wd road)

Five Mile Bay

HARRISON Creek

FIR

Clear

CREEK

MAIN

7

Corn Cr Bridges 64.5km

Tretheway

WEST

500 m

Lake

bridge unsafe 55km

Kaiyama Petroglyphs Doctor's Point

MT. BREAKENRIDGE FSR

gate

CLEAR FSR

CLEAR 7.6km

WMU 2-19

A · 122° 05' · B · 570,000m E · 122° 00' · C · D · 121° 55' · 580,000m E · E · 121° 50' · F · G · 121° 45'

25 Nahatlach Lake

© Mussio Ventures Ltd.

Scale 1:150,000

1.5km · 0 · 3km

N

Two Squaws Mtn

Nahatlatch River Route

Boothroyd

Sho-ook IR

NORTH AINSLIE-MOWHOKAM FSR

The Nipple
2291m

Chaumox

Mt Laughlan

Canyon Alpine

Sam Adams IR

WMU 3-15

North Bend

Stoyoma Creek Eco Reserve

STOYOMA

Mt McEwan

Boston Bar

Scuzzy Mtn
2217m

Fraser Peak

Boston Bar IR

UZTLIUS

Hicks

Komo

4wd only

rough bridge

Scuzzy Creek Rec Site

Scuzzy Rapids

Anderson

Mt Nesbitt

China Bar

WMU 3-14

road system deactivated

Busteed

Hells Gate

Hells Gate

Hells Gate fishways

Ferrabee Tunnel

Gate Mtn

Walsh Lake

Tsileuh

THREE

TSILEUH

ANDERSON

CLEAR CR FSR

Alexandra Tunnel

1858

tunnel

Spuzzum Mtn
1910m

Chapmans

1848 First Brigade Trail

road system deactivated

Tikwalus

Alexandra Bridge Prov Park

WMU 2-18

Spuzzum

SPUZZUM-HANGING VALL FSR

FOREST SERVICE

no thru

WMU 2-17

Stout

WMU 3-13

WMU 3-14

WMU 8-5

WMU 17

27 Coldwater River

Scale 1:150,000

1.5km   0   3km

N

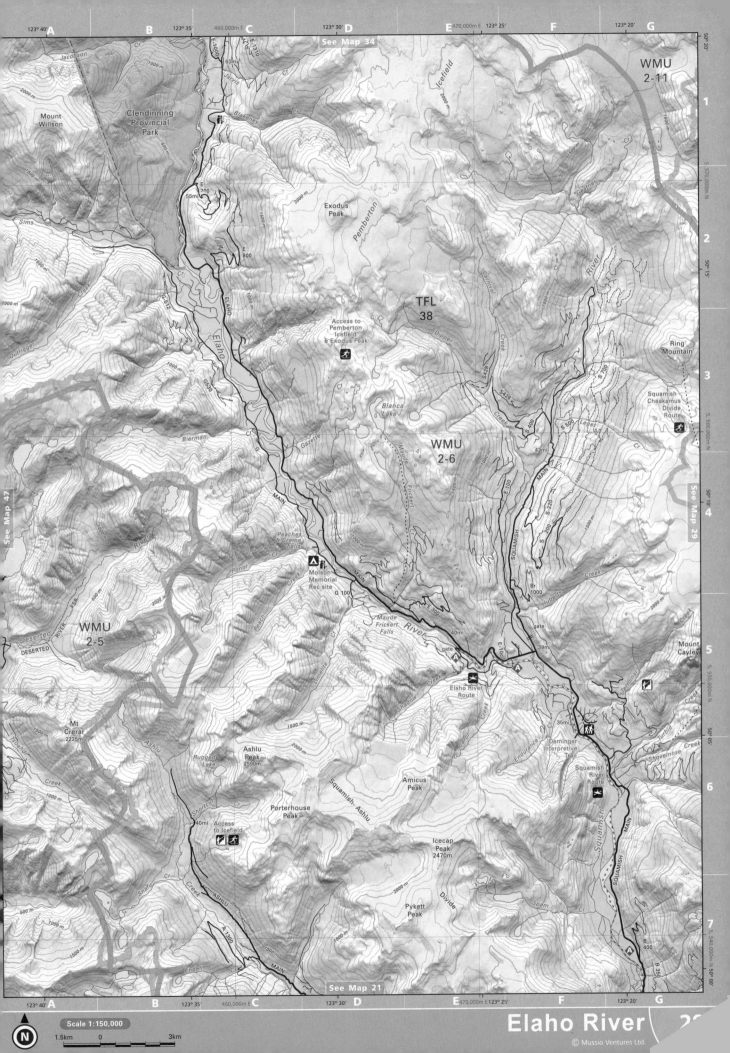

WMU
2-11

WMU
2-6

TFL
38

WMU
2-5

WMU
2-6

Mount
Willson

Clendinning
Provincial
Park

Exodus
Peak

Access to
Pemberton
Icefield &
Exodus Peak

Blanca
Lake

Ring
Mountain

Squamish
Cheakamus
Divide
Route

Peaches
& Creme
Falls

Molson
Memorial
Rec site

Maude
Frickert
Falls

Mount
Cayley

Mt
Crerar
2225m

Rugged
Lake

Ashlu
Peak
2590m

Porterhouse
Peak

Amicus
Peak

Deminger
Interpretive
Trail

Squamish
River
Route

Elaho River
Route

Access to
Icefield

Icecap
Peak
2470m

Pykett
Peak

Squamish-Ashlu

Deserted

See Map 47

See Map 29

Scale 1:150,000

1.5km   0   3km

N

Elaho River

© Mussio Ventures Ltd.

Whistler

© Mussio Ventures Ltd.

Scale 1:150,000

See Map 35
See Map 28
See Map 22

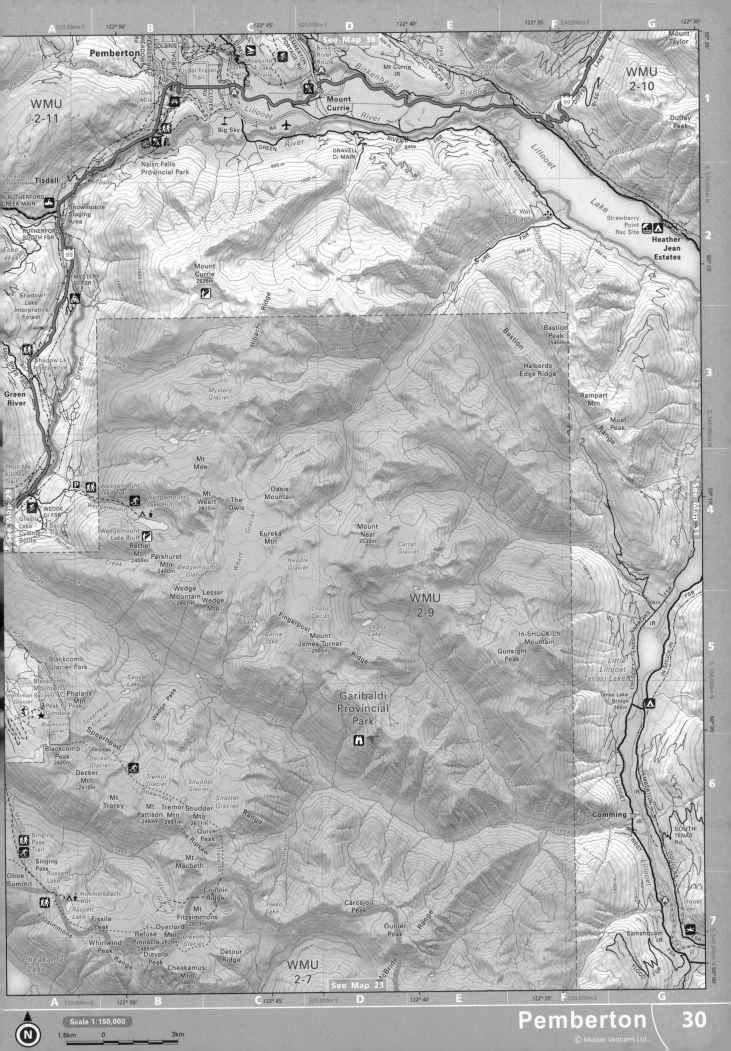

© Mussio Ventures Ltd.

Scale 1:150,000

1.5km 0 3km

Stein River

32

Scale 1:150,000

1.5km   0   3km

N

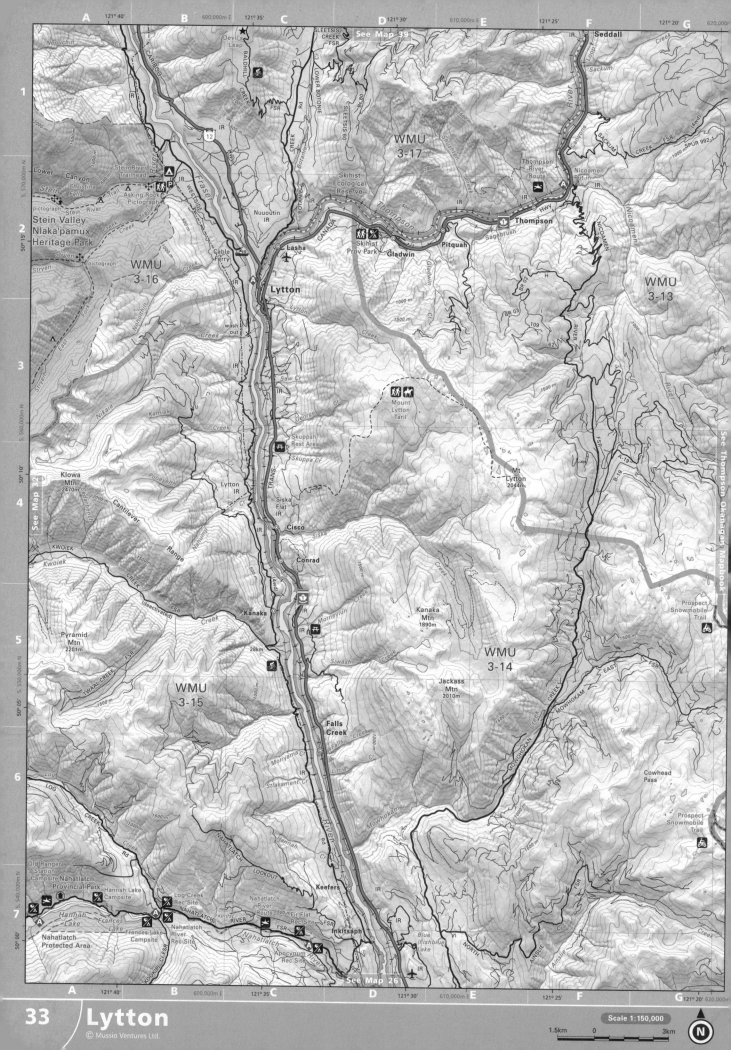

Lytton
© Mussio Ventures Ltd.

Scale 1:150,000

1.5km 0 3km

N

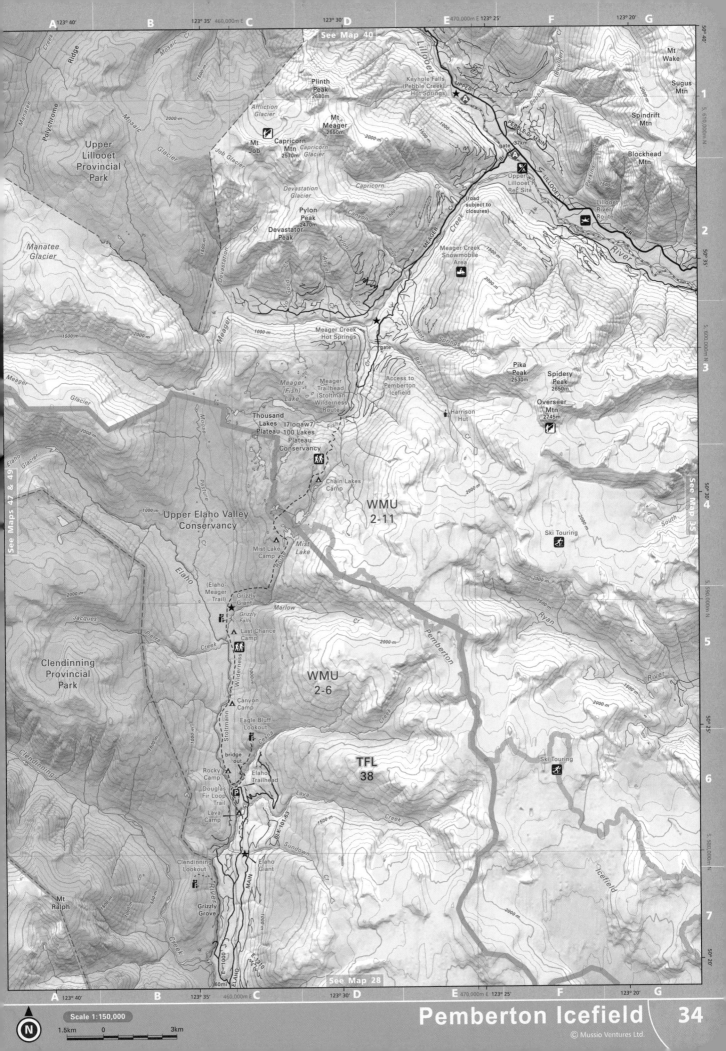

See Map 40

Lillooet

1 Mt Wake

Sugus Mtn

Keyhole Falls
(Pebble Creek)
Hot Springs

UPPER

Plinth
Peak
2680m

Affliction
Glacier

Mt
Meager
2650m

Spindrift
Mtn

PEBBLE CR MAIN

gate 37km

Blockhead
Mtn

Mt Job

Mt
Job

Capricorn
Mtn
2570m

Capricorn
Glacier

Upper
Lillooet R
Rec Site

2

Devastation
Glacier

Capricorn

(road
subject to
closures)

Lillooet
River
Route

FSR

Pylon
Peak
2470m

Canyon

MEAGER Creek

Meager Creek
Snowmobile
Area

Devastator
Peak

Manatee
Glacier

Angel

Pylon Cr

3

Good Cr

Meager Creek
Hot Springs

gate

Pika
Peak
2530m

Spidery
Peak
2650m

Meager

Glacier

Meager

1000 m

Meager
(Fish)
Lake

Meager
Trailhead
(Stoltman
Wilderness
Route)

Access to
Pemberton
Icefield

Harrison
Hut

Overseer
Mtn
2745m

Hot Springs Cr

Barr

Thousand
Lakes
Plateau

Fish

17loqaw7
100 Lakes
Plateau
Conservancy

Moose

Chain Lakes
Camp

4

Pasture

Upper Elaho Valley
Conservancy

WMU
2-11

Ski Touring

Elaho

Jacques

Mist Lake
Camp

Mist
Lake

Route

Pemberton

5

Glacier

Clendinning Provincial Park

Grizzly
Giant

(Elaho-
Meager
Trail)

Marlow
Cr

Grizzly
Falls

Last Chance
Camp

Ryan River

6

Pierre

Elaho

Wilderness

Canyon
Camp

WMU
2-6

Eagle Bluff
Lookout

Cessna

Stoltmann

bridge
out

TFL
38

Ski Touring

Rocky
Camp

Lava

Douglas
Fir Loop
Trail

P

Elaho Trailhead

Clendinning

Lava
Camp

BLK 101-63

Clendinning
Lookout

Sundown

Mt
Ralph

Elaho
Giant

7

Grizzly
Grove

ELAHO MAIN

RIVER

See Map 28

Icefield

See Maps 47 & 49

See Map 35

N

Scale 1:150,000

1.5km 0 3km

Pemberton Icefield

34

© Mussio Ventures Ltd.

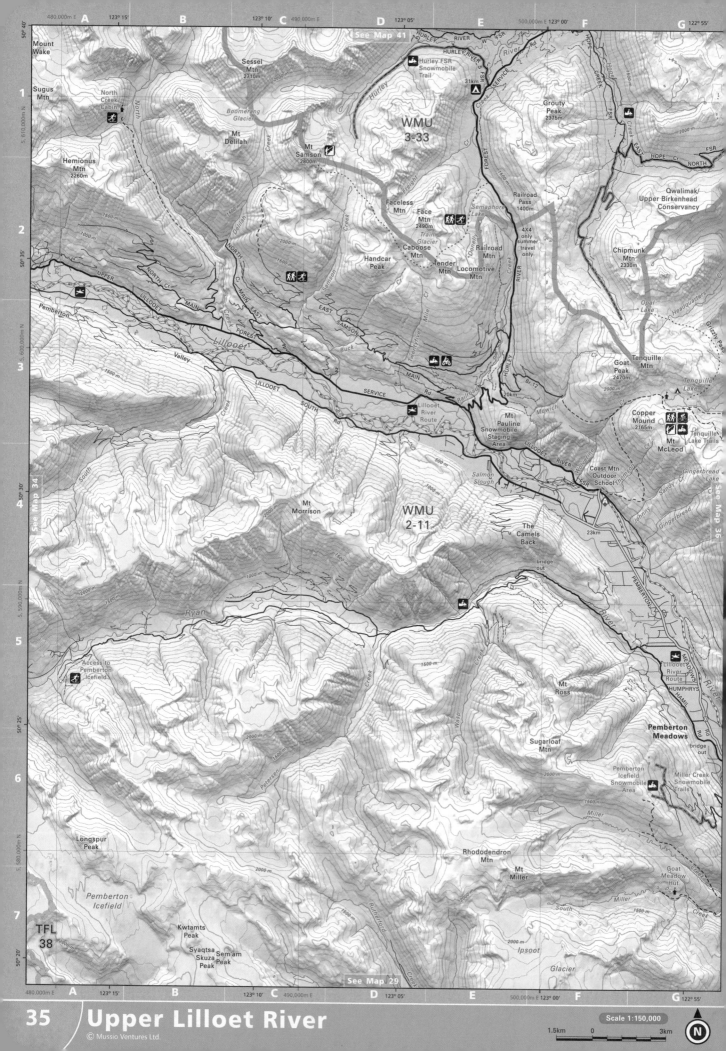

Mount Wake

Sugus Mtn

North Creek Cabin

Hemionus Mtn 2260m

Pemberton

Sessel Mtn 2710m

Boomerang Glacier

Mt Delilah

Mt Samson 2800m

Faceless Mtn

Face Mtn 2490m

Train Glacier

Caboose Mtn

Handcar Peak

Tender Mtn

NORTH Cr

C MAIN EAST

Creek Valley

UPPER LILLOOET

Lillooet

MAIN FOREST

LILLOOET SOUTH Rd

SERVICE Rd

Twentyfive Mile

EAST SAMSON

Samson Creek

Buck Cr

MAIN

Hurley FSR Snowmobile Trail

31km

WMU 3-33

Railroad Pass 1400m

Semaphore Lake

Donelly Cr

Railroad Mtn

Locomotive Mtn

4X4 only summer travel only

Grouty Peak 2375m

HURLEY RIVER S FSR

Creek SERVICE FOREST

Railroad

HOPE CREEK

Qwalimak/Upper Birkenhead Conservancy

Chipmunk Mtn 2330m

HOPE Cr NORTH

HOPE Cr EAST FSR

Opal Lake

Headquarters

Grizzly Pass

Lillooet River Route

Mt Pauline Snowmobile Staging Area

Lillooet River

Mowich

Salmon Slough

20km

Br 12

Goat Peak 2470m

Tenquille Mtn

Copper Mound 2165m

Mt McLeod

Tenquille Lake

Tenquille Lake Trails

Gingerbread Lake

Coast Mtn Outdoor School

23km

Johnny Cr

Sandy Cr

Gingerbread Cr

Mt Morrison

WMU 2-11

The Camels Back

bridge out

Mt Ross

Sugarloaf Mtn

Ryan Creek

South Creek

Wasp Creek

Access to Pemberton Icefield

Longspur Peak

Pemberton Icefield

Rhododendron Mtn

Mt Miller

Petersen

Rutherford Creek

Ipsoot Glacier

Miller South Creek

Lillooet River Route

HUMPHRYS

Pemberton Meadows

bridge out

Pemberton Icefield Snowmobile Area

Miller Creek Snowmobile Trails

Goat Meadow Hut

TFL 38

Kwtamts Peak

Syaqtsa Skuza Peak

Sem'am Peak

Scale 1:150,000

1.5km 0 3km

N

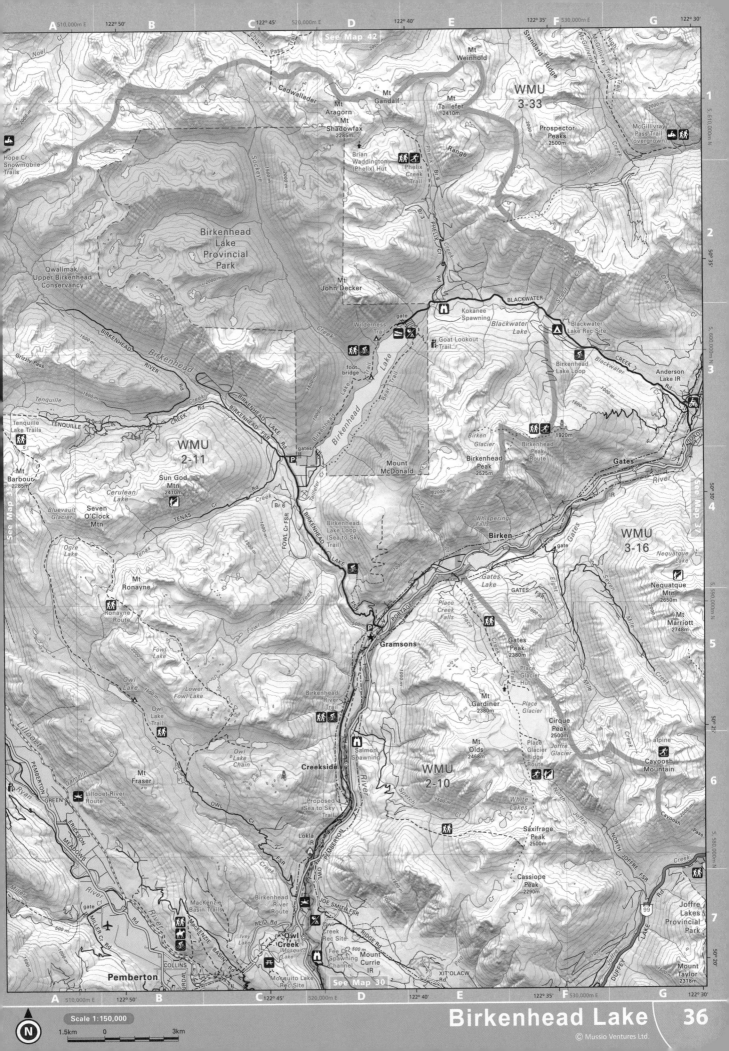

A 510,000m E   122° 50'   B   122° 45'   C   520,000m E   D   122° 40'   E   122° 35'   F   530,000m E   G   122° 30'

Noel Cr

Chism Pass Trail

Cadwallader

Mt Weinhold

WMU 3-33

Standard Ridge

McGillivray Trail

McGillivray Pass Trail (overgrown)

Hope Cr Snowmobile Trails

Mt Aragorn
Mt Shadowfax 2285m

Mt Gandalf

Mt Taillefer 2410m

Prospector Peaks 2500m

Qwalimak/ Upper Birkenhead Conservancy

Birkenhead Lake Provincial Park

Brian Waddington (Phelix) Hut

Phelix Creek Trail

Range

Br. 6

Sockeye

Grizzly Pass

Birkenhead River

Tenquille

Mt John Decker

Wilderness Trail

gate

Kokanee Spawning

BLACKWATER

Blackwater Lake

Blackwater Lake Rec Site

Anderson Lake IR

Tenquille Lake Trails
TENQUILLE

Birkenhead Lake Rd

BIRKENHEAD FSR Rd

CREEK Rd

foot bridge

Goat Lookout Trail

Birkenhead Lake Loop

Birkenhead CREEK

Mt Barbour 2285m

WMU 2-11

Sun God Mtn 2410m

Birkenhead Lake Trail

Bear Trail

Birken Glacier

Birkenhead Peak Route

1920m

Gates

ROAD

Cerulean Lake

Bluevault Glacier

Seven O'Clock Mtn

TENAS

Br 6

gates

P

Mount McDonald

Birkenhead Peak 2525m

See Map 37

Ogre Lake

Mt Ronayne

FOWL Cr FSR

BIRKENHEAD LAKE

Birkenhead Lake Loop (Sea to Sky Trail)

Whispering Falls

Birken

gate

WMU 3-16

Nequatque Lake

Nequatque Mtn 2650m

Ronayne Route

Fowl Lake

Gates Lake

Place Creek Falls

GATES

GATES FSR

Gates Cr

Mt Marriott 2748m

Lillooet River Route

PEMBERTON

GREEN

Owl Lake

Lower Fowl Lake

Owl Lake Trail

Owl Lake Chain

Birkenhead River Trail

Gates River

Place Cr

Gates Peak 2380m

Place Glacier Hut

Place Glacier

alpine

Cayoosh Mountain

Mt Fraser

Creekside

Salmon Spawning

Mt Gardiner 2380m

Cirque Peak 2500m

Joffre Glacier

Place Glacier Ridge Route

Lillooet River

Gamelin Cr

Ryan

Proposed Sea to Sky Trail

River

Mt Olds 2468m

WMU 2-10

White Lakes

North Joffre Cr

Mile Cr

ERICKSON MEADOWS

Lokla IR

PEMBERTON

Saxifrage Peak 2500m

NORTH JOFFRE FSR

99

Joffre Lakes Provincial Park

Miller Cr

Owl Creek

MACKENZIE BASIN

MacKenzie Basin Trails

Birkenhead River Route

IMO

JOE SMITH FSR

RIDGE Rd

Fee Cr Spawning Channel

Mount Currie IR

Cassiope Peak 2290m

DUFFEY LAKE Rd

Cayoosh Pass

REID Rd

Pemberton

COLLINS

URDAL

Ivey Lake

Owl Creek

Mosquito Lake

XIT'OLACW Rd

Mount Taylor 2318m

Mosquito Lake Rec Site

A 510,000m E   122° 50'   B   122° 45'   C   122° 45'   520,000m E   122° 40'   E   122° 35'   F   530,000m E   G   122° 30'

N

Scale 1:150,000

1.5km   0   3km

Birkenhead Lake   36

© Mussio Ventures Ltd.

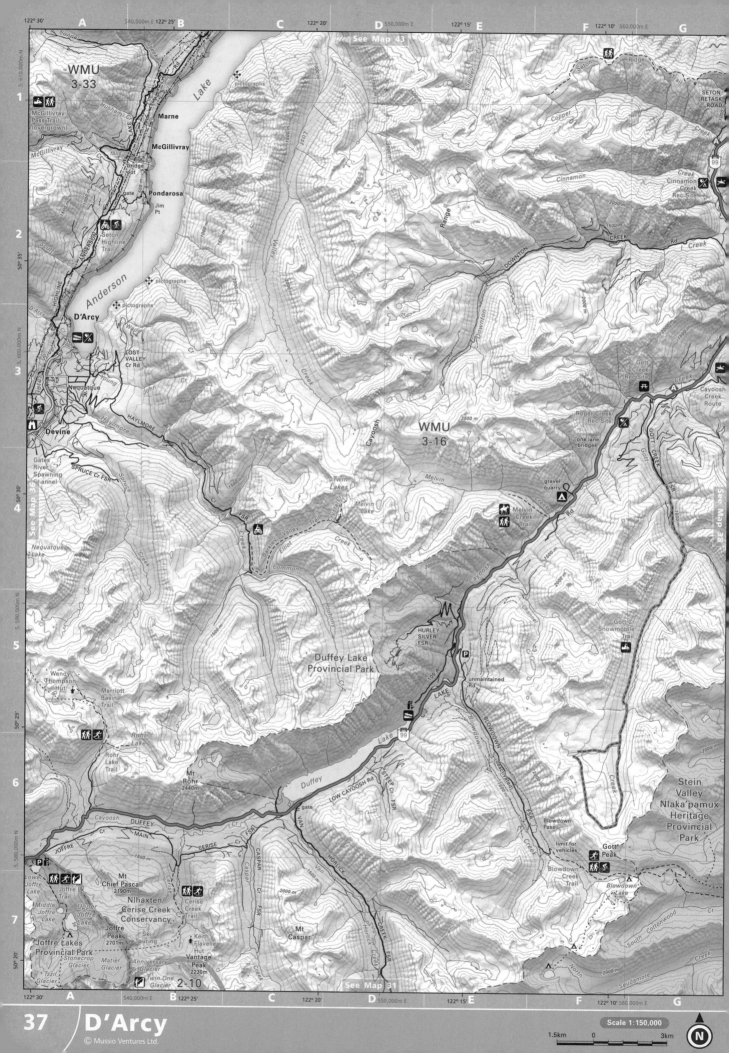

Scale 1:150,000

1.5km   0   3km

N

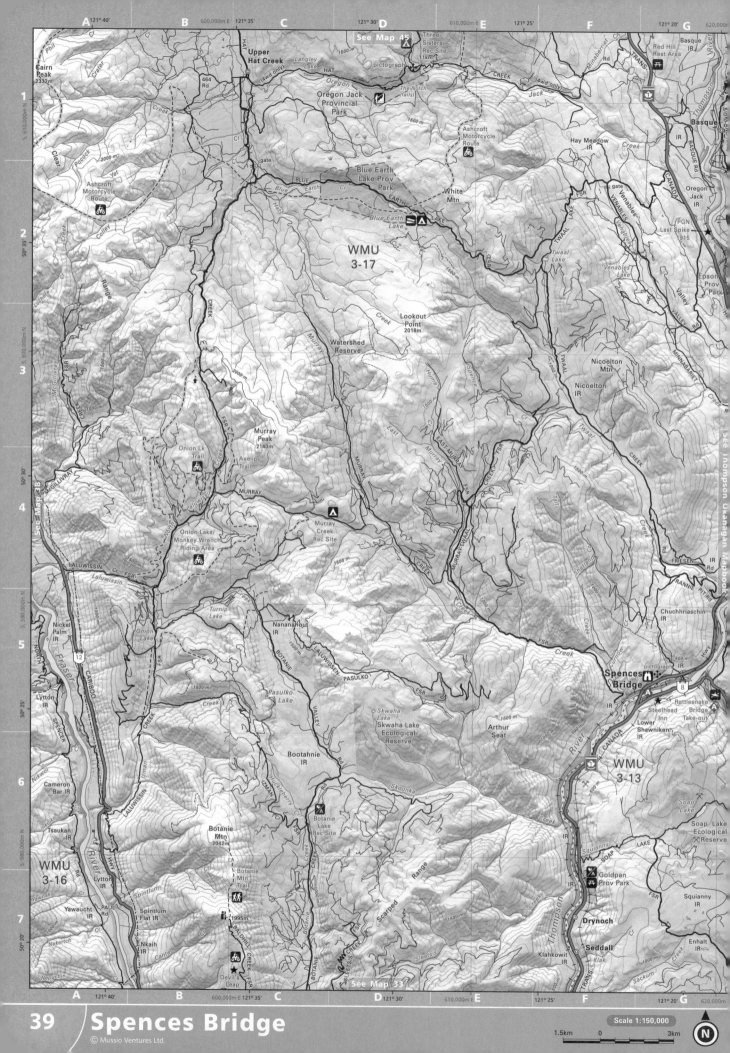

WMU
5-4

Muon
Mountain

Griswold
Pass

Lepton
Mountain

(Closed to
Motor Vehicles)
Restricted Area

Slim
Pass

Socerer
Glacier

Mt
Heaney

Chapman Glacier

Ts'yl-Os
Provincial
Park

Spruce Lake
Protected Area
(South Chilcotin
Provincial Park)

Dickson

Range

WMU
3-32

Lord

Mt Tait

Mount
Wheatley

Mt
Dodds

Mt
Henderson

Bridge

Lord Glacier

Mt
orter

Mt
ills

Bridge

WMU
3-33

Glacier

Ochre
Mtn

Bridge
eak

White Cross
Mtn

WMU
2-11

Mt
Guthrum

Mt
Ethelweard

Icemaker
Mtn

Silt
Lake

Lillooet

Upper
Lillooet
Provincial
Park

Salal

Salal Creek
Athelney Pass
Trail

Mt
Athelstan
2770m

Keystone
Falls

Manatee

Polychrome

Ridge

Mosiac
Glacier

Mosiac

Affliction

Creek

Creek

River

SEC MAN FSR falls

SALAL Cr. FSR

UPPER

LILLOOET

FSR

Pebble

Boulder

Creek

Mt
Wake

41 Spruce Lake

© Mussio Ventures Ltd.

Scale 1:150,000

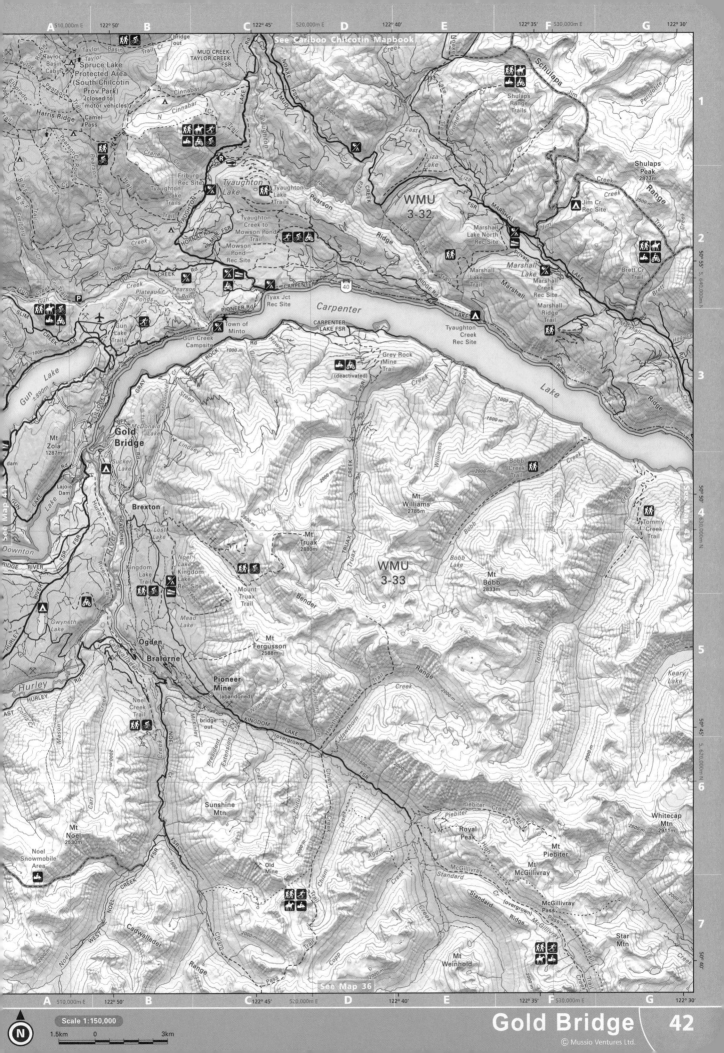

See Cariboo Chilcotin Mapbook

Spruce Lake Protected Area (South Chilcotin Prov Park) (closed to motor vehicles)

MUD CREEK-TAYLOR CREEK FSR

Taylor Basin

Taylor Basin Cabin

Harris Ridge

Camel Pass

Cinnabar Cr

Cinnabar Cr

Friburg Rec Site

Tyaughton Lake Trails

Tyaughton Lake

Tyaughton Lake Trails

Tyaughton Creek to Mowson Pond Trail

Mowson Pond Rec Site

Pearson Pond

Plateau Cr Ponds

Pearson Pond

Tyax Jct Rec Site

Town of Minto

Gun Creek Campsite

Gun Lake Trails

Mt Zola 1287m

Gold Bridge

Brexton

Lajoie Dam

Lost Lake

Sucker Lake

McDonald Lakes

Lindsey

Steep Cr

Kingdom Lake Trail

Kingdom Lake Rec Site

Noel Lake

Mead Lake

Mount Truax Trail

Mt Truax 2880m

Mt Fergusson 2588m

Bender Cr

Ogden

Bralorne

Pioneer Mine (abandoned)

KINGDOM LAKE (overgrown)

bridge out

Noel Creek Trail

Mt Noel 2530m

Noel Snowmobile Area

Sunshine Mtn

Old Mine

WMU 3-33

Grey Rock Mine Trail (deactivated)

Mt Williams 2785m

Bobb Lake

Mt Bobb 2833m

Bobb Creek Trail

Tommy Creek Trail

Carpenter Lake FSR

CARPENTER LAKE FSR

Tyaughton Creek Rec Site

Marshall Lake North Rec Site

Marshall Lake

Marshall Creek Rec Site

Marshall Ridge Trail

Marshall Lake Trail

WMU 3-32

Liza Lake

East Cr

Schulaps Range Trails

Shulaps Peak 2877m

Shulaps Range

Jim Cr Rec Site

Brett Cr Trail

Keary Lake

Whitecap Mtn 2911m

Royal Peak

Mt Piebiter

Mt McGillivray

McGillivray Pass

McGillivray Pass (overgrown)

Standard Ridge

Star Mtn

Mt Weinhold

Piebiter Creek

Hawthorn Creek

Chism Creek

Cadwallader Range

See Map 36

Scale 1:150,000

1.5km   0   3km

Gold Bridge   42

© Mussio Ventures Ltd.

WMU
3-32

WMU
3-33

WMU
3-16

See Map 37

43 / Seton Portage

© Mussio Ventures Ltd.

Scale 1:150,000

1.5km   0   3km

N

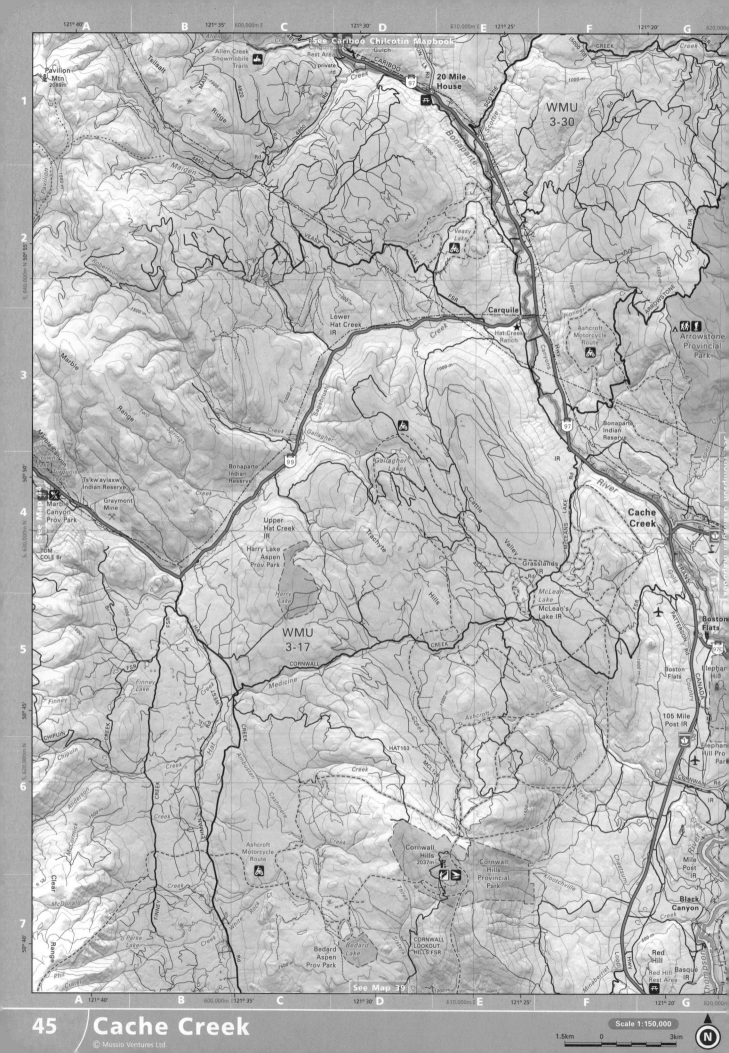

© Mussio Ventures Ltd.

Scale 1:150,000

1.5km 0 3km

N

Scale 1:250,000

2.5km   0   5km

© Mussio Ventures Ltd.

47 Jervis Inlet

Scale 1:250,000

© Mussio Ventures Ltd.

2.5km   0   5km

N

© Mussio Ventures Ltd.

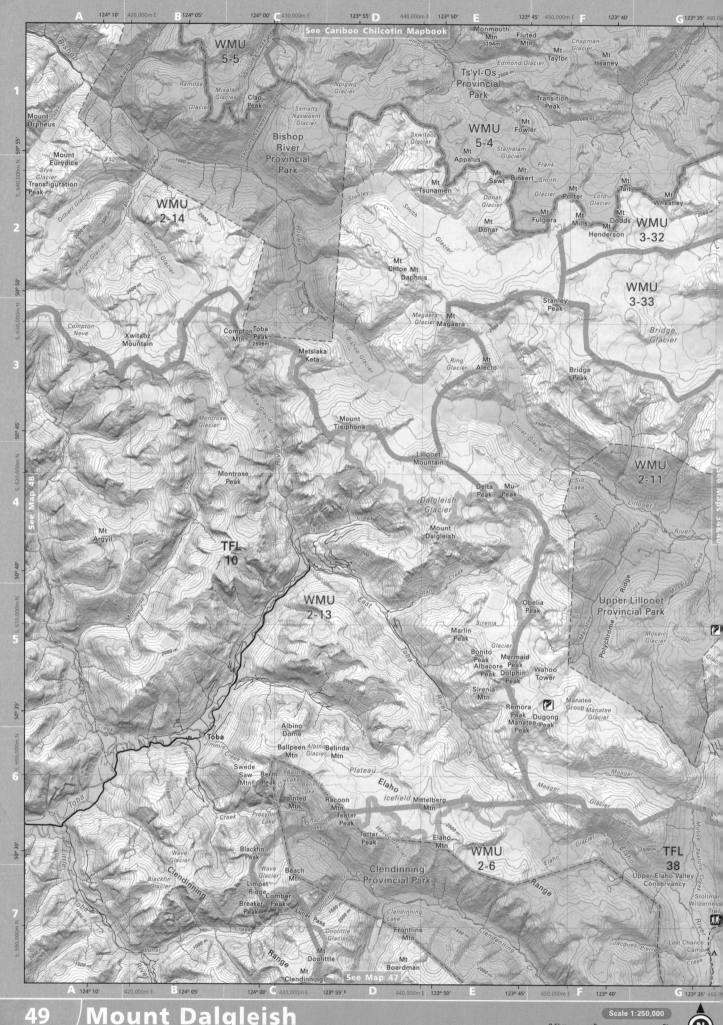

49 / **Mount Dalgleish**

© Mussio Ventures Ltd.

Scale 1:250,000

2.5km 0 5km

N

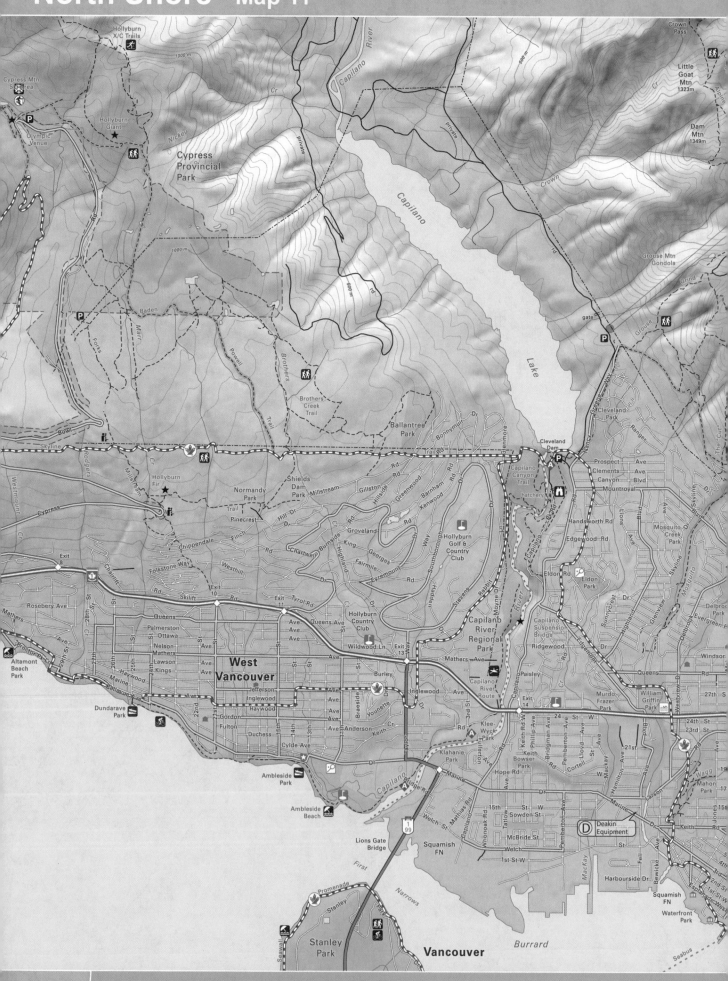

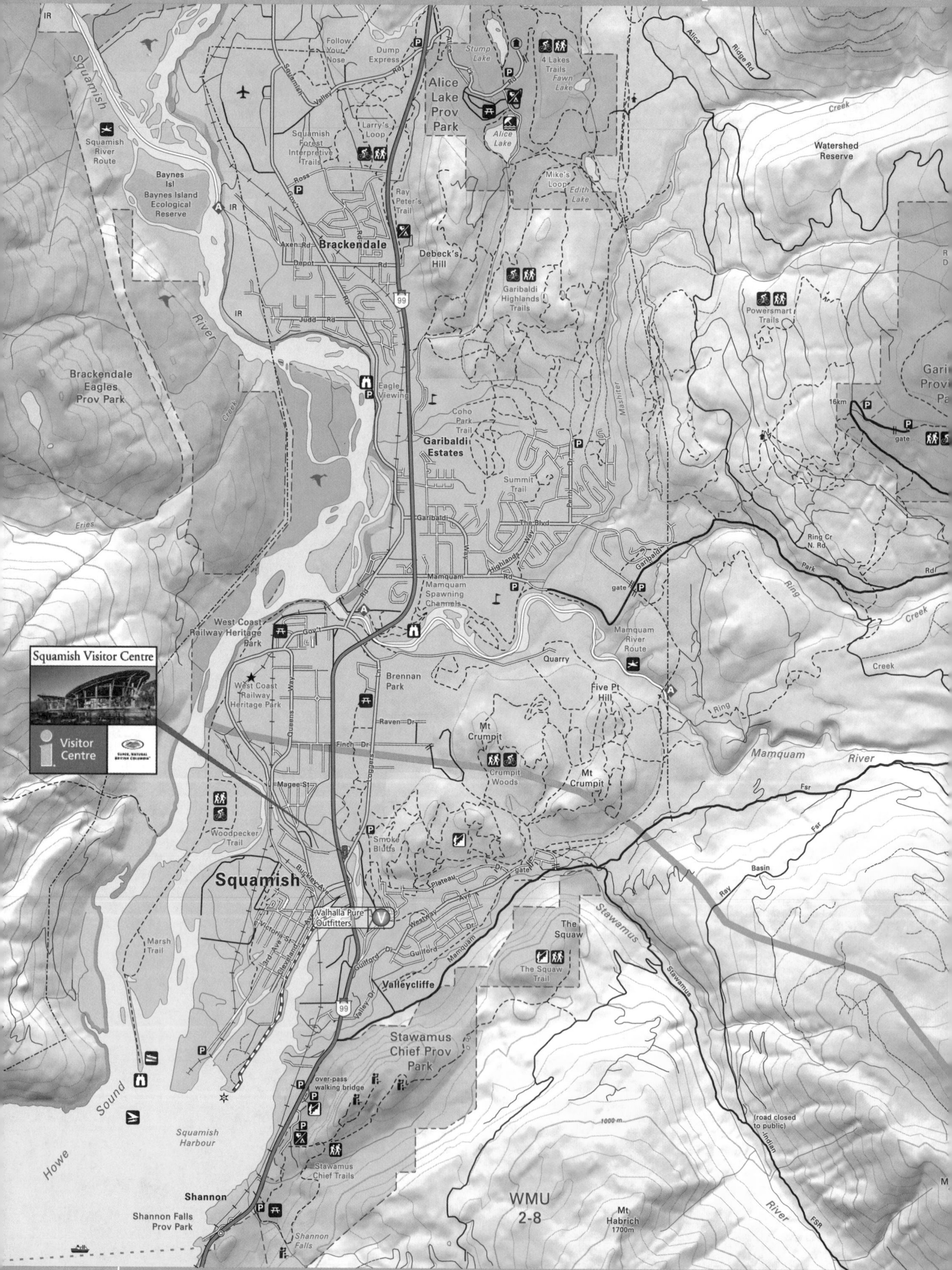

Squamish River Route

IR

Follow Your Nose

Dump Express

P

Stump Lake

4 Lakes Trails Fawn Lake

Alice Lake Prov Park

Alice Lake

Watershed Reserve

Alice Ridge Rd

Creek

Squamish River Route

Squamish Forest Interpretive Trails

Larry's Loop

Ross

Ray Peter's Trail

Mike's Loop

Edith Lake

Squamish River

Baynes Isl Baynes Island Ecological Reserve

A IR

Axen Rd
Depot Rd
Brackendale

Debeck's Hill

99

Garibaldi Highlands Trails

Powersmart Trails

Judd Rd
IR

Coho Park Trail

Gari Prov Pa

16km
P
gate

Brackendale Eagles Prov Park

P Eagle Viewing

Garibaldi Estates

Summit Trail

Ring Cr N. Rd

Ring

Eries

Garibaldi
The Blvd
Highlands Rd
Garibaldi

Park

Creek

Mamquam Mamquam Spawning Channels

P

gate
P

Creek

Mamquam River Route

West Coast Railway Heritage Park

Gov't

A

Quarry

Mamquam River Route

Five Pt Hill

Ring

Mamquam River

West Coast Railway Heritage Park

Brennan Park

Raven Dr

Finch Dr

Mt Crumpit

Crumpit Woods

Mt Crumpit

Fsr

Far

Woodpecker Trail

Magee St

Smoke Bluffs

gate

Plateau

Basin

Ray

P

Squamish

Valhalla Pure Outfitters V

Washington Dr

The Squaw

Stawamus

Marsh Trail

Victoria St
3rd Ave
Cleveland

Guilford Dr
Guilford

Mamquam

The Squaw Trail

Stawamus

Howe Sound

Valleycliffe

99

Stawamus Chief Prov Park

1000 m

(road closed to public)

Indian

over-pass walking bridge

P

Squamish Harbour

Squamish Chief Trails

WMU 2-8

Mt Habrich 1700m

River

Shannon

Shannon Falls Prov Park

Shannon Falls

P

FSR

Vancouver, Coast & Mountains BC

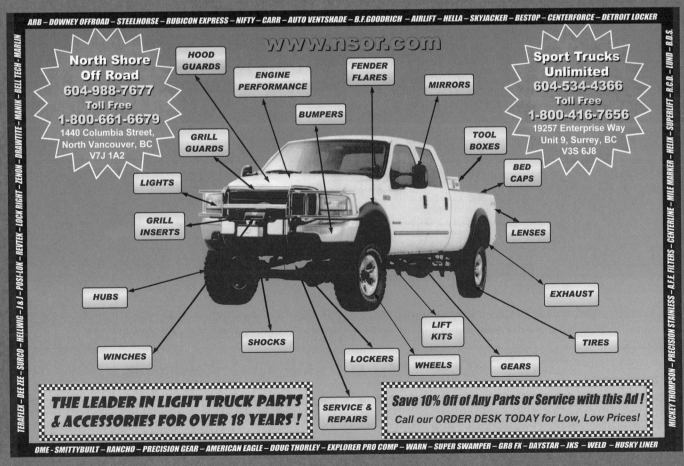

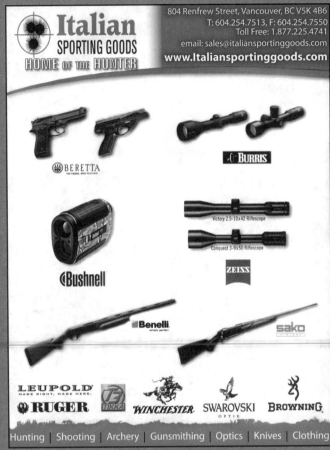

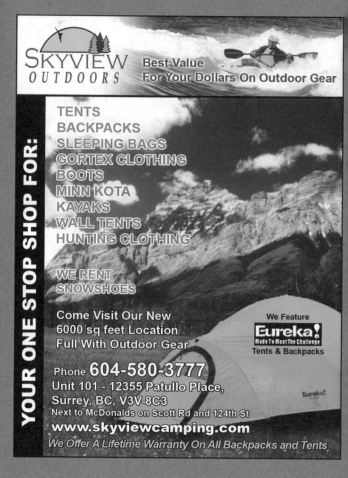
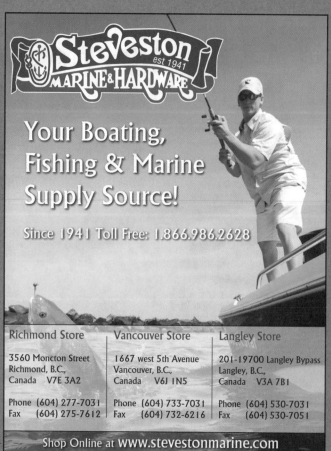

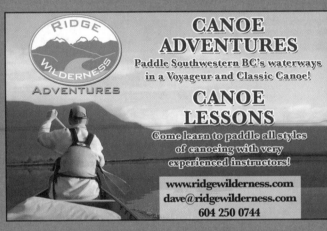

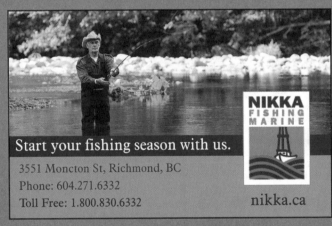

Service Directory

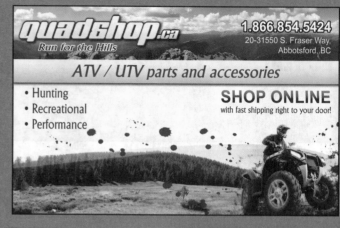

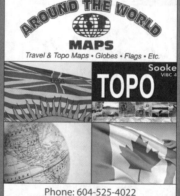

To advertise your business in this section, call **604-521-6277** or **1-877-520-5670**

The hardest part is choosing.

Sky-piercing mountains, glistening glaciers, wild rocky coastlines, lush evergreen forests, smooth sandy beaches, desert-like flatlands, rolling grasslands – British Columbia has some of the world's most dramatic, diverse, and spectacular scenery. When you travel with your own accommodation – tent, trailer, camper, or RV – you are free to follow your spirit from one breathtaking view to the next.

For more visual inspiration, with over 600 campgrounds to choose from, visit **www.rvcampingbc.com**.

CAMPING & RV IN BC

Go where your spirit takes you

British Columbia, Home of the Vancouver 2010 Olympic and Paralympic Winter Games

Share the Excitement!

SUPER, NATURAL BRITISH COLUMBIA®
CANADA

CHRIS HARRIS

PARADISE FUN PARK

Trip Planning Notes:

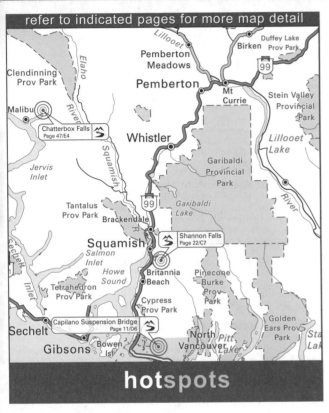

refer to indicated pages for more map detail

Chatterbox Falls
Page 47/E4

Shannon Falls
Page 22/C7

Capilano Suspension Bridge
Page 11/D6

hotspots

There are backroads, as they say, and then there are backroads. For some rugged explorers, getting off the pavement is a backroads adventure. For others, it isn't a real backroad unless you need a winch. Fortunately, there is a mix of both to be found in Southwestern BC.

The loop formed by the Trans Canada and the Sea to Sky Highway is the backbone of the road system in the Vancouver, Coast and Mountains Region of BC. The Sea to Sky leaves the Trans Canada at Horseshoe Bay, passing through Squamish, Whistler, Pemberton and Lillooet before hooking up with the Trans Canada again north of Cache Creek. The Sea to Sky is no longer quite as winding, quite as dangerous a road as it once was. The road has been almost completely upgraded, just in time for the 2010 Olympics, to make it a safer way to get to Whistler. Just like those darn Duke boys, the Ministry of Highways has been hard at work straightening the curves and flattening the hills. Despite these upgrades, the road remains one of the most photogenic roads in Canada and well worth exploring even though no one would call the section to Whistler a backroad anymore.

More adventurous drivers will find the Sea to Sky Highway is still a rustic route past Pemberton, granting access into some great backroading country. The Hurley River Road is one of the most popular routes into the area north of Pemberton and is BC at its finest. While the road is gravel and can be bumpy, it is easily passable by two-wheel drive (2wd) vehicles and is an incredibly scenic route. For the adventurous, many great 4wd routes head off from here.

Another popular road is the West Harrison Lake Forest Service Road. There were rumours of this road getting paved for the Olympics, but it remains a rugged 4wd route that is frequently closed by washouts and avalanches. It is the only road that runs north and south between the Sea to Sky and the Trans Canada.

Unfortunately backroads change. Bridges wash out. Roads are deactivated. And others are gated. We do our best to keep you posted (visit the update page at www.backroadmapbooks.com before setting out), but if in doubt it might be worth calling the local forest district office (numbers at the back of the book) to find out current road conditions. However, if you come across a change that we need to know about, please send an email to updates@backroadmapbooks.com.

If you enjoy exploring backroads, we suggest visiting one of the following featured sites:

MAN MADE ATTRACTIONS

The Lower Mainland is the most populated area in Western Canada. As you might expect, there are man made attractions aplenty. The list offered here hits on most of the highlights but is far from complete.

BC Museum of Mining (Map 11/B1)
Found alongside the Sea to Sky Highway between Whistler and Vancouver, the former Britannia Mines was once one of the world's largest copper mines. Mining artefacts and original blueprints of Mill 3 (a National Historic Site) are available for viewing. Board an authentic mining train and descend underground into a 1910 tunnel; wait for the lights to go off (briefly) to see how miners would have worked. Activities involving fossils, minerals and gold panning are also on site.

Capilano Suspension Bridge (Map 11/D6)
Originally built in 1889, the Capilano Suspension Bridge is suspended 135 metres (450 feet) across and 70 metres (230 feet) above the Capilano River. It is at the heart of a series of adventures here, including the Treetops Adventure, which links a series of giant Douglas firs via elevated suspension bridges.

Domaine de Chaberton Winery/Fraser Valley Wine Tours (Map 2/E7)

One of Langley's oldest and largest wineries, Domaine de Chaberton hosts free public tours year round, at 2 and 4 pm from February to November and at 3 pm in December and January, weather permitting. It is one of the most popular stops on the Fraser Valley winery tours. Visitors can take either a guided tour of the rest of the wineries or stop and pick up a map at a local visitor information centre.

Dr Sun Yat Sen Chinese Gardens (Map 1/C2)

Vancouver's Chinatown is the second largest in North America, while the Sun Yat Sen Chinese Gardens is the largest Chinese garden outside of China. Built in 1986, the garden is the first full-scale Scholar garden built outside of China using traditional techniques. This style of garden was typically for China's ancient elite. It features covered walkways and traditional architecture, making it a delight in any weather.

Fort Langley National Historic Site (Map 2/F4)

Fort Langley is called "the birthplace of BC." In 1827, the Hudson's Bay Company established a fur trading post here. As the post grew, so did its influence. Furs were shipped to Europe via Cape Horn, produce was traded to the Russians in Alaska, local cranberries found their way to California and Fraser River salmon was shipped to Hawaii! In 1858 rumours of gold on the Fraser River caused a massive influx of Americans to the area. Worried that the Americans might annex the area, British Columbia was proclaimed a Crown Colony on this site by James Douglas on November 19, 1858. These days, visitors can see Beaver pelts and HBC blankets and other historical artefacts and watch demonstrations of blacksmithing and barrel-making by costumed interpretive staff.

Gastown (Map 1/D2)

Surrounded by the towering buildings of downtown Vancouver, the historic district of Gastown is Vancouver's oldest neighbourhood, featuring cobblestone streets and beautiful redbrick architecture. It is home to the world's first steam-powered clock and the old Canadian Pacific Railway Station, built in 1912. Here you will get a sense of the design sensibilities of the era.

Grouse Mountain Skyride (Map 11/D6)

The Grouse Mountain Skyride is North America's largest aerial tram system and offers panoramic views over Vancouver and the Coast Mountains as it takes visitors to the top (well, almost top) of Grouse Mountain, high above the city. Once there, take in the sites and visit the Refuge for Endangered Wildlife, where two orphaned grizzly bears and three timber wolves live in a protected sanctuary. Or take in the view from an eagle's perspective at Theatre in the Sky, a high definition tour over the land and sea of Southwestern BC. In summer, enjoy lumberjack shows, hiking trails, guided eco walks, paragliding, falconry demonstrations, scenic chairlift rides, and helicopter tours, just to name a few of the activities found here. In winter, Grouse Mountain offers the finest in local skiing and snowboarding, as well as snowshoeing, ice-skating and sleigh rides.

Gulf of Georgia Cannery (Map 1/B5)

Built in 1894, the Gulf of Georgia Cannery is one of BC's last remaining intact canneries. A collection of buildings including the main cannery, icehouse, drum storage shed and others, sit atop wood pilings and can be toured. There are also 10,000 well-preserved artefacts at the cannery to browse through.

H.R. MacMillan Space Centre (Map 1/C2)

Discover the wonders of the cosmos at the H.R. MacMillan Space Centre. Located across English Bay from downtown Vancouver, the Space Centre offers kids and adult's knowledge and resources about space. One of the major events is the Laser Light shows, from Laser Pink Floyd to Laser Radiohead. Also extremely popular is the planetarium, where visitors can see projections of the night sky, as well as multimedia presentations on the past, present and future of space.

Hat Creek Ranch (Map 45/E3)

The Historic Hat Creek Ranch was a roadhouse, built in the 1860s, which catered to miners, stagecoaches and wagon trains along the Cariboo Wagon Road. The ranch was in operation until 1916, when automobiles were introduced to the Cariboo. These days, visitors can take a tour of the Roadhouse, visit a Native Village, take a stagecoach ride or go gold panning.

Historic Powell River (Map 18/F4)

The Powell River townsite is the only declared National Historic District in western Canada and only one of seven in Canada. The city was first constructed in 1910, and is surprisingly intact, with over 400 original buildings remaining, including the Patricia Theatre, the oldest, continuously running theatre in Canada. The town, while a company town built by the Powell River Company, was pre-planned as a direct response to the excesses of the industrialism of the late 19th Century and designed as a place where families could flourish.

Hope Christ Church (Map 15/F6)

A National Historic Site, the Hope Christ Church is the oldest, continuously operating church on the BC mainland.

Kilby (Map 4/C3)

Located near Mission, Kilby is a reminder of the once thriving community of Harrison Mills, which is now a ghost town. Goods from the 1900s are stocked at the General Store Museum, while it is possible to discover what it was like to live in the rural 1920s at the Manchester House Hotel or even explore the adjacent farm.

Lillooet Golden Mile of History (Map 44/D6)

Not one, not two, but 14 historic locations are found along the main street of Lillooet. From the Bridge of 12 Camels to the Old Bridge, a steel cable and wood bridge built in 1913, there is no shortage of sites from the Cariboo Gold Rush days. Highlights include the Miyazaki Heritage House, the Lillooet Museum and the CNR Station.

Lynn Canyon Suspension Bridge (Map 11/E7)

The tourist trappings of Capilano Suspension Bridge too much for you, but still want the experience of crossing a canyon on a bouncing bridge? Then Lynn Canyon is for you. The suspension bridge is the main feature of the area, but there are waterfalls to view and trails to hike in the popular regional park.

Museum of Anthropology (Map 1/A2)

The University of British Columbia's Museum of Anthropology boasts a vast collection of Aboriginal art and artefacts from BC and around the world. See traditional canoes, masks, jewellery, carvings, longhouse replicas and totem poles – including the world's smallest, which measures just 4.4 cm (1.7 inches), about the size of a pin.

Othello Tunnels (Map 15/G6)

Othello Tunnels (near Hope) are a 1900s engineering feat: they were constructed by slicing through solid granite, almost entirely by hand, to link the Kootenay region of BC to the coast by rail. Named for the engineer's love of Shakespeare, visitors (and Shakespeare buffs) can now trek through the tunnels.

Point Atkinson Lighthouse (Map 1/A1)

The lighthouse at Point Atkinson gives Lighthouse Park its name and can be seen from several viewpoints in the park. It was named in 1792 when Captain George Vancouver charted and named the land where the lighthouse sits. It later became the site of one of Canada's first manned light stations in 1874, although the lighthouse that currently occupies the point was built in 1912. While the original building no longer exists, old military buildings can be found here, remnants of the site's military moment in the sun during World War II.

Point Grey Gun Turrets (Map 1/A2)

The only military force to ever invade Canada actually came from the USA. But during World War II, there was a great fear of attacks by Japanese forces after Pearl Harbour. As a result, places like Point Grey had gun turrets built to defend against invaders. Fortunately, no attack came and the two gun turrets at tower beach serve as a reminder of those times. The concrete turrets also serve as canvases for some rather creative graffiti artist.

Science World (Map 1/C2)

One of Vancouver's most recognizable structures, the geodesic dome is just the shiny shell that holds a variety of hands-on interactive displays. Kids big and small can spend hours and even days exploring the inspirational feature exhibitions and shows in the Science Theatre.

Squamish Lil'wat Cultural Centre (Map 29/F5)

Located in Whistler, this cultural centre was created to celebrate the history of the local Squamish and Lil'wat First Nations. The centre showcases these cultures through art, exhibits, a museum, food, film and live performances. There is also a gallery dedicated to modern Aboriginal art, where visitors can make their own craft.

Stave Falls Power House (Map 3/C3)

The Power House at Stave Falls in Mission tells the story of BC's power industry. Interactive games and informative displays explain how electricity is created. See turbines and generators, as well as a Detroit model electric car, all from 1912!

Vancouver Aquarium (Map 1/C1)
There are over 70,000 creatures housed at Canada's largest aquarium, from the beautiful white beluga whales to dolphins and sea otters right down to star fish and anomies. For those truly interested in a unique experience, the Aquarium offers Animal Encounter sessions where you can help feed and train the animals or get up close with the beluga whales.

West Coast Railway Heritage Park (Map 22/C6)
Found in Squamish, the West Coast Railway Heritage Park is home to BC's most famous train, the Royal Hudson. It is also Western Canada's largest collection of heritage Railway equipment, including Canada's only authentic railway post-office car, as well as cabooses, snowploughs, cranes and other artefacts from the eras of steam, diesel and electric trains.

Westminster Abby (Map 3/E4)
Peek into the life of a Benedictine Monk at the Westminster Abbey Monastery in Mission. On site are the abbey grounds, seminary campus and the monks' farm (which supports their self-sufficient lifestyle). Admire the beautiful stained glass windows and hear the chimes of the 10-bell tower. Visitors are welcome for services.

Whistler Gondolas (Map 29/F5)
In winter, the gondolas at Whistler Blackcomb are mainly the domain of skiers and snowboarders, but in summer, visitors can explore the mountains, aided by the most extensive high-speed lift system in the world. Two gondolas from Whistler Village (Excalibur and Whistler Village), four-person chairlifts at the base of Blackcomb and Whistler mountains and a gondola at the Creekside base, 4 km south of Whistler Village, virtually eliminate line-ups. Add to that the new Peak 2 Peak Gondola, which opened in December 2008 and connects the top of Whistler to the top of Blackcomb.

Xa:ytem Longhouse Interpretive Centre (Map 3/F4)
This 9000-year-old ancient Aboriginal village site features a sacred transformer stone and one of BC's oldest houses. The house offers visitors a chance to learn about Sto:lo history, culture, archaeology and spirituality.

Yale (Map 15/F2)
One of the Gold Rush boomtowns was Yale. In its heyday it was hailed as the largest city north of San Francisco and west of Chicago. Now much smaller, historic Yale still evokes the spirit of the Gold Rush. Explore one of the oldest churches in BC – St. John the Divine – or walk through Pioneer Cemetery with headstones dating from 1862. Want to re-live history? Don a period costume, visit the Saloon and chat with some of Yale's historical characters in the interactive exhibit, "Yale: A Living History".

NATURAL ATTRACTIONS

Southwestern BC is a land formed by volcanoes and great tectonic shifts, then carved by water. There are plenty of natural attractions. These generally take the form of giant trees, hot springs and waterfalls, although there are plenty of other interesting sites too.

Alexander Falls (Map 29/C5)
While nearby Brandywine Falls is a tourist magnet, this waterfall is seldom visited. That's mostly due to the fact that it isn't right along the highway; instead it is 8 km (5 miles) up a poorly signed road. There is a recreation site here, with a nice viewpoint overlooking the 42 metre (140 foot) high falls.

Black Tusk (Map 22/E1)
Black Tusk gets its name from it deep black colour and it's sharp, tooth-like appearance. The 2,319 metre (7,608 foot) peak is visible from points along the Sea to Sky Highway, as well as from the hiking trail to its peak. The distinct peak is one of the most recognizable in the Coast Mountains.

Brandywine Falls (Map 29/D7)
One of the most photographed waterfalls in the province, Brandywine Falls is an impressive cascade that free falls over the lip of the cliff into a deep bowl. The falls are easily accessible at the top, but difficult to access from the base.

Bridal Veil Falls (Map 4/G4)
There is a very short trail to the base of Bridal Veil Falls, found east of Chilliwack. The 60 metre (195 foot) falls don't really fall; they get their name from the fact that the water runs down the face of the cliff, spreading out thinly like a veil.

Cascade Falls (Map 3/F2)
Located outside of Mission, there is a pair of falls here. The upper falls are 28 metres (91 feet) high and the lower falls are about half that. The lower falls are no longer readily accessible as the trail has been re-routed.

Cascade Lookout (Map 7/D5)
Manning Provincial Park sits in the heart of the Cascade Mountains. The turnoff to the Cascade Lookout and Sub-Alpine Meadows is located across the highway from Manning Park Resort. The 16 km (10 mile) drive ascends a steep and winding road right into the mountains. At the 8 km mark, the Cascade Lookout provides spectacular must-see vistas of valleys, lakes and rivers. Visitors who drive the remaining 8 km will be treated to a myriad of flower-clad meadows. If you experience the sensation of being on top of the world, it's because you are! The road is open June to September, weather permitting.

Chatterbox Falls (Map 47/E4)
The remote access to this hidden inlet discourages most visitors from ever venturing to Princess Louisa Park. What a shame, the spectacular fjord-like setting and world famous Chatterbox Falls (only a ten minute excursion from the ocean) are certainly worth the visit. The falls drop 40 metres (120 feet) almost directly into the ocean.

Chilliwack Lake Provincial Park (Map 5/F6)
This provincial park recently grew to include the old growth forest at Sapper's Park at the southeast end of the lake. This area features old growth fir and balsam trees.

Clear Creek Hot Springs (Map 25/G7)
Clear Creek is often packed on summer weekends. The soaking pools are located just off the Clear Creek Main, about 13 km (7.9 miles) from its junction with the Harrison East Forest Road. Access changes frequently, so go prepared to hike or bike in. Even at the best of times, the springs are only accessible by 4wd or ATV. There are four soaking pools, the hottest of which is 43°C (109°F), which range from an old cedar-box to a porcelain bathtub.

Cypress Falls Park (Map 11/A7)
This tiny, out of the way park has one of the largest stands of remaining old growth trees in the Lower Mainland.

Harrison Hot Springs (Map 4/F1)
While the humble (well, it never was really humble) hotel at Harrison Hot Springs has morphed into a destination resort complete with a marina and a golf course, at its heart remains the hot springs. The springs in no way retain any of their natural character, but coming here is the easiest way to have a soak in a hot springs in western BC. There are five separate pools here, at a variety of temperatures, two indoor and three outdoor.

Hell's Gate (Map 26/E5)
Anyone who has driven the Trans Canada through the Fraser Canyon between Hope and Cache Creek knows about Hell's Gate. But if you haven't stopped to see the site, where the entire Fraser River is squeezed through a 35 metre (114 foot) wide gorge at a rate of over 200 million gallons of water during spring run off, it is certainly worth it. The best way to see Hell's Gate is via the Airtram, which brings travellers 150 metres (500 ft) from the highway down to near river level. As you watch the raging river, think back to Simon Fraser's trip through here (sans highway and Airtram) in 1808, becoming the first non-native through the region.

High Falls (Map 22/A2)
The father of trail building in the Lower Mainland, Halvor Lunden, discovered these falls while working on a nearby power station. He is the one to blame for the steep, sometimes perilous trail to a viewpoint over the falls. The impressive falls cascade into a narrow canyon, over 100 metres (325 feet) high and sometimes less than 2 metres (6 feet) wide. Unfortunately, due to the narrow, winding canyon, it is impossible to see the falls from top to bottom.

Hollyburn Fir (Map 11/C7)
At the junction of the Old Brewis Trail and the Crossover Trail, (both in the Brother's Creek area) you will find this giant fir, standing 43.7 metres high, with a diameter of 2.96 metres. The tree is well over 1100 years old. Access is found from the west side of Lawson Creek Bridge on Pinecrest Drive or Eyremount, Crestwell and Millstream Roads.

Hollyburn Giant (Map 11/C7)
Located along the Old Strachen Trail, this is the oldest tree in a grove full of 800 year old trees. It shattered years ago, but is still standing and is estimated to be over 1300 years old, although some would place it's age at closer to 1700, which would make it one of the oldest (if not the oldest) living tree in the country.

Icecap Falls (Map 21/G1)
One of the largest falls in the Squamish area, this fall cascades around 450 metres (1,500 feet) down a cliff in the Squamish River Valley. In periods of high rainfall or spring melt, this is an impressive falls, but in the dog days of summer, the flow is very slow. The waterfall is located on an unnamed creek on the far side of the river and accessing the base of the falls is difficult. They can be seen from the Squamish Valley Road near "The Bayou" and km 29.

Keyhole [Pebble Creek] Hot Springs (Map 34/E1)
These wild hot springs are located about 5.4 km (3.3 mile) past the Meager Creek Road, just before the main road leaves the river and climbs steeply east. It is a 1.5 km (0.9 mile) scramble along the banks of the Lillooet River to the springs that bubble out onto the sand about 15 metres (40 feet) above the river on the north bank. The springs are inaccessible in times of high water and chances are you will have to dig your own soaking pool.

Lighthouse Park (Map 11/A7)
Lighthouse Park boasts one of the largest stands of remaining old growth in the Lower Mainland. While none of these trees are record holders, they make up for it in sheer numbers. The largest tree here is a Douglas fir, at 77 metres (253 feet) tall.

Meager Creek Hot Springs (Map 34/D3)
It seems that Meager Creek Hot Springs are more often closed than open. Meager Creek rests in a spectacular, remote and sometimes dangerous area that is prone to landslides, floods, and avalanches. More annoyingly, when it is open, the site is victim to its own popularity and is littered with debris and in the past was often closed due to high fecal coli form counts because people couldn't be bothered to dispose of their poop properly. In 2008 the site was re-opened after a five-year closure and was being managed with a day-use fee. But in September 2009, the bridge over Capricorn Creek washed out again. There is no word yet on when the bridge will be re-opened, although it is possible to access the springs by foot until then.

Norvan's Castle (Map 11/E6)
Found along the Coliseum Trail, this is the biggest of a number of big trees that have been discovered in this area. It is located along Norvan Creek. Again, there is no formal route, except for flagging tape. It is the fourth largest western hemlock (by volume) in the world and the widest, at 2.9 metres (9.5 feet).

Pitt River Hot Springs (Map 23/D7)
Tucked into a nook between the cliffs of the Pitt River Canyon and the Pitt River, these hot springs are one of the most scenic hot spring destinations in Southwestern BC. Unfortunately (or fortunately, depending on your perspective), the 30 km (18.3 mile) paddle/boat ride up Pitt Lake, the long bike ride/hike in and precarious scramble down to the pools from the top of the cliff (ropes are provided) make them a challenge to get to. For the less adventurous, there are also tour operators that will run you up to the hot springs.

Place Creek Falls (Map 36/E5)
Place Creek Falls is one of the most impressive waterfalls in British Columbia, although few people know it. The 412 metre (1,375 foot) high waterfalls cannot be seen all at once, but the parts that can be seen are very impressive. The falls are accessed by the Place Creek Trail, a steep, difficult trail to the Place Glacier. Access to the area is across private land.

Rainbow Falls (Map 29/F5)
One of the largest falls in the Lower Mainland, Rainbow Falls is also one of the most disappointing for waterfall baggers. Despite their height, viewing them is extremely difficult; only about a quarter of the falls can be seen at one time. The falls are estimated to be 380 metres (1,250 feet) high, although the creek drops over 660 metres (2,165 feet) in the space of less than a kilometre. Some would argue that these falls should be considered a single unit, which would make it one of the tallest falls in North America.

Shannon Falls (Map 22/C7)
On the official list of big waterfalls in BC, Shannon Falls places a respectable third. While there are many unofficial waterfalls that are taller, this one wins the popularity contest. Not only are they very easy to access, they are also one of the prettiest falls in the province. The falls tumble 337 metres (1,105 feet) before they come crashing to the ground just east of Highway 99 south of Squamish.

Showh Lakes Ancient Cedars (Map 29/F3)
One of two main stands of ancient trees near Whistler, there is a mix of red cedars and Douglas fir here. The red cedars are estimated at over 1000 years old, with a diameter of over 10 feet. The Douglas fir are over 650 years old. They are accessed by a bike trail and are within an hour's ride of Whistler.

Skookumchuck Narrows (Map 20/D6)
On a 3 metre (9.8 foot) tide, 757 billion litres (200 billion gallons) of water race through the narrows connecting Sechelt Inlet to Jervis Inlet. The result is a crescendo of turbulent rapids renowned for their astounding whirlpools and whitewater. It is an easy 8 km (5 mile) round trip to the viewing point at Roland Point. You will want to arrive here when the tidal surge is at its strongest. Check with the Sechelt Visitor Centre for best time to view.

Sloquet Hot Springs (Map 24/D6)
Due to the popularity of this site, there is now a camping fee being collected from May to September and there is 24-hour security on-site on weekends. The parking area lies 8.6 km (5.2 miles) up a fairly good side road from the Lillooet West Forest Road. From here is a short jaunt down an old road leads to the meadow and trail above the springs. The springs flow over a 10 metre (30 foot) cliff into several progressively cooler pools built out of stones before emptying into the frigid waters of Sloquet Creek. At its source, the water is an extremely hot 68°C (154°F) and is known to have a fairly strong sulphurous odour.

Spipiyus Provincial Park (Map 9/C1–20/C7)
The Caren Range has an old growth forest of yellow cedar, hemlock and balsam. A ring count on a yellow cedar stump, found in a section of the forest that was logged outside the park, showed the tree was over 1835 years old when logged, making it the oldest known yellow cedar in Canada, while a western hemlock stump showed the tree to be over 1200 years old, again, the oldest known tree of its species. While some of the old growth has been logged, much of it is still standing, protected in this provincial park.

St Agnes Well [Skookumchuck] Hot Springs (Map 24/B1)
Located on private land, there is now a fee to camp and use the springs, which are open year round. An A-Frame bathhouse covers the main soaking pool, which is half a fibreglass septic tank, but there are several other soaking tubs outside the bathhouse. The water is hot, 54°C (130°F), but a second pipe brings in cold water, so bathers can adjust the temperature to their liking. The springs are located below the Pemberton-Douglas Forest Service Road, near BC Hydro tower #682, next to the rushing Lillooet River. Access here can be rough in wet weather.

Stanley Park (Map 1/C1)
Tucked away in Stanley Park in Vancouver are two of BC's largest red alder, six of BC's biggest Bigleaf Maple (including the tallest) and a whole mess of other big trees. They are obviously are among the easiest big tees to access in the region. But even if big trees aren't your thing, Stanley Park is the green heart that beats within the breast of Vancouver, a verdant isthmus surrounded on three sides by water. The park offers a little bit for everyone, from man made attractions like the Vancouver Aquarium (see above) to plenty of trails that pass through lush rainforest, past large trees (and even larger tree stumps) and into places where the noise and rush of the city fade away, if only for a moment.

Stawamus Chief (Map 22/D7)
A granite monolith towering 700 metres (2,297 feet) over Squamish, the Chief is one of the most popular climbing destinations in Canada. The 3 sq km granite monolith is thought to be the second largest such geological feature in the world, after Yosemite's El Capitan. The Chief can be viewed from a variety of angles: from Squamish looking up, from the end of a hiking trail looking down or from up close and personal by experienced rock climbers. The most notable features of the Chief are named, including the Grand Wall and a trio of gullies that separate the Chief into three distinct peaks.

Temple of Time (Map 11/F7)
A grove of 100 metre (300 foot) tall trees found in the Lower Seymour Conservation Reserve became the impetus behind a push by a number of local environmental groups to see the Conservation Reserve turned into a park. That hasn't happened, but the grove has developed somewhat of a cult following. While there is no formal trail, a rough flagged route climbs steeply to these trees. These trees can be hard to find, but are worth the effort.

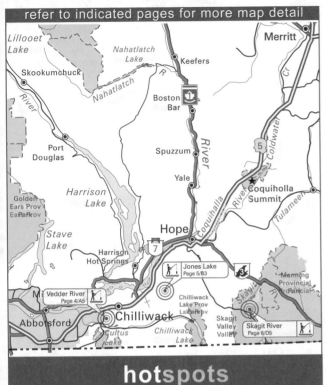

refer to indicated pages for more map detail

hotspots

*T*he fishing in Southwestern BC is simply outstanding. The breadth and variety is unparalleled, the scenery is amazing and there is good fishing throughout the entire year. From winter steelhead to summer trout and char, from spring cutthroat to fall salmon there is always an active fishery to entice you. There are also some pretty impressive fish that roam in the lakes, streams and ocean around the area.

We have divided the fishing opportunities into three sections: Lake, River and Ocean Fishing. The Lake section covers a tremendous variety of waterbodies that range from easily accessible urban lakes to remote boat access or hike-in lakes. The Sunshine Coast to Powell River area is the self-proclaimed cutthroat capital of the world, while fishing around Whistler and in the Fraser Valley is equally promising. Each write up contains the species and a few other important tidbits, such as stocking information, to help you pick a lake that will suit your wishes.

The River (or stream) section is a collection of all the major rivers and a selection of creeks in the area. If you cannot find the stream of interest, look for the major tributary it feeds. Most creeks have similar characteristics. River fishing is easily the most popular fishery in the region since there always seems to be a good run of salmon, steelhead or sea-run cutthroat. Add in the resident trout and char and you will see why anglers come from around the world to test these waters.

The final section is for Ocean Fishing. Once again we are not able to cover every hole, but we have done our best to include the more popular and productive salmon hot spots. By listing the popular fishing holes and when the fish are running, you should be able to pinpoint a place to start.

Combining this information with our detailed maps should help you get out and enjoy a few hours, days or even weeks of fishing. But if you want even more details on the better lakes and streams in the region, we recommend picking up the Southwestern BC Fishing Mapbook. This book is loaded with fishing tips, depth charts and hot spot maps and includes even more alternatives than this book. It is the perfect complement to this mapbook.

Remember, it is essential to review the fishing regulations before heading out. In particular, the regulations for steelhead and salmon change frequently; visit the recreational fishing section at www.pac.dfo-mpo.gc.ca for up-to-date information.

LAKE FISHING

There are a multitude of good lake fishing opportunities in the region that range from remote walk-in lakes to some fine large trolling lakes. As a general rule of thumb, the smaller lower elevation lakes offer better fishing beginning in early April until late June. When the low elevation lakes warm, anglers should focus their efforts on higher elevation lakes. These lakes usually open up in early June and remain productive over the summer months. Into the fall, the lower elevation lakes pick up again and by late fall, the higher elevation lakes begin to ice over. However, fishing pressure in the urban areas can be heavy. You will often find better luck with the stocked lakes. For this reason we have marked the lakes that have been stocked in the last few years with the 🐟 symbol.

Alice Lake (Map 22/D5) 🐟
Alice Lake is the titular feature of Alice Lake Provincial Park. It is a popular recreation lake with a large, grassy picnic site and two sandy beaches. It is a good place to bring a family to try to catch small trout in the spring or swim and sunbath in the summer. The lake has Dolly Varden as well as rainbow and cutthroat. The fish, particularly the stocked rainbow, remain small (a 30 cm/12 inch fish would be a good-sized catch) but numerous. The best time to fly fish is during the black ant hatch in May. A man-made wharf at the east end is a good spot to try but it is closed to fishing from May 15 to September 1.

Alouette Lake (Map 3/A1–13/D7) 🐟
Alouette Lake is a large lake that is the main feature within Golden Ears Provincial Park. The lake has benefited from a fertilization program that aids the intensive stocking program. With the fertilization, the kokanee numbers have picked up and as a result the size of the cutthroat, rainbow, Dolly Varden and lake trout have shown improvements. Some of the lake trout can grow to over 10 kg (22 lbs) and are caught by trolling a plug below the 60 feet (18 metre) level. The other species can be found by trolling along the drop-offs at one of the creek estuaries or in one of the many bays. The lake is very deep (up to 130 metres/423 feet deep) and the fish can be scattered.

Alta Lake (Map 29/E5)
Alta Lake is the biggest of a chain of lakes found in the heart of Whistler and produces the best fishing in the valley. Recent reports boast of cutthroat to 60 cm (24 in) that are being caught on sinking lines around the weed beds, near docks and around the drop-offs using minnow imitation flies. Rainbow to 30 cm (12 in) are also fairly active, while kokanee and dollies also roam the lake but in smaller numbers. The lake is glacier fed and the fishing is best in June to early July particularly near the inflow and outflow creeks (south and north ends of the lake). Fishing is much more effective from a boat or float tube, but be wary of sudden winds that can blow up. There is also a spring/fall speed restriction of 12 km/h (7 mph).

Alpha Lake (Map 29/E5) 🐟
This lake is found in Whistler, to the south of the larger Alta Lake. It is home to substantial development on its shores. The main public access points are from the Valley Trail and Alpha Lake Park, which are both found on the east side of the lake. The lake still offers some good fly-fishing in June and early July for fair sized trout, while trolling (electric motors only) can produce a few small kokanee and Dolly Varden.

Anderson Lake (Map 37/B1)
This large lake is accessed from D'Arcy or Seton Portage. The lake offers good fishing for rainbow and dollies mainly by trolling. There are a number of private residences that line the lake.

Anne Lakes (Map 12/B3)
Located in Pinecone Burke Provincial Park, Anne Lake is reached by a 6 km hike along a logging road and trail. Little Anne Lake is located north of Anne Lake. Given the rough road access, bringing a boat into the lakes is a challenge. The lakes (and road) are not ice free until early May. At this time, the small rainbow are quite aggressive. Fishing should remain steady through the summer and into the fall.

Belknap Lake (Map 12/B3)
This small lake is the first lake on the trail to Anne and Joseph Lakes. The remote access allows for some good fishing for generally small rainbow, especially after the lake opens up in spring.

Birkenhead Lake (Map 36/D3)
Birkenhead Lake is home to a provincial park complete with a beach, boat launch and camping facilities. The lake contains fair numbers of rainbow, dollies, kokanee and whitefish. Trolling is the mainstay of the lake with the best time to fish being in the early summer or fall. The water is surprisingly clear, making fly-fishing exciting when you see a fish rise. Private cabins are found along the northwest shore of the bigger lake. While there is a trail along the western shore, there are very few places that are open enough to fish from.

Black Lake (Map 46/A4)
This lake is located on West Redonda Island and receives very little fishing pressure. To reach the lake, you must boat to Roscoe Bay Marine Park and then bushwhack your way in. Once you reach the lake, try trolling or fly-fishing for the cutthroat that reach 2 kg (4.5 lbs). There is a tenting site in the marine park.

Blackwater Lake (Map 36/F3) 🐟
Blackwater Lake is indeed dark coloured but clear lake located just east of D'Arcy. It is stocked annually with rainbow, which allows the fishing to remain steady for fairly small fish, though the lake is prone to winterkill. Your best bet is to fly fish or spincast from a boat or a float tube during the spring or fall. There is a recreation site with camping on the northeast end of the lake.

Blue Earth Lake (Map 39/D2)
Protected by parkland, this lake is located south of Upper Hat Creek on the Earth Lake Road (2wd access). The lake is not overly popular despite its scenic surroundings, crystal-clear water and prominent shoals. It offers a good fishery for rainbow trout to 1 kg (2 lbs) by fly-fishing or trolling. There is rustic camping and a place to launch small boats at the lake.

Blue [Fishblue] Lake (Map 33/D7) 🐟
Located in the Fraser Canyon, north of Boston Bar, Blue Lake is more nutrient rich than lakes farther south and west. The fishing starts in late April and tails off in early July for rainbow, which are stocked annually. By September, the fishing picks up again in this low elevation lake and continues into November. The small lake is a decent fly-fishing lake with a resort to base your activities.

Bob's Lake (Map 8/D2)
This small Texada Island lake is home to a recreation site and small rainbow trout. The lake is best fished in the spring and fall as shallow waters warm significantly during summer.

Botanie Lake (Map 39/D6)
This lake is accessed by the Botanie Valley Road north of Lytton. It provides decent fishing for rainbow, but access is limited as the lake lies on an Indian Reserve (private property).

Brohm Lake (Map 22/C4) 🐟
Brohm Lake is located next to Highway 99 and receives heavy fishing pressure throughout the year. The lake contains lots of Gammarus shrimp and chironomids, which feed the stocked rainbow, cutthroat and dollies. You can take advantage of the small hand launch, though it is possible to fish from shore. The number of trout stocked here has decreased in the last few years, presumably to encourage the natural cutthroat trout population.

Brown Lake (Map 20/C6)
A small lake found next to the trail leading to Skookumchuck Narrows that has been stocked with cutthroat in the past. Rumour has it that some of these fast growing fish top the scales at 7 kg (17 lbs). That's a big fish for such a small lake and more likely than not just an angler's tale. More recent (and more reliable) reports indicate the fish average 25–30 cm (10–12 inches) in size.

Browning Lake (Map 11/B1) 🐟
Located in Murrin Provincial Park next to Highway 99, this small lake is stocked frequently with 20–25 cm (8–10 inch) rainbow. It is not uncommon to see several fishermen lining the shores as you drive past on the way to (or from) Squamish. The lake is stocked with catchable-sized fish, which are usually fished out by the end of the year. The lake is blessed with a nice day-use area.

Buntzen Lake (Map 12/A7) 🐟
Buntzen Lake is a BC Hydro Reservoir, and is subject to dramatic and sudden changes in water level, although at 200 metres (650 feet) deep, you won't have to worry about them draining the lake dry. The lake is easily accessed from loco and is a very popular recreational area. Anglers will find stocked rainbow, cutthroat, dollies and kokanee, all averaging about 30 cm (12 inches) in size. Since there is a powerboat restriction, it is best to bring a float tube or canoe and try spincasting or fly-fishing from the edges of the lake. The lake has steep drop-offs and a trail circles the lake making shore fishing quite easy.

Burnaby Lake (Map 1/G2)
Located in central Burnaby, this lake has a few fish to tease ardent anglers. It is not a destination type lake but if you are out paddling with the family why not bring a fishing rod along and try for carp.

Burkholder Lake (Map 43/C1)
Located to the west of Yalakom River, this small lake receives light fishing pressure. As a result, it offers some good fly-fishing for small rainbow.

Butterfly Lake (Map 22/B2)
Difficult access makes this small lake a very good fly-fishing destination. Rainbow average 25 cm (10 inches) in size and are best caught in the spring and fall.

Callaghan Lake (Map 29/B3)
Accessed by the Callaghan Forest Road southwest of Whistler, this bigger lake provides decent fishing for rainbow to 1 kg (2 lbs). Given the high elevation, the fishing starts in early summer and continues through to the fall. Trolling is the primary method of fishing. The scenic lake is now part of a provincial park complete with a rustic camping area and boat launch. The lake was once stocked, but the rainbow trout have established a self-sustaining population.

Campbell Lake (Map 4/F1)
Campbell Lake is a small, shallow lake, found in the mountains west of Harrison Hot Springs. The lake can be accessed by a rough 4wd road, then a short hike in. Alternately, you can access it via a long hike from Harrison Hot Springs. The lake contains a few small rainbow best caught in the early spring or late fall.

Carlson and Dragon Lakes (Map 9/D3)
These two lakes are accessed off the Halfmoon Forest Road (4wd recommended) on the Sunshine Coast. Despite the size difference, both lakes have fair numbers of cutthroat to 30 cm (12 inches). Due to the elevation, fishing is certainly better in the early spring or fall.

Carpenter Lake (Map 42, 43)
Carpenter Lake is a long, narrow man-made lake, which provides reasonably good fishing for dollies, rainbow and kokanee that reach 2 kg (4 lb) in size. Trolling is the mainstay of the lake although it is possible to shore fish at the creek mouths. Boaters should be wary of deadheads and draw down on the lake.

Cat Lake (Map 22/D5)
This tiny, low elevation lake is one of the first lakes to be fishable in spring and sees heavy pressure throughout the year, though the fish are usually quite small. Despite the low elevation, the fishing remains good through summer as the lake is deep and the thick trees shelter the lake from too much direct sunlight. The popularity of the scenic lake has resulted in a new development on the recreation site and trails in the area. There is a wharf for those who do not have a floatation device.

Cerulean Lake (Map 36/B4)
Nestled below Sun God Mountain, Cerulean Lake is seldom fished, as the only access is via helicopter or bushwhacking up a creek draw from the Birkenhead Lake Forest Road. The best fishing is around the northern and western shores where the lake drops off steeply. The high elevation lake is deep, cold and contains a fair number of rainbow in the 15–30 cm (6–12 inch) range.

Chadsey Lake (Map 3/G5)
Chadsey Lake is found within Sumas Mountain Park and is accessed by trail. The illegal introduction of largemouth bass has all but wiped out the rainbow fishery. Bass anglers can expect fair fishing for average size largemouth. Since the small lake is hard to shore fish, bringing a float tube or pontoon boat is recommended.

Cheakamus Lake (Map 29/G7–23/A1)
Cheakamus Lake is the easiest lake in Garibaldi Provincial Park to access and the earliest to open up (in May). The lake is accessed by a gentle 3 km (1.8 mile) trail from the end of the Cheakamus Lake Road that allows anglers to haul in a float tube or canoe. The scenic lake contains rainbow in the 20–30 cm (8–12 inch) range, as well as a few larger dollies. The lakeshore is heavily forested, limiting access for shore fishing.

Chehalis Lake (Map 14/B5)
North of Harrison Bay on the Chehalis Forest Road, this lake is 10 km (6 miles) long and has historically provided spotty fishing throughout the year for cutthroat, rainbow or dollies, averaging 20–30 cm (8–12 inches). However, the lake was recently hit by a giant mudslide, which has probably impacted the quality of fishing. We say probably, as access to the lake is now closed indefinitely.

Chilliwack Lake (Map 5/F6)
Chilliwack Lake is a big, popular lake that forms the heart of Chilliwack Lake Provincial Park. The lake features a number of camping areas and former recreation sites, which have now been consolidated as part of the provincial park. While the former Paleface and Depot Creek recreation sites and Sappers Provincial Park still grant access to the lake, camping is not allowed. The lake contains rainbow, cutthroat, dollies and kokanee, all growing to 2 kg (4.5 lbs). Since the lake is glacier fed, the waters remain cold throughout the summer, while the fishing remains steady. The fish here are notoriously difficult to catch, with trolling being your best bet.

Clerf Lake (Map 6/A5)
Clerf Lake is a small high elevation lake located to the south of the Silver Skagit Road. It is reached by a long trail off the Upper Klesilkwa Creek Road. Due to the high frequency of winterkill, it is unconfirmed whether there is still a rainbow fishery.

Clowhom Lake (Map 21/D6)
This remote lake is found at the north end of the Salmon Inlet and requires a boat to access. From there, it is advised to pack a canoe into the lake and paddle to the north end where the Clowhom River enters the lake. Because of the difficult access, the lake provides very good fishing during the fall (September–early October) for cutthroat to 2 kg (4.5 lbs) in size as well as a few large dollies. It is possible to fish from shore, although using a floatation device is better.

Como Lake (Map 2/A2)
An urban lake in the heart of Coquitlam, Como Lake is well stocked with rainbow to offset the heavy fishing pressure. The lake also holds brown catfish and carp and there are still rumours that people still pull out cutthroat and brook trout. During the spring and fall, the fishing is usually pretty good but in summer, the lake warms up and the fishing slows down. Most people spincast or fly fish from shore (there is no fishing on the lake's northern shore) or from the two docks. No motors are allowed on the urban lake.

Coquihalla Lakes (Map 16/F1)
The Coquihalla Lakes receives little fishing pressure, despite the fact that they lie alongside a major highway and are home to a resort with a campground. Even more surprising, the lake offers good fishing for rainbow trout to 1 kg (2 lbs) by trolling. The fishing season, given the high elevation, begins in early summer and lasts to the fall.

Cranberry Lake (Map 18/G3)
Cranberry Lake is located just east of Powell River and provides marginal fishing for cutthroat to 40 cm (16 inches) in size throughout the spring and early summer. There is a beach and boat launch at the lake, which is easily accessed by paved road.

Crown Lake (Map 45/A4)
Crown Lake lies in Marble Canyon Provincial Park and offers stocked rainbow. The best fishing is found throughout the spring or fall.

Crowston Lake (Map 9/E4)
A rough logging road leads from Highway 101 just south of Trout Lake to this small lake. The lake is best fished in the spring and fall as the waters warm significantly in the summer. Since the shore is lined with weeds, fly-fishing or spincasting from a small boat or float tube for the stocked cutthroat is your best option. The fish average 20–40 cm (8–16 inches) in size.

Cultus Lake (Map 4/C6)
Accessed by a paved road south of Chilliwack, this popular recreational lake is noted more for its boating and jet skiing than fishing, although trolling in the early spring or late fall can produce small rainbow and the odd larger cutthroat and dollies. The large lake remains relatively cool in the summer and while fishing does slow a bit, it does not suffer the doldrums to the same extent as smaller, shallower lakes in the area. Shore anglers can try working around one of the five main inflow creeks, around the Main Beach, or in Maple Bay. Provincial parks, stores, resorts, water slides and all manner of tourist traps are available at this popular summer retreat.

Davis Lake (Map 3/E1)
To the east of Stave Lake, Davis Lake is home to a provincial park complete with a campground, beach and boat launch. The lake provides an opportunity to catch small cutthroat (to 30 cm/12 inches) primarily in the spring. This is a low elevation lake and is stocked regularly with cutthroat. You will need to carry a boat or canoe in since the access road is gated.

Deeks Lake (Map 11/B4)
Located at the north end of Cypress Provincial Park, the lake is reached along the Howe Sound Crest Trail from the south or the Deeks Lake Trail from the northwest. Either way, it involves a strenuous hike to the lake. To save your back hauling a float tube, you can produce by casting from shore at the inflow and outflow creeks. Given the elevation, fishing for the small cutthroat begins in late spring and extends into the summer.

Deer Lake: Burnaby (Map 1/F3)
Deer Lake isn't a great fishing lake, but it is an easily accessible oasis from the city. The lake is regularly stocked with cutthroat and rainbow, but these fish are usually muddy and do not make good table fair. Alternatively, visitors can have a lot of fun fishing for black crappie, which become much more active in the summer. The lake can be fished from the shore, or by float tube or canoe/small boat, which are available to rent in summer.

Deer Lake: Sasquatch Park (Map 15/A7)
Located in Sasquatch Provincial Park, Deer Lake has both rainbow and cutthroat in the 20–35 cm (8–14 inch) range. The lake is best fished by boat, although shore fishing along the road is possible. Since the fish are plentiful, they are easily caught using a number of methods. Note that electric motors only are allowed on the lake.

Dennett Lake (Map 12/D7)
A small lake located in Pinecone Burke Provincial Park. Reports are mixed on this lake. Some say there are no fish; some say you will find cutthroat and brook trout. If you want to find out for yourself, you will have to hike a steep 4 km (2.4 miles) one-way trail to find out. Nearby Munro Lake is all but a distant memory since the dam let go.

Devil's Lake (Map 3/C2)
A short trail leading downhill from the 4.9 km (3 mile) mark on the Florence Lake Forest Road accesses the popular lake. It is a definite advantage to pack in a canoe or float tube as the western shore is very brushy and the deeper, more productive area is off the northeastern shoreline. The low elevation means better fishing for the cutthroat occurs in the early spring or fall.

Dodd Lake (Map 19/D1)
Dodd Lake is one of the larger lakes in the Powell Forest Canoe Circuit that can also be accessed by vehicle along the Weldwood Main. It holds cutthroat that can reach 3 kg (6.6 lbs) and some small kokanee. Trolling is the preferred method of fishing although casting a fly or a lure in one of the small bays can be productive. There are a few recreation sites on the low elevation lake, with the main (Dodd Lake) site sporting a boat launch.

Duck Lake (Map 19/A3)
Duck Lake is a low elevation lake, easily accessed on the Duck Lake Forest Road. It provides fair fishing for cutthroat in the 25–30 cm (10–12 inches) range as well as some small kokanee. Trolling is the preferred method at this lake.

Duffey Lake (Map 37/D6)
This large, beautiful lake is accessed by Highway 99 northeast of Pemberton. The lake has rainbow and dollies (to 2 kg/4.5 lbs), which are best caught by trolling. There is a campsite and a boat launch at the north end of the lake.

Eaton Lake (Map 5/G2)
Located on a steep trail off the Silver Skagit Road, Eaton Lake holds many small rainbow and cutthroat, averaging 20–30 cm (8–12 inches). This is a high mountain lake that is noted for its cold water and limited shore fishing opportunities.

Echo Lake (Map 22/B7)
This mountain lake is located west of Squamish. The difficult access should ensure a peaceful fishing experience for anglers.

Edith Lake (Map 22/D5)
Edith Lake contains stocked rainbow (to 30cm) and a few wild cutthroats. Fly-fishing is very difficult from shore due to the encroaching vegetation and the expansive muddy shallows. Bait fishermen are able to pick their spots and cast a bobber out far enough to get some action. There are some nice submerged logs, which can be seen in the murky water. Sink a wet fly next to one of the logs and you have a good chance for success.

Elbow Lake (Map 4/C2)
Found along the Chehalis Forest Road north of Harrison Mills, Elbow Lake is a small, steep-sided lake that is stocked regularly with rainbow. Access is found at the south end of the lake. The Chehalis Forest Road runs along the lake's west side, creating a clearing where shoreline anglers can fish.

Elsay Lake (Map 11/G6)
This high elevation lake is found towards the north end of Mount Seymour Park. A long challenging trail passes beneath Mount Seymour and Mount Elsay before reaching the lake. Elsay Lake has good numbers of small rainbow for the brave angler willing to venture in during the late summer.

Emily Lake (Map 18/F5)
Like other lakes on Texada Island, Emily Lake is a very nutrient rich lake, which leads to vibrant insect and aquatic vegetation growth. This means plenty of food for the fast growing cutthroat. The lake is found at the north end of the island by a short trail that leads through private property (permission necessary to access the lake).

Evans Lake (Map 22/C4)
Evans Lake is surrounded by private property, limiting access. But ardent anglers can take advantage of the trail system found near Evans Lake Camp. The lake opens up early in the year and offers small rainbow. The lake is suffering from a white worm infestation and it is not recommended that you keep any fish caught here.

Falls Lake (Map 16/E1)
Located west of the Coquihalla Toll Booth, Falls Lake is accessed by a gentle 2 km (1.2 mile) trail from Exit 221 on Highway 5. Not many anglers venture into this scenic mountain lake, which can provide fast action for small rainbow during the summer.

Fire Lake (Map 24/C4)
This long, narrow lake has many small rainbow to 30 cm (12 inches). The remote, high elevation lake is found just outside the Garibaldi Provincial Park

boundary. The final kilometre or so to the lake is along a hiking trail. The rainbow here come readily to a fly or lure in the summer through fall.

Flash Lake (Map 7/C6)
Located southwest of Lightning Lake along the Lightening Lake Chain Trail, Flash Lake holds a good number of rainbow averaging 20–25 cm (8–10 inches).

Flora Lake (Map 5/F5)
A most difficult hike reaches Flora Lake. Given this, fishing pressure is not heavy. For those willing to carry a float tube 7 km (4.3 miles) to the lake, the fishing can be fairly good for small rainbow in the 20–25 cm (8–10 inch) range primarily by fly-fishing.

Foley Lake (Map 5/D4)
This scenic, low elevation lake is quite unique. It has crystal clear, cold waters that are more common in high elevation lakes. The lake makes a good family destination due to the relatively easy access and stocked rainbow trout. In addition to stocked rainbow, the lake has Dolly Varden, which grow to about 35 cm (14 inches) or 2 kg (4 lbs). There is an electric motor restriction on the lake.

Fountain [Kwotlenemo] Lake (Map 44/E6)
Fountain Lake is the most popular of the lakes in the Three Valley Chain. It is home to several popular recreation sites complete with boat launches. The fishing is fairly good for stocked rainbow to 2 kg (4.5 lbs) by trolling slowly (electric motors only). If fishing is slow, nearby Chilhil and Cinquefoil Lakes may be worth a try.

Francis Lake (Map 14/E7)
Accessed by a rough 4wd road off the Harrison West Forest Road, this small lake is home a small recreation site. The stocked rainbow are best caught in the spring and fall. The lake can be fished from the shore, though expansive shoals make it a bit difficult.

Freda Lake (Map 19/D2)
Located on the Stillwater Main (good 2wd access), this fair sized lake has a fair number of cutthroat trout in the 25–35 cm (10–14 inch) range. The lake provides decent trolling throughout the spring and fall.

Garden Bay Lake (Map 9/B1)
Found next to Pender Harbour, Garden Bay Lake sees more attention from paddlers since most of the anglers devote their attention to the saltwater fishery. This is a shame. The pretty lake has stocked cutthroat to 35 cm (14 inches) best caught in the spring or the fall.

Garibaldi Lakes (Map 20/E2)
Located in Garibaldi Provincial Park, these two spectacular sub-alpine lakes are accessed by the steep but well maintained Black Tusk Trail. The lakes are fairly high in elevation and fishing is possible from June through the summer and fall. Garibaldi Lake provides excellent fishing for small rainbow that can reach the 45–55 cm (18–22 inch) range. Shore fishing is possible. Lesser Garibaldi Lake holds rainbow that are smaller (25–30 cm/10–12 inches) and fewer in number.

Garrison Lakes (Map 7/E2)
A poorly maintained trail leads off the Sunday Summit Forest Road to two scenic sub-alpine lakes. The lakes produce rainbow to 2 kg (4.5 lbs) by fly-fishing. Given the elevation, fishing is best left to the early summer through fall. The remote access limits fishing pressure.

Gates Lake (Map 36/E4)
Gates Lake is located along the road to D'Arcy and holds rainbow and dollies to 2 kg (4.5lbs), as well as smaller kokanee and cutthroat. Given the easy access and the private residences that line the lake, this lake receives heavy fishing pressure. A resort is located at the lake, offering accommodation.

Gillis Lake (Map 27/G2)
This popular lake is easily accessed off the Coquihalla Highway (Highway 5). As a result, the recreation site with a cartop boat launch can be busy on weekends. Fishing for rainbow trout to 1.5 kg (3 lbs) in size remains steady due in part to the stocking program. The best time for fishing is during the spring and fall using a fly or by trolling.

Glacier Lake (Map 24/B3)
A rough 4wd road leads to this remote lake on the boundary of Garibaldi Provincial Park. The difficult access means that there is fairly good fishing for rainbow trout, kokanee and Dolly Varden throughout the spring and fall. Trolling is your best bet, although sampling the shoreline with a fly or small lure can be effective.

Goat Lake (Map 46/G5)

Goat Lake is a low elevation lake containing small kokanee, cutthroat to 2 kg (4.5 lbs) and rainbow trout. The big lake offers excellent fly-fishing and spincasting for rainbow when they congregate near the mouth of Eldred River in late April-mid May in preparation for spawning. The rest of the year, rainbow are best caught by trolling, as are the kokanee. There is a pair of rustic campsites along the southeast shore of the lake, which is part of the Powell Forest Canoe Circuit.

Grace Lake (Map 14/E7) 🐟

Grace Lake is a small, marshy lake found on the west side of Harrison Lake. The lake has poor shoreline access for people on foot and is too small and shallow to troll effectively. Anglers wishing to chase the stocked rainbow (up to 35 cm/14 inches) should use a float tube or a small boat in the spring and fall. Found next to the Harrison West Forest Road, the lake and recreation site are busy places.

Green Lake (Map 29/G4)

Located just north of the Whistler Village Centre, this emerald-coloured lake has rainbow to 1 kg (2 lbs), dollies to 3 kg (6.6 lbs) and some smaller kokanee. The lake is best trolled, but fly anglers will find good fishing at many places around the lake, including the River of Golden Dreams Inlet. The lake is single barbless, no bait only.

Greendrop Lake (Map 5/F4)

Greendrop Lake has fair numbers of small rainbow that can reach 30 cm (12 inches) in size. These trout are best taken on the fly from a float tube. The deep water and high elevation ensures that the water temperature remains cold throughout the summer and the 6 km (3.6 mile hike) keeps out all but the most avid angler. The lake makes a fine overnight destination.

Green Timbers Lake (Map 2/B4) 🐟

Found in the heart of Surrey off of 96th Avenue, most people would be shocked to know that this small lake produces some trophy trout. Rumours are that a 4.5 kg (10 lb) rainbow was caught here. The lake is stocked annually with catchable sized trout and is only accessible on foot. There is good shore access allowing fly anglers to practise their trade.

Gun Lake (Map 42/A3)

Gun Lake is a popular recreational lake to the west of Goldbridge. The big lake is lined with cabins, has a resort, a boat launch and even a recreation site on the west side of the lake. The lake offers fair fishing for rainbow to 1 kg (2 lb), small kokanee and dollies to 4 kg (9 lbs). Trolling is the mainstay of the lake.

Gwyneth Lake (Map 42/A5)

Located next to the Hurley River Forest Road, Gwyneth Lake is a shallow lake that can be fished using a dry fly or by spincasting.

Hammil [West] Lake (Map 19/A4)

Hammil Lake is a medium sized water body found east of Powell River. Given the low elevation, it provides decent fishing for cutthroat in the spring and fall. There is a boat launch as well as a good trail system to provide access for shore fishers.

Hanging Lake (Map 5/E7)

Located high up in the mountains on the border between Canada and the USA, this lake is reached by a steep trail from the south end of Chilliwack Lake. The lake holds rainbow that grow over 45 cm (18 inches) in size. Fly-fishing and spincasting can be a lot of fun on this lake.

Harrison Lake (Map 4, 14, 24, 25)

Harrison Lake is a huge lake that is 55 km (33.5 miles) long and averages a couple kilometres wide. The best boat access is from Harrison Hot Springs or Green Point. The town also provides full facilities including hotels and camping. Although mainline logging roads run up each side of the lake, there are few access points. You can find cutthroat to 40 cm (16 inches) and rainbow to 1.5 kg (3 lb) by trolling. The best locations to fish near the south end of the lake are at the mouth of Cascade Bay or along the shores north of the Harrison River outflow. The lake is very deep (up to 200 metres/650 feet) and is known for its hostile winds.

Haslam Lake (Map 19/B2)

This big lake is easily accessed northeast of Powell River. The lake provides fairly good trolling for cutthroat, rainbow and kokanee that average 30 cm (12 inches) in size. The odd fish can grow to 2 kg (4.5 lbs). Despite its size, the low elevation lake has an electric motor only restriction.

Hatzic Lake & Slough (Map 3/E4)

Hatzic can easily be found by travelling 6 km (3.7 mi) east of the town of Mission on Highway 7. Not known as a great fishing lake, Hatzic Lake does support rainbow, cutthroat, black crappie, carp, juvenile Coho and sturgeon. Rainbow are the most numerous and will reach up to 0.5 kg (1 lb). You might also try your luck in the Hatzic Slough, which features similar fishing as the lake.

Hayward Lake (Map 3/C3)

Hayward Lake is a man-made lake easily accessed to the west of Mission. The lake had been extensively stocked with steelhead and rainbow in the past but the fish population has not really grown. The lake is best fished for small rainbow (to 35 cm/14 inches) towards the south end by boat near the Ruskin Dam where there is a deep hole. Shore fishing is possible along the western shores or at the north end where the Stave River empties into the lake. There are day-use facilities at the lake together with a concrete boat launch.

Hicks Lake (Map 15/A7) 🐟

Hicks is the hub of Sasquatch Provincial Park, with its camping, beach and warm water. The lake contains fairly good numbers of rainbow, kokanee and cutthroat, which are larger than those in the other lakes in the park. Better fishing is found around the small island or at the mouth of one of the four bays in the spring or fall. When the water warms in the summer, the sandy beach may be more appealing than the fishing. At this time, it is best to try trolling deep near the centre of the lake. The nearby Beaver Pond (found to the north) produces surprisingly well. It isn't unusual to catch rainbow or cutthroat up to 40 cm (16 inches) if you can get beyond the logs and vegetation.

Hoover Lake (Map 3/D2)

This small trail accessible lake is set in a thick forest and is rarely visited. Visitors need to hike nearly 4 km (2.4 miles) to get to the lake. The lake tends to warm up in the summer but in the spring and fall you can expect good fishing from a float tube for rainbow and cutthroat that average 20–30 cm (8–12 inches) in size. Shore fishing is very difficult due to debris except for a few spots along the east shore.

Horseshoe Lake (Map 19/D2)

Most anglers access this lake from the recreation site on Nanton Lake. Horseshoe has many small cutthroat, rainbow and kokanee that are best caught by fly-fishing or trolling. The cutthroats are known to grow up to 2 kg (4.5 lbs) in size although catching a fish this size is rare. It is best to concentrate your fishing efforts in the channel between Horseshoe Lake and Nanton Lake or in one of the many bays or weed beds that line the western shore of the lake. There are a couple of rustic (and quite lovely) camping spots, developed for canoeists on the Powell Forest Canoe Circuit.

Hotel Lake (Map 9/A1) 🐟

Hotel Lake has stocked cutthroat to 35 cm best caught in the spring or fall by fly-fishing or spincasting. The low elevation lake is electric motor only.

Hut Lake (Map 22/B4)

This small lake has numerous small rainbow that come readily to a fly, bait or small lure. The road up to this lake is very rough and overgrown and you may have to walk or bike in from Levette Lake.

Inkwathia Lake (Map 15/D1)

A high elevation lake northwest of Yale accessed along the Inkwathia Forest Road. If you have a high clearance 4wd vehicle, you'll only need to walk about 2 km (1.2 miles) to the lake, which is home to plenty of rainbow.

Inland [Loon] Lake (Map 18/G2)

A popular recreational destination, this pretty lake is located northeast of Powell Lake. Given the low elevation, it is best to troll in the spring or early summer (there is no boat launch, but a short carry with a cartopper will bring you to the lake). The lake provides good fishing for cutthroat up to 50 cm (20 in) in size as well as for a few small kokanee. A well maintained, wheelchair accessible, trail circles the lake allowing shore fishing. The lake is heavily regulated to help protect the vulnerable cutthroat.

Ireland Lake (Map 19/C2)

Ireland Lake is one of the smaller lakes along the Powell Forest Canoe Route. There is no vehicle access to the lake but you can bushwhack from the Goat Lake Main, or hike along either of the portage trails to the lake. The lake offers good fishing for small cutthroat and kokanee throughout the spring and into the early summer. It is best to fish near the creek inlet leading to Dodd Lake or at the outlet to Nanton Lake.

Isabel Lake (Map 12/G4)

Isabel Lake is worth a try if you want a multi-day excursion into rarely visited country. The lake is accessed by an unmarked trail from the shores of Pitt Lake, which, in turn, is only accessed by boat. Once you reach the lake, you will be rewarded with very good fishing for rainbow on a fly or by spincasting. Given the elevation, the fish remain active throughout the summer months.

Ivey Lake (Map 30/C1)

It is catch and release only in this small lake, which can be heartbreaking if you happen to land one of the monster rainbow that inhabit this trophy lake. The trout, which grow to 4 kg (9 lbs), are cagey. There are also some small cutthroat.

Jane Lakes (Map 29/E6)

The main access route to the Jane Lakes, a series of three mountain lakes, is now blocked by a fence built by BC Rail. You can still trudge in by bike or foot along the old washed out road. The lakes provide good fishing throughout the spring and fall since they are stocked regularly. There are rumours of rainbow to 50 cm/18 inches (2 kg/4.5 lbs).

Joffre Lakes (Map 37/A7)

Off the Duffey Lake Road near Cayoosh Pass, a trail leads past three sub-alpine lakes. Upper Joffre Lake is the highest of these high elevation lakes and has the best fishing for small rainbow beginning in July and running to October. Middle and Lower Joffre Lakes also have small rainbow but the fish are not as plentiful. Rustic camping is possible at each lake.

Jones [Wahleach] Lake (Map 5/C2)

This man-made, high elevation lake is found tucked in at the base of Mount Cheam. The road rises sharply from the valley bottom to the lake where you will find fair fishing for small rainbow and big cutthroat trout and excellent fishing for small kokanee that can reach 1 kg (2 lbs) in size. Trolling is the mainstay of the fishery. Visitors will find a nice campsite, day-use area and boat launch near the north end of the lake.

Joseph Lake (Map 12/B3)

Found by a trail leading past Anne and Little Anne Lakes, this lake also has fair numbers of small rainbow. The rough logging road network into the lake is not open until late April-early May due to snow accumulation.

Katherine Lake (Map 9/A1)

Katherine Lake is located in Katherine Lake Park and offers cutthroat to 35 cm (14 inches) in size. The lake is best fished in April and May and again in the fall. Katherine Lake Park has a beach and camping.

Kawkawa Lake (Map 15/F6)

Found just east of Hope, this lake and park are a popular place for locals. In addition to a boat launch, the park offers picnicking facilities and a beach. Most of the fishing action comes from the kokanee, which can grow to fairly large sizes (to 40 cm/16 inches). Cutthroat and dollies are the other main species, although there are rumours that people are pulling smallmouth bass out of this lake. Shore fishing is limited so it is best to bring a boat and try some trolling. The lake is closed to fishing in the winter.

Kelly Lake (Map 44/E1)

North of Pavilion, this small, windy lake offers fairly good fishing for rainbow to 1 kg (2 lbs). The scenic lake is home to Downing Provincial Park, which has camping and day-use facilities.

Khartoum Lake (Map 19/G3)

Khartoum Lake does not receive heavy fishing pressure and provides good fishing for cutthroat to 2 kg (4.5 lbs). Concentrate your efforts at the inflow of Lois River or in the channel between Lois and Khartoum Lake. Most anglers access the lake via the Third Lake Road, at the recreation site that sports a boat launch.

Killarney Lake (Map 10/F6)

Killarney Lake is a small lake on Bowen Island, about 2 km (1.2 miles) from the Snug Cove Ferry Terminal. This low level lake warms up in summer, so spring and fall are the best times to come here for rainbow and cutthroat.

Kingdom [King] Lake (Map 42/B5)

Kingdom Lake is a pretty lake, sporting a nice recreation site with small boat launch. The lake contains many small rainbow.

Klein Lake (Map 20/B6)

Klein Lake is accessed off the North Lake Road, to the east of Earl's Cove. The small but deep lake has many small cutthroat easily caught by trolling, fly-fishing and spincasting. Its scenic surroundings and good fishing make it

a popular destination for locals. A recreation site on the north end of the lake provides camping and cartop boat launch facilities.

Kokomo Lake (Map 20/A7)

Kokomo is reached by portaging a canoe from Sakinaw Lake. Given the difficult access, fishing for small cutthroat can be quite good. The lake has an electric motor only restriction.

Lafarge Lake (Map 2/C2)

Also known as the Coquitlam Pit, this former gravel pit has been dammed to create an urban fishing hole and picnic site. The small, low elevation lake is located between Pinetree Way and Pipeline Road in Port Coquitlam. The lake contains rainbow (the odd one up to 35 cm/14 inches) and carp. The lake is intensively stocked with rainbow. A great place from is the fish way along the western shore.

Lajoie [Little Gun] Lake (Map 41/G4)

Located just south of Gun Lake, this lake provides good fishing for stocked rainbow trout and a few dollies that both reach 1 kg (2 lbs). There is a cartop boat launch here, but an electric motor only restriction.

Lake Errock [Squakum Lake] (Map 4/B3)

Lake Errock is located alongside Highway 7 and is known more as a recreation lake than a fishing lake. It does have small cutthroat and rainbow best caught in the spring or fall, as well as course fish like catfish and bullheads.

Lake Lovely Water (Map 22/A5)

To reach this scenic sub-alpine lake, you will have to somehow cross the Squamish River. Then you will have to endure a perilously steep 5 km (3 mile) hike along a poorly maintained trail. The reward is great views and good fishing for rainbow. Shore fishing is possible.

Lake Lucille (Map 22/C1)

Lucille Lake is located west of Highway 99 across the Cheakamus River Bridge and requires a short hike when you reach the powerline crossing (the road is blocked by the railway tracks). The lake has an electric motor only restriction and produces brook trout and the occasional rainbow in the 30–40 cm (12–16 inch) range. There are reports of fish as large as 2.5 kg (5.5 lbs).

Lake of the Woods [Schkam Lake] (Map 15/F5)

Off Highway 1 north of Hope, this lake is stocked annually with rainbow, which can grow to 35 cm (14 inches). Spring and fall are the best times to fish here. The Lake of the Woods Resort offers accommodation and a boat launch (electric motor only).

Levette Lake (Map 22/B4)

The steep road may deter anglers without a 4wd vehicle, but the number of small rainbow that grow to 30 cm (12 inches) should make the drive worthwhile. There are a few private cabins along with a steep cartop boat launch at the south end of the lake. Although fishing from the shore is possible, you may wish to bring a float tube or small boat in order to get away from the trees and debris around the shoreline.

Lewis Lake (Map 19/C1)

Located off the rough Tin Hat Road, you'll need a 4wd to get to Lewis Lake. The lake provides good fishing for cutthroats to 2 kg (4.5 lbs) in summer and early fall. A small recreation site is found on the lake.

Lewis Lake (Map 22/B3)

An old gated 4wd road leads along Pillchuck Creek up to this small lake. Due to the difficult access, anglers can expect a good fly-fishing lake during the spring and fall. The stocked rainbow average 25 cm (10 inches) in size.

Lightning Lake (Map 7/C6)

Lightning Lake is the most popular lake of the Lightning Lake chain, due in no small part to the nice campsite, boat launch and trail system. It is slightly higher in elevation than the others and fishing is steady throughout the summer. The lake contains many small cutthroat and rainbow.

Lillooet Lakes (Map 30, 31)

By May, spring run-off causes these lakes to murk up and the water does not begin to clear until late August. The best time to fish for the rainbow, cutthroat and dollies in these poor producing lakes is in April. Work the narrows between the two lakes at the creek mouths. There are several recreation sites offering boat launches and camping along the bigger lake.

Lindeman Lake (Map 5/F5)

Lindeman Lake is a cold, emerald green lake that is reached by a fairly steep 3 km (1.8 mile) trail. The moody lake has good numbers of rainbow trout that average 20–30 cm (8–12 inches) in size and are best caught on the fly. Although it is possible to fish from shore, a float tube is more effective.

Ling Lake (Map 5/D3)
It is a long hike from Foley Lake to Ling Lake along a washed-out road, then trail. Once you reach the high elevation lake, you will be rewarded with good fishing for rainbow to 1 kg (2 lbs) throughout the summer months and into the fall. The lake is best fished using a float tube and casting a fly or small lure.

Liumchen Lake (Map 4/E7)
You will need a 4wd vehicle to access the trail into this small lake. Due to the difficult access and the high elevation, the fishing is quite good for trout into the summer. Some nice trout (to 35 cm/14 inches) are caught here annually.

Liza Lake (Map 42/E1)
Liza Lake is located off the Marshall Lake Forest Road and offers good fishing for small rainbow that are best caught by fly-fishing.

Lizzie Lake (Map 31/C5)
The road up to this scenic sub-alpine lake is water barred and/or washed out making access a challenge (or a long walk). However, the lake does offer good fishing for small rainbow best caught by fly-fishing or spincasting. Despite the good trail system along the northern end, shore fishing is difficult.

Lodestone Lake (Map 17/B4)
Lodestone is a lovely little lake located at the end of the Lodestone Forest Road (as well as by foot or horse along the Hope Brigade Trail). The high elevation lake offers fair fishing for small rainbow beginning in early July through to October. A recreation site at the lake provides a cartop boat launch and camping.

Loggers Lake (Map 29/E6)
Found in the Whistler Interpretive Forest, Loggers Lake can only be accessed by foot or bike. The small, scenic lake offers reasonable fishing for stocked rainbow that are rumoured to grow to 45 cm (18 inches) in size.

Lois Lake (Map 19/E3)
Lois Lake is one of the larger lakes in the Powell River area. Most people doing the Powell Forest Canoe Circuit start here. The lake is home to cutthroat to 2 kg (4.5 lbs), as well as small kokanee. It is best fished by trolling, but you can also try spincasting or fly-fishing at the inflow and outflow of the lake, around the islands or in one of the sheltered bays.

Lookout Lake (Map 14/D4)
Located off the Harrison West Forest Road, a 4wd is recommended to access the lake. The lake contains a good number of rainbow and cutthroat to 35 cm (14 inches). Try working the bays at the south end of the lake. Shore fishing is difficult, but not impossible.

Lost Lake (Map 29/G5)
Found near Whistler, this tiny lake is a popular year round destination with a picnic area and beach as well as an excellent trail system that includes part of the Valley Trail. The lake is stocked with catchable-sized rainbow that reach 30 cm (12 inches) but are usually quickly fished out. There are bull trout in the lake as well.

Lyon Lake (Map 9/C1)
Follow the Halfmoon Forest Road north from Highway 101 to this small lake. The road deteriorates significantly as you approach the lake making a 4wd vehicle a must. There are stocked cutthroat in the 20–40 cm (8–16 inch) range as well as a few larger fish. Fly-fishing and spincasting in the spring or fall are your best bets. There is a recreation site at the south end of the lake providing camping.

MacKechnie Lake (Map 19/F6)
Located on Nelson Island, this small, low elevation lake provides fairly good fishing for cutthroat to 1 kg (2 lbs) in the spring and fall. Old logging roads from Hidden Basin reach the lake.

McDonald Lake (Map 42/B4)
Home to rainbow, most prefer to troll this small lake east of Gold Bridge. The difficult access may deter some from bringing in a boat.

Madeley Lake (Map 29/C3)
Found to the northwest of Whistler on the Madeley Lake Road (4wd/bike access), this lake produces very well for small rainbow, up to 30 cm (12 inches). There is a small campground at the north end of the lake with a rough cartop boat launch. It is highly recommended that you bring a float tube or a boat you can pack-in as the lake is difficult to shore fish except at the south end.

Mamquam Lake (Map 22/G4)
Located well inside Garibaldi Provincial Park, this lake is accessed by a 22 km (13.4 mile) hike along the Diamond Head Trail. The lake is seldom fished

so it offers good fishing for generally small rainbow from shore. If you can get out on the water, there are rumours of nice trout as large as 50 cm (20 inches). This is a high elevation lake and the water doesn't open up until early summer.

Marion/Phyllis Lakes (Map 11/B3)
To reach these two mountain lakes, you must walk or bike a gated road from Highway 99 just north of Furry Creek. The lakes do not receive heavy fishing pressure and so you can do quite well for small cutthroat and dollies particularly in the spring and fall. It is possible to fish from the shore, but it is recommended to bring a float tube.

Marshall Lake (Map 42/F2)
Marshall Lake has good fishing for stocked rainbow to 1 kg (2 lbs) primarily by trolling. There are two recreation sites, one at the south end of the lake, the other at the north.

Mead Lake (Map 42/B5)
Just south of Kingdom Lake, this small lake is accessed by a 4wd vehicle or by a hike. It provides good fishing for small rainbow throughout the spring and fall.

Mike Lake (Map 2/G2)
This tiny lake is found in Golden Ears Park and has stocked rainbow and wild cutthroat that grow to 30 cm (12 inches), best caught in the spring. Fishing from a canoe or float tube is your best bet as the shoreline is shallow and marshy. There is a fishing dock for people with no way out onto the water.

Mill Lake (Map 3/D6)
Located in the heart of Abbotsford, next to the Seven Oaks Shopping Centre, this urban lake is heavily stocked with rainbow. The marshy lake also contains bullheads, crappies and largemouth bass. You will need a boat (electric motor only) or tube to get to the deepest hole. The best place to fish from shore is off the dock or from the beach.

Mixal Lake (Map 9/A1)
Mixal Lake offers fishing for small cutthroat mainly in the spring and Coho in the fall. The low elevation lake has an electric motor only restriction.

Moon Lake (Map 44/A6)
This tiny lake is noted for having large rainbow that reach 2 kg (4.5 lb) in size. The remote lake has poor access and requires hiking or biking in from a 4wd logging road.

Morgan Lake (Map 13/D7)
Morgan Lake is a catch-n-release and fly-fishing only lake that sports brook trout and cutthroat to 2 kg (4.5 lbs). For best results, bring a float tube as shore fishing is very difficult and the lake is quite deep in the middle.

Morris Lake (Map 4/E1)
Morris Lake is connected to the Harrison River just east of the Weaver Creek spawning channel by a rather large channel and is accessed via a rough road that most people will have to walk up. The fishing isn't great here, but you might catch a cutthroat to 50 cm (20 inches).

Mosquito Lake (Map 36/C7)
Located just east of Ivey Lake near Pemberton, Mosquito Lake has a recreation site with a picnicking area. The small lake has stocked rainbow and cutthroat to 30 cm (12 inches), but the fishing is usually slow.

Moss Lake (Map 15/A7)
If you want to get to Moss Lake, you'll have to hike at least 1.5 km (1 mile) and you'll want to pack a float tube with you. If you don't have a 4wd vehicle, the hike will be longer, but these obstacles have kept this small lake a viable fishing destination in Sasquatch Provincial Park. The lake features rainbow in the 25–35 cm (10–14 inch) range.

Mowson Pond (Map 42/C2)
This lake used to offer very good fishing for stocked rainbow. We say used to, as the Tyaughton Lake Fire has burned the landscape surrounding this former fishing hot spot, which has adversely affected the water levels and fishing. Hopefully the fishing will return back to the glory days when trout to 36 cm (14 in) were a real joy to catch on the fly.

Murphy Lakes (Map 17/A3)
Off the Lawson-Britton Creek Forest Road, these popular mountain lakes contain rainbow and brook trout that can grow to 1.5 kg (3+ lbs) in size. The eastern lake has larger fish. The lakes are home to rainbow that somehow withstand some fairly heavy fishing pressure.

Murray Lake (Map 27/F4)

Murray Lake is easily accessed off the Coquihalla Highway (Highway 5). As a result, the two recreation sites and boat launch get frequent use. Trolling and fly-fishing are your best bet to catch the rainbow that reside here.

Nahatlatch, Hannah & Frances Lakes (Map 32/G7–33/A7)

Strung together like pearls on a string by the Nahatlatch River, these three lakes are wonderfully scenic, although the fishing is not very good. The lakes hold limited numbers of rainbow, dollies and cutthroat. If you're going to make a serious effort to catch something, your best bet is to go trolling in the spring or fall. Several former recreation sites along the Nahatlatch River Road provide camping for the paddlers and fishermen that frequent the area.

Nanton Lake (Map 19/C2)

Nanton Lake is accessed off the Goat Lake Main and is really an extension of Horseshoe Lake. In addition to kokanee, the lake has developed a reputation for holding some pretty large cutthroat to 3 kg (6.5 lbs). Try fly-fishing or trolling near the channel from Horseshoe Lake or at one of the inflow creeks. There is camping on its western shores.

Nicomen Lake (Map 7/B3)

As the crow flies, Nicomen Lake is 10 km from the nearest road, but the hike in is nearly double that, along the Hope Pass Trail/Grainger Creek Trail. Given the tough access, you can usually expect some good fishing for rainbow that average 20–30 cm (8–12 inches). A small, scenic tenting site is located at the lake.

Nita Lake (Map 29/E5)

The smallest in a chain of three lakes in Whistler, Nita is a deep, cold lake that offers fairly good fishing even in the warm weather of summer. Nita Lake has an electric motor only restriction and offers good fishing for small, stocked rainbow and some kokanee.

North Lake (Map 20/B6)

North Lake is a well developed lake that is the highest elevation lake on the north end of the Sechelt Peninsula. The lake provides slow fishing for cutthroat averaging 25–30 cm (10–12 inches). April and May or October is the best times to fish. The lake has full facilities and has an electric motor only restriction.

Norton Lake (Map 12/A3)

Norton Lake is noted for having the largest rainbow of all the lakes in the Hixon Creek area, getting up to 2 kg (4.5 lbs). It is also the easiest to find but you will need a 4wd vehicle to drive in. Fishing is best in the late spring and fall, from a float tube.

Olive Lake (Map 14/A5)

You'll have to bushwhack your way to Olive Lake from the end of the North Statlu Forest Road, a distance of about 3 km. The lake contains cutthroat to 25 cm (10 inches) as well as some rainbow.

Onion Lake [Ruddocks Dam] (Map 39/B5)

You wouldn't expect to find a private catch and release lake this far from the city, but that is what is here. Anglers willing to pay can enjoy fishing for wild trout here.

Owl Lake Chain (Map 36/B5)

From the Owl Creek Forest Road (4wd access), a steep trail leads to Owl Lake as well as several other lakes in the watershed. These lakes have small rainbow (to 30 cm/12 inches) that rarely see a lure. Owl Lake sees most of the action and casting from shore is possible. Further north, Ogre and Fowl Lakes will require some bushwhacking through rugged terrain to access. Due to their remote sub-alpine setting, fishing with most small lures and flies is good through the summer for generally small rainbow. The odd trout can reach 50 cm (20 inches) in size.

One Mile Lake (Map 30/B1)

South of Pemberton and right next to Highway 99, One Mile Lake sees more than its share of anglers. There are a few rainbow and cutthroat (to 30 cm/12 inches) that are best caught by spincasting or fly-fishing from a small boat or float tube throughout the spring and fall.

Otter Lake (Map 17/D2)

This popular recreation lake has private cabins, camping as well as a boat launch and a beach at the Otter Lake Provincial Park. A good gravel road skirts the west side of the lake, while the Kettle Valley Railway runs along the east side. Despite stocking of rainbow and brook trout in the lake, fishing still remains fairly spotty. There are also some lake trout, kokanee and whitefish

available. The best method of fishing is trolling during the early spring or late fall as the lake warms due to the low elevation.

Pavilion Lake (Map 44/G3)

Pavilion Lake, the largest lake in the Marble Canyon Area, has fair fishing for stocked rainbow to 1.5 kg (3.5 lbs), primarily caught by trolling. The lake also offers good ice fishing. A cartop boat launch is available, as is camping and a resort.

Paxton Lake (Map 18/G6)

This small lake can be accessed by a 4wd vehicle off the Iron Mine Road. The lake contains cutthroat to 2kg (4.5 lbs), which can be caught in the early summer by spincasting or fly-fishing.

Pearson Pond (Map 42/B2)

The fishing at Pearson Pond was adversely affected as a result of a fire, which blazed through the area in 2009. Hopefully the fishing will improve in the near future. For now, the fishing is very slow for stocked brook trout that can reach 1.5 kg (3.5 lb) in size. The lake also makes a fine ice fishing destination.

Petgill Lake (Map 11/C1)

This lake is accessed by a steep 11.5 km (6 hour) return trail leading from Highway 99. Since the lake is no longer stocked, it is unclear whether the small trout have survived. Shore fishing is possible for those still willing to haul up fishing gear.

Pierce Lake (Map 5/B6)

This lake is reached by a steep, difficult trail leading from the Chilliwack Lake Road. The hike is worth the effort given the beautiful mountain scenery, but the fishing can be hit and miss. Some report good fly-fishing or spincasting for larger trout (over 50 cm/20 inches), while others say it is slow for only small trout in the 20–30 cm (8–12 inch) range. Regardless, the lake is quite deep and allows for decent shore fishing.

Pitt Lake (Map 12/E3–F7)

At the south end of Pitt Lake, Grant Narrows Park provides the main boat launch onto this large lake. The lake contains resident rainbow, dollies, sturgeon and whitefish but the action picks up when the salmon species and steelhead migrate through the lake. In particular, in the spring (April–May) sea-run cutthroat cruise to the north end of the lake looking for salmon fry returning to the ocean. When boating, watch for the sandbars, deadheads and sudden winds.

Plateau Ponds (Map 42/B3)

Found by trail to the east of Gun Lake, these small waterbodies are stocked with rainbow. During the spring and fall, fishing can be quite steady here.

Poland Lake (Map 7/A5)

This high elevation lake is accessed by the Poland Lake Trail in Manning Provincial Park. The small lake contains many small rainbow to 20 cm (8 inches). There is a rustic campground next to the lake.

Powell Lake (Map 46/E5)

Powell Lake is a big lake that resembles an inlet or a fjord, running narrow and deep into the heart of the Coast Mountains. The lake is notoriously difficult to fish and is subject to strong winds. If you're lucky, you might manage to catch one of the cutthroat or rainbow that can reach up to 4 kg (9 lbs). Your best bet is trolling around Goat Island, near Olsen's landing, or near Haywire Bay.

Priest Lake (Map 18/F5)

Priest Lake is the biggest lake on Texada Island. As a result, trolling is the preferred method for cutthroats to 2 kg (4.5 lbs) in late spring or early summer.

Rice Lake (Map 11/E7)

Found in the Seymour Demonstration Forest, Rice Lake is best accessed by trail from the end of Lillooet Road. The irregularly shaped lake is stocked annually with catchable sized rainbow to help maintain the fishery.

Richardson Lake (Map 9/F2)

Surrounded by a provincial park, this picturesque lake is best accessed by 4wd vehicle or ATV. A former recreation site provides camping at the west end of the lake. The lake is stocked with cutthroat, which grow to 30 cm (12 inches). Trolling is the preferred method of fishing.

Rolley Lake (Map 3/C2)

Rolley Lake is home to a popular provincial park complete with camping, a boat launch and a beach. The lake has stocked rainbow (to 30 cm/12 inches) as well as a few larger dollies and cutthroat. It is best fished near the north end where there is a deep hole. No powerboats are allowed in this low elevation lake.

Ross Lake (Map 6/F7)
At the end of the Silver Skagit Road, Ross Lake sits on the border between Canada and the USA. The lake is quite shallow on the BC side of the border during draw down and the lake is little more than a mud flat. Earlier in the year, the lake is best trolled for rainbow and Dolly Varden that average (12–18 inches). Around mid-August the dollies are preparing to spawn and can be found near the snag infested estuary. There is camping, a boat launch and a beach at the provincial park. Be wary of stumps and debris as well as special regulations.

Ruby Lake (Map 20/B6)
Ruby Lake is a popular recreation lake with many summer and permanent residents lining the lake. The lake also has a resort, boat launch and camping. Despite the heavy fishing pressure, the lake produces well for cutthroat, usually to 25–35 cm (10–14 inches) and small kokanee, mainly by trolling. In the summer, the waters in this low elevation lake warm up, making water sports more enjoyable than fishing.

Sakinaw Lake (Map 20/A7)
Sakinaw is a large, deep lake lined with private residences and summer cottages. Salmon and sea-run cutthroat can be caught in the fall near the channel flowing into the ocean at the southwest end of the lake. With patience, it is also possible to catch large cutthroat (to 60 cm/24 inches) and some small kokanee in the spring.

Salsbury Lake (Map 13/E7)
Salsbury Lake is found north of Davis Lake and offers small, stocked rainbow and kokanee to 30 cm (12 inches). Shore fishing is difficult due to the debris, while trollers should stick with shallow presentations. Former recreation sites provide access and a gravel boat launch to the lake.

Sardis Pond (Map 4/D5)
Located in Sardis Park on Vedder Road south of Chilliwack, this pond is open year round to seniors, BC disabled and anglers under 16. It is heavily stocked with both rainbow and cutthroat trout to ensure a good fishery. The shallow nature of the lake does result in slow fishing during warmer months.

Sasamat Lake (Map 2/A1)
Sasamat Lake is located within Belcarra Regional Park and is better known for its great beach and picnic facilities than its fishing. In the early spring and late fall it to catch wild cutthroat or stocked rainbow that can grow to 45 cm (18 inches). Powerboats are restricted on the lake from May to September so bring a float tube and spincast or fly fish near the middle of the lake, where there is deep hole, or along the western shoreline. For shore fishermen, a 200 metre (650 foot) long floating dock at the south end of the lake or two docks at the outflow are excellent spots.

Sayres [Cedar] Lake (Map 3/D1)
This low elevation lake is accessed by short trail from the Florence Lake Forest Road. Visitors will still find a dock where you can launch a small boat or canoe, but the fishing is not what it once was. The lake can be fished from shore but it is better to fish with a float tube or small boat in order to cast/troll towards the centre of the lake. There average rainbow tends to be quite small (less than 30cm/12in) and there are also some small dollies and brook trout. There is a bait ban as well as a catch limit and a single barbless hook restriction on the lake.

Seton Lake (Map 43/D6–44/B7)
Seton Lake holds large rainbow (to 2 kg/4.5 lbs), lake trout (to 5 kg/11 lbs) and dollies to 6 kg (13 lbs). Trolling a large spoon at the drop-off of one of the creek estuaries such as Madeleine, Tsee or Machute Creeks is particularly effective. Casting a large spoon off the Seton Lake Canal Dock just east of Lillooet can also be very effective. Steelhead anglers will find Seton Portage, the short river between Anderson Lake and Seton Lake, fairly productive. Rainbow and dollies to 2 kg (4.5 lbs) are also found in the river.

Showh Lakes (Map 29/F3)
Despite the difficult 4wd/trail access, this catch and release fishery has really increased in popularity recently. The main lake provides for stocked, rainbow that reach some impressive sizes. In fact, 50 cm (20 inch) are not uncommon. Due to the elevation, this fishery heats up in the early summer and maintains through the fall.

Silver Lake (Map 5/F1)
This lake is home to a provincial park complete with camping, a boat launch and picnic facilities. The lake has small rainbow, cutthroat and kokanee as well as a few larger dollies (to 2 kg/4.5 lbs). Small steelhead come into the lake in the winter and Coho come through in the fall. For best results, you can cast a float with bait from the southern shoreline, fly fish at the creek outflow, or troll the shallow lake.

Silvermere Lake (Map 3/C4)
This man-made lake next to the Lower Stave River is easily accessed by Highway 7. The lake is very marshy and shallow making it better for water skiing or catching catfish and bullheads than rainbow. More recently, the lake has become a popular largemouth bass fishery. The best place to fish is near the highway, either from shore or by boat. Private residents line the east side of the lake, making access difficult.

Sliammon Lake (Map 18/F2)
Found close to Powell River, this lake provides fair fishing for cutthroat to 2.5 kg (5.5 lbs) and for small kokanee. Trolling is the preferred method although it is possible to catch fish by fly-fishing or spincasting in the many bays.

Slollicum Lake (Map 15/A6)
Reached by a three kilometre trail off a 4wd road on the east side of Harrison Lake, this lake has numerous small rainbow. Try fishing at the north end of the lake where the fish tend to congregate.

Stacey Lake (Map 4/E2)
Found west of Agassiz, watch for a spur road to this lake after kilometre 7 off the rough Mount Woodside Forest Road. The lake is stocked with rainbow and the fishing here is decent in late spring and again in fall. The lake is subject to winterkill.

Statlu Lake (Map 14/B4)
Statlu Lake is located to the north of Chehalis and is reached by a rough 4wd road and then a short hike. Rainbow tend to be small but plentiful in this scenic lake set below some majestic peaks.

Starvation Lake (Map 22/C3)
Starvation Lake is a tiny lake that is reached by an overgrown road leading from the very end of the Paradise Valley Road. The spring-fed lake produces rainbow as large as 2 kg (4.5 lbs) in the spring. Rustic camping is available at the lake.

Stave Lake (Map 3, 13)
Stave Lake is a large lake, stretching 27 km (16.5 miles) through the mountains north of Mission. Despite its size, access is limited. Most boaters launch near the Stave Falls Dam. There are also a few places that get to the water from logging roads on either side of the lake. The low elevation lake has been damned by BC Hydro resulting in fluctuating water levels and spotty fishing. There are a few rainbow, cutthroat, kokanee, Dolly Varden and whitefish in the lake. Most of the trout remain small, but the odd 50 cm (20 inch) cutthroat is reported, while dollies up to 5 kg (11 lbs) also roam the lake. Trolling is preferred because the fish are scattered but watch for debris and high winds that can make boating treacherous at times.

Strike Lake (Map 7/C6)
Strike Lake, one of the Lightning Lakes in Manning Park, contains many small rainbow (to 20 cm/8 inches) best caught by spincasting, bait fishing or fly-fishing.

Stump Lake (Map 22/D5)
Stump Lake is nestled in a thick, second growth hemlock/cedar forest in Alice Lake Provincial Park. A trail circles the lake, offering access for shore fishermen, though is difficult to cast from shore except in a few limited areas. However, the lake has a muddy bottom, murky water and shallows that extend far out from shore making it best to have a float tube. The lake contains stocked, sterile rainbow (to 30 cm/12 in), though as of 2007 they are no longer being stocked. Instead, the lake is now being stocked with cutthroat. In addition, the lake also holds pumpkinseed sunfish.

Sunrise Lake (Map 14/E4)
Sunrise Lake is another in a series of small lakes found in the hills above Harrison Lake. The lake is quite deep and cold and can provide good shore fishing or trolling (electric motors only). There is a recreation site and a boat launch that is maintained by the local 4wd club. Access to the lake itself is by very high clearance 4wd vehicles or by foot.

Surrey [Latimer] Pond (Map 2/D6)
Also known as Stokes Pit or Latimer Pond, this man-made waterbody is stocked with rainbow. As with most urban ponds, pressure can be heavy and fishing slow. But the fact it is so close to home is hard to beat.

Swanee Lake (Map 5/F2)
This small lake is accessed off a long, rough bushwhack from the Silver Skagit Road near where it crosses the Silverhope Creek just south of the Eaton Lake Forest Service Site. The lake has fair fishing for small rainbow from June to early fall.

Tannis Lake (Map 10/A2)
Located along the Mount Steele Backcountry Trail System, this small lake is one of a series of small mountain lakes in the area. It provides good fishing for rainbow in the 20–30 cm (8–12 inch) range, in fall or early summer by trolling.

Tenquille Lake (Map 35/G3)
This scenic sub-alpine lake is found beneath Tenquille Mountain. It is reached by any one of three trails leading from surrounding logging roads. The lake is a popular hiking and mountaineering destination, but it also has good fishing for rainbow in the 20–30 cm (8–12 inch) range. Fly-fishing with a dry fly can be a lot of fun. There is a lakeshore camping area as well as a cabin in the area.

Thomas Lake (Map 13/B3)
Located well and truly back in Golden Ears Provincial Park, Thomas Lake is a fly-in lake. The fact that few anglers ever make it into this lake, which has been stocked in the past with rainbow, means fishing should be excellent.

Thunder Lake (Map 7/C6)
Thunder Lake is the farthest lake along the Lightning Lake Chain Trail and sees a lot less action than the other lakes in the chain. The lake also contains many small rainbow (to 20 cm/8 inches) best caught by bait or fly-fishing.

Trout Lake (Map 1/D2)
Looking at this urban lake, you wouldn't figure there would be good fishing here. But the lake is stocked every year with catchable sized rainbow and people seem to do okay. Don't expect anything big and you will need to fish this one in the spring or fall before it heats up.

Trout [Halfmoon Bay] Lake (Map 9/D4)
This small, productive lake is located next to Highway 101 just to the east of Halfmoon Bay on the Sunshine Coast. Despite its easy access, the lake has lots of stocked cutthroat up to 2 kg (4.5 lbs). The lake is best fished by casting towards the weeds on the north end of the lake. An electric motor only restriction is in place.

Trout Lake (Map 15/A7)
Fishing from the bushy, marshy shoreline of this shallow lake is not an appealing proposition. Instead, bring a float tube, or a small boat with an electric motor. The lake is in Sasquatch Provincial Park and contains many small rainbow that easily take to flies. The lake gets quite warm in summer.

Turquoise Lake (Map 45/A4)
This small lake has good fishing for stocked rainbow growing to 1 kg (2 lbs) primarily by casting a small lure or by fly-fishing. The lake sports a cartop boat launch.

Twenty Minute Lake (Map 7/C6)
This tiny lake is located right along the Gibson Pass Road just east of Lightning Lake. Fishing is slow for small rainbow.

Tyaughton Lake (Map 42/C2)
Tyaughton is native for flying fish. On any given evening, you will know why. The lake is quite deep and clear making fly-fishing difficult, but casting towards shore with a fly or small lure can be effective for the stocked rainbow. There are also unconfirmed reports of dollies in the lake, which hosts a recreation site and fine resort.

Unwin Lakes (Map 46/C4)
Unwin Lakes are located in Desolation Sound Marine Park via a short trail. It is possible to portage a canoe or small boat in. The lakes are rarely fished and provide excellent fishing for cutthroat to 30 cm (12 inches). The lakes are best fished in late fall or early summer with bait.

Venables Lake (Map 39/G2)
This lake supports rainbow that can reach 1 kg (2 lbs). Trolling in the spring or fall is your best bet. A cartop boat launch is at the lake, which is accessed via the Venables Valley Road (2wd access).

Waugh Lake (Map 20/C6)
Waugh Lake is found on the Egmont Road and is frequently fished for cutthroat and rainbow to 40 cm (16 inches). The cutthroat are a little more abundant as they are stocked regularly. An electric motor only restriction applies at the lake.

Weaver Lake (Map 14/E7)
Weaver Lake has good numbers of rainbow and cutthroat that reach 50 cm (20 inches). The lake receives heavy pressure during the summer, due in no small part to the scenic recreation site complete with a beach, boat launch and trail around the lake. Trolling is popular although the lake, given its numerous bays and undulating shoreline, is well suited to spincasting or fly-fishing. Fishing is best on the western side because the water is deeper. Better fishing is found in May and June or in September and October.

Welcome Lake (Map 2/A2)
This small, unmarked lake is located in the city of Coquitlam on Gatensbury Street. The lake is stocked with rainbow and cutthroat.

Wells Lake (Map 17/B6)
To reach this tiny mountain lake, requires a long hike along the Whatcom Trail or a high clearance 4wd vehicle. When you reach the lake, you will be rewarded with good fishing for small rainbow that holds steady through the summer and early fall. A very rustic recreation site offers camping at the lake.

West Lake (Map 19/G6)
Located on Nelson Island, West Lake is reached along a network of old logging roads from Hidden Basin. It is a big lake for the island. The low elevation lake has some surprisingly large cutthroat, growing up to 3 kg (6.5 lbs) as well as rainbow. The lake is best fished in the spring or early summer using a boat. There is a resort on the lake.

Whonnock Lake (Map 3/B3)
Whonnock Lake is an urban lake located northwest of Mission off of 276th Street. It is a marshy lake that is very shallow and notably dark but clean water. The lake has cutthroat, crappies, carp and stocked rainbow which all grow to 25 cm (10 inches). The marshy shoreline makes shore fishing very difficult so bring a canoe or float tube (no powerboats). There are day-use facilities at the lake making it a popular summer lake.

Widgeon Lake (Map 12/E5)
Widgeon Lake is a tough lake to access, but it provides good fishing for rainbow trout to 2 kg (4.5 lbs). The lake is very deep and cold. Anyone making the long hike up should carry a float tube, as casting a line from the shore is difficult, if not impossible.

Wilson Lake (Map 14/A5)
Wilson Lake is west of Chehalis Lake along a long series of rough backroads that may need to be walked due to washouts. Trolling seems to be the preferred fishing method for the rainbow that reside here.

Windsor Lake (Map 46/G6)
Windsor Lake can be reached either along the Goat Lake Main or by boat from Dodd Lake (there is a short portage trail). The cutthroat in this lake are very small but the numbers allow fast fishing particularly in the spring.

Wood Lake (Map 14/E5)
Access into Wood Lake is gated when the campsite is not open. This small lake, not much more than a pond, contains good numbers of stocked rainbow up to 40 cm (16 inches) best caught in the spring or fall. Electric motors only.

Wormy Lake (Map 9/E3)
Wormy Lake is accessed by 4wd road off the Honeymoon Forest Road on the Sunshine Coast. The cutthroat in the lake average 35–45 cm (14–18 inches) and are usually difficult to catch. The best time to fish is during spring.

Wotten Lake (Map 15/D3)
Wotten Lake is a remote lake, containing rainbow. The lake receives very little fishing pressure and can offer exceptional fly-fishing and spincasting for rainbow.

Young Lake (Map 12/A3)
Young Lake is a small, remote lake that offers small rainbow that usually come readily to most flies and small lures after the lake opens up in spring.

STREAM FISHING

In Southwestern BC, there is an incredible selection of rivers and creeks that provide good fishing for the various salmon species as well as sea-run cut-throat and steelhead. Most of the fishing occurs in the fall or over the winter, but there is a limited opportunity to fish resident cutthroat, Dolly Varden and rainbow from the spring through fall. Please note that the rivers and creeks in the region are heavily regulated to preserve the fishery. Some of the regulations are noted below. However, regulations for steelhead and salmon change frequently, visit http://www.pac.dfo-mpo.gc.ca/fm-gp/rec/fresh-douce/index-eng.htm for salmon regulations and http://www.env.gov.bc.ca/fw/fish/regulations/ for non-salmon for up-to-date information.

Alouette River (Map 2/D2–3/A1; 13/C6)
This urban river flows from the Alouette Lake into the Pitt River. All five species of salmon return to the Alouette system, however, regulations only allow the harvest of Chinook and Coho at certain times and limits. There is a small run of steelhead in December through March, cutthroat in the spring and fall, pink in August and September, Coho in late September and October and chum and Chinook in October and November. Given its easy access, pressure is heavy and the fishing is marginal.

American Creek (Map 15/E5)
American Creek is accessed by Highway 1 and the American Creek Road. It has small resident rainbow best caught in July and August after spring runoff. In early summer (June to early July), the odd salmon can be caught near the mouth of the creek.

Anderson River (Map 26/E4–G7)
Anderson River flows into the Fraser River north of Hell's Gate. The river has resident dollies and rainbow, which can be caught by bait fishing or spincasting. There is also a small run of steelhead in the late winter to early summer.

Ashulu River (Map 21/C1–G2, 28/B7)
Most of its length can be accessed by 2wd vehicle except the upper reaches, which are best left to a 4wd vehicle. Due to the falls, the migratory fish are only found in the lower 3 km of the river. Steelhead and dollies can be caught here from March through May. There is also a Coho run in October. Resident rainbow and dollies can be caught above the falls by bait fishing or spincasting.

Big Silver Creek (Map 14/F2, 25/E4–E7)
This creek flows into Harrison Lake near the Silver Creek Camp. It is easily accessed by an extensive network of logging roads. The creek is only fishable below the falls 7 km upstream. Steelhead can be caught in the winter months and resident cutthroat throughout the year.

Birkenhead River (Map 30/D1, 36/A2–D7)
The Birkenhead River flows into the northwest end of Lillooet Lake and is accessed by the road to D'Arcy or the Birkenhead Forest Road. Sockeye and Chinook salmon enter the river in good numbers in the fall, as well as some large rainbow trout that follow the salmon upstream. Glacial silt entering the river during spring runoff restricts fishing in May through July. There is no fishing for salmon from August 1 to September 15 to protect spawning Chinook as well as a bait ban year round.

Brem River (Map 48/C7)
Located far, far away from anything resembling civilization, this remote river is fly or boat only. Logging roads (which can be hiked or biked) provide access to upper reaches of the river. The river is best known for its winter steelhead but it also has resident cutthroat, a Chinook run in summer, and a Coho run in fall. Note that there is no fishing area below the falls, 1.5 km (.9 miles) from the mouth of the river.

Bridge River (Map 40/C3–41/C4; 43/E5–44/C5)
This small river flows into the Fraser River to the north of Lillooet. Outside of the upper reaches, good access is found along most of the river. Steelhead, Coho and Chinook in the fall as well as resident rainbow offer a good variety of fishing.

Brittain River (Map 47/C6)
Brittain River is a remote river in Jervis Inlet, which is accessed by boat. Due to its limited access, the river is very good for steelhead from November through March as well as resident cutthroat in the spring and fall. The farther you walk/bike up the river the better the fishing becomes.

Brunette River (Map 1/G2–2/A3)
The Brunette is a dark river that drains Burnaby Lake. Efforts to clean the river up has seen cutthroat and stocked steelhead taking up residence here again.

The green space protecting the river also provides good access for anglers from Cariboo Road and North Road. When fishing for trout no fishing is allowed from Cariboo Dam to Cariboo Road, and it is catch and release on all steelhead. The stream is closed to salmon fishing.

Capilano River (Map 1/C1–11/C7; 11/C5)
The Capilano is perhaps the most popular fishing river on the North Shore. Hundreds of anglers gather here during the prime fishing months. The river has a small summer steelhead run, and a small winter run from December to April. The real action begins in August when the Coho start to return to the Capilano Hatchery. There is a bait ban restriction from August 1–October 31 and you must release all steelhead. The river is heavily regulated, so make sure you check the regulations before heading out.

Chapman Creek (Map 9/G5–10/B2)
Chapman Creek is located west of Sechelt and flows into the ocean at Wilson Creek. The creek is accessed by the West Road along most of its length and provides fishing for steelhead in February to April, Coho in the fall and resident cutthroat year round.

Cheakamus River (Map 22/C1–5; 29/D7–F7)
The upper reaches of the Cheakamus River flow beside Highway 99 and provide fishing for small resident rainbow, which are best fished using bait. Beyond the canyon, most of the upper reaches are impassable. Even below the canyon, fishing should be restricted to when the river is not swollen with spring runoff (September–May). The lower Cheakamus, between Fergie's Lodge and up the Paradise Valley Road, offers a fairly good spring steelhead run (April–May) which must all be released. There is no retention of pink, Chinook and chum and only hatchery Coho may be retained. Coho enter the river in October and can be caught throughout the winter. Resident dollies and cutthroat are also present year round.

Chehalis River (Map 4/C1, 14/C7)
This river flows from Chehalis Lake southward into the Harrison River and is considered one of the best local steelhead rivers. The river provides a good run of winter steelhead beginning in December until March as well as a few steelhead in June and July. Both fisheries are enhanced by hatchery stock. In addition to steelhead, there are some summer Chinook running in July through August as well as a very good Coho run (to 7 kg/15 lbs) in October through early December so long as there are fall rains. Since the river is mostly walled in by a steep canyon, most anglers are usually found along the gravel bars near the Morris Road Bridge. Those that make it into the canyon will find it less crowded but difficult to fly-fish. Water levels affect the quality of fishing, so check the local fishing websites for fishing reports on this river.

Chilliwack River (Map 4/C6–5/E5)
This river is known as the Chilliwack River above the Vedder Bridge and the Vedder River below the bridge. The total fishing length is about 36 km (22 miles), all the way to Slesse Creek. The Chilliwack is easily accessed along the Chilliwack Lake Road and therefore receives heavy fishing pressure. The best place to fish the river is above the bridge as there are numerous pools to sample. The river has an excellent steelhead run from December through March as well as a few steelheads in the summer months. Chum and Coho fishing can be very good in September to October due to hatchery enhancement. Cutthroat fishing can be very good beginning in July until October and Chinook fishing can be decent in July through September. Because of its popularity, the Chilliwack is a heavily regulated river including an annual closure of the "limit hole" near Slesse Creek from August 1 to September 7.

Clowham River (Map 19/C3–E5)
Clowham River is a remote stretch of water that flows southward into the northeast end of Clowham Lake. It provides sea-run cutthroat fishing in the spring and fall as well as Coho fishing in the fall. There are also resident cutthroat and dollies available.

Cogburn Creek (Map 14/G3–15/B2)
Cogburn Creek flows into the Harrison River just north of the Bear Creek Camp. It has steelhead in January to April as well as some resident cutthroat throughout the year. A set of impassable falls limits fishing to the first 3 km of the creek. There is no fishing from May 1 to June 30.

Copper Creek (Map 7/D2–G3)
Copper Creek crosses Highway 3 about 10 km north of the Manning Park East Gate. The creek contains small rainbow.

Coquihalla River (Map 15/F6–16/F1)
The Coquihalla is a medium sized river flowing into the Fraser River at Hope. Access to lower reaches is via Kawakawa Lake Road east of Hope; further

upstream access is found off Highway 5. Dolly Varden are available all year throughout the system and a small run of winter steelhead are present in the lower reaches from February through March. A bigger run of summer steelhead occurs from June through September, while a few Coho also show up in the lower reaches in October and November. Check the regulations for restrictions, including closures around the infamous railway tunnels.

Coquitlam River (Map 2/C1–12/C7; 12/C4)
Flowing from Coquitlam Lake into the Pitt River, this shallow, urban river has a small run of steelhead in December to April, Coho in November and December and chum in the fall. There are a few small cutthroat and dollies that reside in the river year round. The Coquitlam River Trail provides good access to the various holes. There is no fishing above the Mary Hill Bypass bridge from May 1 to June 30.

Deserted River (Map 28/A5, 47/F5)
Deserted River is a remote river flowing into the Jervis Inlet that can only be reached by boat and then bushwhacking up the river. Given its difficult access, there is a good run of steelhead in the winter as well as Coho in the fall.

Elaho River (Map 28/B1–F5, 34/A1–C7)
The Elaho River flows into the Squamish River and is easily accessed along most of its length by the Elaho Road. A few steelhead are found in March to May as well as a few Coho in September and October. The river is noted more for its resident Dolly Varden, which can reach 2 kg (4.5 lbs), as well as smaller rainbow. There is a bait ban restriction in place year round and all steelhead must be released.

Emory Creek (Map 15/E4)
Emory Creek crosses Highway 1 about 18 km north of Hope where a provincial campsite provides good access. The best fishing is during late spring and fall for dollies or in the summer for rainbow trout. The creek also has Chinook salmon, which are best caught near the mouth in June and July, and a fall run of Coho. A few steelhead are known to show up in late winter.

Fraser River (Map 1–5, 15, 26, 33, 38, 39, 44)
The Fraser River, between Coquitlam and American Creek, offers excellent fishing for Pacific salmon and the mighty sturgeon. Most of the fishing occurs off one of the many gravel bars that line the river. The easily accessible areas are very busy, so having a boat to access the quieter bars for salmon and the back eddies for sturgeon is helpful. Perhaps the busiest time on the river is when the sockeye run from mid-July to late September, but the Chinook fishery beginning in June after the spring runoff subsides and lasting until October is also popular. Coho enter the river in late September and provide excellent fishing until December although retention is limited to hatchery origin fish and only after mid-October. Chum are caught in October and pink in August and September. Sturgeon, which can exceed 450 kg (1000 lbs), are also caught throughout the river system, while sea-run cutthroat are caught throughout the fall until early spring and steelhead from November to March. In addition to paying attention to the current restrictions, anglers in boats need to be wary of the many sandbars that line the river.

Gold Creek (Map 3/B1–13/B6)
This creek is found in the Golden Ears Provincial Park and flows southward into the Alouette Lake. The creek is accessed by a series of trails and can be fished for small cutthroat, rainbow and dollies, which reside in the creek year round. After spring runoff is the best time to fish.

Gray Creek (Map 9/G3–10/A2)
Gray Creek flows from a series of mountain lakes into the Sechelt Inlet south of Tuwanek. The creek has cutthroat in the spring and fall and Coho in the fall.

Green River (Map 29/G4–30/D1)
Green River flows northwest from Green Lake and enters the Lillooet River to the east of Pemberton. Most of the length of the river is easily accessed off Highway 99. Glacial silt entering the river makes it difficult to fish. It is possible to catch a few larger dollies (to 1.5 kg/3 lbs) and a few small rainbow.

Harrison River (Map 4/D2–F1)
This is a popular and productive river. At the Highway 7 bridge near Harrison Mills, it is not uncommon to see 20 to 40 fishermen lining the banks in the late summer and into the fall. In addition to casting from shore, anglers often launch a boat at Kilby Park off Highway 7. Sockeye start their annual migration in July, while Pink run every other year between August and October. Chinook and Coho are caught during the fall, with the best time being in late October. Chum also offer an excellent fishery in late October and November. Cutthroat fishing can be particularly effective from December through March, although during spring runoff (May–June) the fishing tails off because

the waters are quite murky. The river also offers decent steelhead fishing in December and January as well as whitefish in June. There are different regulations for fishing above and below the Highway 7 bridge so please check the government websites noted above.

Hope Slough (Map 4/F4)
Hope Slough is a slow moving meandering waterway near Chilliwack that is surrounded by private property. The slough can be accessed by a canoe and contains cutthroat, which can be best caught in spring and fall, as well as a run of Coho in fall.

Hunter Creek (Map 5/D1–15/D7)
Hunter Creek is a small creek that flows northward into the Fraser River to the west of Hope. Chinook are available at the mouth of the creek in June and July whereas cutthroat and steelhead frequent the estuary in the winter.

Indian River (Map 11/F2–12/A5)
Indian River is a beautiful, clear river that flows into the north end of the Indian Arm. Anglers access the river near the estuary by boat. There are also resident cutthroat and Dolly Varden that are best caught in the spring when they follow the salmon fry migration. However, the best time to visit this river is in late summer and fall when pink and chum run. The pink run every odd year and enter the river in large schools from August until September, while the chum enter the system in October and November. There is non-retention of any salmon year round and a bait ban on the river from December 1 through September 30.

Kanaka Creek (Map 2/G3–3/B2)
This is a small urban creek in Maple Ridge which has a few steelhead in January to March, cutthroat in September to April and a few Coho in the fall. Most of the creek can be easily accessed by paved roads and a good trail system however there is no fishing for salmon upstream of the 112th Street bridge.

Lang Creek (Map 17/C5)
Lang Creek flows from Duck Lake into the ocean just southeast of Powell River. There are steelhead in January to March as well as cutthroat in the spring and fall in the river. However, the best fishing is now in the shallow estuary for hatchery Chinook averaging 20 kg (44 lbs). They are fished in mid September to late October, while the occasional Coho and chum can also be caught.

Lawless Creek (Map 17/B2)
Lawless Creek drains the slopes of Mount Thynne towards Tulameen where it flows into the Tulameen River. Lawless Creek Forest Road accesses most of the lower reaches, but access to the upper reaches is by bushwhacking. Small rainbow trout are found here.

Lillooet River (Map 30/E1–34/E1, 40/B7; 24/G6–30/G6)
The Upper Lillooet River is a slow meandering stream that is easily accessed from Pemberton. South of Little Lillooet Lake, the Lower Lillooet River is a much faster flowing stream that extends all the way to Harrison Lake. It contains steelhead (March–May), resident dollies, Coho (October) and Chinook (April–May). However, the river is very silty during spring runoff and fishing is poor during May through October, although the estuaries such as Rogers Creek offer cleaner water at this time. Chinook are closed from July 30 to September 30.

Little Campbell River (Map 2/C7–F7)
This river flows into Georgia Straight near Mud Bay and, given its urban setting, does not offer great fishing opportunities. There is a very small run of winter steelhead as well as Coho, Chinook and cutthroat entering the river in late fall (October–November). It is possible to catch the cutthroat until the spring as they often winter within the river system to spawn. The Little Campbell River has been extensively rehabilitated by the community hatchery and this has helped somewhat in increasing the salmon, trout and steelhead returns. Access to the river is where 16th Avenue crosses the river near the Peace Portal and Hazelmere Golf Courses.

Lynn Creek (Map 1/E1–11/E6)
Lynn Creek is a difficult river to access and only has 5 km of fishable waters. There are a couple trails that bring you to some nice holes that hold a small run of winter steelhead in December to April and small runs of Coho and Chinook in the fall. There is a bait ban restriction year round.

Mamquam River (Map 22/C6–G7)
Mamquam River flows westward into the Squamish River just south of Brackendale. The best places to try are at the mouth of the river where it enters the Squamish River or at the estuary of Mashiter Creek. The Mamquam contains

fair numbers of steelhead in March to May with April being the best time to fish. Coho and dollies are also present in October to early November, while all four species of salmon return to the Mamquam. There is no retention of pink, Chinook and chum and only hatchery Coho may be retained.

Maria Slough (Map 4/G2, 5/A1)
This water body is an extension of the Fraser River near Agassiz. The Seabird Island Road provides access along most of its 10 km length. The slough offers some very good fishing for sea-run cutthroat (to 2.5 kg/5 lbs) in October through March along with resident cutthroats and dollies throughout the year. There is also a good run of Coho beginning in late October until mid-December.

McNab/McNair Creeks (Map 10/C3; 10/E2)
These two small creeks flow into the Thornbrough Canal near Port Mellon. McNab Creek is accessed by boat, while McNair Creek is accessed by Highway 101 and logging roads. Look for cutthroat in the spring and fall, Coho in October and November and steelhead in the winter.

Miami River (Map 4/G1)
This stream runs into Harrison Lake at Harrison Hot Springs. In the summer months anglers will find rainbow and in late October cutthroat and Coho. Although the mouth of the creek is the most popular spot, some of the larger pools upstream can be particularly good for Coho and cutthroat in late November when the waters have risen due to rainfall.

Nahatlach River (Map 26/D1–33/A7; 25/A1–F1)
The Nahatlach flows into the Fraser River south of Lytton. The fast flowing stream contains resident rainbow and dollies, as well as steelhead in the winter, Chinook in the late summer and Coho in the fall.

Nikomekl River (Map 2/A6–F5)
This river flows into Georgia Straight near Mud Bay and, given its urban setting, does not offer great fishing opportunities and is heavily regulated. There is a very small run of winter steelhead as well as Coho and sea-run cutthroat that enter the river in late fall.

Nicomen Slough (Map 3/F4–4/A4)
This slough attaches to the Fraser and provides access for Coho up into Norrish Creek in October and November and chum in October and November. The slough is also a good place to go looking for cutthroat in spring and fall.

Norrish [Suicide] Creek (Map 3/G3)
A falls at 7.5 km restricts fishing to the lower reaches. There are steelhead in December to March, cutthroat in the spring and fall and Coho in fall. Small resident rainbow trout are available year round; however, there is no fishing permitted from May 1 to June 30

Pasayten River (Map 7/G4)
Easily accessed along the Pasayten River Forest Road, this river is home to small rainbow, which can be caught by fly-fishing or spincasting.

Pitt River (Map 2/C3–12/E7; 12/E3–23/C4)
While you can lay down a line in the heavily industrialized, lake-like Lower Pitt River, you won't want to. At least, not if you can get to the upper reaches. The Upper Pitt River offers some of the best fishing in the Lower Mainland and is basically one 65 km long (40 mile) fishing hole. The bottom 24 km or so of the Upper Pitt is where most of the action takes place. The river is home to rainbow trout, bull trout, steelhead (in spring), sockeye (in August), and Coho (in October). Unfortunately, there is no way to the Upper Pitt other than boat or plane. There is a lodge on the river, but note the bait ban and it is encouraged to practice catch and release.

Potlatch Creek (Map 10/G2)
A boat access only river north of Anvil Island in Howe Sound, Potlatch River is a good cutthroat stream in spring.

Rainy River (Map 10/C2–D3)
Rainy River is accessed by Highway 101 to Port Melon and then along a deteriorating logging road. The river has steelhead in February to March, cutthroat year round and Coho in October and November.

Roberts Creek (Map 10/B6–C4)
Roberts Creek is found west of Gibson and contains steelhead and cutthroat. Those fish are best caught near the estuary.

Ruby Creek (Map 15/B6)
Ruby Creek flows southward into the Fraser River east of Agassiz. The creek has resident rainbow and cutthroat as well as steelhead in the winter and

Coho in the fall. Most of the creek can be accessed by gated logging roads that may or may not be drivable.

Salmon River (Map 2/F4–3/B6)
A slow, meandering river that flows into the Fraser near Fort Langley, the Salmon River is closed to fishing above 232 Street. Resident cutthroat and Dolly Varden along with a good run of Coho in fall, and winter steelhead draw anglers.

Sawmill [Five Mile] Creek (Map 15/E2)
This small creek crosses Highway 1 approximately 6 km north of Yale. You will find Chinook salmon near the mouth of the river in June and July.

Scuzzy Creek (Map 26/B4–E4)
Scuzzy Creek flows eastward into the Fraser River south of Boston Bar. An extensive logging road network provides access along most of the creek length. There are small resident cutthroat in the creek that are best caught by bait fishing.

Sechelt Creek (Map 21/C7–E7)
Sechelt Creek is a remote creek located towards the north end of the Salmon Inlet. The creek is accessed by boat and then following a logging road, preferably with a bike. Anglers will find resident cutthroat as well as Coho in the fall and steelhead in the winter.

Serpentine River (Map 2/B6–C4)
This river flows into Georgia Straight near Mud Bay and, given its urban setting, does not offer great fishing opportunities and is heavily regulated. There is a very small run of winter steelhead as well as Coho and sea-run cutthroat that enter the river in late fall.

Seton River & Pond (Map 44/C7; 43/D6)
There are two distinct sections on the Seton River. The lower river is a dam controlled river that connects Seton Lake with the Fraser River. It is easily accessed from the Duffey Lake Road (Highway 99) at Lillooet. There is a fish hatchery on this section of the river, which offers a variety of species. Trout (brook, bull, cutthroat and rainbow), Dolly Varden and whitefish offer year round fishing opportunities, while the salmon (Chinook, Coho, pink and sockeye) and steelhead run in the river in the fall and winter.

The short river between Anderson Lake and Seton Lake called Seton Portage offers steelhead as well as rainbow and dollies (to 2 kg/4.5 lbs). Steelhead anglers should try near the inflow and outflow, while the rainbow and dollies are caught at the mouth of Whitecap Creek.

Seymour River (Map 1/E1–11/F5)
The Seymour River has a small run of winter steelhead from late December to early April. There is also a small summer steelhead run in June until late July. All steelhead must be released. In fall, Coho and some Chinook head up the river. The Seymour River is the easiest of the North Shore rivers to fish since a trail system extends north along the river to the Seymour Dam.

Silverhope Creek (Map 5/G5–15/E7)
This large, fast flowing creek reaches the Fraser River just west of Hope. It has a small steelhead run in the summer (June–August) and again in the winter (January–April). There are also a few salmon that enter the river in the fall and there are some resident cutthroat and dollies. For best success, fish at the mouth of the creek or try some of the deep holes along the creek.

Similkameen River (Map 7/B3–G4)
The Similkameen River begins near Allison Pass in Manning Park and flows in an easterly direction some 160 km (97 miles) before entering the United States near Osoyoos. Most of the river length is accessed by Highway 3. The river produces well for rainbow on a (dry) fly. There is a bait ban from April 1 to October 31 as well as a catch and release fishery for rainbow between the Highway 3 bridge at Princeton and 31 km south of Princeton. A good whitefish fishery is offered in the winter season.

Skagit River (Map 6/E7–7/B5)
Offering some of the best rainbow trout fishing in southwestern BC, the Skagit is a slow meandering river. Fishermen either walk along the Skagit River Trail from Sumallo Grove or float down the river to sample some of the more remote pools. Other access is through the Skagit Valley just west of Hope. Day-use and campground facilities exist close to fishing access points. Fishing is restricted until July with the best fishing being towards August and September, after the runoff has subsided. The rainbow in the Skagit River average 20–30 cm (8–12 inches) but can grow as large as 50 cm (20 inches). Dollies enter the Skagit from Ross Lake and can grow as large as 5 kg (10 lbs). These fish are in the river in the fall but some remain year round.

Skwanka River (Map 47/B3)
The Skwanka is another remote river with a logging road that follows the river valley. The river contains cutthroats, Chinook, Coho and a small run of winter steelhead.

Sloquet Creek (Map 13/B1–24/F6)
Sloquet Creek flows northeast into the Lillooet River. A deteriorating logging road accesses the lower portions of the creek. There are steelhead in January to April, resident dollies and Coho in the fall. While in the area, why not visit the hot springs for a relaxing après fishing soak?

Spuzzum Creek (Map 26/A6–F7)
Spuzzum Creek is a small creek that crosses Highway 1, 25 km north of Yale. Like most of the small creeks that flow into the Fraser, the closer you get to the Fraser, the better the fishing is. The creek has a steelhead fishery from January to April, Chinook salmon in June and July, and rainbow throughout the year.

Squamish River (Map 21/G2, 22/A3–C7, 28/G2–G7)
This large river flows southward into Howe Sound at Squamish. It has a total of 60 km (36.5 miles) of fishable water. Due to glacial silt and spring runoff, the Squamish is very difficult to fish from early May to the end of July. Also, the lower reaches of the river below Brackendale are very unproductive. As a result, the best time to fish is in the fall to early spring from the Ashulu Creek estuary to below the Cheakamus River. The river offers steelhead beginning in January with the best time being in late March. Four species of salmon return to the Squamish: pink, Coho, Chinook and chum. There is no retention of pink, Chinook and chum and only hatchery Coho may be retained. These Coho are present in October and November, while dollies are available year round.

Stave River (Map 3/B4; 13/A1–F5, 24/A6)
The Stave has two distinct sections. The Lower Stave River is a short, broad river that flows out of Hayward Lake, which in turn falls out of Stave Lake. The lower section offers the typical migratory species including; pink (odd years), summer Chinook, fall Coho and chum and winter steelhead. The Upper Stave River flows into the north end of Stave Lake and can only be reached by boat and then biking or hiking up the Stave River Forest Road. There are resident cutthroat and dollies in the river. Given the remote access, the upper river can be very productive, particularly in the late fall.

Stawamus River (Map 11/E2–22/C7)
Stawamus River is a small stream that flows into Howe Sound at Squamish. It provides slow fishing for steelhead in April and May and Coho in the fall. There are also resident cutthroat and dollies.

Stein River (Map 31/E4–33/B2)
Although the Stein offers very good fishing for steelhead in the winter, Chinook and Coho in the fall and rainbow year round, few visitors to the valley bring along fishing rods. This makes the fishing all that better.

Sumas River (Map 3/F7–4/A5)
This river parallels Highway 1 for a good stretch and provides a few cutthroat in the spring and fall, resident dollies year round, Coho in the fall (mid-September to December) and steelhead in the winter. There are even carp in the canal. A boat launch is available at the Sumas Pumping Station.

Sumallo River (Map 6/B3–E3)
The upper reaches of the Sumallo River are easily accessed from the Sumallo River Forest Road. The lower reaches parallel Highway 3 east of Sunshine Valley. The river offers good fishing for rainbow and dollies in summer. Although small, the rainbow trout receive most of the attention and can be by fly, bait or small spinner.

Texas Creek (Map 38/C5–E2)
Texas Creek is found south of Lillooet and flows to the northeast into the Fraser River. Texas Creek Road provides access but if you want to reach the upper portion of the creek you will need a 4wd vehicle and a lot of patience (due to water bars). The creek provides excellent fishing for small rainbow.

Theodosia River (Map 46/C5–D3)
This remote river flows into the Theodosia Inlet near Desolation Sound. The river is accessed by boat and then by following the Theodosia Main logging road up the river. The river provides steelhead and cutthroat in the spring and fall as well as Coho in September and October.

Thompson River (Map 33/C2–39/G5)
This large river is renowned for its excellent steelhead fishery. However, in recent times (despite conservation measures), the fishing has declined. Regardless, anglers come from around the world to try to hook into one of these mighty trout (some reach 13 kg/30 lbs) during the late fall (October–December). The pools around Spences Bridge are legendary. Other species in the river include several salmon runs, rainbow trout, sturgeon, Dolly Varden and whitefish. Please check the regulations as the river is closely regulated to help preserve the fishery.

Tingle Creek (Map 13/B3–D5)
This small, remote creek flows into Clearwater Bay on Stave Lake. Accessed by boat, it provides resident rainbow, dollies and cutthroat.

Tulameen River (Map 17/A7–G5)
The Tulameen flows from the Cascade Mountains before arcing past the town of Tulameen and spilling into the Similkameen River at Princeton. The 81 km (49 mile) long river contains a number of species, most notably rainbow and brook trout and mountain whitefish. Although most sections of the river are easily accessed, there are some remote, wild sections that offer excellent fishing.

Tzoonie River (Map 20/G5–21/B3)
Tzoonie River is a remote river flowing southward into Narrows Inlet. It is accessed by boat and then by following the Tzoonie River Road preferably by mountain bike. The river provides steelhead fishing in December to March as well as Coho fishing in the fall. There are also resident Dolly Varden and cutthroat in the river system.

Vancouver River (Map 20/D2–G2)
The Vancouver River is yet another remote river that flows into Jervis Inlet. A mountain bike can be used to access the length of the river along an old rail line/road from Vancouver Bay. The river has steelhead in January to May, cutthroat in October and November and Coho in the fall. There are also resident dollies available.

Vedder River (Map 4/A5–C5)
Below the Vedder Bridge, Chilliwack River is called the Vedder River as it slowly flows into the Vedder Canal. This section of the river is the most popular stream to fish in the Fraser Valley if not the province. It is not uncommon to see hundreds of anglers lined up shoulder-to-shoulder trying for the winter steelhead, chum and Coho fishing in September to October as well as Chinook in July through September. Some anglers will launch a boat at the Sumas Pumping Station to avoid the crowds. Water levels definitely affect the quality of fishing so be sure to watch the weekly fishing reports on the local fishing websites. Also be sure to check the current restrictions before heading out.

Weaver Creek (Map 4/E1, 14/E7)
Home to the Weaver Creek Spawning Channel, this small creek has a good run of steelhead in December to March and cutthroat all year. Sections of the creek are closed to fishing.

Whonnock Creek (Map 3/B3)
Whonnock Creek crosses Highway 7 between 272nd Street and 280th Street. The river contains cutthroat, has a small run of Coho in fall and a small run of winter steelhead.

Widgeon Creek (Map 12/E6)
This creek drains Widgeon Lake southward into Pitt River. It is accessed by canoe from Grant Narrows and has resident cutthroat as well as steelhead in the winter and Coho in the fall.

Whipsaw Creek (Map 7/D1–17/G6)
Whipsaw Creek crosses Highway 3 south of Princeton and is a rainbow stream. You can access the northwest banks of the river from the Whipsaw Creek Forest Road or you can access the southeastern shore from the Friday Main.

Yale Creek (Map 15/E2)
This small creek is off Highway 1 just north of Yale. The creek offers Chinook in June through July at the mouth of the Fraser River.

OCEAN FISHING

As with all coastal areas of BC, there are seemingly endless areas to fish for Pacific salmon, as well as sea-run cutthroat, shellfish and groundfish. However, this is a very popular area and keeping track of the fishing regulations can be as much a challenge as actually catching the fish. You will need to confirm openings with the Department of Fisheries and Oceans. Their website is http://www.pac.dfo-mpo.gc.ca/fm-gp/rec/tidal-maree/index-eng.htm or call 1-866-431-3474. You should also note the many rockfish conservation areas in the area. Again the DFO website provides maps and descriptions of these areas. Listed below are the many hot spots off the Vancouver and Sunshine Coasts.

Howe Sound/Vancouver Area

The real advantage of the Howe Sound and Burrard Inlet is the easy access from Vancouver and Gibsons. Boat launches are available near the entrance to False Creek, at Ambleside Beach in West Vancouver, at Horseshoe Bay, at Sewell's Marina, at MacDonald Park in Richmond, Rocky Point Park in Port Moody and several locations along the Fraser River. It is also possible to access the Howe Sound from the Sunshine Coast. The closest boat launches are at Langdale and Gibsons.

Bowen Island (Map 10/F7)

Due to its close proximity to Vancouver, Bowen Island is a popular fishing destination. The southern end of the island seems to get most of the attention but there are many areas to drop a line in. Collingwood Channel produces very well for winter Chinook in December–April, while Cowan Point to Cape Roger Curtis is another good area for wintering Chinook on a deep (25–35 m/80–120 ft) troll. Cowan Point also produces well for Chinook in May through July, Coho in late August to October, pinks in late August to September (odd years) and sockeye in September with trolling being your best bet. Snug Cove is often trolled southward to the Copper Mine for Chinook from December to March and from June to August. Coho can be found from July to September. Watch out for heavy traffic in the area, especially ferries.

Capilano River (Map 1/C1)

The mouth of the Capilano is an incredibly popular area to fish, especially for the Coho that congregate at the river mouth. It is possible to cast from shore for the Coho beginning in June until November or anchor a boat 20–30 metres off the lighthouse and mooch on a tide change. A number of Chinook in the 10–15 kg (30–40 lb) range also come into the area in late summer until mid-October. These fish are best caught by trolling during flood tides. In December through April, winter Chinook frequent the mouth and can be caught by mooching 60–80 metres offshore. Care must be taken to ensure you are not fishing in the navigational channel.

Fraser River Estuary (Map 1/A2-C7)

The Fraser River is the pathway for millions of migrating salmon. It is no wonder the river mouth can provide some of the best fishing anywhere. Between Point Grey Bell Buoy and the QA marker off the North Arm, the T-10 marker off the Middle Arm, around the Sand Heads off the end of the Steveston Jetty in the tide lines and from Roberts Bank to the Tsawwassen Ferry Terminal all seem to produce at particular times (just follow the crowds). The Chinook fishery beginning in the spring and lasting until the end of September gets most of the attention. The waters of the Fraser are murky making it necessary to attract the fish. Other salmon species include pinks every odd year in August-September, sockeye in July and August and hatchery Coho from August to October, while chum are present in October to November.

Hole in the Wall (Map 11/A6)

This is a very popular fishing spot just north of Horseshoe Bay and is so named because of a mining test hole on the granite cliff rising above the ocean. The area is notoriously fickle with mooching near the cliffs where you will find a 150 metre ledge the best bet for Chinook in November through March and again in July through September. Troll deep (25–35 m/80–120 ft) in the winter months. The occasional Coho is caught in the area between July and September.

Indian Arm (Map 11/G1–12/A6)

Indian Arm produces an excellent fishery for pinks in late August–early September, during odd numbered years (2003, 2005, etc.). These fish congregate just south of the Vancouver Yacht Club against the rock cliff. It is best to drift fish and casting into the school of fish. Another good fishery occurs in late October when chum enter the arm.

Keats Island (Map 10/E6)

This small island to the west of Bowen Island is best fished for wintering Chinook in November through April off Cotton Point. The point can also produce well for Chinook and Coho in June–October. Nearby Home Island is a small rock outcrop also known as Salmon Rock. This area receives heavy fishing pressure because it is a constant producer for Chinook in March and April and Chinook and Coho in June–September.

Point Atkinson (Map 1/A1–C1)

The lighthouse in Lighthouse Park marks Point Atkinson. A rock shelf extends off the point to the 18–25 metres (60–90 feet) level before dropping off to 60 metres or more. It is at this drop-off that trolling is most effective for Chinook in the winter and July to September as well as for a few Coho and pinks in August through September. Due to strong currents, it is best to troll in a circular manner around the point. If fishing is slow, trolling along the West Vancouver Waterfront, about 300 metres (1,000 feet) offshore at the notable underwater bench, can be effective all the way to the Ambleside boat launch.

Sunshine Coast/Powell River Areas

The fishing on the Sunshine Coast is similar to what is found on the East Coast of Vancouver Island. As a general rule, fishing is better here than around Vancouver, but not as good as places farther north or west. Of course, that's just a general observation and there are lots of good places to fish along the coast, from the popular Pender Harbour to the remote corners of Jervis Inlet.

Copeland Islands (Map 46/A6)

The Copeland Islands are north of Lund and offer some good fishing for Chinook and Coho. The best location to fish is on the inside passage either by trolling a plug at 15–25m (60–90 feet) or by fishing from shore. Chinook begin to appear in mid April and can be caught until July. Coho tend to be near the islands in July and August.

Earls Cove (Map 20/B6)

From May to August, Earls Cove is a good destination for Coho and Chinook. It is sheltered from the winds of Jervis Inlet so it makes a good place for smaller crafts. If you are fishing for Chinook, it is best to try a deep mooch (20–45 metres/65–100 feet). Smaller Coho (bluebacks) come into the area in May and then you can catch mature Coho until August.

Egmont Area (Map 20/C5)

In order to get into the Sechelt Inlet, fish must first pass Egmont Point. Fishing can be quite good throughout the year for Chinook and Coho. Moochers tend to stay closer to Earls Cove than the point, whereas the trollers tend to troll toward Egmont.

Gower Point/Gibsons Gap (Map 10/C7)

Gower Point is considered one of the premier Coho areas on the Sunshine Coast as the fish must pass by the point on their way to the Fraser River or other rivers of the Burrard Inlet. Locals fishing the area usually anchor near the drop-off at the south end of the point and try mooching or strip casting. The Gap is a shallow rock shelf that extends from the south end of Keats Island to Cape Byng west of Gibsons. The water on either side of the shelf drops off rapidly to 45 metres (150 feet) and it is at the drop-off where the fish hold. Coho are caught from June–September and the occasional Chinook is caught here in May–September. There are also good numbers of pinks caught during late July and early August in odd years

Halfmoon Bay (Map 9/C4)

This bay is one of the best fishing areas on the Sunshine Coast, producing Chinook from November through to March as well as in June and July and again in September. Coho are present in July through September. Both species are best caught by trolling around the points leading into the bay.

Harmony Island/Granville Bay (Map 20/B3)

This area is popular for Chinook in April through early June as well as Coho fishermen later in summer (July and August). The best place to fish is at the north end of the islands or near the estuary of Freil Lake. Mooching is by far the method of choice.

Harwood/Vivian Islands (Map 18/D3)

To the east of Powell River, Harwood Island marks a good area for salmon fishing. The best spots to fish for Coho and Chinook are off the east and southwest sides of the island using a deep troll. Nearby Vivian

Island offers Chinook in July and August primarily by trolling. There are also Coho in June through August.

Lasqueti Island (Map 8/E5)

By far the best location to fish around Lasqueti Island is off Young Point, which attracts many moochers. Trollers can circle the point or work their way up to Bull Passage with reasonable success. Coho are the most common fish here, with July being the best month to catch them. Off the northeastern end of Lasqueti Island from Fegen Islets to False Bay, fishing produces Coho and a few Chinook primarily by a shallow troll. At the south end of Jenkins Island is a good spot to troll for Coho in June through October with the bigger northerns coming through in September to October. The occasional Chinook can be caught in July and August.

Mystery Reef/Grant Reefs (Map 18/A2–C2)

Mystery Reef is situated to the northwest of Harwood Island. It is known to produce good numbers of Coho in May through June as well as a few Chinook in July and August. If the bait is near the reefs, anchor off the north or south end of the reef and try some mooching or jigging. Otherwise, try trolling around the reef as the fish are likely scattered. Finding Grant Reefs is half the fun as they are submerged but marked by a series of kelp beds. The reefs provide good fishing for Coho from May to July and Chinook in July and August.

Nelson Island (Map 8, 19)

Nelson Island is the large island that is found at the northwest end of Sechelt Peninsula. Scattered around the island are several good fishing holes. Ackland Reef, which is several hundred yards off the mouth of Quarry Bay, provides one of the best fisheries for Coho throughout July and August. The area is difficult to find but once you do, it is best to anchor at the edge of the reef in 15–30 metres (50–100 feet) of water and try jigging or mooching. Chinook are around in May through August. Fearney Point provides a popular fishery for Chinook, pink and Coho. Most fishermen troll around the point, while moochers can anchor near the point. Green Bay is located in Agamemnon Channel on the southeast side of the island. This area offers good fishing for Chinook as well as Coho and bluebacks. Moochers do well by concentrating in the inlet to the bay or on the point to the north of the bay where there is a nice tide rip caused by the point. For trollers, it is best to troll around the point. Quarry Bay is a good area to troll for Coho in July and August or for Chinook in April to July.

Pender Harbour (Map 9/A1)

The shear number of resorts and guides in the immediate area is proof of the fine fishing around Pender Harbour. There are several hotspots to try. Francis Point is a good location for trolling for both Chinook and Coho from May through September. The Gap leading into Pender Harbour is extremely popular with fishermen to mooch with live herring for Chinook throughout the year. Lee's Bay is located between Daniel Point and Irvines Landing and is another popular mooching areas for Chinook throughout the year. A bit further north, Sakinaw Estuary, or the A-Frame, is best trolled or mooched near the point south of the actual estuary. The best fishing for the Chinook is in December through March and for the Coho in July and August.

Powell River (Map 18/F4–19/A5)

The old boat breakwater, known as The Hulks, marks the location of some good Chinook fishing in May through August. Most fishermen begin trolling near the Hulks at dawn and then work their way outward throughout the morning. The opposite is true for the evening fish. Another area to try is the Westview Waterfront. The occasional wintering Chinook can be caught in December to April on a deep (25–40 metre/80–130 feet) troll. The better fishing, however, is in May through July for Chinook and Coho. Grief Point is located south of Powell River and can be good year round. The focus, however, is in May to August when the Chinook are found off the point in good numbers. Trolling or mooching are the primary fishing methods. Myrtle Point/Rocks are found between Powell River and Brew Bay and offer good fishing for Chinook from May to July and for Coho in July. Trolling along the shoreline from Myrtle Rock all the way to the point is the most common method of catching fish.

Roberts Creek Area (Map 10/B6)

The shoreline extending from Wilson Creek all the way to Gower Point can be a very productive trolling area for Coho from June to October and for Chinook in June and again in September–October. It is also possible to catch wintering Chinook in December to March. Moochers tend to focus their efforts approximately 200 metres (650 feet) from the wharf at Roberts Creek where there is a noticeable drop-off. The area is subject to large swells.

Saint Vincent Bay (Map 19/G4–20/A4)

Saint Vincent Bay has a number of fishing holes all the way out to Elephant Point and Culloden Point. Both points are best for Coho (bluebacks beginning in April until May and then mature Coho throughout the summer) whereas Saint Vincent Bay is best for Chinook. This area can be extremely busy during the summer months with both moochers and trollers.

Sarah Point (Map 46/A5)

Sarah Point marks the northern tip of Malaspina Peninsula. It is a good spot for fishing because fish entering Desolation Sound must pass by the point. There are some wintering Chinook but the main fishery is from May and June for Chinook and late August to early September for Coho. Trolling around the point seems to work the best.

Savary Island (Map 18/A1)

In July and August, the south side of Savary Island can be trolled using a typical Coho lure. The Coho can be found in good numbers all the way along the south side of the island and northward to Hernando Island. Jigging or casting along the kelp beds on the south side of the island can also be effective.

Scotch Fir Point (Map 19/D6)

This point marks the beginning of Jervis Inlet and migratory salmon must pass here to get into the Inlet and its system of creeks and rivers. As a result, it offers good fishing throughout the summer months for Coho and in December–March and May for Chinook.

Sechelt Inlet (Map 9/F4–20/D6)

This long narrow inlet leads all the way from Egmont south to Sechelt. Porpoise Bay sees the most pressure, as it butts up against Sechelt, but there are a number of other places to fish the sheltered inlet. Coho start running through this area in July and Chinook in August. In odd years the inlet sees a good fishery for pinks, too. Some areas to try include Snake Bay, Tillicum Bay, Carlson Point and Highland Point.

Texada Island (Map 8, 18, 19)

Texada Island is a popular destination for residents of the Sunshine Coast and beyond. Larger boats can cross Malaspina Strait, while smaller boats usually base their activities from one of the scenic campsites around the big island. Anderson Bay is located on the southeast side of Texada Island and offers some good trolling and mooching for Chinook in April to July and Coho beginning in May until August. Just north of the bay, the series of pilings mark another good mooching area for Chinook throughout the year and Coho. The best place is between 30–60 metres (100–200 feet) out from the pilings. Blubber Bay to Davis Bay provides a good trolling area for Coho and Chinook in May through September. Grilse (Coho) Point is located at the northern tip of Texada Island and is considered a premier Coho area in August. Mouat Bay is known primarily as a trolling area for Coho found anywhere from Gilles Bay to Mouat Islets. The area is quite exposed to winds. Sturt Bay is found near Van Anda and provides a holding area for Chinook in the summer months when bait is present in the bay. Given the confined area, mooching and jigging are your better choices. Outside the bay, Coho can be caught from July to September by trolling in the tide lines. Upwood Point is the southernmost point of land on Texada Island. Coho can be found from July to October whereas Chinook cruise the area year round. The area is best trolled.

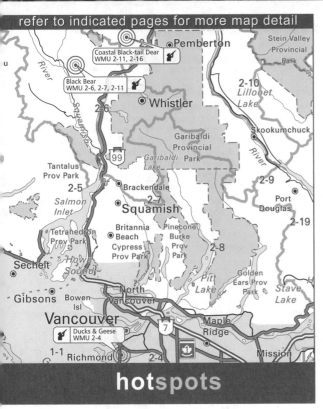

hot**spots**

*B*C hunters enjoy some of-if not the-widest variety in game animals anywhere on the continent, many of which can be found within this book. This diversity of wildlife is made possible by the range of habitats from riverbank to alpine and desert to rainforest.

Regardless of habitat though, winter is normally the bottleneck for survival of wild animals.

The Coastal area of BC is blessed with a temperate climate that usually ensures a lower than average winter mortality rate for both bird and beast. As a result, the coast has the largest population of overwintering waterfowl and raptors in the country. However, the farther inland you go, the thicker the snowpack becomes.

Hunters can expect some of the best big game hunting this region has ever produced. This is because the winters for the last decade or two have been the mildest in a hundred years and most game populations are thriving. Further, there is easier backcountry access, and, unlike many outdoor pursuits, the number of hunters is actually on the decline.

Ducks and geese don't do well in mountainous terrain and much of the low-lying wetland areas are protected by parks. While Canada geese have reached nuisance numbers in urban areas, many of the best hunting areas are closed by Municipal bylaws. Still the birds are there and the seasons are long.

There are also few upland game species in this region, save for the eastern sections of the book. These bird species prefer the drier climes of the interior as opposed to the wet coastal weather.

A person wanting to hunt in BC first needs a Hunter Number, which he can get after completing the Conservation and Outdoor Recreation Education course (see http://www. bcwf.bc.ca/programs/core/index.html). You then need a hunting license and a species tag for each big game animal you intend to hunt. More details on licensing are at http:// www.env.gov.bc.ca/fw/wildlife/hunting/regulations/. Some game animals are controlled though Limited Entry Hunting (http://www.env.gov.bc.ca/fw/wildlife/hunting/resident/ leh.html), while non-resident hunters must be accompanied by a licensed guide. Licenses can be picked up at many sporting good stores, as well as Service BC locations.

Because Wildlife Management Units (MU) 2-4 and portions of 2-8 overlap with the most heavily populated area in the province, hunters in these areas need a Fraser Valley Special Area Hunting License in addition to the other hunting licenses. Further, hunters need to carry at least $1,000,000 in Public Liability and Property Damage Insurance.

BIG GAME ANIMALS

Bighorn Sheep

Bighorn rams are one of the most distinctive animals in the province, with their large, spiral horns. They are generally brown or grayish brown in colour, with lighter undersides and rump. Ewes and young rams have spike-like curved horns. They have soft hooves with hard outer rims that give them good footing in mountainous terrain. They have incredible eyesight and are able to detect movement over a kilometre away. This, coupled with their mountainous habitat makes them some of the most difficult and most challenging species to hunt. Many, even most, people who hunt bighorn come away disappointed.

Bighorns are the largest wild sheep in North America, with rams weighing up to 135 kg (300 lbs). Ewes average 70 kg (150 lbs). They spend their summer high in the alpine; while in winter they migrate to south facing slopes where snow cover is minimal. They are often found around mineral or salt licks.

California Bighorn are found on the eastern facing slopes of the Coast Range and into the interior. There is Limited Entry Hunting in all the Thompson (Region 3) Management Units found in this book, but no openings in the Lower Mainland Region.

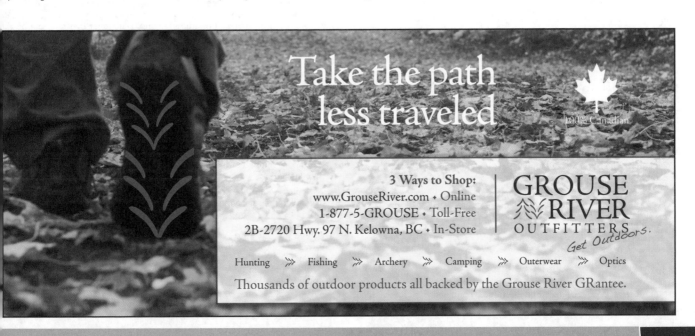

Black bear

Black bears (Ursus americanus) are the most common predator in the Lower Mainland and can be found in good numbers in almost any habitat from river flat to mountain top. Adult male bears weigh up to 300 kg (660 lbs) and females about 200 kg (440 lbs). They get to that size by eating almost anything, from grass, roots and berries to freshly killed meat and rotting fish.

"Black" is the name, and black is the most common colour of the pelage (hair), but this animal can come in a true amazing variety of colours, from jet black through various shades of red and brown to bluish or pure white. There are both spring and fall hunting seasons for bear. In spring, the right habitat is just about anywhere that there is new green growth. Logged openings, recent wildfires and utility corridors are good areas to start. The south facing slopes of major river valleys green up quickly, so are a prime choice to hunt bear in the early season. By fall, bears are working hard to fatten up for the winter hibernation and can be found anywhere that there is an abundance of food. Good places to start a fall bear hunt are wild berry patches or along streams, particularly those with spawning salmon.

Coastal Black-tail Deer

Deer in BC are either white-tailed (Odocoileus virginianus) or black-tailed (Odocoileus hemionus). Black-tailed deer are further divided into mule deer and coastal (or Columbian) black-tails. Of all the species, the most common in Southwestern BC is the Columbian black-tail. These deer inhabit a thin strip of land and are generally not found more than 200 km (120 miles) inland, preferring to inhabit the dense rainforest found nearer the ocean.

Columbian black-tail deer are a smaller sub-species with a good-sized buck weighing a mere 90 km (200 lbs) and some females as small as 40 kg (90 lbs). But what they lack in size, they make up in cunning. These deer can be elusive as they make their way though the farmland of the Fraser Valley and get lost in the thick underbrush of the coastal mountains. They have almost no rump patch, but have a wide, black tail. When startled, they run with a stiff legged bounce like a mule deer.

Cougar

This largest member of the cat family in BC provides hunting recreation during the winter when little else is open. Cougars (puma concolor) are tawny coloured with lighter coloured hair under their chin, throat and belly. An adult male cougar is about the same size as an adult human although an adult female is usually less than 40 kg (90 lbs). Both sexes have a muscular tail, about as thick as a man's wrist and can be almost as long as the rest of the body.

Cougars kill and eat a wide range of prey, but deer are preferred, and their distribution and migration generally follows that of deer. Cougar hunters mainly use trained dogs to chase and tree the big cats. Pursuit only, a kind of "catch and release" hunting is popular with some hunters. The hunting season is November to March, but January has the most reliable conditions with fresh, soft snow and the most productive hunting.

Elk

Elk are one of the most distinguished and distinguishable members of the deer family, especially the bulls, with their large, sweeping antlers and dark brown heads. Elk are also known as wapiti and, while they are smaller than moose, they are much larger than most of the other members of the deer family, with bulls weighing up to 450 kg (1,000 lbs) and cows to 270 kg (600 lbs). Bulls challenge each other for possession of cows and the elk is the only member of the deer family in BC that collects a harem.

Elk are found in areas of woodland mixed with grassland as is found at the edges of forests and in mountain meadows. They forage on forbs and grasses in the summer and aspen bark and twigs in the winter.

In the Lower Mainland, the only species of Elk found are Roosevelt Elk, which are slightly larger than Rocky Mountain elk found farther east. Also, the antlers of bulls sometimes terminate in a crown of three or four points.

Elk were extirpated in the Lower Mainland area, but small populations have been re-established on the Sunshine Coast and in the Pitt River and Indian River drainages. While these populations are still small, there is a Limited Entry Hunt on the Sunshine Coast. In the next few years, LEHs may open elsewhere in Region 2 as the herds introduced in the Pitt and Indian drainages are doing quite well.

Moose

Moose are one of the most prized animals to hunt in BC. They are the largest member of the deer family and the largest ungulate in North America. Because of their size, they have few predators. Wolves will sometimes attack young or infirmed moose, but a healthy, grown moose is rarely targeted. There are currently estimated to be about 170,000 moose in the province.

Moose are quite distinctive looking (some would say downright ugly). They have long legs, a large, drooping snout and a flap of skin in the shape of a bell under their throats. The have broad hooves and are usually dark brown to black. Male Moose have large, broad antlers that are extremely prized among hunters. A full sized bull moose can stand 2.75 m (9.25 ft) tall.

Moose are usually found in wooded areas next to swamps, lakeshores and streams. They feed on leaves, grass and water plants in the summer. During the winter, moose browse on aspen bark and around the edges of dense forests where there is less snow. In spite of their large size, moose can move through the underbrush quickly and quietly. Moose cannot see very well, but they have an acute sense of smell and hearing. When frightened, they will trot away with long smooth strides, threading their way through bush and trees that you wouldn't think they'd be able to navigate.

They are not usually found in the thick coastal forests of southern BC, but have been found at the head of inlets from Bute north. Still, their main range is the northern interior and the farther northeast you travel, the more likely you are to find moose. There are no openings for moose in the Lower Mainland Region, but there are openings in all the Thompson (Region 3) MUs.

Mountain Goat

One of most unique mammals in North America, with no close genetic relatives, the mountain goat is known for its sure-footedness and ability to navigate some of the country's steepest terrain. However, while the steep cliffs protect the goats from predators, it makes them extremely vulnerable to poaching and over hunting.

Billies can weigh up to 120 km (260 lbs) while nannies average about half that. Other than size, it can be difficult to tell the two apart, as both male and female have narrow, sharply pointed horns. Technically, the female's horns are slightly narrower at the base and curve more.

Because the goats have the thickest covering of hair of any animal in BC, they do not do well in hot, arid areas. They are also only found in limited numbers in the Coast Mountains, but become more common in the mountains as you head east. There is an extremely Limited Entry Hunt, for hunting mountain goat on Mount Meager (MU 2–11), as well as more limited alternatives in Regions 3 & 8.

Goats do not migrate more than a few kilometres, usually just moving from the valleys to the alpine as winter turns to spring, then summer. This makes them fairly easy to find, though, considering their preferred habitat, easy is a relative term. Goats have low reproductive rates and, since mortality rates can be as high as 50% in the first two years of a goat's life, they do not bounce back very quickly.

Mule Deer

Mule deer are the one of the most widely distributed big game animals in the province. In the Vancouver, Coast and Mountains region they are not found near the coast, but are found farther inland. Mule deer bucks weight about 100 kg (220 lbs) with does about 2/3 that weight. Both sexes have a grey/brown coat and oversized ears (hence the name) and a light cream coloured rump patch with a narrow, black tipped tail. Mule deer antlers are bifurcated, that is, continuously branched into two as they grow. When startled, instead of running, mule deer often move with a bounding leap called "stotting" in which all four feet spring the animal forward and come down together.

Mule deer prefer generally open country and can be found in the alpine and in forest openings created by logging or forest fire. Hunters should be constantly glassing the hillsides with binoculars when hunting mule deer. Autumn snow forces these animals to lower elevation where they concentrate on south facing slopes for winter. Young mule deer can be remarkably unwary regarding humans but big mulie bucks can be shy, although even they become less cautious in the rut (during mid November).

In the area where both mule deer and Columbian black-tail are found, interbreeding is common, and a hybrid species–slightly larger than the Columbian, but smaller than the mule deer–are frequently found.

Wolves and Coyote

Wolves are the largest wild dogs found in the province, indeed, anywhere in the world. A full-sized male wolf can get up to 60 kg (130 lbs). Wolves are often grey with dark shading, but fur colour can range from pure black to pure white. Their fur is thick and dense. Wolves have large feet that help them travel over snow in wintertime.

Perceptions of wolves vary wildly. Some people consider wolves to be the epitome of the noble beast, fierce, brave and loyal, while others consider them little more than pests that prey on domestic animals. The truth, if it is to be found, lies somewhere in the middle.

Coyote are usually considered more of a pest than a popular species for hunting. Coyote are larger than foxes, but smaller than a wolf. An adult coyote weighs between 10 to 23 kg (22 to 50 lb). They are usually grey or reddish grey, with black markings on the back and tail, and lighter colouration underneath. The ears are long and the muzzle is slender and pointed. The busy tail is usually carried low and close to the hind legs.

Wolves are a pack animal, traveling in groups that can be as small as two to over twenty. Pack sizes tend to be larger in winter. The primary food of wolves is moose, deer, elk and caribou, but can include beaver, hare, fish and even some plant material. In areas where wolves and ranchers occupy the same territory, there is often some predation. Ranchers and landowners often view wolves with suspicion and sometimes with downright contempt.

Coyotes are not pack animals, and usually hunt alone or in pairs, though several may gather at carcasses or other communal feeding sites. They are opportunists, feeding on carrion of livestock, especially in winter. They will also feed on chickens, cats and other small farm animals, reinforcing their reputations as nuisance creatures. In the wild, they feed on hare and mice as well as blueberries and other fruit.

Despite the often-aggressive attempts to destroy as many coyote as possible by landowners, coyote still survive and thrive. Coyotes can even be found in urban centers like Vancouver, and are found in all regions in the province.

There is a compulsory report of all wolves taken in region 2.

GAME BIRDS

Grouse
Not known for being the most cunning bird on the block, grouse are still a popular bird to hunt. What they lack in brains they make up for in colouring. You can nearly step on one of these birds before they take off in a chaotic explosion of feathers. On a still autumn morning, whilst sneaking through the forest watching and listening for the slightest hint of movement, this burst of activity can get the heart racing and the hands shaking. Once in the air, grouse are quick, and often fly a random pattern through the forest, making them hard to hit.

In fact, that's grouse hunting in a nutshell: walk through the woods until you flush a grouse and then try and shoot it down in the two second (at most) window you have. More often than not, grouse hunters will walk for hours without success.

There are three game species of grouse found in this region. Ruffed grouse have a ruff of black features about their neck and are usually about 43 cm (17 inches) long. Blue grouse are usually a slate gray colour (and not, as you might expect, blue) with a solid black tail and are usually about 53 cm (21 inches) long. Spruce grouse are smaller, only 38 cm (15 inches) long and usually mottled grey, brown and black.

Ducks
There are, broadly speaking, two types of ducks, dabbling and diving.

Dabbling ducks are typically found in fresh, shallow marshes and rivers rather than large lakes and bays. They are good divers, but usually feed by dabbling or tipping, rather than diving underwater, thus the name. The speculum or colored wing patch is generally iridescent and bright and often a telltale field mark. Dabbling Ducks include blacks, mallards and green winged teals are most commonly found in the many open wetlands and lakes. In areas where there aren't many open wetlands there also aren't a lot of ducks.

If dabbling ducks are so named because they don't go beneath the surface to feed, it seems logical that diving ducks get their name from their feeding habits as well, diving deep below the surface of the water to find food. They feed on fish and aquatic plants. Diving ducks include canvasbacks, redheads, ring-necked ducks and greater and lesser scaup.

Diving ducks are sometimes found in small marshes (especially ringnecks), but are more frequently found in larger lakes. They favour deeper open water areas where there is a good growth of underwater vegetation.

Any ducks feeding on land will likely be a dabbling duck, as these birds are sure-footed and can walk and run well on land. Their diet is mostly vegetables and they are just as likely to be found in a farmer's field as they are in a marsh.

Geese
There are two main species of geese that are hunted in Southwestern BC: snow geese and Canada geese, although there are open seasons for brant, Ross's geese and cackling geese as well.

Canadian geese are one of the most popular waterfowl and the most common species of goose in the province. They are not usually found in areas where there are a lot of trees and little open water or food, which describes much of this region. However, they can be found in agricultural areas, especially where there are lakes and wetlands nearby, especially in the wetlands around the Fraser River.

Hunting geese in a field is like similar to hunting dabbling ducks. Find an area, put out decoys, and get under cover, either with camouflage gear or with netting. Geese like to land near where other geese are feeding, so set your decoys up so that you lead the birds to where you want them. The more decoys you use, the more likely geese are to land, as they find security in numbers. Feeding geese tend to make lots of noise, especially when they see competition approaching, so a goose call usually helps.

VANCOUVER, COAST AND MOUNTAINS MANAGEMENT UNIT HIGHLIGHTS

MU 2-1 (Map 6, 7)
This wildlife management unit bounds are within Manning Provincial Park, which is closed to hunting.

MU 2-2 (Map 5, 6, 15, 16)
The Skagit Silver Hope area encompasses the drainage of the Skagit River east of Hope. Here hunters will find a mix of coastal and interior wildlife species. Near Ross Lake, for instance, hunters will find an interior type ecosystem that is more typical of the Cascade. The management unit offers fair hunting for Columbian black-tail deer, mule deer, as well as a hybrid species. The area offers good black bear hunting and fair hunting for cougar and bobcat. However, the region is not known for its bird hunting, but there are some grouse hunting opportunities towards the dryer eastern section of the area.

MU 2-3 (Map 4, 5, 6, 15)
Encompassing the drainage of the Chilliwack River, this management unit sits on the interface between wilderness and urban areas and between the Cascade Mountains and the lowlands of the Fraser Valley. Hunters need to be aware of private land and not trespass or hunt on these lands without express permission from the landowner. Columbian black-tail deer are tough to find but they are here. The area also offers good black bear hunting and fair hunting for cougar and bobcat. The region is not known for its bird hunting, although there are some band-tailed pigeons to be found. The northern portions of this area also abut the Fraser River, where hunters will find some good spots to hunt waterfowl.

MU 2-4 (Map 1, 2, 3)
This management unit is made up of the south Fraser Valley, including the cities of Abbottsford, Surrey and Richmond. There are regulations regarding the discharge of firearm in municipal areas, so if you are planning on hunting in this region, make sure you know what the rules are. Also note that there is literally no public land save for some intertidal zones so if you are planning on hunting, you will need landowners' permission. Here you will find the largest wintering population of waterfowl in Canada. Snow geese have increased in populations and are becoming a real nuisance in some areas, feeding on crops and invading public spaces, although most of these areas are closed to hunting. There are plenty of ducks, too. Although very few upland birds exist, there are some private pheasant farms in the region. Being so close to urban development, big game populations are limited to a few deer that can be found here.

MU 2-5, 2-12 (Map 8, 9, 10, 11, 18, 19, 20, 21, 28, 46, 47)
These two management units are comprised of the watersheds that drain the Sunshine Coast. There is a fair amount of human habitation along the coastal fringes of these units and hunters need to be wary of private land issues. But there are also vast tracts of land that have no settlement, no roads and some of the most difficult access on the continent (there is a reason the Sunshine Coast is only accessible by ferry; if they could have built a road, they would have…). There are relatively good populations of deer, although these are in decline right now, due to a strong population of predators, including

coyote, wolves, cougars and bears. This means that there is good hunting for these species as well. Unlike management units with easier access and stronger hunting pressure, there is actually a limited opening for mountain goat. As well, the Roosevelt elk population, re-introduced in the early 1980s, is large enough to support a limited entry hunting season.

MU 2-6, 2-7 (Map 11, 12, 21, 22, 23, 28, 29, 30, 34, 47, 49)
Making up both the eastern and western drainages of the Squamish River, these two management units are part of the coastal ecosystem. Despite the heavy snowpack, there are a couple openings for goat as well as good black bear and moderate deer population. Although there are a lot of waterfowl in the Squamish area, there is no hunting allowed. Hunters will be happy to note elk have moved into 2-6 from top end of 2-5 and can expect a limited entry season soon.

MU 2-8 (Map 1, 2, 3, 4, 11, 12, 13, 14, 22, 23, 24)
Containing the largest population of people in the province, finding a place to hunt here is going to be the hardest part of hunting in this management unit. Much of the area is private land and the portions that aren't are generally provincial or regional parks that are closed to hunting or watersheds that are closed to access. If you can find a place to hunt, opportunities are good. There is a large resident population of Canada geese and other waterfowl, some band-tailed pigeons and even some lager ungulates like deer. Roosevelt elk have been reintroduced into this region over the last decade and will very soon have a small open season, barring any unforeseen circumstances.

MU 2-9, 2-10, 2-11 (Map 13, 23, 24, 28, 29, 30, 31, 34, 35, 36, 40, 41, 49)
These three management units take up a large swath of the interior regions of this book. Similar in characteristic, each unit has high elevation areas that are difficult to access along with a mix of coastal and interior climates. There are good deer populations that include a mix of coastal black-tail, mule, and the hybrid of the two. For mountain goat hunters, there is a limited entry hunt on Mount Meager, with a very low success rate, maybe one goat every few years taken. Coastal hunters will be surprised to see some moose here, but it is not a large enough population to support an opening. Wolves are on the increase, as are black bear, which are becoming a nuisance in the agrarian areas of the Pemberton Valley. The valley also has some wetlands and hunters will find okay hunting for Canada geese. These regions are also popular areas for cougar and bobcat hunting.

MU 2-13, 2-14, 2-15 (Map 46, 47, 48, 49)
These remote management units are boat access only along the mid-Coast and are comprised of the drainages in the area that empty into Toba Inlet and Bute Inlet. And, let's be honest. Nobody is going to head go through all the effort of making the trek to this area for a spot of band-tailed pigeon hunting. Which is good, because populations of both upland game birds and waterfowl are thin, the latter being found in the marshes and wetlands and the head of these inlets. There is, however, some good big game hunting, including goat, deer and black bear.

MU 2-16 (Map 8, 10, 11, 18, 19, 20)
Made up of the Howe Sound Islands, such as Bowen, Gambier, Anvil, as well as some of the Northern Gulf Islands such as Texada and Nelson, this is a unique area to hunt deer. There are no natural predators and the deer tend to thrive on the islands. So much so that in winter, there is a high mortality rate as there is too much competition for food. As a result, this management unit has one of the most liberal open seasons for deer. Hunters who make the trip to Texada Island have a 50-50 chance of going home with a deer, which is the best success rate in the province. However, the downside is that it is a full day and three ferries from the Lower Mainland just to get there. There are no bear, cougars, wolves or coyotes and little in the way of waterfowl or upland bird hunting. Please note it is against the law to discharge a firearm on Bowen, although the island is still open to hunting.

MU 2-17 (Map 26, 27)
This management unit is more interior than coast and encompasses the Coquihalla drainage. The area has a lot of deer (mule deer), but heavy snowpack can have a negative impact on populations. There are also lots of black bear, and some good cougar hunting, but the limited number of backroads in this area can make access difficult. The drier interior climate offers better conditions for grouse, too.

MU 2-18, 2-19 (Map 4, 5, 13, 14, 15, 24, 25, 26)
These two management units are comprised of the Harrison Lake drainage 2-18 on the east side of the lake, 2-19 on the west. This area is far enough inland to not experience the same degree of moderate weather as the west coast, although it still experiences nearly the same amount of precipitation, and as a result, the snowpack is much heavier. This makes it harder for deer to survive, a situation that hasn't been helped by logging in the area that has mostly decimated the deer's winter ranges. There is some human habitation and private land to worry about, but mostly Crown land. The area is best known for its great black bear hunting, while there is some decent cougar hunting, too. Grouse can be found in the eastern portions of 2-18 and some waterfowl hunting along the Harrison River and around the islands in the Fraser River.

MU 3-13 (Map 27, 33, 39)
In this area, hunters find a wide diversity of habitats from low elevation grasslands through dry forest to alpine. Mule deer, cougar and black bear are abundant. This is a good choice for upland birds, including grouse and ptarmigan but sharp-tailed grouse are closed for conservation.

MU 3-14, 3-15 (Map 16, 24, 25, 26, 27, 31, 32, 33)
These management units straddle the Fraser River and consist of steep, rugged habitats from low elevation dry sage-steppe to coastal transition forests and alpine. Access is somewhat limited west of the Fraser. Black bear are abundant and mule deer common. Elk are present and increasing, but not yet open for hunting.

MU 3-16 (Map 31, 32, 33, 36, 37, 36, 43, 44)
Steep, rocky, forested slopes and bare rocky peaks characterize this area. The terrain and provincial parks limit access, but hunters can find good numbers of mule deer and some of the best opportunities for mountain goat in the region.

MU 3-17 (Map 38, 39, 44)
This management unit holds a diversity of dry forest types from low elevation grassland to scattered alpine. This is a good choice for bighorn sheep hunters because both sub-species are present, while mule deer and cougar are also plentiful. This area also provides a high harvest of black bear.

MU 3-30 (Map 45)
This management unit includes the dry slopes of the South Thompson and Fraser and the gently rolling forested slopes of the Bonaparte Plateau. Mule deer and moose are abundant, while shot gunners will find good to excellent numbers of virtually every game bird available in the region. Both upland birds and waterfowl provide good sport.

MU 3-32, 3-33 (Map 35, 36, 37, 40, 41, 42, 43, 44, 49)
These management units consist of the steep forested slopes of the coastal/interior transition. The rugged country rewards experienced hunters with excellent mule deer hunting. Mountain goat and bighorn sheep are also taken through limited entry. These areas are among the best choices in the region for blue grouse and ptarmigan hunting.

MU 5-4, 5-5 (Map 40, 49)
The southern tips of these two management units are found on these maps, but very few people are willing to make the trek into these remote areas. Traditionally popular for both alpine deer and California Bighorn sheep, recent populations have been down and the regulations have changed accordingly. There are some moose, mule deer and grouse in the lower valleys, which are a little more popular north of these maps.

MU 8-04 (Map 7)
With forests of lodgepole pine, Douglas fir and spruce, this area has seen extensive logging and is laced with logging roads. You can find mule deer, moose, black bear, cougar and occasionally elk in the logged openings. The mix of old and young forest also favours ruffed and blue grouse.

MU 8-05 (Map 6, 7, 16, 17)
This is a large management unit capturing the pine and spruce forests in the drainages of the Tulameen River and Otter Creek. There is plenty of logging road access for hunters to pursue mule deer, moose, black bear, cougar, elk and forest grouse. This is a productive area but sees high hunting pressure.

refer to indicated pages for more map detail

Toba

East Redonda
Isl Prov
Marine
Park

Clendinning
Prov Park

Desolation
Sound

Malibu

Powell
Lake

Jervis
Inlet

Squamish River
Page 28/F6

Whistler

Desolation
Sound Prov
Marine Park

Lund

101

Powell
River

Powell Forest Canoe Route
Page 19/E4

Tantalus
Prov Park

99

Saltery
Bay

Strait

Texada
Isl

101

Brackendale

Squamish

Sechelt Inlet
Page 9/E2

Salmon
Inlet

Tetrahedron
Prov Park

Britannia
Beach

Cypress
Prov Park

Sechelt

Howe
Sound

19

Parksville

Gibsons

Bowen
Isl

Georgia

Vancouver

hotspots

T from the rush of whitewater rafting and kayaking to the serenity of sea kayak touring, to just plain cruising around on a lake in a canoe, Southwestern BC provides an endless array of water-based recreational fun. In fact, you will find many of these activities within an easy drive from Greater Vancouver. Of course, accessibility often means many other people will be out enjoying themselves. It's true, some of these routes are often busy, but it's not as bad as you might expect. Besides, if you truly want to get away from the crowds, there are places covered by this mapbook where few people ever go. If you really want to be alone with your paddle, you only need to travel a little further a field.

Flatwater or Lake Paddling enthusiasts have literally hundreds of lakes and sloughs to choose from in the area. We have selected a good sampling of the small lakes and ponds as well as canoe routes and multi-day destinations. The standout destination is the Powell Forest Canoe Route, but there are a few other fantastic circuit routes on the Sunshine Coast that involve lake and ocean travel. The Parks and Recreation Sites section of this book highlights many of the other smaller lakes that are more easily accessed.

Ocean Paddling along the southwestern coast of the mainland is a mixed blessing. Vancouver Island absorbs the brunt of the wind and waves, and while it certainly can get stormy, it is nothing like on the wild west coast. However, there are other issues. The narrow channels between islands can create strong rip tides, creating whirlpools and other hazards to navigate. And the large population in the Lower Mainland means that there's lots of activity in the area, especially the Burrard Inlet.

River paddlers can pick and chose from a mix of easy floats to hardcore whitewater descents. The variety is fantastic. Serious whitewater paddlers will find the rivers in top form during winter and spring. By the time summer rolls around, many of the smaller volume rivers have lost their spunk.

Below we have listed a few of the best-known areas for all three types of paddling opportunities. Please note that these descriptions given in this book are limited, and may not contain enough detail to navigate certain routes safely, especially rivers with higher ratings. Check current conditions with local canoeists/kayakers or local outdoor stores before heading out. It is also essential to scout rivers, since conditions can change daily.

LAKE PADDLING

There are hundreds of lakes and sloughs scattered throughout Southwestern BC and many if not all make a fine place for a day or overnight paddling venture. Below, we have provided some of the most popular destinations for canoeists. As an added convenience, we have indicated which lakes have rentals available nearby. As a general rule, big mountain lakes tend to attract wild weather patterns and wind, which funnels down through the narrow valleys. Although you can expect wind at any time, it is often calmer in the morning. Always stay close to shore.

Alice Lake (Map 22/D5)
Alice Lake is a small lake, north of Squamish and the namesake of Alice Lake Provincial Park. This is a popular vacation spot for families. Because there are no motorized boats permitted, the lake is a haven for canoeists. Rentals are available.

Alouette Lake (Map 3/A1–13/C6)
A fjord-like lake that runs 17 km (10.4 miles) into the Coast Mountains, Alouette Lake is an extremely popular cruising lake. There are a number of destinations to aim for from the boat launch and rental area near the south end of the lake: Campers Beach (4.5 km/2.7 miles) away, Moyer Creek Campground 9 km (5.5 miles) along and the Narrows at 10.5 km (6.4 miles). All these are found on the western shore.

paddlingadventures

Birkenhead Lake (Map 36/D3)
Nestled in the mountains north of Pemberton, Birkenhead Lake is a great place to paddle. There is a nice wilderness campsite at the mouth of Sockeye Creek as well as good fishing. The lake is open to powerboats and can be windy, especially in the afternoon.

Buntzen Lake (Map 12/A7)
It's 9 km (5 miles) around Buntzen Lake, making this a nice afternoon canoe trip. The long, narrow lake provides the illusion of paddling on the ocean since mountains to the east and west surround it. If you ever do run into trouble, you can put to shore almost anywhere and walk back to your car along the trail that circumnavigates the lake. With a powerboat restriction in place, Buntzen Lake is a peaceful place to ply the paddle.

Burnaby Lake (Map 1/G2)
A return trip from the Still Creek Footbridge at the west end to Cariboo Dam at the east end is 10.8 km (6.6 miles). This urban lake provides a recluse for a wide variety of wildlife including; beavers, muskrats, coyotes, geese, ducks, herons and ospreys.

Chehalis Lake (Map 14/B5)
Chehalis Lake is the smallest of the long, narrow lakes that run generally north and south along the North Shore/Fraser Valley (a series that includes Harrison, Stave, Alouette and Pitt Lakes). There are three recreation sites on the lake that provide possible access to the lake.

Chilliwack Lake (Map 5/F6)
A big mountain lake, located near the BC/Washington State border at the end the scenic Chilliwack Lake Road, which is paved to the park campsite. Chilliwack Lake is deep, cold and often windy, but it is fairly remote and quite scenic. The wilderness feel makes this a popular destination with canoeists, most of who are prepared to spend more than a day here.

Deer Lake: Burnaby (Map 1/F3)
Deer Lake is a small lake in Burnaby. It is a pretty urban lake, though sometimes hard to get to, with all the traffic controls in the area. Your best bet to get to the lake is off Canada Way. Rentals are available.

Green Lake (Map 29/G4)
The biggest of the lakes to be found in Whistler, Highway 99 follows the northwest shores of the lake on its way to Pemberton. There is a boat launch (powerboats are allowed) and some great views of Blackcomb and Whistler Mountains.

Harrison Lake (Map 4, 14, 24, 25)
Harrison Lake is a big, big lake. At 60 km (36.6 miles) long and 9 km (5.5 miles) wide in places, it is a big, windy, exposed lake. It's not a lake to be taken lightly, especially by canoeists. Still, it is a lovely lake, and, as long as you paddle in groups, stay close to shore and keep an eye on the weather, you shouldn't have any problems.

Haslam Lake (Map 19/B2)
A fair sized lake, Haslam Lake is much less paddled that the lakes of the Powell Forest Canoe Route that surround it. This is not necessarily a bad thing, especially if you're looking to do something different. If you don't mind carrying a canoe, you can do a mini-circuit. There is a short portage from Haslam to the tiny Giavanno Lake and from there, a rather long portage down to Powell Lake.

Hatzic Lake (Map 3/E4)
Hatzic Lake is a doughnut-shaped lake with an island in the middle. It doesn't seem like a big lake, but you will travel 9.5 km (5.8 miles) around the outer shore or 5 km (3 miles) around the island. If that's not enough paddling, you can head into Hatzic Slough (at the northern end of the lake) or into nearby Chilqua Slough, both of which attach to the lake.

Hayward Lake (Map 3/C3)
Although Hayward Lake is only 4.3 km (2.6 miles) long and 1 km (0.6 miles) wide, you will cover more than 12 km if you paddle along the shoreline. This is a lake with lots of nooks and coves to explore. Be warned that the dams at both ends of the lake are off limits.

Inland [Loon] Lake (Map 18/G2)
A popular paddling lake, there are several boat/trail access campsites. The Anthony Island site is by far the most beautiful of the bunch and the most popular with paddlers.

Lightning Lakes (Map 7/C6)
A chain of four lakes–Thunder, Strike, Flask and Lightning Lakes– are threaded together by Lightning Creek. Only the last three, Strike, Flask and Lightening, are reasonably canoeable. There is a 15 minute portage between Lightning and Flask lakes and a 30 minute portage between Flask and Strike Lakes.

Nahatlatch Lakes (Map 25/G1–33/A7)
The most common paddlers out on Nahatlatch Lake are rafters, practicing their strokes before heading down the wild and woolly Nahatlatch River. However, there's nothing to say that canoes or kayaks can't explore the long narrow lake as well. There are three recreation sites on the lake and two more on Hannah Lake, which is a short stretch of Grade II/III whitewater away.

Pender Harbour Canoe Route (Map 9/A1)
While Pender Harbour is a popular destination for sea kayakers, some (mostly canoeists) choose to do a 13 km (7.9 miles) circuit that includes three portages. The portages are: 200 metres from Agamemnon Channel to Sakinaw Lake (please ask for permission to cross the Indian Reserve), 800 metres between Sakinaw Lake and Mixal Lake and 700 metres from Garden Bay Lake to Pender Harbour. It is also possible to tag the Mixal Lake/Garden Bay leg of this route to the Agamemnon Channel Route above.

Pitt Lake (Map 12/E3–F7)
Pitt Lake is the second largest lake in the region, second only to the monstrous Harrison Lake. The end of the Pitt Valley opens up to the Fraser Valley, and all the way to the open ocean, so the lake can get pretty windy, especially in the afternoon. It is a couple kilometres longer up the eastern shore (30 km/18.3 miles in total), but it has more places that a canoe/kayak can pull into if the wind blows up. Zealous paddlers have been known to bring along bikes to cycle the 15 additional kilometres to the oh so beautiful Pitt River Hot Springs. Rentals are available.

Pitt Polder (Map 2/F1–12/F7)
Once a flood plain, dykes were constructed back in the 1950s to keep the lower Pitt River flooding under control. A polder is actually the land reclaimed from underwater, so you're not actually canoeing on it, but on the parts still under water. The water levels rise and fall with the tides.

Powell Forest Canoe Route (Map 18, 19, 46)
Easily one of the best canoe circuits in the province, the Powell Lake Canoe Route can be done in as few as three days. Most take up to a week or more to paddle the 90.4 km (54.8 mile) route. Paddle is a bit of a misnomer; 10.7 km (6.5 miles) of the route is spent carrying your canoe, including one 2.4 km (1.5 mile) hump from Windsor Lake down to Goat Lake. Down being the operative word: losing over 100 metres (300 feet) packing a canoe. Only suicidal folks would want to carry up this hill. This is why most travel this route counter clockwise. This route features great canoeing and some sweet spots to camp. Lois Lake and Powell Lake are both big lakes and can be very windy. It's best to travel these lakes early in the morning. For folks who don't want to canoe the entire circuit, it is possible to double back on your route from Dodd Lake, via the tiny Beaver and Little Horseshoe Lakes.

Ruby Lake Canoe Circuit (Map 9/A1–20/B6)
This is a 31 km (18.9 mile) circuit route that starts and ends at Earls Cove or at Dan Hosch Park at the south end of Ruby Lake. Expect to take two or three days to finish the route. Starting in Ruby Lake, paddle to the south end, where there is a rustic 750 metre portage to Sakinaw Lake. Between Sakinaw Lake and the Agamemnon Channel is a 200 metre portage that crosses Sechelt Indian Band land. Please ask for permission to cross before you set out. Dangers en route include high winds on Sakinaw Lake and strong tidal currents out in the channel. It's best to travel with the tide so check the tide charts. Near the south end of Sakinaw Lake you may see Indian pictographs painted on the rocks. When you get back to Earls Cove, you're only about a kilometre from the starting point. Smart people will have left their car at the cove.

Sakinaw Lake (Map 9/A1–20/B7)
A long, narrow lake, Sakinaw is a popular getaway from Vancouver for a lot of people, many who own cabins on or around the lake. There is no formal camping on the lake, which is part of two canoe circuit routes described above.

Sasamat Lake (Map 2/A1)
Sasamat is an extremely popular lake in the summer. So popular that, during the peak hours the parking lot for the beach is always packed and usually gated. Wiley canoeists have been known to find other places along Bedwell

paddlingadventures

Bay Road to launch from. It's a small lake, which means two things. The first is that it is usually unaffected by wind. The second is that it is one of the warmest lakes in the Lower Mainland.

Stave Lake (Map 3/E2–13/E5)
The third-largest lake in the area, you would travel over 70 km (42.7 miles) circumnavigating the whole lake. To put that in perspective, the Powell Forest Canoe Route is only about 10 more kilometres (6 more miles) of actual paddling and takes up to a week to explore. The big lake does not see as much boat traffic as nearby lakes but the wind can still kick up without warning.

Widgeon Slough (Map 12/E7)
This is one of the most popular places for canoeists in the Lower Mainland and for good reason. It is a spectacular trip, canoeing from the open floodplains of the Upper Fraser Valley into a mountain valley, with Burke Mountain towering on your left hand side. The scenery is phenomenal, the wildlife plentiful (part of the slough is one of only five National Wildlife Areas in the country), the canoeing easy and the options of exploring the other channels and nearby trails are endless. Crossing the narrow channel of open water from Grant Narrows Park past Siwash Island to the entrance of the channel, can be difficult when it is windy. From Grant Narrows to the Widgeon Creek Campground is 4.5 km (2.8 miles).

OCEAN PADDLING

An endless coast with numerous sheltered inlets makes ocean paddling a peaceful and scenic way to explore Southwestern BC. We have included a number of popular routes, but this is just a fraction of the places you can go by sea kayak or, sometimes, canoe.

Boundary Bay (Map 1/F7)
Extensive tidal flats make this a difficult place to explore by boat at low tide. From Boundary Bay Regional Park to Crescent Beach, it is 22 km (13.4 miles) one-way. It is often windy here, sometimes too windy to safely paddle. The best time is early in the morning.

Copeland Islands Marine Park (Map 46/A6)
Known locally as the Ragged Islands, the Copeland Islands are a fairly easy 8 km (5 miles) paddle north of the boat launch at Lund. The islands are home to colonies of seals and a diverse array of tidal life. The marine park also offers campsites. An easy circuit route for novice kayakers would be to paddle to the Copeland Islands, then around the tip of Malaspina Peninsula and down Okeover Inlet.

Desolation Sound Provincial Marine Park (Map 46/B4)
Desolation Sound is BC's largest and most popular marine park. It has warm, sheltered waters, spectacular scenery and lots of nooks and crannies to explore. Marine life flourishes in these waters, which can reach temperatures of 26° Celsius (79°F) in summer. The park is rich in native history as well as natural beauty. Birders will find this area a delight, with loons, kingfishers, eagles, gulls, plovers, murrelets, grebes, herons, oyster catchers and more. It is also possible to explore past the park and all the way into the emerald green Toba Inlet. En route you can visit Homfray Channel, which features the second deepest waters off the coast at 730 metres (2,394 feet).

You can launch from two locations. From Lund, the paddle is more exposed but it takes you past the Copeland Islands Marine Park. If you choose the more sheltered Okeover Inlet route, you will need to paddle during slack tide to avoid tidal currents up to 10 knots in Malaspina Inlet. It can take anywhere for three days to two weeks to explore this area, and even then, you will feel like you've only scratched the surface.

False Creek (Map 1/D2)
An extremely protected inlet, False Creek is slowly outgrowing its commercial roots and becoming an urban playground. The most prominent feature here is the Science World Globe, but on the water you will see sea kayaks, dragon boats, canoes, paddle cycles, row boats and even Hawaiian Outriggers.

Hotham Sound (Map 20/A3)
Located off Jervis Inlet, Hotham Sound is a peaceful destination, easily accessed from Saltery Bay. The Sound offers sheltered paddling, with many coves and bays to explore. On the way from Saltery Bay, you will pass through St. Vincent's Bay, then round Elephant Point, where the sound opens up before you. In addition to the majestic Coast Mountains as a backdrop, one of the highlights of this trip is the 444 metre (1,456 foot) Freil Falls, which are across from Elephant Point. There is a marine park on Harmony Islands where you can camp.

Howe Sound (Map 10, 11, 22)
Howe Sound stretches north from Horseshoe Bay to Squamish and is framed by the rugged, towering peaks that have always tormented the road builders on the Sea to Sky Highway. Before that road went in, the only way to Squamish was by boat. Even today, some would argue it's still the only way to get to Squamish. There are a number of great destinations in the Sound, including Gambier Island, which can be circumnavigated in about two days and Anvil Island, a good one-day trip. The most popular places to launch are Porteau Cove, on Highway 99, followed by Port Mellon, on the Sunshine Coast.

Indian Arm (Map 1/G1–12/A5)
The northernmost reaches of Indian Arm are protected inside the boundaries of the Indian Arm Marine Park. This is a gorgeous place to paddle that is well protected from the winds but sees a lot of small boat traffic that can kick up some chop. Regardless, this is the domain of the recreationist, with many sites to see (Silver and Granite Falls), places to camp (Twin Islands, Bishop Creek) and places to just stop and enjoy the stillness of nature. Its 23 km (14 miles) up the west side of Indian Arm, from Deep Cove to the Indian River. Add another kilometre if you travel the east side from Belcarra Park.

Jervis Inlet (Map 19, 20, 47)
There are three good launching points into this undeveloped fjord, which stretches deep into the rugged Coast Mountains and neatly divides the Sunshine Coast into two. Edgemont is one, Earls Cove is the second and Saltery Bay the third. Highlights include the Princess Louisa Inlet and Chatterbox Falls near the head of Jervis Inlet and of course the endless views of the majestic mountains. The inlet can be a dangerous place to be caught if the weather blows up, as the steep cliffs that plunge into the water for long stretches at a time offer no place to take shelter. It will take one to two weeks to explore the inlet.

Jedediah Island (Map 8/E4)
Sheltered from all but the most persistent winds by Texada to the north and east and Lasqueti Island to the south and southwest, this 26 hectare (64 acre) island is a favourite of kayakers. The archipelago of islands is often referred to as a string of pearls. This is BC kayaking at its best. Jedediah Island is accessible either from Secret Cove on the Sunshine Coast or Texada Island. There is no water available on Jedediah.

Pender Harbour (Map 9/A1)
Pender Harbour is a well-sheltered harbour, with many small islands and bays to explore. There is no formal camping here, but there are some places that a tent can be pitched.

Port Moody (Map 2/A1)
Port Moody, the bay, is a large, sheltered finger poking into the Lower Mainland from Burrard Inlet. This is a working harbour, so there is lots of traffic and not many places to land or launch a boat from.

Redonda Islands (Map 46/B3)
Warm water, secluded coves, the BC's tallest island mountain (outside of Vancouver Island) and excellent fishing make West and East Redonda Islands great paddling destinations. These islands are very large and it will take the better part of a week to circumnavigate even one. You can launch from Lund or Okeover Inlet and paddle up Desolation Sound before crossing over. Maybe it is time needed or the exposed crossings, but the islands are not popular paddling destinations.

Savary Island (Map 18/B1)
Savary Island has long, curving and dazzling white beaches. It is a summer Shangri-la, attracting kayakers from around the world. This is also where the great tidal currents from the north and south meet, creating a unique environment of warm water, unlike anywhere else on the Coast. If you don't feel comfortable with the 3 km (1.8 mile) crossing, a water taxi at Lund will transport you across. Be warned: there is no fresh water on Savary, so pack what you will need.

Sechelt Inlet (Map 9, 20)
This sheltered inlet that is almost a lake is a popular destination and a great place for novice kayakers to get their sea legs. From Porpoise Bay you can travel a few hours or a few weeks into the inlet, exploring its many marine parks and sheltered bays. You can do a round trip or start at Porpoise Bay and arrange for a shuttle at Egmont. This area is home to many marine birds and animals; there is even the occasional killer whale spotted by fortunate sea kayakers.

Skookumchuck Narrows (Map 20/C6)

Some people do silly things. Like surfing the waves that set up in this narrow bore, which has been clocked at up to 16 knots, creating standing waves over 2 metres (6 feet) high. This is a great spot for playing in big waves, but at anything except slack tide should only be attempted in whitewater kayakers with appropriate skills.

Thornanby Islands (Map 9/B4)

North and South Thornanby Island guard the western entrance to Halfmoon Bay. The two islands are home to a pair of provincial parks and the islands offer secluded campsites overlooking Vancouver Island, some great beaches to explore and lots of marine wildlife.

RIVER PADDLING

From lazy rivers that meander though the Fraser Valley lowlands to raging whitewater streams, there are routes to satisfy every paddler. For each route we have listed where the best place(s) are to put-in, as well as take-out. We have also included the length of each run and some general comments.

We use a modified version of the international scale to grade rivers. The grade of a run tells you how difficult the overall stretch of river is while individual rapids, chutes and other features are rated by class. A run might be rated Grade II overall, but one section might feature a Class IV drop. Water flow also effects how difficult a run is. For this reason we have provided the difficulty of grade and class at both low water and high water. If a run is rated Grade II/III, it means that at low flows the run is Grade II, while at high flows it is Grade III. Most of the challenging features have portages to help less experienced paddlers negotiate the route more safely.

Alouette River (Map 2/D2–3/A1)

The Alouette River (or South Alouette River) flows 23 km from the BC Hydro Dam on Alouette Lake to its confluence with the Pitt River. While the upper reaches are the most interesting and provide some whitewater, it is also very shallow and obstructed. This section of river is impassable to all but the most determined of paddlers. On the other hand, the lower section is a perfect family style (grade 1) paddle. Some folks put-in at the 206 Street bridge, but it is better to put-in 2.5 km (1.5 miles) below, at the Neaves Road Bridge. By this point in time, the river has left the mountains and is constrained by dykes. The paddling is easy and it is possible to paddle upstream as well as down. For people looking to do an out-and-back trip, it is recommended that they start at the Harris Road Bridge and paddle the 5 km (3 miles) upstream to the Neaves Road Bridge while they are still fresh before paddling back down with the (ever so slight) current. The last stretch of river is 1.6 km (1 mile) from the Harris Road Bridge to the plodding Pitt River.

Big Silver Creek (Map 14/F2)

An easy river, with a couple Class II features, Big Silver Creek is a great place for novices to learn their whitewater chops. Access to the put-in is west from the junction of the Harrison East/Clear Creek roads, along a difficult, but mercifully short (ten minute) trail. The take-out is just south of the Silver River Logging Camp on Harrison Lake; watch for a small road leading down to the lake off the Harrison East Forest Road.

Birkenhead River (Map 36/D7–30/D1)

From the put-in where the D'Arcy Road crosses the river north of the Owl Creek Recreation Site, to the take-out north of Mount Currie, this is a 5 km (3 mile) Grade III+ romp along the turquoise waters of the Birkenhead. The river is quite shallow and moves quickly through almost continuous rapids. By late July, the water volume has fallen significantly and it can be a fairly bumpy ride through even shallower water.

Capilano River (Map 1/C1–11/C7)

At high water levels, the Capilano is a beast, rated up to Grade V and sometimes (at very high water levels), unrunable. At low to medium water, it is Grade III run. The Capilano is one of the most popular rivers in the entire province. Partly due to the location and partly due to the fact that it doesn't freeze in winter (though it gets pretty darn cold–only attempt with appropriate clothing). The Cap is a dam controlled drop-and-pool river that flows through North Vancouver in a surprisingly wild valley. From the fish hatchery just below Cleveland Dam to Ambleside Park, it is 5.6 km (3.4 miles), but there are a number of other take-out points, including Park Royal Mall and Klahanie Park. Watch for people fishing from the riverbanks.

Cayoosh Creek (Map 37/G3–38/A1)

Like most small volume rivers, the character of the Cayoosh changes tremendously with water. As the water level rises, the difficulty increases; taking it from a Grade III run up to Grade IV at higher water levels. The Cayoosh runs alongside the Duffey Lake Road from Cayoosh Pass to the small town of Lillooet. The most common section for paddlers to run is a 5.8 km (3.8 mile) section between Boulder and Copper Creek. There are two put-ins; one about 2 km (1 mile) south of Boulder Creek and the other about 1 km south of the Cottonwood Recreation Site. The take-out is found at a logging road bridge just before Copper Creek.

Cheakamus River (Map 22, 29)

This glacier-fed river has many, many possible put-ins and take-outs and is never more than a few hundred metres from a road. Easy access makes this a popular river. There are three main runs, getting progressively easier as you move towards its confluence with the Squamish. The most difficult section is from the Westside Main/Black Tusk Road to the Westside Main Bridge over the Cheakamus. This is a fast, technical 1.5 km (1 mile) section of river that is popular with Whistler boaters (experts paddle in playboats as there are rodeo holes all over the place). The river is rated Grade IV, with some Class V features at high water levels and there is a more difficult run upstream.

An easier run is from the Highway 99 Bridge south of Daisy Lake to the Highway 99 salt sheds. This is a 4 km (2.4 mile) section of Grade III/III+ whitewater, with a Class IV drop near the mid-point of the run. Despite the fact that this section is below the Daisy Lake Dam, it still acts very much like a wild river; there is just so much water coming down during spring run-off, that BC Hydro usually keeps the gates fairly wide open. Please note that the canyon stretch below Daisy Lake is not navigable.

Even easier is the section from the end of Paradise Valley Road to the North Vancouver Outdoor Centre. This Grade II/III route that runs 12 km (7.3 miles) through the forests north of Squamish. There are a number of alternate take-out (or put-in) spots along the way to shorten the run or you can continue onto the Squamish River. At higher water, eddies can disappear and more of the run is Grade III making this river appropriate for intermediate kayakers and experienced open boaters. There are plenty of play spots including a great surfing hole right at the put in and an exciting drop at Culliton Creek. As with all rivers in this region, watch for logjams and sweepers.

Chehalis River (Map 14/C7–4/C1)

The put-in for this Grade III+ river is at about 1.7 km past the Statlu Creek Bridge. More advanced paddlers can put in at the Statlu Creek Bridge and run Statlu Creek down to the Chehalis (expect Class IV+ boulder gardens). The Chehalis has lively and almost continual drops with rodeo holes and surfing waves to make this a fun river to run. When you have a chance to breathe and look around, you will notice that the scenery is pretty spectacular, too. Due to challenging canyons and few places to escape, this is a great river to explore if your skills are up to it.

Chilliwack River: Upper (Map 5/C5–5A6)

The Chilliwack River Valley offers good fishing, abundant camping sites, easy access and phenomenal scenery. This upper section of the Chilliwack is 9 km (5.4 miles) of steep, demanding and non-stop whitewater action. Rated Grade IV at higher water, with some even more difficult features, expect to take about four hours to complete this exhilarating stretch from Foley Creek Forest Road to west of Slesse Creek.

Chilliwack River: Middle (Map 5/A6–4/E6)

This 18 km (11 mile) stretch of up to Grade III water (with a Class IV drop) and a 1 km (0.6 mile) stretch that features some challenging whitewater, including the Tamihi, Campground and Sawmill Rapids. Many people choose to portage the rapids, especially in high water, but for expert paddlers, this section is one of the highlights of the four hour plus trip between Slesse Creek Bridge and Chilliwack River Provincial Park.

Chilliwack River: Lower (Map 4/E6–4/C6)

Like many rivers, the Chilliwack starts to calm down as it gets closer to its final destination, the mighty Fraser. By the time it reaches Vedder Crossing, the Chilliwack has basically run out of steam. From Chilliwack River Provincial Park to Vedder Crossing, this is a 6.5 km (4 mile) run along relatively easy Grade II waters. A great testing ground for novices or as a warm up before tackling some of the bigger water upstream, the river is medium flow, with lots of braiding and gravel bars. It is runable from spring to fall. Allow about two hours to run it. Longer if you wish to continue on the Vedder River (see below).

Cogburn Creek (Map 14/G3)
From the Harrison East Forest Road Bridge to the Bear Creek Logging Camp, it is a mere 3 km (1.8 miles), but they are a wild 3 km, indeed. Rated Grade III/IV with lots of boulder gardens and technical manoeuvring, during spring runoff, it is almost continual whitewater from the put-in until you hit Harrison Lake. It is a short but peaceful paddle south on the lake to the camp.

Coldwater River (Map 27/F5–east of maps)
Yes, the name is a pretty fair indication of the river, but you will be wearing a wetsuit, right? The river flows beside and occasionally under, the Coquihalla Highway for 34.5 km (21 miles) from Juliet Creek to Merritt. Access is fairly good along the winding, fast moving Grade II/II+ river with one Class IV drop after the bridge near the 18 km (11 mile) mark. It is possible to break this river up into a number of bite-sized pieces (common put-ins/take-outs are Larson Hill, Coldwater Interchange and Patchet Road) or to do it in one long run. The first section between Juliet Creek and Larson Hill is easy (Grade I) and is often skipped by kayakers looking for a bit more excitement. Watch for sweepers.

Coquitlam River (Map 2/C1–C3)
The Coquitlam is more of a winter run than a summer run, when the river all but disappears. It offers an 8 km (4.9 mile) route through Grade III water during high and medium water levels. This is a great place for intermediate paddlers to practice their skills, as there are lots of places to bail. The put-in is off of Pipeline Road, while the take-out is off Shaughnessy Street.

Elaho River (Map 28/D4–G7)
This fast, silty and ice-cold river begins its source in the giant Elaho Glacier, well removed from any signs of civilization. The Upper Elaho is a difficult, rarely run river, while, to our knowledge, the far upper reaches of the Elaho has only been run once. Most trips on the Elaho start about 3.5 km (2.1 miles) upstream from its confluence with the Squamish River and finish their run after the canyon section of the Squamish. The Elaho is Grade III/IV and has some really great surfing waves at moderate water flow. This scenic stretch of river offers some great cliff jumping opportunities and is very popular with the rafting companies. The Elaho is subject to flash flooding, especially during spring rains.

Fraser River (Map 1-5, 15, 26, 33, 38, 39, 44)
Southwest BC captures the mighty Fraser's two extremes. The Fraser Canyon, which begins north of Hope, is a Class IV water body that should only be attempted by commercial rafters. On the other hand the lower reaches, from Hope to Vancouver, offer a more placid river. Although this stretch does not have any whitewater, it can still be dangerous (up to Grade III) due to the speed and volume of water. In particular, watch out for boils and standing waves between Hope and the Highway 9 Bridge at Bridal Falls. As you get closer to the mouth, watch out for the Pitt River confluence and the commercial traffic (fishing boats, tug boats, barges, etc.) plying these waters.

Harrison River (Map 4/D2–F1)
An easy Grade I paddle takes you from Harrison Hot Springs to the Highway 7 Bridge, just before the Harrison flows into the Fraser. While this 15 km (9.1 mile) trip is scenic and enjoyable (except when the wind picks up on the broad river), the best time to go is in the fall, when the salmon are spawning. Eagles. Fish. Fishermen. Fall leaves. What more could you ask for?

Kanaka Creek (Map 2/G3–3/B3)
Kanaka Creek is a mostly slow moving river–hardly more than Grade I, with a couple really slow Grade II sections. For the most part, Kanaka Creek is perfect for an idyllic family float close to Maple Ridge. There are a handful of places to put-in or take-out along the sprawling Kanaka Creek Park or the more adventurous can head out onto the Fraser and cross to Derby Reach Park. If you don't want to shuttle, you can put-in at the Highway 7 bridge and paddle upstream for as far as you want, then return. Be careful not to venture above 112 Ave, as there are a pair of waterfalls a few hundred metres upstream.

Lillooet River: Upper (Map 34/E1–34/F1)
The Lillooet is a long, large, windy and cold river that starts deep in the heart of the Coast Mountains before eventually spilling into Harrison Lake. It is faster in its upper reaches. Travelling the Lillooet often feels remote, although in truth the river is paralleled by logging roads for its entire run-able length. As an added bonus, there is a number of hot springs near the river, a great way to end a hard day's paddle. The section found 2.9 km past the Pebble Creek Bridge to Meager Creek Bridge is a short (5 km/3 mile) stretch of Grade III/IV whitewater, about the toughest stuff you will find on the Lillooet.

It features lots of rock gardens and standing waves and one really nice hole to play in. Expect to take the better part of two hours to do this section, which can be done on its own or as the start to a longer expedition down the tamer sections of the Lillooet.

Lillooet River: Middle (Map 34/F1–35/F4)
After the Meager Creek confluence, the Lillooet meanders along a broad, flat floodplain with lots of braided channels. While this is a Grade II-III route, picking the right route can be tricky due to the many false channels. Downed trees are very frequent in this river. Expect to take at least 8 hours to do this 35 km (21.4 mile) section of the river between the Meager Creek Bridge and the bridge on the Upper Lillooet River Road.

Lillooet River: Pemberton Section (Map 35/F4–30/C1)
As the Lillooet approaches Pemberton, the river widens and slows down. The 23 km (14 mile) section between the bridge on the Upper Lillooet River Road to the Highway 99 bridge east of Pemberton is little more than a scenic float, which usually takes about 6 hours to complete.

Lillooet River: Lower (Map 30/G6–24/E5)
South of Pemberton, the Lillooet turns into a long, narrow lake or rather, two lakes, separated by a short section of moving water. Most kayakers skip this section, though folks (usually canoeists) who are doing a multi-day trip from beginning to end do paddle this section as well. Below Little Lillooet Lake, is a 33.9 km (21.1 mile) float to the final bridge/take-out before Harrison Lake. Most of this section is Grade II, but there are some Class III features, just to make it interesting. The hot springs at St. Agnes Well is a popular and relaxing alternate take-out spot about halfway down this run. Although most trippers take-out at the last bridge before Harrison Lake, long distance canoeists/kayakers can continue on into Harrison Lake. From the big (and often windy) lake it is possible to continue down to the Fraser and even out to the Pacific Ocean.

Mamquam River (22/D6)
A short, interesting Grade II/III route is found just south of Squamish. With great scenery and easy access, the Mamquam is a great river to practice on and short enough to run two or three times in a day. From the upper put-in off the Mamquam Forest Road (take the side road at approx 3.5 km), to the Government Road Bridge (just west of Highway 99), this is a 5.8 km (3.3 mile) stretch.

Nahatlatch River: Hannah Lake to Francis Lake (Map 33/A7)
The Nahatlatch is a challenging river that flows through a series of canyons on its way from Hannah Lake to the Fraser River. Access is from the Nahatlatch Forest Service Road on the north bank of the river. It is popular during the summer months and those who have done it consider it one of the premier whitewater rivers in North America. Not surprisingly, the river is a popular commercial rafting destination. There's good paddling from June to August, with the best time coming mid-summer, when the river has passed its peak flow, but hasn't slowed to a trickle yet. This first section from the Old Ranger Station on Hannah Lake to the west end of Francis Lake is a short, warm up route. The shallow 1.5 km (.9 mile) section is rated Grade II/III, with steady rapids.

Nahatlatch River: Middle (Map 33/A7–C7)
The 8 km (4.9 mile) section of Grade III whitewater found between the east end of Francis Lake and Apocynum Campground offers a number of Class IV features, including some of the most storied rapids in the province. Some of the names include the Rose Garden, Meat Grinder and Head Wall. This last one is worth noting; if you do not execute a sharp turn, you and your boat will get stuffed under an overhanging ledge. Needless to say, this is not a route for the faint of heart.

Nahatlatch River: Lower (Map 33/C7–26/D1)
Grade IV, with a number of Class IV+ features makes the last stretch of river between Apocynum Campground and the former bridge site 500 metres east of Reo Resort, if anything, even more exhilarating than the previous section. The Canyon is a 5.3 km (3.3 mile) epic section of whitewater that is equal to anything, anywhere. This is not a place you want to go if you don't know what you're doing. But for those with adequate skill, this is a riot. The best time to go is later in summer after the levels dropped substantially.

Nicomekl River (Map 2/A6–F5)
From Old Yale Road to Crescent Beach, the Nicomekl travels 25 lazy km (15.3 miles). While the trip is all flat water, the river itself is small, narrow and often blocked by obstructions, making this a tough trip to complete in a day.

Portaging around obstacles is difficult; the banks are steep and often overgrown. A trio of pipes cross the river. Two of you will have to carry it around; one of you may be able to squeak under. There is also a flood control dam to portage around. While parts of this river are pretty, it has seen a lot of abuse over the years, especially on the lower sections. This river provides an accurate picture of the state of urban rivers in the Lower Mainland.

North Alouette River (Map 2/D2–F2)
While the North Alouette River begins at Jacobs Lake in the UBC Research Forest, it isn't until the 232 Street Bridge in Maple Ridge that it is even feasible to put-in, and even then, from 232 Street to Neaves Road, the river is shallow and congested with rocks, logs and vegetation. Lining and sometimes carrying, the canoe is a must. From 232 Street to Neaves Road is 7 km (4.3 miles); from Neaves Road to Harris Road is a much nicer 7.1 km (4.3 miles). Those that do travel the river will find a tranquil setting with abundant waterfowl to enjoy.

Pitt River (Map 2/C2–12/E7)
Although this is a flat-water paddle, the Pitt moves a lot of water and sees a fair bit of boat traffic, making it a sometimes dangerous place to be. The Pitt is also a tidal river so it is advised to consult tide charts so you won't have to fight against the current paddling downstream. From Grant Narrows to the Port Mann Bridge on the Fraser is a 23.8 km (14.5 mile) paddle through a farmland type setting.

River of Golden Dreams (Map 29/F5)
Flowing through the heart of Whistler, from Alta Lake to Green Lake, this is a great river for a lazy summer day float. There are two parks on Alta Lake, Wayside and Lakeside, where you can launch your boat. The river winds its way though a marshy area between the two lakes. This is also a popular float trip on inner-tubes and air mattresses.

Salmon River (Map 2/G4)
Like many Fraser Delta rivers, the Salmon is difficult to paddle in its upper reaches. Not because of whitewater, but because it is narrow and overgrown. The first good launch point comes at McMillian Park on Glover Road near Fort Langley. At low water, the Salmon looks more like a flooded ditch than a river, but don't despair, it gets bigger. Most people take-out at the 96 Avenue bridge about 8 km (4.9 miles) downstream where there is a pump station/flood box blocking the river.

Seymour River (Map 1/E1)
The Seymour is a great challenge for novices looking to hone their skills or for experts looking to get in a bit of paddling during winter. In summer, the Seymour is a little too shallow to paddle, but it is fine the rest of the year. The Seymour is a Grade II/III river, with boulder gardens at low water and lots of play holes at high. The river is certainly not wild, but it does flow through a pleasant suburban paradise. From Seymour Park on Riverside Road to Burrard Inlet it is 4 km (2.4 miles). In summer, contact the GVRD regarding keys for the gate on Riverside Drive.

Skagit River (Map 6/E3–E7)
A Grade III/IV route through a scenic valley at the base of sheer mountain faces, the Skagit is a beautiful river to run, though plagued by logjams. The river is best run after spring runoff, from July to October. Most people put in at 26 Mile Bridge and take out at Ross Lake. For the most part though, the river follows the Silver Skagit Road and you can put in and take out at leisure. The exception is the section from the confluence with the Sumallo River to Silvertip Park, where the Skagit flows through a wild valley.

Squamish River: Upper (Map 28/F5–G6)
The Squamish River is a cold, murky, big volume river that makes its way from the Pemberton Icefield south to Howe Sound at the city of Squamish. The river is never too far from a road but for the most part, it feels like you are in another world, far from civilization. In late winter along with salmon, the area is home to thousands of bald eagles. The uppermost section, from the bridge near the 37 km sign to the log sort near the 29 km sign, is an 8.2 km (5 mile) run through the scenic Squamish Canyon. This Grade III/IV section features some great big standing waves including the Steamroller Rapid, which can get as big as 3 metres (10 feet) during high water levels. While this is a river for rafting and advanced kayakers in peak season, at lower levels (April or October), it is a great run for advanced open boaters. Watch for logjams and sweepers. This run is often combined with the Elaho.

Squamish River: Middle (Map 28/G6–21/A2)
The mid section of the Squamish offers an easy float through a broad valley.

Most start at the confluence with the Elaho and take out at the Steamroller Rapid near the forestry campsite and the bridge. This section avoids all the really challenging features on the river and is rated Grade I/II. This is a 12 km (8 mile) section of the river and can easily be done in conjunction with the next segment of river.

Squamish River: Lower (Map 21/A2–22/C5)
The 32 km section between the Powerhouse and Brackendale is mostly a Grade II route. Closer to Brackendale many people like to run the river in January to get an up close view of the Bald Eagles. Be wary of obstacles such as deadheads and logjams as well as braiding channels.

Sumas River (Map 3/F7–4/A5)
From just about the US border (Vye Road Bridge) to Hougan Park (13 km/7.9 miles from Vye Road), the Sumas is a slow moving river. By the time you reach Hougan Park, almost all forward momentum has stopped and you will have to paddle the remaining 10 km (6.1 miles) to the Sea Dam, just upstream from the confluence with the Vedder Canal. The Sumas is a nice easy paddle, but a little too close to Highway 1 for some people's tastes.

Thompson River: Goldpan Campground to Nicomen Confluence (Map 39/F7–33/F2)
The southwest reaches of the Thompson River are one of the kayaking and commercial rafting hotspots in the province. This is not an area for the inexperienced (unless you are on a guided trip), but it is THE place for some whitewater thrills. The 12 km (7.3 mile) Grade II/III route from Goldpan Campground to the Nicomen River confluence has plenty of turbulence and large waves but few rock obstacles. Through this section, the river is fast flowing and offers a scenic paddle through dry ponderosa pine country. The paddling season extends year round except during peak flows.

Thompson River: Lower (Map 33/F2–C2)
As the Thompson River approaches the Fraser River, it becomes more difficult to paddle as the water level and flow of the river increases. Between Nicomen River and Lytton, the river extends 24 km (14.6 miles) through the dry pine country and is rated as a Grade III-IV expert kayak route. The paddle is not technically difficult but is intimidating due to its large waves, rapids and holes. It is recommended that the route only be tried after a local has shown you the best line to take through the difficult sections. The route is best paddled during late summer and fall.

Tulameen River: West of Tulameen to Tulameen (Map 17/B3–D3)
The Tulameen area is an area rich in history. From the gold mines to the historic Kettle Valley Railway stops, there are many sites and sounds to see along the way. The Hoodoos and rich red clay banks of the river are certain to be a highlight of the trip. The section from the bridge 7 km west of Tulameen to Tulameen flows through the Tulameen Canyon. The first rapid, visible from the put-in, is a Class II+ with rocks, large waves and holes. It is the calling card for the canyon about 200 metres (600 feet) beyond, which is also full of Class II+ features. Past the canyon, the trip to Tulameen mellows to a Grade I or so float.

Tulameen River: Tulameen to Coalmont (Map 17/D3–E3)
Between the famed Coalmont Hotel (B.C.'s oldest operating hotel) and Tulameen, the Tulameen River Road provides good access to the river. But most paddlers choose to run this Grade I–I+ stretch of river from town to town.

Tulameen River: Coalmont to Princeton (Map 17/E3–east of maps)
This 21 km (5 hours) section of the Tulameen is an easy Grade II paddle, with one major exception. Tulameenie Falls, which should be portaged (the portage is through the KVR Tunnel), is a Grade IV+ drop that is particularly dangerous in low water. Below the falls, the river is mostly Grade I, with a few easy Grade II sections. Throughout the route, the river is quite variable with many pools, rock and boulder gardens. Along the way, admire the history of the Kettle Valley Railway, marvel at the hoodoos or stop and relax on the sandy beaches. The best time to paddle the route is in May or June, during spring runoff.

Vedder River (Map 4/A5–C5)
From Vedder Crossing to Number Three Road, the Vedder River is Grade II run. Not as challenging as the Chilliwack upstream, but still enough to provide lots of fun, especially for open boat canoeists. This section is 8 km (4.9 miles) long. Beyond Number 3 Road, the Vedder becomes an easy float down to the Sumas confluence along the slow moving Vedder Canal. Not particularly difficult, but a nice family outing, with great views of Sumas Mountain.

parkadventures

BCParks
The Best Place on Earth

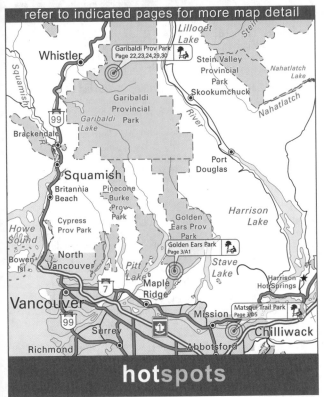

refer to indicated pages for more map detail

Garibaldi Prov Park
Page 22,23,24,29,30

Golden Ears Park
Page 3/A1

Matsqui Trail Park
Page 3/D5

hotspots

Parks and recreation areas are our frontline to the outdoors and no other region of the country offers the breadth and variety that Southwestern BC does. From dynamic city and regional parks to remote and wild provincial parks, these areas are the best, or at least the easiest, places to experience the Great Outdoors.

There are a number of large, wilderness parks in this area, some of which see surprisingly few visitors, considering their proximity to the largest population centre in British Columbia. Then again, these parks have few, if any, facilities and access into these areas can be difficult. Obviously, it is much easier to head for a well-developed park like Cultus Lake than to bushwhack your way deep into the wilds of Pinecone Burke Provincial Park.

This mix of large wilderness areas and popular recreation areas is what makes the park system so great: no matter what it is you love to do outdoors—camp, boat, fish, hike, climb mountains or just lay on a beach all day—you're sure to find a site that will meet your needs.

Provincial and Regional Parks are set aside for a variety of reasons. Two of the biggest reasons are to protect the environment and to provide recreational opportunities for residents and visitors. To make things easier when planning a trip, we have added recreational symbols beside each site name. The symbols will show you some of the more popular activities pursued in the area, while the description will provide you with a good background of the park or recreation site.

In recent years, there have been many changes to the provincial park system. One of the most notable changes was the institution of parking fees at many of the most popular parks and camping fees at the more popular recreation sites. While there was much debate around the parking fees, especially, it looks like they're here to stay at parks like Golden Ears, Alice Lake, Brandywine Falls, Cypress and Cultus Lake.

Most campgrounds operate from early spring through fall. Some stay open all year. Most charge a fee for overnight stays and, as mentioned, the most popular parks have day-use parking fees as well. The camping fees vary according to the facilities and services provided. If you want even more details, the government has put together a fantastic website. Visit www.bcparks.ca. We have noted the parks that currently offer a call-in reservation system through Discover Camping (www.discovercamping.ca).

Aldergrove Lake Regional Park (Map 3/A7)
This regional park is centred around the man-made Aldergrove Lake, tucked away in the rolling hills beside the US border. The park is 280 hectares and contains both the lake and the surrounding forests and fields. There are 9.5 km worth of trails, most of which are open to horseback riding and biking. During the hot summers, most people come here to swim in the warm waters or lay back on the white sand beach that surrounds the lake.

Alexandra Bridge Provincial Park (Map 26/F6)
A small, 55 hectare day-use park is located high above the Fraser River. The original Alexandra Bridge dates back to 1926 and you can still walk across to the other side of the river. A short distance downstream, highway traffic uses a more modern crossing. In addition to walking back and forth across the steel grate bridge and throwing stones into the water, there is a picnic area just off the highway.

Alice Lake Provincial Park (Map 22/D5)
Alice Lake is a popular provincial park, 13 km north of Squamish. There are 108 campsites here, over half of which have electrical hook-ups. Showers, a playground and interpretive program and sani-dump are some of the campground amenities here. Alice Lake is one of four lakes that dominate this park

and water sports like swimming, fishing and canoeing are the most popular activities here. There are a number of trails in the park, ranging from a stroll around Alice Lake, to the 6 km Four Lakes Trail. The park covers 396 hectare and now charges a daily parking fee.

Anderson Bay Provincial Park (Map 8/F4)
Anderson Bay is an extension of South Texada Island Provincial Park. The 35 hectare parcel of land provides well-protected anchorage and access to some trails in the area, but other than that, there are no developed facilities.

Apodaca Marine Park (Map 10/G7)
Apodaca is an 8 hectare marine park located on the eastern shore of Bowen Island. There are no developed facilities, but it is a good place to moor your boat and explore the shore. The park protects the shoreline, which consists of scenic cliffs and rocky knolls.

Arrowstone Provincial Protected Area (Map 45/G3)
Located in the foothills northeast of Cache Creek, this protected area is accessed off the Arrowstone Forest Road and Highway 1. The park protects the Arrowstone Creek Drainage as well as the Cache Creek Hills. There are no developed facilities in the park, but is fairly accessible for hikers, hunters and nature lovers to explore.

Bedard Aspen Provincial Park (Map 45/D7)
Located about 40 km west of Cache Creek, this diverse, trail access only area is centred around a small lake that contains rainbow trout. The lake lies in the heart of the Ashcroft Motorcycle Trail system allowing for ATV's and other motorized vehicle access.

Belcarra Regional Park (Map 1/G1)
Protecting the eastern flanks of the entrance to Indian Arm, this 1,116 Regional Park is the second largest of the Greater Vancouver Regional District (GVRD) parks, second in size only to Lynn Headwaters. Belcarra is a popular recreation destination in summer, with 22 km of trails (only 6 km open to horseback riding and 9.5 km open to mountain bikers). There are two main recreation areas in the park. The first is Sasamat Lake, a popular beach and swimming lake, looped by a trail. The second area is down at Belcarra Bay where a nice picnic site and a second series of trails are found. Trails link the two areas as well as joining to nearby Buntzen Lake Park.

Birkenhead Lake Provincial Park (Map 36/C2)
This recently expanded park encompasses the turquoise-coloured Birkenhead Lake, as well as the rugged mountains that surround the lake. This is truly a beautiful spot, located 55 km northeast of Pemberton via the Blackwater Lake Road. In addition to a popular 94 site campground, there is a daily parking fee. There is also a boat launch, a beach and hiking/biking trails. The rustic 10,439 hectare park is home to many animals, including bobcat, moose, deer and black bear. An additional 4,888 hectares have been protected in the Qwalimak/Upper Birkenhead Conservancy that preserves a significant First Nations site and old growth forests as well as moose, salmon and trout habitat.

Bishop River Provincial Park (Map 49/C2)
This provincial park is about as remote a place as you could ask for in this corner of the province. The closest road is a boat access logging road. From here you will have to hike or bike 75 km (46 miles) up the Southgate River. Most people who come here (and there are not a lot of them) get here by helicopter. This is an area of big mountains and glaciers and should be left to experienced mountaineers.

Blackcomb Glacier Provincial Park (Map 30/A5)
This is one of most popular provincial parks in the Whistler area, by sheer virtue of its location, adjacent to both Garibaldi Provincial Park and Whistler Village. The 250 hectare park is a popular hiking destination in summer. In winter, the area is accessed via a series of chair lifts and thousands of people a day pass into, then out of, the park as they ski Blackcomb.

Blue Earth Lake Provincial Park (Map 39/D2)
Blue Earth Lake Park is located in a deep valley and offers fishing and rustic camping for five or so groups between two sites. There are a few small areas of old-growth Douglas fir and mature aspen, while spawning trout may be seen in the shallow channel between the lakes in early summer. The 705 hectare park is bisected by the rough Blue Earth Lake Forest Road to the east.

Boundary Bay Regional Park (Map 1/E7)
The biggest draw to this 182 hectare regional park is the sandy beaches and the warm waters of Boundary Bay. When the tide goes out, almost all the water in the bay disappears, leaving a magical intertidal world to explore. The shallow pools fill with marine life and you can walk for miles on the mud flats. The park is also the start of the multi-use 16 km Boundary Bay Regional Trail.

Brackendale Eagles Provincial Park (Map 22/C6)
Brackendale Eagles Provincial Park lies in the Squamish River watershed, a large low lying valley through the Coast Mountains. This valley has long been recognized as one of the most significant areas of wintering bald eagles in North America. These majestic birds can be seen feasting on the spawned out remains of Chum Salmon from November to February each year. A new 755 hectare provincial park was developed to protect habitat for the eagles. There are no developed facilities in the park and it is recommended that people view the eagles from outside the park boundaries. The park is located on the west side of the Squamish River, but one of the best viewing locations is across the river at the municipal dyke on Government Road in Brackendale.

Brae Island Regional Park (Map 2/F4)
This park was developed in an area previously occupied by a private campground called Fort Camping. In addition to a day-use area, the park features a large campground with over 140 sites, 4 km of trails, a group camping area, walk-in yurt camping and canoe launching facilities. The park is located on Brae Island, across Bedford Channel from Fort Langley.

Brandywine Falls Provincial Park (Map 29/D7)
One of the fallouts from the Sea to Sky Highway being expanded for the 2010 Olympics is a reduction in the size of this park. So much so that BC Parks has closed the campsite here and converted the park to a day-use only site. There is a picnic site, but most visitors will continue to do what they've always done: come in, look at the 70 metre (227 foot) high Brandywine Falls, take a few pictures, then continue on their way. There are a number of trails in the area, including a section of the Sea to Sky Trail.

Bridal Veil Falls Provincial Park (Map 4/G4–5/A4)
Bridal Veil Falls Park is a 32 hectare day-use area located just off Highway 1 east of Chilliwack. The landscape encompassing the park is characterized by low elevation valleys and lush, rounded mountains. The falls tumble 60 metres (195 feet) over a smooth rock face and make a fine hiking destination.

Buccaneer Bay Provincial Park (Map 9/B4)
Buccaneer Bay is a tiny one hectare park with a broad sandy beach at the southern tip of North Thormanby Island. The large sheltered bay provides safe anchorage in most summer conditions for small boats or kayaks. This is also a popular scuba diving location. There is random beach camping (with space for about 8 groups) allowed.

Burnaby Lake Regional Park (Map 1/F2)
The majority of this 311 hectare regional park is Burnaby Lake itself, but the really interesting part of the park is where the marshy area water meets the land. It is here where birds and small mammals tend to hang out. You can explore this area from shore, along the 19 km of trails or from the water in a canoe or kayak.

Burnaby Mountain Conservation Area (Map 1/G2–2/A2)
Originally logged in the early 1900's, the mountain has long been a popular trail destination for city folks. Today, many simply come to enjoy the manicured gardens, Japanese sculpture and high-class restaurant at the top of the mountain. Further east, there is a large, wild swatch of mountain captured within the park boundaries, too. There are great views over both the city and Burrard Inlet from the top and an established trail system cutting through the forested slopes of the hill. The Trans Canada Trail also runs through the park.

Burns Bog Regional Park (Map 1/G4)
For years, Burns Bog was at the centre of a raging debate over development in the area. If Stanley Park is the Lower Mainland's green heart, Burns Bog is its lungs and kidneys. The 40 square km domed peat bog is the largest on the west coast of North America. The bog actually acts like a filter for fresh water and stores carbon dioxide. In 2004, much of the bog was protected as a regional park and is closed to public access. However, the Delta Nature Reserve next door is being developed as the focus of both access and education about the bog and trails, including an elaborate boardwalk system, have been developed. They connect with the Delta South Surrey Greenway.

Callaghan Conservancy (Map 29/A3)
Originally named Sea to Sky Conservancy (I), this area has now been given the much more meaningful designation of Callaghan Conservancy. As you might expect, the conservancy butts up against Callaghan Lake Provincial Park and protects part of the Callaghan River drainage.

Callaghan Lake Provincial Park (Map 29/B3)
Callaghan Lake is a high mountain lake at the end of a rough two-wheel drive road. In addition to ten rustic campsites, the lake and nearby Cirque Lake offer fishing for rainbow and lake trout. There are also numerous small wetlands and small lakes, especially in the southern and eastern areas of the park and in the upper headwaters of Callaghan Creek. A zone has been designated for snowmobile use, providing an access corridor to the bowls north of the park, while cross-country and backcountry skiing are also popular here due to the abundant snow levels. Abutting the 2,667 hectare park is a new conservation area that protects more of the Callaghan Creek drainage, as well as some recent 2010 Olympic development.

Campbell Valley Regional Park (Map 2/E7)
There are 20 km of trails in this 549 hectare regional park, 14 km of which are open to horseback riders. The trails are the most prominent feature in the park, winding their way through forest and field, marsh and meadow. Campbell Valley is also home to a number of historical sites. The park is accessed at the end of 208th St south of Langley.

Capilano River Regional Park (Map 11/D7)
The Capilano River cuts deep into the North Shore. The steep canyon walls, the view from the Cleveland Dam and the few pockets of old growth trees are just some of the highlights of this spectacular area. There are 14 km worth of multi-use trails to help you explore. In the fall, the Capilano Fish Hatchery becomes the centre of attention, as people flock to watch the returning salmon spawn up the river. Anglers also line the banks of the river and more than a few have landed more than a giant fish. The Cap is a great whitewater river and the odd kayaker has been hooked by errant lures.

Cascade Falls Regional Park (Map 3/F2)
This 9.5 hectare site is one of the three nature parks in the Fraser Valley Regional District. The park's main feature is a series of waterfalls on Cascade Creek. The largest of which, the upper falls, plunge 28 metres (90 feet) to a large pool. Below the pool a series of smaller falls, in a deep, narrow gorge, drop the remaining 18 metres to the valley floor.

Cascade Recreation Area (Map 6, 16, 17)
This big, 11,858 hectare recreation area is bounded by both the Skagit Valley Recreation Area and Manning Provincial Park. One can access the area from either the Cascade Recreation Area Parking Area or along the Whipsaw Creek Road. This pristine backcountry wilderness area has seen very little development over the years, although there are 7 backcountry campsites ranging from the bigger 10 site camping areas at Snass View and Marmot City Camps to the small Fido Camp. These sites offer space for 2 to 10 groups and usually provide a pit toilet, fire ring and food cache. The Hubbard, Tulameen and Warburton Camps also provide horse corrals and hitching rails, while the Backcountry Horsemen maintain a cabin at Tulameen Camp. In winter the northeast corner of the Granite Mountain area is open to snowmobiling.

Central Park (Map 1/E3)
Central Park is a patch of green space near the ever-expanding glass and concrete of Metrotown. If you can't get out of the city, this is a good place to go to relax. Only in the heart of the park will the noise of the city fade, but it is easy to ignore the traffic whizzing by on Boundary Road as you relax on the grass beneath the shade of a Douglas fir. The park also hosts 8.5 km of multi-use trails winding their way through a small urban forest.

Cheam Lake Wetlands Regional Park (Map 4/G3)
Located just east of Highway 9, this 93 hectare park is mostly lake and wetlands. This is a BC Wildlife Watch site and there are plenty of birds and small mammals in the area. There are a number of trails in the park to explore, some of which are under water in spring and early summer.

Chilliwack Lake Provincial Park (Map 5/F6)
Chilliwack Lake Provincial Park has recently been expanded to 9,122 hectares. The expansion includes the east side of the lake where former recreation sites at Depot Creek, Post Creek, Sappers Park and Paleface Creek have been deactivated. At the head of the lake, campers will find 144 drive-in campsites in four separate loops, an adventure playground, boat launch and sani-dump open from early May until mid October. Day visitors can enjoy the beach, while backcountry campsites are found at Greendrop, Lindeman, Flora and Radium Lakes. Chilliwack Lake is ideal for boating, canoeing, kayaking, swimming (although it doesn't get very warm) and fishing. There are over 40 km of established trails, including parts of the recently established Trans Canada Trail and the historic Centennial Trail, as well as some unmaintained routes. The park is located 64 km southeast of Chilliwack at the end of the paved Chilliwack River Road.

Chilliwack River Provincial Park (Map 4/E6)
A popular spot for anglers and kayakers, this day-use site is also a nice place for a picnic. It is found a short distance from Vedder Crossing, on the north side of the river.

Clendinning Provincial Park (Map 28, 34, 47, 49)
Protecting the Clendinning Creek drainage and parts of the Elaho River Valley, the south end of this 30,330 hectare park is road accessible by a long, lonely drive up the Squamish Main, then the Elaho Main. There are no facilities, but the deep, forested valleys and rugged glaciated peaks do attract hardcore backpackers and mountaineers looking to explore this dramatic landscape. There is an unmaintained trail through the old growth to Clendinning Lookout, but most mountaineers, the parks main user group, access the mountains at the north end of the park by helicopter.

Cliff Gilker Regional Park (Map 10/B6)
This small regional park is easily accessed off Highway 101 adjacent to the Sunshine Coast Golf & Country Club. It provides a series of popular hiking trails through a forested setting with little elevation gain. Wooden bridges cross several small streams and Roberts Creek in amongst some large second growth timber. There are four well-maintained and easily followed trails within the park.

Colony Farm Regional Park (Map 2/B3)
This is a recently developed 262 hectare parcel of land near the Fraser/Coquitlam River confluence. There are a series of dyke trails to walk or bike and viewing platforms for the nature lover. From Highway 7, turn south onto Colony Farm Road and continue to the parking area at the end of the road.

Copeland Islands Marine Park (Map 46/A6)
Located northwest of Lund, this provincial park encompasses the scenic Copeland Islands. The area is a sanctuary for birds, as well as an excellent spot for scuba diving. The park is often used as a stopover point by sea kayakers heading into Desolation Sound, but the islands also make a nice two or three-day destination themselves.

Coquihalla Canyon Provincial Park (Map 15/G6)
This park is situated around the Othello Tunnels built in the early 1900s as part of the historic Kettle Valley Railway. The tunnels are impressive, as are the great views of the canyon, a 93 metre (300 foot) deep gorge of near-vertical granite. The old rail bed is part of the Trans Canada Trail. A daily parking fee applies.

Coquihalla Summit Recreation Area (Map 16/E2)
To the south of the tollbooth, at the summit of the Coquihalla Highway (Hwy 5), is a lovely picnic area for highway travellers. Most visitors will enjoy the incredible views of Zopkius Ridge and Needle Peak before moving on, but the 5,750 hectare park offers much more. It is possible to explore the subalpine terrain around the toll booth, fish at Falls Lake or challenge the many surrounding peaks along mountain routes best left to experienced mountaineers.

Cornwall Hill Provincial Park (Map 45/E7)
To the west of Ashcroft, the Cornwall Lookout Road can access this undeveloped park. The summit of Cornwall Hill is a popular launch for hang gliders and offers nice views of the surrounding area. There are also a number of unmarked trails through the meadows and rare Engelmann Spruce in the 1,188 hectare park.

Crippen Regional Park (Map 10/F6)
Bowen Island has been a popular getaway for people from the Vancouver area since the early 1900s. People come here to get away from the city and spend a few hours living on island time. The most prominent feature in this 242 hectare park is Killarney Lake. It is possible to walk off the ferry, walk around the lake and return to the ferry in an easy afternoon stroll. There are 11 km of trail here.

Cultus Lake Provincial Park/International Ridge Recreation Area
(Map 4/C6)
This 656 hectare park, located 13 km south of Chilliwack, sees a lot of water-based activity. There are four well developed campgrounds in the park: Clear Creek (82 sites), Delta Grove (57 sites), Entrance Bay (52 sites) and Maple Bay (104 sites) that are open from early April until mid October. In summer the beaches are often packed and the lake is positively abuzz with power-boats and jet skis. There are canoe rentals, but the lake can be a dangerous place to be in an open craft, as winds can pick up at any time. There are five main trails in the park, ranging from the interpretive stroll along the Maple Bay Trail to a 5 hour hike along the Edmeston Road to Road 918 Trail. The trails also hook up with trails outside the park. A daily parking fee applies.

Adjacent to Cultus is the International Ridge Recreation area, which adds another 2,080 hectares to the co-joined parks. If Cultus Lake is the popular front country, International Ridge is the nearly forgotten backcountry, featuring a couple of lesser known trails.

Cypress Falls Park (Map 11/A7)
The main features of this park, a little known gem of a park near Horseshoe Bay, are a series of waterfalls on Cypress Creek. There are a number of trails in the park and the most popular destination is, of course, the falls.

Cypress Provincial Park (Map 11/B6–B4)
Cypress has the distinction of being the most popular provincial park in the province. Most of the visitors to the park come in winter, as Cypress is home to a popular ski hill, just 15 minutes from downtown Vancouver. This will be the site of the Freestyle Skiing and Snowboard Venue for the Vancouver 2010 Olympic Winter Games. On a clear day the views from the top of Mt. Strachen (pronounced Strawn) are spectacular! To the south is the sprawling metropolitan area of Vancouver, while to the southeast is snow clad Mount Baker in the Cascade Mountain chain. To the west and southwest lie the Gulf Islands and Vancouver Island with Georgia Strait in the foreground. But the park is much more than just the ski area and covers nearly 3,000 hectares. There are many trails in the park, including the strenuous but rewarding Howe Sound Crest Trail. A daily parking fee applies.

Dakota Ridge Regional Winter Recreation Area (Map 10/C3)
This recently established recreation area is one of the prime areas for cross-country skiing on the Sunshine Coast. In the summer, the 12 km of trails are open for hikers, although the access road may be closed in spring.

Dan Bosh Regional Park (Map 20/B6)
This popular day-use park is found on Ruby Lake next to Highway 101. Swimming, fishing and paddling are the typical activities, although the site is popular with birders and naturalists as well. Viewing the birds and the painted turtles is easy, but Roosevelt elk, deer and even bear frequent the area.

Daniel Point Regional Park (Map 9/A1)
Daniel Point is a small point that juts out from the Sunshine Coast. This small park protects a fragile ecosystem of mosses and lichens. The main feature for visitors is a short but difficult trail to a viewpoint over Malaspina Strait.

Davis Lake Provincial Park (Map 3/E1)
Davis Lake Provincial Park is located 19 km north of Mission. Continue from Sylvester Road past the park boundary and look for a side road that descends south, down the slope to the short trail into Davis Lake. The 192 hectare park surrounds the small, warm water lake with pretty beaches, a scenic waterfall and good fishing. While it is primarily a day-use park, walk-in camping is permitted.

Deas Island Regional Park (Map 1/D5)
A relatively small, 72 hectare park on the Fraser River, Deas Island isn't actually an island, but a peninsula, jutting out into the Fraser. While thousands of commuters pass by here every day, fighting back the road rage that threatens to envelop them, most have no idea that just a few metres away lies a peaceful riverside park. There are 9 km of trails through the park, taking you along Deas Slough, along the banks of the Fraser and past the heritage buildings. The picnic area is a fine place to enjoy a sunset from.

Deer Lake Park (Map 1/F3)
An urban park, protecting Deer Lake—an oasis of calm in the midst of the city—Deer Lake is home to arts, culture and history, as well as the natural beauty of the park itself. There are canoe rentals for folks who want to get out on the lake for a lazy paddle, as well as well developed trails, a beach and a surprising amount of wildlife for a park surrounded by city. To get to

the park from Highway 1, take the Kensington South turnoff. Turn west on Canada Way and follow the signs to Deer Lake Park.

Derby Reach Regional Park (Map 2/F3)
Edgewater Bar, located in this park, is considered by many to be one of the best, if not the best, fishing bars on the Fraser River. In August and September, this section of the riverbank is choc-a-block with anglers, while the channel just off shore is stuffed with salmon. Besides fishing, this is one of just two regional parks with public camping. There are 37 campsites, all of which have access to the river. There are two trails—the 1 km Edge Trail and the 4 km Houston Loop trail that skirts Derby Bog. Derby Reach was the original site of Fort Langley. Although the fort is no more, there are a few historical buildings.

Deroche Regional Park (Map 4/A3)
Established in 2004, this small, 4.4 hectare park is located on the north side of the Fraser River east of Mission. There is a boat launch here and fishing is very popular. In the fall and winter, it is a great place to watch bald eagles, while shorebirds and seals can also be seen here.

Desolation Sound Provincial Park (Map 46/A5)
Desolation Sound is one of the most popular yachting and sea kayaking destinations in the world. It is also BC's largest marine provincial park encompassing Gifford Peninsula and several small islands. Despite its remoteness at the end of the Sunshine Coast, with no access other than by water, it can be busy in the summer. Boat cruisers, sea kayakers and anglers all flock here from Lund or Okeover Inlet. There are several developed camping areas throughout and the shallow bays are famous for warm waters and oysters. For more information, consult the fishing and paddling sections of the book.

Dewdney Nature Regional Park (Map 3/F4)
This 7 hectare nature park is located outside the dyke on the east side of the south end of River Road South in Dewdney. This is a popular spot for bar fishing along the Fraser River, especially during the fall Coho runs. There is also a concrete boat launch as well as a chance to see shorebirds, seals and bald eagles in the fall and winter. Swimming and canoeing in the slough is also possible.

Don Bosch Regional Park (Map 20/B6)
Ruby Lake is a beautiful roadside lake that entices many people to stop at this small park. In addition to the nice beach, there is boat launch for paddlers and anglers to enjoy.

Duck Lake Protected Area (Map 19/A3)
Located 5 km east of Powell River, south of Haslam Lake, this protected area is an important nesting area for a variety of bird species. As you might expect, bird watching is a popular pursuit in the 768 hectare park and canoes can be launched on the lake from the Duck Lake Road. There are also 9 km of hiking and biking trails in the park.

Duffey Lake Provincial Park (Map 37/D6)
Located about 35 km east of Pemberton, Duffey Lake is nearly halfway to Lillooet along the Duffey Lake Road (Highway 99). Duffy Lake is a beautiful lake, surrounded by snow capped mountains. There is a boat launch at the east end of the lake for boaters. Be wary of afternoon winds.

E.C. Manning Provincial Park (Map 6, 7)
Encompassing over 70,844 hectare of rugged mountains, valleys, meadows, lakes and rivers, Manning is a four season outdoor paradise. Trails of all shapes and sizes, lakes for canoeing and fishing, wildlife for viewing and downhill and cross-country skiing in winter are just some of the popular activities enjoyed here. Highway 3 runs through the park providing good access to the park. Campers will find four campgrounds in the park. Lightning Lake Campground is the most popular site in the park with 143 reservable sites, showers and interpretive programs available from June to early September. There is also a boat launch for non-motorized boats. Coldspring, Hampton and Mule Deer Campsites, with 212 sites between them, are all available on a first come first serve basis. The camping season is weather dependent but generally opens in early May (at Mule Deer) and goes to early October (at Coldspring), although the 2 sites at Lone Duck group campsite are open in winter. Trail users will also find several designated areas for backcountry camping ranging from 3 to 10 tent pads, with outhouses, bear caches and fire rings usually available. Day visitors will find 7 sites around the park including West Gate, Sumallo Grove, Lightning Lake and the popular Sub-Alpine Meadows area.

BCParks
The Best Place on Earth

parkadventures

Edge Hills Provincial Park (Map 44/D1)
This large park protects panoramic vistas over the Fraser River canyon as well as ravines, forested valleys and grassy uplands. There are unmaintained and unmarked trails in the park, but that's about it for infrastructure.

Elephant Hill Provincial Park (Map 45/G5)
This park protects a pair of prominent hills in a naturally dry grassland area, which are home to rattlesnakes. The grasslands are closed to vehicle traffic and no camping or day-use facilities are provided. There is random hiking in the 979 hectare park, which is a popular destination with wildlife watchers. The park is easily accessed off Highway 97C south of Cache Creek.

Emory Creek Provincial Park (Map 15/F4)
Emory Creek is a roadside park next to the Fraser River, 18 km north of Hope. There are 34 campsites in this 15 hectare park. This is a popular spot with anglers.

Epsom Provincial Park (Map 39/G2)
Located on the west bank of the Thompson River, north of Spences Bridge, this 102 hectare park provides access to the river, mostly for anglers. There is no road access to the park, so anyone wishing to visit must scramble down to the river from Highway 1 along a rough trail. Be careful crossing the railway tracks.

Este-Tiwilh/Sigurd Creek Conservancy (Map 21/F2)
Found adjacent to Tantalus Provincial Park's northern tip, this conservancy protects much of the Sigurd Creek drainage. The Sigurd Creek Trail passes through the new conservancy, but otherwise, there is no access. The phrase Esté-tiwilh (pronounced us-tut-ee-wayth) means "the great beauty and power that surrounds us and that we should strive to be in harmony with." This conservancy protects an area that is used by mountain goat, grizzly bear, marbled murrelet, bald eagle, spotted owl as well as spawning areas steelhead and salmon.

F.H. Barber Provincial Park (Map 5/B1)
This is a small day-use area between Highway 1 and the Fraser River.

Francis Point Provincial Park (Map 9/A2)
Francis Point protects 73 hectares of coastal forest, wetland and open area, as well as about 6 km of undeveloped coastline on the Sechelt Peninsula. There is a short walking trail from the end of Merrill Road to a rocky knoll just past the Francis Point Beacon. The area was set aside to protect a number of rare plant species and caution is needed in this area. However, it is one of the best diving areas along the Sunshine Coast and is a popular sea kayaking area.

Fraser Foreshore Park (Map 1/E3)
This picturesque riverside park is located south of Marine Way tucked between an industrial park and the river. The park is long and narrow, and, once you get away from the manicured lawns of the picnic area (off Bryne Road), there are some interesting sites to see and many side trails to explore.

Garden Bay Marine Provincial Park (Map 9/B1)
Located around Mount Daniels, this small marine park has a dock, a picnic area and hiking trails. It can be accessed by water, or by land, off Garden Bay Road. On the rock bluffs next to the ocean is a stand of juniper trees, a rare site on the Sunshine Coast.

Garibaldi Provincial Park (Map 22, 23, 24, 29, 30)
A huge 194,650 hectare wilderness park located next to Squamish and Whistler, Garibaldi is a popular destination with outdoor enthusiasts. Day trips are possible (a parking fee applies), but most people who visit plan on spending a few days, or even a few weeks, exploring this alpine paradise. The main access points into the park from south to north are the Diamond Head Trail, The Black Tusk Trail, The Cheakamus Lake Trail, the Singing Pass Trail and the Wedgemount Lake Trail. The park has an interesting geological background; volcanic action formed many of the park's peaks. Lava from Clinker Peak created The Barrier, a natural dam that created the 300 metre deep Garibaldi Lake. The Barrier has been declared a Civil Defence Zone and there is no camping or stopping while travelling through the Zone. There are many popular, developed backcountry camping areas, like Garibaldi Lake, Taylor Meadows, Diamond Head, Singing Pass and Wedgemount Lake. During winter there are also several huts or cabins for backcountry skiers to use. Mountain bikes are only allowed as far as Elfin Lakes on the Diamond Head Trail and no dogs are allowed in the park. For more information check out www.garibaldipark.com.

Glen Valley Regional Park (Map 3/B4)
This park is a thin strip of land along the Fraser River to give access to Two Bit, Poplar and Duncan Bars. Anglers frequent the area and there is a canoe launch, a couple picnic tables and even some short walking trails to enjoy.

Golden Ears Provincial Park (Map 2, 3, 12, 13, 23, 24)
Although less than a third of the size of the massive Garibaldi Provincial Park to the north, Golden Ears, at 55,590 hectares is still one of the largest parks in the province. Most of the recreational usage happens in the southern portion of the park, around Alouette Lake. There is swimming, windsurfing, water skiing, canoeing, boating, fishing or just lazing about the beach. There are two vehicle accessible campgrounds in this park, Alouette (205 sites) and Gold Creek (138 sites) complete with showers, a playground and sani-dump. Backcountry or walk-in camping is allowed at North Beach on Alouette Lake, Alder Flats on the West Canyon Trail and Lake Beautiful on the Alouette Mountain Trail. A number of trails push deeper into the park including the popular Golden Ears Trail and the overnight route to Hector Ferguson Lake. There is a large boat launch at the south end of Alouette Lake along with three day-use areas with nice beaches. A daily parking fee applies.

Goldpan Provincial Park (Map 39/F7)
Located right next to Highway 1 (and between 2 busy railroads), this 5 hectare provincial park is best used as a stopover for travellers on Highway 1. The day-use area is open year round and is popular with people who wish to explore the Thompson River for fishing or paddling opportunities. In addition, there are 14 rather noisy campsites. The provincial park is set within the dry sage brush country typical of the Thompson River Valley.

Grant Narrows Regional Park (Map 12/F7)
While Grant Narrows Park is a mere 6 hectares with little to offer other than a boat launch, it bounds on a number of interesting ecological areas and low-lying wetlands. The 1,500 hectare Pitt Wildlife Management Area lies to the south of Grant Narrows, to the east is the UBC research forest and across the narrows is the Widgeon Slough. All of these areas are prime wildlife habitat and home to a wide variety of birds and other creatures. From the park, there are almost 14 km worth of dykes that can be walked or biked, as well as the 4 km Mountainside Trail. In addition to viewing platforms, there are canoe rentals available for folks who want to canoe across to Widgeon Creek.

Green Timbers Urban Forest (Map 2/B4)
Known as the birthplace of reforestation in British Columbia, Green Timbers Urban Forest is a natural oasis in the middle of Surrey. The area was replanted in 1931 and now offers a series of approximately 5 km of trails through second growth forests, grasslands, wetlands and around Green Timbers Lake. The lake itself is a very popular fishing hole that has produced some surprisingly big trout. Access is best off 100 Avenue.

Halkett Bay Provincial Park (Map 10/G5)
Located on Gambier Island, this park is only accessible by boat. There are ten picnic sites and a trail leaves from here and up to Mount Artaban. There are mooring buoys and dingy floats for boaters.

Hardy Island Marine Provincial Park (Map 19/E6)
Originally called Musket Island Provincial Park, the name of this park was changed in 2004, as the anchorage is known as Hardy Island Anchorage. The area is boat accessible only and is a popular shelter for boaters. The waters here are clean, green and warm, making it a popular swimming spot. Outside of a park bench, there is little development here.

Harmony Islands Marine Provincial Park (Map 20/B3)
These small, sheltered islands are just north of the towering Freil Falls in the sheltered Hotham Sound. Swim, go snorkelling, fish or just appreciate nature.

Harry Lake Aspen Provincial Park (Map 45/C4)
This small, remote park has no developed facilities, but the grasslands are known for a small but colourful bloom of wildflowers in summer.

Haywire Bay Regional Park (Map 18/G2)
Part of a regional park, Haywire Bays' main feature is the big campsite, that is usually full of drive-in campers. There used to be camping on an island

tucked away in this sheltered bay, but it was abused and ultimately removed. Canoe circuit travellers well schooled in no-trace camping might want to think about staying here, rather than trying to find a place in the main site. The park also offers a good boat launch for visitors to Powell Lake.

Homathko Estuary Provincial Park (Map 1/B6)
Because of its location and the fact that water access is hindered by extensive mud flats, this park offers few recreational opportunities. It is possible to explore the beach area at low tide or observe grizzly bears from a distance.

I7loqaw7/100 Lakes Plateau Conservancy (Map 34/ C4)
The hundred lakes plateau is an important part of the Elaho River drainage and the wetland complex is a feeding ground for many species, including waterfowl, moose, mountain goat and grizzly bear. The area can be accessed by trail, but is otherwise inaccessible.

Indian Arm Provincial Park (Map 2, 11, 12)
Indian Arm is a long, narrow fjord that extends north from Burrard Inlet. The 6,821 hectare park protects the upper portion of the inlet and is primarily accessed by water. The landscape is spectacular, with rugged, forested mountains, alpine lakes and numerous creeks and waterfalls, including the 50-metre high Granite Falls. The Arm is ideal for motor boating, kayaking, canoeing and scuba diving, while the Indian River and the lower reaches of some of the creeks are great for fishing. The flat beach areas along the shorelines of Bishop Creek provide a good area for rustic camping or even picnicking. Granite Falls is another popular area for camping and picnics. There is a day-use area on the north side of the falls, near a small dock, while tenters will often set up on the south side of the falls. At the south end of the arm, a marine park also protects Raccoon and the Twin Islands. Although camping is possible on Twin, be wary of private property on the island. Day moorage for small craft can be found at Granite Falls and North Twin Island.

Inland Lake Provincial Park (Map 18/G1–19/A2)
This park has taken over the former, very popular Forest Service Recreation Site and trail north of Powell River. There is a 13 km wheelchair accessible trail around Inland Lake, along with less developed connecting trails to nearby Powell Lake. The main campsite offers 16 campsites with picnic tables, cabins for disabled people as well as a wharf. Tenting only sites spread around the lake, including the scenic boat access only sites on Anthony Island.

Iona Beach Regional Park (Map 1/B3)
While the park is built around the beach, the most noticeable feature here is the 4 km long jetty, jutting far into the Strait of Georgia. For many years, this out-of-the-way corner of the Lower Mainland was the sewer of the Strait and it was a nasty, disgusting, unpleasant place. But in the late 1980s, pipes were added to carry the sewage farther out into the strait, well away from this area. Now it is quite a pleasant place to be and a testament to the recovery powers of nature. It is an isolated green space and home to many birds and small mammals. There are tidal flats to explore, as well as marshes, grasslands and the beach, for which this park gets its name. The beach is a great place for a picnic or to go sunbathing and some people even go swimming.

Island 22 Regional Park (Map 4/C3)
This is a popular equestrian area, complete with riding ring, corrals, jumps and several equestrian events throughout the year. The park is also a fishing hot spot when the salmon are running. It features a good bar to shore fish from and one of the largest boat launches in the Lower Mainland. There are 80 campsites, six of which have electrical hook-ups. Call 604-792-5567 for reservations.

Jedediah Island Provincial Park (Map 8/E4)
Jedediah Island has long been the destination of boaters and kayakers. It is the largest and most diverse island of a chain of over thirty islands and islets located north and west of Lasqueti Island. Some of the best camping areas are near the shoreline around Long Bay. Small bays on the east side of the island provide campers with a little more privacy, especially during the summer when the island can get quite busy.

Joffre Lakes Provincial Park (Map 31/A1–37/A7)
This 1,460 hectare wilderness park contains the lovely Joffre Lakes and the towering (2,701 metres/8,778 feet) Joffre Peak. The trail leading past the three lakes is a fairly rough 5 km mountain route. Beyond the rustic campsite at Upper Joffre Lake is only recommended for mountaineers prepared for

travelling on glaciers and snowfields. Another popular backcountry destination in the area is the Cerise Creek area where trails and a backcountry hut are located. The Nlhaxten/Cerise Creek Conservancy has been recently established to protect this significant area for local First Nations.

K'zuzalt/Twin Two Conservancy (Map 31/B2)
Twin Two Creek flows into Lillooet Lake and is one of a very few drainages that hasn't been logged out. There is some young growth forest, but also some old growth as well. The area offers good habitat for a variety of species from spotted owl to grizzly bear.

Kanaka Creek Regional Park (Map 2/G3–3/B3)
Kanaka Creek Regional Park follows the valley of Kanaka Creek for 11 km. This is not a popular recreation park, but it does see its fair share of picnickers, trail users, canoeists and nature lovers. There are a couple picnic sites, one just above Cliff Falls and one at the Bell-Irving Fish Hatchery. The hatchery is a fine place to see spawning salmon in fall, while the mouth of the creek is another nice place to watch for wildlife. There are also several walking trails in the 413 hectare park, totalling 10 km but these do not all connect.

Katherine Lake Regional Park (Map 9/B1)
Located off Garden Bay Road, Katherine Lake is a pretty lake with sandy beaches and a thickly forested shore. The park has 26 campsites that are large enough for an RV and 10 sites that are tent only. These sites are open from the May long weekend to the October Long Weekend. There is also a nice family friendly beach that makes a nice place to spend a hot afternoon. Call 604-883-9557 to reserve a site.

Kawkawa Park (Map 15/F6)
Formerly a provincial park found just east of Hope off the Kawkawa Lake Road, Kawkawa Park is a day-use park on the west side of the warm lake. In addition to the popular beach, anglers will find excellent fishing for kokanee.

Kilby Historical Provincial Park (Map 4/C2)
Tucked away in a rural pastoral setting, Kilby Provincial Park is located just past the historical Kilby General Store. This provincial park is a great place to watch wintering bald eagles, trumpeter swans, geese and small songbirds. This scenic riverfront park has 38 camping units as well as the main boat launch onto the Harrison River.

Klein Lake Regional Park (Map 20/C6)
This regional park, a former recreation site, is found on Klein Lake south of Earls Cove. It offers 23 small campsites, which can be used by small trailers or tents, but are not large enough for big RVs. Fishing and trails are found in the area.

Lost Lake Park (Map 29/G5)
Once a local hideout, Lost Lake Park is now a popular year round destination in Whistler. The elaborate cross-country trails can be used by everyone from hikers and bikers in summer to skiers and snowshoers in winter. There are also a couple beaches, barbeque pits, picnic tables, washrooms and an off-shore dock to enjoy.

Lower Seymour Conservation Reserve (Map 11/F6)
Formerly known as the Seymour Demonstration Forest, this 5,668 hectare site was renamed in 1999. This valley is sandwiched between the ridges of Lynn Headwaters Regional Park and Mount Seymour Provincial Park. The main recreational feature of the park is the new trail that parallels the service road from the parking lot to Seymour Dam. This paved trail leads 10 km (6 mile road) one-way and is a popular walking/biking/roller blading path. But there are many other trails in the park, some official, others not, leading to various spots in the park. Most of the official trails are in the southern corner of the park, including the Fisherman's Trail. This trail runs along the Seymour River providing access for hikers, mountain bikers and, of course, anglers. Another popular but unofficial trail, is the Temple of Time, which leads to some of the largest old growth trees still standing in the Lower Mainland. No dogs are allowed in the park.

Lynn Canyon Park (Map 1/E1)
The majority of visitors to this park are here for one thing: the suspension bridge. It's like a mini version of the Capilano Suspension Bridge and you don't have to pay to come here. Some continue on, but most admire the view into the deep gorge below, then leave. After crossing the suspension

bridge, the majority of foot traffic heads north, to a rocky area just below a waterfall through a narrow canyon. In summer, this is a popular destination for families and bolder individual's cliff dive in the pool at the base of the falls (not a recommended activity). To the south, a trail follows the canyon for a few kilometres, then crosses over Lynn Creek and returns on the other side, above the canyon.

Lynn Headwaters Regional Park (Map 11/E6)
Lynn Headwaters is the biggest of the regional parks in the Lower Mainland and it helps protect parts of the famed North Shore Mountains. One of the nice things for visitors is that buses stop just a few hundred metres outside the park, making it accessible to everyone. You only have to walk a short way into the park along the access road to have the sounds, smells and sights of the city fade away, to be replaced with the sensations of this verdant park. There are a number of fabulous hiking trails including the Headwater Trail (15.5 km/9.5 miles return) and the Hanes Valley Loop, which takes you over to Grouse Mountain and back on the Baden Powell Trail (15 km). The trails in Lynn Headwaters also hook up with trails in the Lower Seymour Conservation Reserve to the east. In winter, when there is snow, the trails are taken over by backcountry skiers.

Malaspina Provincial Park (Map 46/B5)
Located at the north end of the Malaspina Peninsula, this park is water accessible only. There are no developed features in the park.

Manning Provincial Park (Map 6, 7)
See E.C. Manning

Marble Canyon Provincial Park (Map 44/G3–45/A4)
A small provincial park just east of Pavilion on Highway 99, Marble Canyon is set at the base of 1,000 metre (3,250 feet) high limestone cliffs. The 335 hectare park contains a trio of lakes, Crown, Pavilion and Turquoise Lakes, with a 34 unit campsite found between tiny Turquoise and Crown Lakes. This park is popular with fishermen and birders.

Matsqui Trail Regional Park (Map 3/D5–F5)
Located along the Fraser River beneath the Mission/Abbotsford Bridge, this 117 hectare park is thin and long, stretching 10 km along the south bank of the Fraser. The park is threaded together by a dyke trail, which runs the length of the park. There are six formal campsites, a popular picnic area and plenty of space for bar fishing. But the main feature of the area is the scenic Matsqui Trail. Part of the Trans Canada Trail, this broad multi-use trail can be stretched into a multi-day (or week or month) adventure.

Mehatl Creek Provincial Park (Map 25, 31, 32)
The 23,860 hectare Mehatl Creek is a wilderness getaway for backcountry adventurers. During the summer, visitors can trek 3 km up the park's only established trail to Mehatl Falls, which is nestled in a sub-alpine bowl. Parking is available adjacent to the 48 km bridge of the Nahatlatch River Forest Road in a vacant dry land log sort area. Other activities include fishing in the lower creek and wildlife viewing.

Minnekhada Regional Park (Map 2/D1)
Minnekhada occupies an interesting parcel of land. Part of the park is in the mountains and is forested and rocky. Part of the park is in the lowlands, and is marshy, with dykes providing access to the Addington Lookout. In fall, when the wild berries are ripe, it is not surprising to see black bears around the Minnekhada Farm area. There are over 12 km of trails through the park, from easy dyke walks to fairly stiff climbs up to the rocky knolls.

Mount Elphinstone Provincial Park (Map 10/B5)
Three separate parcels make up this 139 hectare park. The most notable is the piece on the southwest slopes of Mount Elphinstone, where old-growth forests contain some of the oldest trees in the province. Mount Elphinstone is also home to a prolific number of mushrooms, some of which have yet to be properly identified. Tread carefully and take only photographs. The other parcels are found near Roberts Creek and north of Gibsons.

Mount Richardson Provincial Park (Map 9/F2)
Located north of the town of Sechelt, this park is accessibly by a rough forest service road (4wd recommended). There is a former recreation site at Richardson Lake, where you'll find good fishing and wilderness camping. There are a number of hiking trails in the area, including a couple routes up the

mountain, while boat-accessible camping is offered at Oyster Beach, Nine Mile Point and Tuwanek on Sechelt Inlet.

Mount Seymour Provincial Park (Map 1/F1–11/G6)
The 3,508 hectare Mount Seymour Provincial Park is located 30 minutes northeast of downtown Vancouver. The park is notorious for winter recreation. The downhill ski area is popular with snowboarders and family skiers, while backcountry skiers and snowshoers have endless areas to play in. During summer, Mount Seymour, Mount Elsay and Mount Bishop all make great hiking or backpacking destinations (wilderness camping is permitted in the sub-alpine north of Brockton Point). A daily parking fee applies.

Mundy Park (Map 2/B2)
This is a suburban park with 12 km of multi-use trails weaving their way through cool, lush forest of the 180 hectare park. The heart of the park is Mundy Lake, but the smaller Lost Lake is also a popular destination. The park is found off Como Lake Road and makes a pleasant year round destination.

Murrin Provincial Park (Map 11/B1)
This small park surrounds tiny Browning Lake and is a very popular stop for travellers on the Sea to Sky Highway. In addition to picnic tables and a good fishing hole, rock climbers can be seen testing their skills on the bluffs rising above the parking lot. A daily parking fee applies.

Nahatlatch Provincial Park (Map 25/D1–33/A7)
Nahatlatch Provincial Park is a long and narrow 1,695 hectare park. The natural beauty of this spot, nestled in the glacier covered mountains, with old growth forest and a lake and river system like no other in the Lower Mainland. A series of small streams flow into, out of and between the three lakes in the park. Their waters drain into the Nahatlatch River, one of the best whitewater rivers in the province. For those not interested in these high adrenaline antics, they can canoe in and between the lakes. There are six former Forest Service Recreation Sites that provide camping in the park. From east to west they are; Frances Lake, Hannah Lake, Old Ranger Station, Nahatlatch Lake, Salmon Beach and Squakum. The park entrance is located on the Nahatlatch Forest Road (an active logging road) approximately 25 km northwest of Boston Bar. It is identified with a park information shelter.

Nairn Falls Provincial Park (Map 30/B1)
The waterfall for which this park is named plummets 60 metres (195 feet) into the valley below. They are accessible by a short, easy trail. The scenic park is not as busy as some of the others in the area. There are 88 campsites next to the Green River, a good fishing river for Dolly Varden and rainbow trout.

Neilson Regional Park (Map 3/E4)
A 4 hectare park on the west side of Hatzic Lake, Neilson Park provides public access to the lake. There has been some development, including a cookhouse, picnic tables, improved beach area and approximately 2 km of walking trails. The park looks out across the Fraser Valley, with Mount Cheam in the distance. There is also a private campsite on the lake.

Nicolum River Provincial Park (Map 16/A7)
Located east of Hope on Highway 3, the 24 hectare Nicolum River Provincial Park is set in dense forest cover next to a small, fast flowing river. There are only nine campsites here and they fill up quickly.

Nlhaxten/Cerise Creek Conservancy (Map 37/B7)
This conservancy is found abutting the eastern boundary of Joffre Lakes Provincial Park. The area is a popular destination for backcountry recreation and is a culturally significant area for local First Nations, who historically used the area for cultural, ceremonial and spiritual practices.

Okeover Arm Provincial Park (Map 46/B6)
On the east side of the Malaspina Peninsula, this 4 hectare park is used as a launching point for sea kayakers heading out into Desolation Sound. There are 14 vehicle/tent sites open seasonally and four small, sites open all year. These sites are usually full and are located close together so there is not much privacy. There is also an undeveloped boat launch and a government wharf here.

Oregon Jack Provincial Park (Map 39/D1)
Easily accessed on the Hat Creek Road, this undeveloped park preserves the Notch, a limestone canyon and falls on the Oregon Jack Creek drainage. An Indian Pictograph can be seen in the canyon.

Pacific Spirit Regional Park (Map 1/B2)

Pacific Spirit has the distinction of being the only clothing optional park in the Lower Mainland and while most of the naturalists hang around Wreck Beach, the entire foreshore area, around the point to Acadia Beach, is clothing optional. It is possible (though difficult in places) to walk the 6 km foreshore at low tide. The biggest part of this park is the southeast corner, which has become a haven for mountain bikers. There are over 90 km (55 miles) of trails in the park, of which 60 km are open to mountain bikers and horseback riders.

Peace Arch Provincial Park (Map 2/C7)

The Peace Arch sits on the International Boundary, where BC's Highway 99 and Washington States' Interstate 5 meet at the Canada/United States border. There are 41 picnic tables throughout the day-use park. This is not a wilderness park, but is pretty nonetheless, an elegant, well-manicured park with lovely flower gardens.

Pinecone-Burke Provincial Park (Map 2, 11, 12, 23)

A large, still undeveloped park is tucked in between (and behind) Pitt Lake and the Coquitlam Lake Watershed (and Indian Arm Park and Golden Ears…). It's a big 38,000 hectare park, capturing some of the rugged territory to the west of Pitt Lake and Upper Pitt River Valley. The park protects a number of sites that have been historically popular, but unprotected, like Burke Mountain in Coquitlam, Widgeon Slough and Widgeon Valley (which are accessible only by canoe or kayak from Grant Narrows). Most visitors make Widgeon Lake, a pretty lake in a hanging valley, their ultimate destination. But if you keep right instead of heading left to Widgeon Lake, you will follow the Fool's Gold Route north and west to hook up with the Mamquam River Forest Road southeast of Squamish. This route is infrequently travelled (and sees one or two groups a year).

Plumper Cove Provincial Park (Map 10/D6)

A small marine park on the northwestern shores of Keats Island, this park is accessible by canoe/kayak, boat or by the infrequent foot ferry from Gibsons (the Dogwood Princess). From Keats Landing, it is 2 km to the park. The park offers a snug anchorage for boaters and a good overnight destination for sea kayakers out of Gibsons. The park has a developed area with forested walk-in campsites, fire rings and water. Marine facilities include a wharf and mooring buoys, while the pebble beach is great for swimming and picnicking.

Porpoise Bay Provincial Park (Map 9/F4)

Located on the shores of Porpoise Bay in Sechelt, this popular provincial park has space for 84 campers from mid April to mid September. Showers, a playground and a separate day-use area are available. The large sandy beach is the main feature in the park, but there are trails that lead to the estuary of Angus Creek, offering great views over the inlet. In the fall, this is a good place to watch spawning salmon. Reservations are recommended for camping and a daily parking fee applies.

Porteau Cove Provincial Park (Map 11/B3)

Howe Sound is the southern most fjord in North America. Porteau Cove offers 44 scenic campsites stretched out along the shores of the sound, plus a popular walk-in beach area with 16 sites just south of the main campground. The campsites are open from March 1 through October, offering everything from electric hook-ups and showers to interpretive programs and a sani-dump. Mooring buoys, dock facilities and two boat launches are also available for boaters. An old ship has been sunk to attract marine life for scuba divers, making this one of the most popular diving spots in BC. The park is sandwiched between the BC Rail Line and the ocean and many campers have awoken to the rumbling of trains passing by. Be careful around the tracks. Reservations are recommended for camping and a daily parking fee applies for those interested in exploring the beach.

Princess Louisa Provincial Park (Map 47/E4)

Princess Louisa Inlet is located far inland, accessed by way of Jervis Inlet some 48 km (36 miles) from Egmont. The 8 km long inlet is in a magnificent granite-walls gorge; mountains rise sharply from the water's edge to heights in excess of 2,100 metres (7,000 feet). Up to mid-June, the warm sun melting the mountain snow pack creates more than sixty waterfalls that cascade

down the steep granite cliffs, straight into the ocean. The most famous of these, Chatterbox Falls, tumbles 40 metres (120 feet). Beyond the seven to ten knot Malibu Rapids at the entrance, the inlet is as placid as a mountain lake. Wilderness campsites are provided with toilets and picnic shelters nearby. Mooring buoys and docks are provided, while walking trails provide access to nearby scenic features.

Qwalimak/Upper Birkenhead Conservancy (Map 36/A2)

Established in 2008, this 4,888 hectare conservancy protects a portion of the Upper Birkenhead River's drainage. The river is an important watershed for spawning salmon, trout, Dolly Varden, whitefish, bull trout and suckers. The area is also a good wintering habitat for ungulates, especially moose, which are also found here in summer. Old-growth forests are found along the river and in the upper reaches of the watershed. This area is important to First Nations for resource gathering and historically has been used for cultural, ceremonial and spiritual practices. There are numerous significant First Nations site within the conservancy, including rock art, burial sites, culturally modified trees and village sites.

Richmond Nature Park (Map 1/D4)

The Richmond Nature Park protects a relic example of the raised peat bogs that once covered more than 25 per cent of Richmond. In addition to the bog flora, bog creatures like snakes, turtles, coyotes and deer are often seen. A 5 km network of trails allows you to explore the park.

Roberts Point Regional Park (Map 2/D3)

Located on Barnston Island, this park is accessed by ferry and by foot or bike. There are 2.5 km worth of trails in the park, though not all of the trails are open to bikes.

Roberts Creek Provincial Park (Map 9/G5–10/A5)

Located off Highway 101 west of Gibsons, this 14 hectare park has two separate sites built around a cobblestone beach. The campsite is home to 21 sites open from mid June to mid September. The nearby Flume Beach is a better destination for picnickers and swimmers. Beachcombers can find an interesting display of marine life at low tides, while orca (killer) whales or harbour seals can often be spotted here.

Rolley Lake Provincial Park (Map 3/C2)

Less than an hour's drive from Vancouver, Rolley Lake Provincial Park is a quick escape from urban life. The small, warm water lake provides opportunities for swimming, fishing and canoeing. For campers, there are 64 popular sites nestled in the trees with showers, a playground and sani-dump. There is a trail that circles the lake and leads down to Rolley Falls. Reservations are recommended for camping and a daily parking fee applies for day visitors.

Roscoe Bay Marine Provincial Park (Map 46/B4)

A popular place for boating, kayaking, fishing and camping, Roscoe Bay also features a hiking trail to Black Lake and an annual congregation of Moon Jelly Fish. There is space for a couple of small groups to tent here.

Sabine Channel Provincial Park (Map 8/D4)

Sabine Channel is the channel between Texada and Lasqueti Island. This park protects a chain of small islands and islets that are popular with kayakers and boaters. Wilderness camping is possible.

Saltery Bay Provincial Park (Map 19/E5)

This provincial park is found just west of the Saltery Bay Ferry Terminal. There are 42 campsites at the east end of the park. There are also two day-use areas, one adjacent to the camping area and one 2 km west. There is great scuba diving in Saltery Bay, with the famous Emerald Mermaid, a 3 metre (9 foot) bronze statue at 10 fathoms in front of Mermaid Cove and a disabled access ramp. From the shore, visitors can sometimes see killer whales and sea lions in the distance. Mounds of seashells, called middens, indicate that this was a traditional gathering area for First Nations.

Sargeant Bay Provincial Park (Map 9/D4)

This tiny park is known for its abundance of intertidal and marine life. In fall, this is a great place to watch fish spawning up a fish ladder. In addition to

the picnic area and beach next to the sheltered, undeveloped cove, there is a good trail system. One trail leads through a cedar forest to the tidal pools, another trail leads inland past Triangle Lake and the many swamp creatures found there.

Sasquatch Provincial Park (Map 14/G7–15/A7)

Sasquatch Provincial Park is located north of Harrison Hot Springs, close to Harrison Lake. There are over 175 campsites available in three popular campgrounds around Hicks and Deer Lakes. There are also day-use areas around these lakes and at Green Point on Harrison Lake. Amenities range from boat launches and a sani-dump to a playground and interpretive program in summer. Hicks and Deer Lakes are ideal for small motorboats and canoeing while Trout Lake provides a more tranquil fishing experience. Reservations are recommended for camping and a daily parking fee applies.

Sechelt Inlets Provincial Park (Map 9, 10, 20)

This park is actually made up of nine different marine access sites scattered throughout Sechelt, Salmon and Narrows Inlets. From south to north to east the sites are: Piper Point, Tuwanek Point, Oyster Bay, Skaiakos Point, Nine Mile Point, Halfway Islet, Kunechin Point, Thornhill and Tzoonie Narrows. The inlets are a popular sea kayaking destination and the HMCS Chaudiere was sunk off Kunechin Point to create a wonderful artificial reef for scuba divers. All of the sites, with the exception of Skaiakos, have some development such as tent pads.

Seton Portage Historic Park (Map 43/D7)

Now site of Seton Portage Tourist Information Centre, this site commemorates the location of the first railway in British Columbia. The info centre is housed in an old railway caboose. No facilities are provided.

Shannon Falls Provincial Park (Map 22/C7)

Shannon Falls are the third highest falls in the province, at 335 metres (1,089 feet) and are truly an amazing site as they cascade down a steep mountainside. The park offers a small day-use area that allows highway travellers a place to picnic beneath the falls. Many people also explore the trails that lead up and behind Shannon Falls or to the top of nearby Stawamus Chief. Climbers, looking to get to the top of The Chief by a slightly more direct route, also use the park. A daily parking fee applies.

Shelter Point Regional Park (Map 8/A1)

On Texada Island, this regional park is easily accessed south of Gillies Bay, about 27 km from the Blubber Bay ferry terminal. The campsite has been expanded to 47 sites, offering showers, a spectacular beach and wonderful views. A scenic 2 km trail leads along the ocean through some large wind-swept Douglas-fir.

Silver Lake Provincial Park (Map 5/F1; 15/F7)

Situated in the scenic Fraser Valley, just down the Silver Skagit Road, Silver Lake Provincial Park is a small, largely undeveloped lakefront area 12 km southwest of Hope. There is a gravel boat launch and plenty of scenic beauty. This area is renowned for its fly-fishing. There is a 50 unit campground next to the lake.

Simson Provincial Park (Map 9/B4)

South Thormanby Island is a fairly dry island with a rocky shore and number of small bays. Rising above the ocean is Spyglass Hill. This park is accessed by small boat or kayak, as there are no docking facilities. A trail traverses the island starting at Farm Bay, on the southeast corner of the island.

Skagit Valley Provincial Park (Map 6/D3–F7)

This newly defined park is part of a larger protected area complex that includes the US North Cascades National Park and the Ross Lake and Lake Chelan National Recreation Areas. This is a large protected area, at 32,577 hectares, in a valley that was carved by glaciers. The valley is an excellent outdoor recreation destination with 50 km (30 miles) of trails, great fishing and 142 campsites (between the Silvertip and Ross Lake Campgrounds and the less known Whitworth Meadows Horse Camp). Ross Lake is the biggest with 88 sites, a boat launch, separate day-use area and playground and is open the longest from early May to mid October. Visitors should note that drawn down on the lake outside of July and August (call 1-604-869-7080 for water level information) can create lake access issues. There is also backcountry camping throughout the area, including more developed sites at Delacey Camp, Large Cedar Camp and Galene Lakes.

Skihist Provincial Park (Map 33/D2)

Just northeast of Lytton on Highway 1, this 33 hectare park is mainly used as a stopover for travellers on Highway 1 or by folks heading out rafting on the Thompson. It has 56 campgrounds and full facilities for camping and picnicking. The park is located well above the highway and railway tracks in a dry ponderosa pine forest. A loop trail leads to the bench above the campsite and offers fine views of the canyon or even mountain goats and elk in the surrounding hills.

Skookumchuck Narrows Provincial Park (Map 20/D6)

Skookumchuck Narrows are an impressive site during tide changes. The water is so constricted that standing waves up to 2 metres (6 feet) high and currents up to 30 km per hour are the result. Several unwary vessels have been lost in the whirlpools, yet you often see extreme kayakers surfing the waves. This 123 hectare park is found south of Egmont along an easy 4 km one-way trail. The best viewing times are one hour before or after the tide change.

Smuggler's Cove Provincial Park (Map 9/C4)

The name of the cove comes from rumrunners, who in days gone by used this bay as a staging area for trips down into the US. You can still visit the area by boat or kayak but many people come overland, which requires a 1.3 km hike from Brooks Road to the ocean. Along the forested shoreline, you will find five tent pads and a hiking trail along the shoreline.

Soames Hill Regional Park (Map 10/D6)

This day-use park is found northeast of Gibsons. To get here, take North Road towards the Langdale Ferry Terminal. Turn right onto Chaberlin Road and then onto Bridgeman Road. It is not a huge park, but there are about 4.2 km of trails around and to the top of the titular feature. There are three viewpoints from the top.

South Texada Island Provincial Park (Map 8/F3)

Essentially a boat access park, the shoreline is steep and rocky with few places boaters can land. Visitors can enjoy the fine hiking, kayaking and fishing in the area. A separate parcel of the park is located at Anderson Bay, on the island's southeastern shore. Anderson Bay is a much more protected anchorage for boats.

Sprockids Regional Park (Map 10/D5)

This park is a popular mountain biking destination; indeed, it was set aside specifically for mountain biking, although hikers will sometimes be seen on the more outlying trails. The park has over 14 km of trails, some featuring jumps, teeterbars and ramps.

Spruce Lake Protected Area [South Chilcotin Park] (Map 40/G1–42/B2)

The Spruce Lake area is hiking heaven. It's also biking, horse packing and fishing heaven. There are 164 km (100 miles) of wilderness trails in the area, which traverse gentle mountain passes and meander through lush alpine grasslands and flowers to destination trout lakes. The park was finally designated in the late 1990s after nearly 60 years of debate and lobbying. There are campsites at the north and south ends of Spruce Lake, Hummingbird Lake, Trigger Lake, Jewel Bridge and Gun Creek Grassland. The main access points into the area are the Gun Creek Road, Mud Creek-Taylor Creek Forest Road and the Slim Creek Forest Road. Or if you prefer, you can always charter a floatplane into Spruce Lake itself. The area is still at the centre of controversy. In 2004, the park boundaries were reduced about 20% from 72,000 hectares to 56,540 hectares, to open up areas for mining exploration. There is a proposal to see the area combined with a number of other parks in the area to create a National Park.

Squitty Bay Provincial Park (Map 8/F5)

Located at the southeast end of Lasquiti Island, this small park protects a sheltered anchorage. The entrance to the bay is a little tricky and the small dock is often occupied as the destination is quite popular.

Sunnyside Acres Urban Forest (Map 2/B6)

Found off 24th Avenue near Softball City in south Surrey, this 130 hectare urban forest is being managed for its intrinsic values. Home to a wealth of animal and plant life visitors can see birds, coyotes and black-tailed deer or even the rare orchid and rattlesnake-plantain. To the north, there are about 4 km of trails to explore, while the nearby Semiahmoo Trail to the northeast can also be explored.

Stanley Park (Map 1/C1)

Stanley Park is the life and love of the city of Vancouver whose reputation is built on the beauty of its natural surroundings. Stanley Park is wilderness light, an introduction to some of the magic of nature without ever having to leave the city. With many developed areas like Lost Lagoon, the Aquarium, the Zoo, the totem poles... it is easy to forget that there are still fragments of the wilderness here. It is impossible to name all the recreational activities–from roller blading the Sea Wall to playing pitch and putt to relaxing on one of the beaches to hiking the trails on the west side of the park, to splashing in the kids water park, to watching the marine life in the Aquarium. Stanley Park is one of the great urban parks in North America and, despite its' popularity on a sunny summer Saturday, it is still a wonderful and worthwhile place to visit.

Stawamus Chief Provincial Park (Map 22/C7)

The Chief is Canada's rock climbing mecca. After years of climbers sleeping in their VW Vans in the parking lot, BC parks finally developed an actual campground at the base of The Chief. There are 15 vehicle access sites and 47 walk-in sites open from May to mid October. There are trails in the park, leading up and around the backside of the large granite monolith.

Stein Valley Nlaka'pamux Heritage Park (Map 31, 32, 33, 38)

The Stein Valley area has for centuries had a very special and spiritual meaning to the aboriginal people in this region. This is clearly shown by the many unique pictographs and petroglyphs on the rock faces of the valley. As a result, the valley is protected and the provincial government and the Lytton Indian Band jointly manage the park. It is a spectacular 107,191 hectare wilderness park, with 150 km (92 miles) of hiking trails, cable crossings, cabins and established backcountry campsites. Although a day hike is possible, most people who visit the area spend a few days. The Stein River is a hardcore white water rafting/ kayaking river. These folks hike in from the west side (off Horlick Creek Road) and arrange for a shuttle on the other side.

Sumas Mountain Regional Park (Map 3/G5–4/A5)

Sumas Mountain is the monolith that dominates the eastern part of the Fraser Valley. The park covers 1,445 hectares and is best known for its hiking trails leading to the viewpoint overlooking Chilliwack and the eastern Fraser Valley. Fishing and swimming is possible in tiny Chadsey Lake, while biking and wildlife viewing are also popular. The main access is off Batt Road. Although a service road that is used by ATV's and bikers climbs to near the summit, the hiking trails are separate.

Surrey Bend Regional Park (Map 2/C3)

This park, jointly owned by the City of Surry and the Metro Vancouver Regional District, captures a unique section of relatively untouched, flood plains on the Fraser River. There are a few trails here, used mostly by anglers to access the river. Across the waters of Parsons Channel, on Barnston Island, is the Roberts Point Rest Area, which has washrooms and a picnic area. Cyclists often cycle counter clockwise around the island road, stopping at the scenic point for a picnic lunch. From the ferry to Roberts Point is 2 km if you head west and 8 km if you head east (counter clockwise).

Tantalus Provincial Park (Map 21/F3–22/B5)

Built around the former Lake Lovely Water Recreation Area, this elaborate 11,351 hectare park now includes the Tantalus Range, a popular mountaineering area. Hikers and backcountry skiers frequent the area and the Alpine Club of Canada Cabin, which can be reserved for a fee, makes the stay that much more enjoyable. Ambitious anglers will also be rewarded with good fishing in a spectacular setting. The new Este-Tiwilh/Sigurd Creek Conservancy to the north protects the creek and the many wild animals (goats, grizzlies, bald eagles and salmon) that can be seen there on occasion.

Teakerne Arm Provincial Park (Map 46/A3)

A popular place for boating, kayaking, fishing and camping, Teakerne Arm is home to a 30 m (95 foot) high waterfall that plunges straight out of Cassel Lake and into the ocean. There is a short hiking trail up to the lake.

Tetrahedron Provincial Park (Map 10/C2)

At 6,000 hectares, Tetrahedron is the largest provincial park on the Sunshine Coast. It features some dramatic terrain that includes Tetrahedron Peak, Panther Peak and Mount Steele and an extensive trail network that leads to the peaks and some terrific backcountry huts. The area also makes a great rock climbing or backcountry skiing destination.

Thacker Regional Park (Map 15/F6)

Found in Hope, this 9 hectare park is home to a new spawning channel, built in 2001 for Coho, pink and chum salmon. The trail along the channel is park of the Trans Canada Trail and is very popular in fall when the salmon spawn. In summer, there is a popular swimming hole at the confluence of Sucker Creek and the Coquihalla River.

Thompson Regional Park (Map 4/E6)

Established in 2004, this park provides interpretive panels and maps of the area. It is found 6 km from the Vedder Bridge on Chilliwack River Road. There is a short loop trail around a salmon restoration project.

Ts'yl-os Provincial Park (Map 40/B1; 49/E1)

Better covered in our Cariboo Chilcotin Coast mapbook, Ts'yl-os (pronounced "sigh-loss") Park encompasses rugged mountains, clear blue lakes, glaciers, alpine meadows and waterfalls. It is bordered by the rugged peaks of the Coast Mountains to the west and the dry Interior Plateau to the east. The heart of the park is the turquoise-coloured Chilko Lake, which is found north of our maps.

Tynehead Regional Park (Map 2/C4)

Located just off Highway 1, Tynehead is a 260 hectare park in the centre of North Surrey. The park contains the headwaters for the Serpentine River and is a popular place to watch salmon spawning in fall. The park is also home to the unique Butterfly Garden. They have grown plants here that attract butterflies and have even provided viewing platforms.

Upper Elaho Valley Conservancy (Map 34/B4)

This new conservancy protects the headwaters of the Elaho River not far from the Stoltmann Wilderness Trail. The river has carved a canyon 80 metres deep, with sheer volcanic rock cliffs rising on either side. The conservancy protects areas of importance for local First Nations, but also attracts grizzly bear from Fiordland and even as far north as Tweedsmuir Park. After spawning in Kimsquit Lake, adult sockeye salmon carcasses are often frozen in the lake. In the spring when the lake thaws, the salmon carcasses are released, providing an important protein source for the roaming grizzlies. The area is also home to deer, mountain goat and even moose, one of the few coastal drainages that have moose.

Upper Lillooet Provincial Park (Map 40/B7; 49/G5)

This remote 19,996 hectare park is not accessible by road or trail. The few visitors that do explore this area usually access base camps in the alpine portions of the park via helicopter. The park was developed to protect the old-growth forests, wetlands and high alpine ridges and glaciers around Lillooet River. Salmon spawn in the many tributaries and wildlife such as black-tailed deer, moose, grizzly and black bears, mountain goat and wolverine are abundant.

Upper Rogers Kolii7 Conservancy (Map 31/E5)

Protecting an area that is important to the in-SHUCK-ch First Nation, this conservancy also protects overwintering habitat for mountain goats, grizzly and wolverine. The name Kolii7 is a reference to the area's meadows, with the connotations of a verdant landscape.

Upper Soo Conservancy (Map 29/C2)

Originally named "Sea to Sky Conservancy (II)", this area has been renamed to reflect the fact that it protects the upper reaches of the Soo drainage. The conservancy protects an old-growth ecosystem, as well as important habitat for grizzly bear.

Walch Cove Provincial Park (Map 46/A3)

A popular place for boating, kayaking, fishing and diving, visitors to Walsh Cove can see pictographs on the rock faces in the area. There are no developed trails, but people can hike up and down the shoreline.

Welcome Woods Wilderness Regional Park (Map 9/C4)

This park is a destination for hikers and mountain bikers and the trails here connect up with other hiking and mountain biking trails in the Halfmoon Bay area. The park is accessed from Fullerton Road.

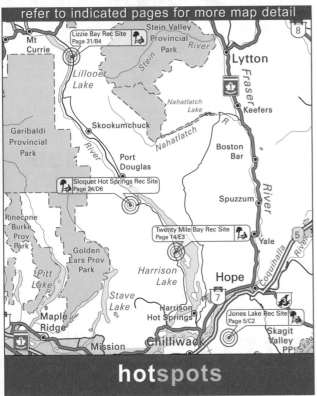

refer to indicated pages for more map detail

Mt Currie
Lizzie Bay Rec Site Page 31/B4
Stein Valley Provincial Park
Stein River
8
Lytton
Lillooet Lake
Nahatlatch Lake
Keefers
Skookumchuck
Nahatlatch
Fraser R
Garibaldi Provincial Park
Port Douglas
Boston Bar
River
Sloquet Hot Springs Rec Site Page 24/D6
Spuzzum
Rinecone Burke Prov Park
Twenty Mile Bay Rec Site Page 14/E3
Yale
5
Golden Ears Prov Park
Coquihalla River
Pitt Lake
Harrison Lake
Hope
Stave Lake
7
Harrison Hot Springs
Jones Lake Rec Site Page 5/C2
Maple Ridge
Skagit Valley PP
Mission
Chilliwack

hotspots

While it is true that you can erect a tent most anywhere that suits your fancy on public land, many of the best sites have already been discovered and at least partially developed. While provincial parks capture the lion's share of attention, there is a host of sites that were originally developed by forestry workers who wanted to be able to access a good fishing lake or interesting hiking trail on their days off.

These days, they are looked after by the Ministry of Tourism, Culture and the Arts, although local recreation groups, forest companies, First Nations or private contractors often maintain the sites. Some of these sites have been developed to rival provincial parks. These enhanced sites do charge a nightly fee (usually around $10/night) and are gated in the off season, which is typically from October to May. In other cases, user groups will look after a site simply because they have a vested interest in keeping the site open and do not charge any fees.

Recreation Sites offer a nice balance between the developed but often crowded provincial park system and a completely undeveloped patch of Crown land. The sites are usually small and rustic, but offer access to some great fishing lakes, paddling routes and scenery that make British Columbia such a beautiful place to explore. Unlike parks, recreation sites are located on Crown land, not inside a protected area, that has been developed to provide recreational opportunities in a forest setting. A site found on the shores of the lake does not usually encompass the lake itself; it merely provides access to that lake. Access to some of the sites can be rough, often leading down active logging roads. Although the remote nature of these sites can be appealing, due take care travelling the backroads and ensure you take necessary precautions.

Most recreation sites have a camping area, although some are day-use only. They usually have toilets and at least one or two picnic tables. Larger sites have trails, firewood and even a caretaker for on-site supervision and maintenance. There is no reservation system and camping is entirely on a first-come, first-served basis.

The majority of these sites are user maintained, where users are responsible for collecting their trash, getting their own firewood and even providing their own toilet paper. Please help keep our province beautiful and pack out any garbage you bring in or that was left by inconsiderate visitors. For current conditions and access details, visit www.sitesandtrailsbc.ca.

Alexander Falls Recreation Site (Map 29/C5)
This is a small, quiet picnic site overlooking the picturesque Alexander Falls. This site is accessed 8 km down the Callaghan Valley Road, which is now paved. The wheelchair accessible site has 3 picnic tables.

Allison Pool Recreation Site (Map 4/F6)
Set in a pretty second growth forest next to the Chilliwack River, this 8 unit campsite is accessed by a short gravel road off the Chilliwack Lake Road and is not suitable for RVs. The area is a popular spot for salmon and steelhead fishing and provides access to the Trans Canada Trail.

Apocynum Recreation Site (Map 33/C7)
Recently upgraded and upsized, this popular site, found 16.5 km along the Nahatlatch River Forest Road, has space for 16 groups and is RV accessible. Whitewater paddling, fishing, hiking and hunting are popular pastimes in the area.

Appleton Creek Recreation Site (Map 18/E2)
A trail access site set in an old growth Douglas fir stand, there is space for about 3 tenters here. In addition to a unique bridge crossing, there is a network of hiking trails leading to Sliammon Lake and Okeover Inlet that can be accessed from here.

Bear Creek Recreation Site (Map 14/G5)
Tucked in a nook created by the Harrison East Forest Road, Harrison Lake and Bear Creek, visitors will find 25 quiet, shady campsites set into a second growth forest. It is a short hike to nearby Bear Falls and the site is popular with windsurfers. Although is open for the October and April long weekends, the site is gated after the Labour Day long weekend until May 1.

Beaver Lake Recreation Sites (Map 19/D2)
A few canoe access sites are found on Beaver Lake and the portage leading to Dodd Lake. The north site is one of the nicest campsites on the Powell Forest Canoe Route with plenty of space to spread out and rarely anyone else around. The southern site is behind the logjam at the lower end of Beaver Lake and has enough space for 1 group to set up. There is also a seldom used site to the southeast the few people carry their canoes up to.

Big Tree Recreation Site (Map 9/D4)
This picnic site is found at the end of a short, wheelchair accessible trail. The site is located below a number of large old growth trees about 2 km down the Crowston Lake Forest Road.

Blackwater Lake Recreation Site (Map 36/F3)
On the road to Birkenhead Lake, this small site is accessed off of a good gravel road, but RVs are not recommended. It is a user maintained site with a hand launch for boats.

Bob's Lake Recreation Site (Map 8/D2)
A small, treed site used mainly by anglers, hunters and 4wd drive enthusiasts on Texada Island. The recreation site is accessible off Hydro Reactor Road. Please stay on the trails in the area and try not to damage the flora, especially a rare species of orchid found here.

Botanie Lake Recreation Site (Map 39/D6)
This small, semi-open recreation site is located next to Botanie Lake off the Botanie Valley Road. The access to the lake is good enough so allow small RVs to reach the site. Please note that the lake is on an Indian Reserve and so access may be restricted.

Brohm Lake Recreation Site (Map 22/C4)
This is a popular day-use site that is found just off Highway 99 north of Squamish. In addition to the extensive trail system, there is a place to hand launch small boats. It is a short walk to the lake, where you can swim, fish or picnic.

Cabin Lake Recreation Site (Map 27/B1)
This is a small, 4 unit site located by rough 4wd/ATV road. Hikers accessing the Heather Basin Trail frequent the area.

Cal-Cheak Confluence Recreation Site (Map 29/D6)
This is a popular trio of enhanced, heavily used recreation sites, near the confluence of Callaghan Creek and the Cheakamus River. There are 55 campsites divided between the three sites, some of which are walk-in (tenting) only, some of which are big enough for RVs. At the south site, a suspension bridge leads across Callaghan Creek and down to the Brandywine Falls.

Camp Foley Recreation Site (Map 5/B5)
This small site is found along the banks of the Chilliwack River, 26.5 km along the Chilliwack Lake Road. The 4 unit campsite is popular for small family groups by reservation only. The access road is paved, but not suitable for larger vehicles like RVs.

Carol Lake Recreation Site (Map 43/A3)
Carol Lake is a small, popular fishing lake, just above Carpenter Lake. This site is a great place for a picnic and there are 9 campsites, which have enough room for RVs. There is a cartop boat launch or if you prefer, there is an extensive trail network to the northwest.

Carpenter Lake Recreation Site (Map 43/E5)
Located along the south shores of Carpenter Lake, this is a small site on a big man-made lake. Noted more as a boat launch than camping area, picnicking is popular here too. The site is RV friendly.

Cascade Peninsula Recreation Site (Map 14/G5)
This medium sized forested site is found on the shores of Harrison Lake in a sheltered bay. The site is popular with boaters, anglers and hikers. To get to this site, turn left at the 11 km mark of the East Harrison Forest Service Road and follow the signs.

Cat Lake Recreation Site (Map 22/D5)
Cat Lake Road is found down a narrow, winding road north of Alice Lake Provincial Park. The 36 campsites here are all walk-in tenting sites, but they are often busy and a fee is charged to camp here. There is an extensive network of biking and hiking trails, as well as decent fishing in the small lake.

Chehalis Lake Recreation Sites (Map 14/B5)
In December of 2007, Chehalis Lake was hit by a major landslide, which in turn created a wave about 15 m (50 feet) high, impacting all three rec sites on the lake. As a result of the slide, the road to the lake is closed indefinitely, as are the campsites.

Chehalis River Recreation Sites (Map 4/D1)
There are actually three separate RV accessible sites on the banks of the Chehalis, one on the left side of the road, one on the right before crossing the single lane bridge over the river. The third site is on the far side of the bridge, to your left (to your right is private property). Between the three, there are about 65 sites, set in an open forest. From the campsite on the north side of the river, a trail runs up the hill and then follows the edge of a spectacular canyon. There is a nice swimming hole and good access to good river fishing along this trail.

Chipmunk Peninsula Recreation Site (Map 5/B5)
Set in a coniferous forest next to the Chilliwack River, on the Chilliwack Bench Forest Road, visitors will find 21 campsites. There is good access to the river and the site is popular with ATVers and motorcycles riding the local trails.

Cinnamon Creek Recreation Site (Map 37/G1)
There are 11 campsites in this recreation site, located next to the rushing Cayoosh Creek that drowns out the infrequent traffic on the Duffey Lake Road (Hwy 99). There are a number of nice spots right on the banks of the creek in this semi-open RV friendly site.

Cogburn Beach Recreation Site (Map 14/G4)
This long, open stretch of beach is a popular weekend getaway despite (or because of) the trail access. This is the northern most recreation site on the east side of Harrison and the closest one to Clear Creek Hot Springs. There is space for about 25 groups here.

Cottonwood Creek Recreation Site (Map 38/A2)
This site is located along Cayoosh Creek and the Duffey Lake Road has well-spaced campsites giving campers a fair degree of privacy. There are 14 sites that provide good access to the creek and also make a nice picnic site.

Dinner Rock Recreation Site (Map 18/C1)
Located just off Highway 101, down a steep, but paved access road, the Dinner Rock Recreation Site is a 12 unit, semi-open site located on the ocean. There is good salmon fishing in the area, a cartop boat launch and even a popular scuba diving area. This area is wheelchair accessible and makes a fine picnic destination.

Dodd Lake Recreation Sites (Map 19/C1)
The 12 unit site on the shores of Dodd Lake is often busy. Powell Forest canoeists might want to give this one a miss in favour of the Beaver Lake Recreation Site (see above). Wise boaters would head for the other site, less than a kilometre away, to get away from the (usually party) crowds here.

Driftwood Bay Recreation Site (Map 31/A3)
There are ten enhanced tent sites on Driftwood Bay, which are often taken up by large parties. The site is found at km 17 on the In-Shuck-Ch Forest Road, on a driftwood filled beach near the middle of Lillooet Lake.

East Lake Recreation Site (Map 19/A4)
Mainly a day-use site, this is a scenic site found about 4 km down the Duck Lake Forest Road. A short trail leads to the lake where a good chance of seeing waterfowl and other wildlife is possible.

Eaton Creek Recreation Site (Map 5/G2)
A small 3 unit site found 16.5 km down the Silver Skagit Road, this site is mainly used by people wishing to hike to nearby Eaton Lake. Two of the sites are set in the forest next to the creek.

Fir Flats Recreation Site (Map 33/C7)
This 6 unit site is located along the Nahatlatch River, 18 km up the Nahatlatch Forest Road. The site is popular with people hiking and fishing in` the area.

Francis Lake Recreation Site (Map 14/E7)
Francis Lake is a small lake and this is an even smaller 4 unit recreation site. The turn-off to the site is located at the 6.5 km mark of the West Harrison Forest Road. From here it is 3 km along a 4wd drive only road to the popular fishing lake.

Friburg Recreation Site (Map 42/C2)
Friburg is found on the western shore of the picturesque Tyaughton Lake. Natives named the lake Tyaughton or 'jumping fish' due to the incredible aerial display the trout in this lake like to perform. The recreation site has room for about 5 campsites along with a cartop boat launch. This is an open site, with space enough to park an RV or two.

Garrison Lakes Recreation Site (Map 7/E3)
Found north of Manning Park off the Sunday Summit Forest Road, a short 2km trail leads to the lakes. The site is mainly used by anglers.

Gillis Lake West Recreation Site (Map 27/G2)
The Murray Lake Road to the west of Kingsvale accesses this site on the western side of the lake. Visitors will find 4 treed sites as well as a boat launch for anglers testing their luck.

Goat Lake Recreation Site (Map 46/G6)
After carrying your canoe down the long portage from Windsor Lake to the south, the Goat Lake Recreation Site is a sight for sore eyes (and shoulders, and back, and legs…). It is one of the prettier spots on the Powell Forest Canoe Route and Goat Lake is much calmer and less travelled than Powell Lake itself.

Gott Creek Recreation Site (Map 37/G3)
This is one of the series of easy access recreation sites found next to the Duffey Lake Road. The small site has 3 picnic tables that appeal more to the day-tripper than campers.

Grace Lake Recreation Site (Map 14/E7)
This is a 3 unit recreation site on the rocky outcrops next to Grace Lake and the busy Harrison West Forest Road. Grace Lake is a good fishing lake with a short trail that skirts the edge of the lake.

Gun Creek Campground (Map 42/C4)
This 16 unit campsite is located on the Carpenter Reservoir, where Gun Creek flows in. There is good fishing in the area and, at low water, you can explore the old town of Minto, which was flooded in 1954. The RV accessible site is operated by BC Hydro.

Gun Lake South Recreation Site (Map 42/A4)
Gun Lake is a popular destination lake found just north of Gold Bridge. This site is easily accessible, with 8 campsites and enough open area to park an RV. There is a boat launch a few kilometres south, near the Lajoie Dam.

Gwyneth Lake Recreation Site (Map 42/A5)
Located at the north end of Gwyneth Lake, just off the infamous Hurley River Road, this user-maintained site has space for 6 groups. There is a cartop boat launch onto the relatively small, marshy lake. This is a good fishing lake and the site sees a lot of use from anglers. There are some great mountain views here.

Hale Creek Recreation Site (Map 14/E4)
This is a secluded site just above Harrison Lake, used mostly by boaters on the lake. However, it is possible to navigate a 4wd drive down to the site. There are 5 partially treed campsites and a large sandy beach.

Hayward Lake Reservoir Recreation Sites (Map 3/C3)
Two different BC Hydro recreation sites are found on this popular recreational lake. The Hayward Lake site is found at the north end, while the Ruskin Dam site is found at the south end. Both sites offer day-use areas as well as boat launches. Hayward Lake is a popular recreation. There is also a boat launch and campground on nearby Stave Lake.

Hope Creek Recreation Site (Map 41/F7)
This small site is used mostly as a resting stop in summer for backroad enthusiasts as well as hunters later in the fall. The Hope Creek site offers one campsite site and picnic table and is located about 1 km off the scenic Hurley River Road.

Horseshoe Lake Recreation Site (Map 19/D3)
Accessed by portage from Lois Lake (or the 10 km mark of Stillwater Main), there is space for about 4 tenters here. Enjoy the Powell Forest Canoe Route or simply fish and beetle about Horseshoe Lake.

Ireland Lake Recreation Site (Map 19/C2)
This is a tiny, one unit site at the north end of Ireland Lake on the Powell Forest Canoe Route. The site is more functional than pretty; the dock on Ireland Lake itself is an amazing place to watch a sunset, but the actual site is tucked back into the enclosed forest and showing signs of abuse.

Jacobson Lake Recreation Site (Map 16/F7)
Found well down the Tulameen River Forest Road, this small 6 unit site is not accessible to hunters in the fall. There is a horse corral and the site acts as the trailhead for the "Treasures of the Tulameen" complete with information kiosk and map.

Jones Lake Recreational Site (Map 5/C2)
Jones Lake is a BC Hydro maintained site located on the shores of Jones (Wahleach) Lake. There are two camping areas on either side of the Wahleach Dam—Jones Lake Main and Jones Lake West—with a total of 55 sites, most of which are big enough for RVs. However, it is not recommended to bring big units up the steep, rough road into the lake. There are launches for cartop boats.

Kenyon Lake Recreation Site (Map 13/E6)
The open again, closed again recreation site at Kenyon Lake is open again, with 1 site accessible by 4wd vehicles only. There is also a small island with a site suitable for overnight camping. Anglers should note the sub-alpine lake is reported barren.

Khartoum Lake Recreation Site (Map 19/G3)
Khartoum Lake Recreation Site is a 9 unit site found down a good 2wd road, although access is controlled. The treed site is also accessible by canoe from Lois Lake, but few visitors to the Powell Forest Canoe Route venture this far out of the way.

Kingdom Lake Recreation Site (Map 42/B5)
Found off the Kingdom Lake Forest Road on the way to Bralorne, this is a treed, lakeside site with nice mountain views. There are 15 campsites at the user-maintained site and a cartop boat launch onto the good fishing lake. There are also trails to nearby Lost Lake and Noel Lake.

Klein Lake Recreation Site (Map 20/B6)
Accessed off the North Lake Forest Road near Earls Cover, this 23 unit site is set in the trees on the northern end of Klein Lake. The campsites are spread out so even on a busy summer weekend you will have at least some privacy. This access is a little rough but this does not deter trailers. There is a floating dock and the lake makes a nice fishing or canoeing destination.

Kwotlenemo [Fountain] Lake Recreation Sites (Map 44/E6)
In all there are four different sites to choose from on Kwotlenemo Lake. The popular lake is also known as Fountain Lake and is the northern most lake of the scenic Three Lake Valley. Visitors will find good road access into the area and should note that the lake is only open to boats with electric motors. The southern site is the largest of the bunch sporting 17 campsites, while the northern site hosts 5 sites and a cartop boat launch. The east and west sites are smaller sites situated in the trees.

Lake La Mare Recreation Site (Map 43/D2)
Lake La Mare is a popular fishing lake. Hikers, horseback riders and ATVers have the option of continuing on a trail to Buckholder Lake or along the Hog Creek Trail to Carol Lake. Campers will find room for about 3 units with a small cartop boat launch at Lake La Mare.

Lang Creek Recreation Site (Map 19/A4)
Accessed off the Lang Creek Trail, this picnic area is located across from the salmon hatchery. This is a great place to watch salmon spawning in September and October. Access to this site is along the Lang Creek Trail.

Lewis Lake Recreation Site (Map 19/C1)
A 4 unit site is available for visitors wishing to explore Lewis Lake or nearby Tin Hat Mountain. The access into the area is rough and best left for 4wd clearance vehicles.

Lightning Lake Recreation Site (Map 27/C1)
This campsite is found in a heavily forested area next to a small mountain lake. There is room for about 3 units. A 4wd vehicle is required to access the lake, which is a popular trail riding and snowmobiling area too.

Little Horseshoe Lake Recreation Site (Map 19/D2)
This small, 1 or 2 unit site is located on Little Horseshoe Lake on the Powell Forest Canoe Route. Access is by canoe. There is a floating dock to enjoy.

Lizzie Bay Recreation Site (Map 31/B4)
At km 15.5 on the In-Shuck-Ch Forest Road, this is probably the nicest site on Lillooet Lake. The access road is a bit rough so RVs probably want to avoid it. There are 15 enhanced sites here, spread out along next to the beach but tucked back into the forest enough to create a sense of complete privacy.

Lodestone Creek Recreation Site (Map 17/B4)
Lodestone Lake is located on a 4wd road south of Tulameen. Used by fishermen and as a stopover for hikers or horseback riders on the Hope Brigade Trail, there are 2 sites located in a semi-open forest.

Log Creek Recreation Site (Map 33/B7)
A small recreation site is situated at the Log Creek/Nahatlatch River confluence, about 23.5 km up the forest road. There is space for 6 groups.

Lois Lake Recreation Site (Map 19/E4)
The starting point of the Powell Forest Canoe Route, this recreation site is used more by RV's and cartop campers than by canoeists. No wonder. The site isn't all that pretty, especially compared to other sites, just a short paddle/portage away. There are 12 well used campsites here, most of which are in an open area near the shore, along with 4 walk-in sites.

Lois Point Recreation Site (Map 19/D4)
Developed to address the issue of Powell Forest canoeists not wanting to share a site with vehicle campers, this site has space for 4 tents. The site is a short 2 km paddle or walk along the southeast shore of Lois Lake from the start of the canoe route.

Long Island Bay Recreation Site (Map 14/F4)
A small tenting area on Long Island, this is a popular spot for boaters making their way down Harrison Lake. The sites are secluded and there is moorage, a beach and dock as well as a barbecue shack.

Lookout Lake Recreation Site (Map 14/E3)
Located at the junction of the West Harrison and the Mystery Creek Forest Road, there is only space for 1 group at this small site. The 4wd access limits visitors here.

Madely Lake Recreation Site (Map 29/C3)
You will have to walk in about 500 metres to get to this beautiful mountain lake. That is if you can negotiate the 16 km of rough road into the lake. The road does deter some, but the site still remains a popular getaway in summer. In addition to a chance to pitch your tent on the beach there is good fishing on the lake and a trail leading up to the Rainbow Lake area. The site is destined to become a part of the Whistler Sport Legacy.

Marshall Creek Recreation Site (Map 42/F2)
Located just below where Marshall Creek flows out of Marshall Lake, this is a small, treed site, with space enough for 3 groups. There is a cartop boat launch at the site that has good road access.

Marshall Lake North Recreation Site (Map 42/F2)
This is a fairly open site on the northeastern shores of Marshall Lake. There are 7 campsites split between 2 sites for anglers and people who are looking for a nice place to camp. Trail enthusiasts will be amazed at the number of trails to choose from in the area.

Middlepoint Recreation Site (Map 19/C2)
An open site carved out of the forest about halfway along the portage trail between Nanton and Ireland Lakes on the Powell Forest Canoe Route. Accessed only by foot (usually by people with a canoe on their back), this site is a great place to stop for an evening, with space enough for 2 tents.

Mission Dam Recreation Site (Map 43/E5)
This 3 unit site is located on the easternmost reaches of Carpenter Lake. The Terzaghi Dam is certainly an impressive sight but the busy Carpenter Lake Road detracts from the peaceful nature of the area. The site is open, with space for RVs and offers a dock for boaters.

Molson Memorial Recreation Site (Map 28/C4)
This small and rustic site is situated beside the Peaches and Cream Falls on Ponor Creek. Found off G Main from Elaho Main, the remote site has one table and stairs to the waterfall viewing area.

Mosquito Lake Recreation Site (Map 36/C7)
This small, forested day-use only site receives heavy use, especially by anglers. The road is rutted and muddy but water enthusiasts will brave the conditions to enjoy a day at the beach. The lake also makes a refreshing stop over for mountain bikers and hikers enjoying the nearby trail system.

Mowson Pond Recreation Site (Map 42/C2)
The Tyaughton Lake Fire in 2009 played havoc with the area and Mowson and nearby Pearson Pond received the brunt of the abuse. The once scenic lake is half its original size and the burned trees create an eerie setting for would be campers. That said; there is space for 6 groups, a boat launch and good road access for RV's.

Murphy Lakes West Recreation Site (Map 17/A3)
There is a recreation site on the western Murphy Lake (a second site, on the East Lake, has been decommissioned) that offers space for 5 campers and a cartop boat launch. The lake offers fishing, while trail enthusiasts and hunters can explore the surrounding area.

Murray Creek Recreation Site (Map 39/D4)
Located on the Murray Creek Forest Road, this is a small 4 unit semi-open site, which requires a 4wd to reach. The recreation site is next to Murray Creek and is used primarily by hunters in the fall, although the nearby Onion Lake/Monkey Wrench Riding Area does attract dirt bikers in the summer.

Murray Lake Recreation Sites (Map 27/F4)
There are two campgrounds found on Murray Lake, which, in turn, is found on the deteriorating Murray Lake Road north of Exit 240 of the Coquihalla Highway. In total there are 13 campsites on the scenic lake, 10 at the north and 3 at the south, with the primary users being anglers and hunters.

Nahatlatch River Recreation Site (Map 33/B7)
This is a 6 unit site on the south side of the Nahatlatch. Recent enhancements have made this a nice campsite to visit. To get to the site, take the Power Puff Road for 3 km, then turn right and follow that road for 4 km to the site.

Nanton-Ireland North Recreation Site (Map 19/C2)
Located on the shores of Ireland Lake at the end of the 2.4 km portage, this 4 unit site is closed in. The shores of the lake are shrubby, and, although the forest is nice, the other two sites on this portage (Nanton-Ireland South, Middlepoint) on the Powell Forest Canoe Route are nicer.

Nanton Lake Recreation Site (Map 19/C2)
Found on the western shore of Nanton Lake, this recreation site has 16 sites, 2 of which are right on the lake and 13 of which have picnic tables. Visitors come by canoe or vehicle along the Goat Lake Road. The site is suitable for smaller RV's.

North Dodd Lake Recreation Site (Map 46/G6)
Located at the north end of Dodd Lake, well away from the main recreation site at the south end, this is a pretty, site, enclosed in the forest. The site is accessible by canoe or by folks willing to do a bit of bushwhacking to get to this remote-feeling recreation site. There is space for 2 tenters and a floating dock.

Owl Creek Recreation Sites (Map 36/C7)
There are two enhanced sites here, one on Owl Creek and the other on the Birkenhead River. The best spot is the one next to Owl Creek, which has 15 well spaced campsites. An old apple orchard and maple trees make this a nice site, but watch for bears in fall. The other site is just a big roadside pullout, with space for about 11 vehicles. These sites are located a few hundred metres off the road to D'Arcy, but don't see much use.

Rainbow Falls Recreation Site (Map 14/G6)
Rainbow Falls Recreation Site is a small boat access site in a protected bay on Harrison Lake formed by Cascade Peninsula. It can also be reached by picking your way down Slollicum Creek. There is space for tenting on the gravel beach, a dock for boaters and a short trail to the beautiful falls.

Riverside Recreation Site (Map 5/C6)
Found 28.7 km along the Chilliwack Lake Road, the site is actually alongside a small tributary of the Chilliwack River. The 11 unit site is suitable for RV's and larger groups. Despite its easy access and nice setting, the road traffic does deter some. The Trans Canada Trail also runs through the area.

Roger Creek Recreation Site (Map 37/F3)
The Roger Creek Recreation Site is actually a pair of small roadside sites, with 11 campsites in total. The northern site has space for 5 campers and is more open, making this a better place for RVs.

Scuzzy Creek Recreation Site (Map 26/D4)
This 9 unit site is found on the banks of Scuzzy Creek. Most 2wd vehicles with enough clearance can make it to this site. Set in a large cottonwood stand, 12.5 km up the forest road, anglers and hunters are the main visitors to the area.

Seton River Recreation Sites (Map 44/C7)
BC Hydro has created a series of lovely recreational sites just southwest of Lillooet off the Duffey Lake Road. The Seton Beach Picnic Site provides picnic tables and a viewing platform to watch the salmon spawn. Seton Dam Campsite is a popular 45 site camping area found near the junction of Cayoosh Creek and the Seton River. Naxwit Picnic Area is a large RV friendly site found 3 km west of Lillooet and is an easy walk from the Seton Dam Campsite.

Shingle Beach Recreation Site (Map 8/C2)
Located right on the ocean, the open grassy site offers a great ocean view. However, it can also get hammered fairly hard by winds and storms. There is good road access off Mouat Bay Road for RVs and the 30 unit site is home to a music festival every July. Boaters also frequent the site, where salmon fishing and scuba diving can be enjoyed.

Silver Lake Recreation Site (Map 27/C1)
Located in a spruce/Lodgepole pine stand next to the lake are 2 campsites and a cartop boat launch. The site is found on a 4wd road west of Spius Creek.

Sloquet Hot Springs Recreation Site (Map 24/D6)
Although very remote, this site attracts all kinds of people due in no small part to the beautiful hot springs below. Thankfully the area has been cleaned up and there is now a nice 7 unit recreation site near the start of the steep trail down to the springs. During the winter, camping is still free, but access can be suspect.

Squamish Riverside Recreation Site (Map 21/G2)
Found close to the Ashlu Creek confluence, this recreation site has recently been upgraded. There are now 10 campsites and a couple new outhouses that are wheelchair accessible. The site is popular with anglers, but is also a destination for swimming, picnicking and kayaking or just hanging out on the beach.

Strawberry Point Recreation Site (Map 30/G2)
This small, enhanced, forested site is found just a few clicks down the In-Shuck-Ch Forest Road. It is a short walk from the parking lot to the beach on Lillooet Lake, where you can set up your tent. This site receives moderate use.

Sunrise Lake Recreation Site (Map 14/E4)
This isolated site is found at the end of a rough 4wd road off the Harrison West Forest Road. Turn left onto access road at the 26 km mark. The BC 4wd association has been maintaining the site for years, which may explain why the road has not been upgraded over the years. In addition to having fun bumping their way in, people will find 4 sites, a cartop boat launch and a nice lake to fish.

Sutter Creek Recreation Site (Map 16/F5)
This site is found on the Tulameen River Forest Road in a quaint little area next to the creek. There are 2 campsites within a fairly open area. Hiking to Treasure Mountain and hunting are popular pastimes.

Tamihi Creek Recreation Site (Map 4/E6)
Set in a large open grassy area ideal for RVs, this is one of the bigger recreation sites in the area. There are 108 sites (depending on how many people want to squeeze into the open area) including some quieter tenting sites in the deciduous forest next to Tamihi Creek. The site is popular with everyone from salmon and steelhead anglers in the fall, to Trans Canada Trail enthusiasts and even ATVers.

Tenquille Lake Recreation Site (Map 34/G3)
A remote, hike in destination, Tenquille Lake is a spectacular backpacking destination. The lake is situated in an alpine meadow with mountains that tower across the lake. The easiest access into the lake is via the 2.5 hour walk from Branch 12, a 4wd road found off the Hurley River Road.

Three Sisters Creek Recreation Site (Map 39/D1)
Located on the Hat Creek Road just north of Oregon Jack Provincial Park, there is a small campsite next to the creek. Visitors to the nearby parks use the campsite, which has 5 sites set in an opening. Alternatively, there are pictographs to explore by following the faint trail at the bend in the road. There is limited access to the site when the area is wet.

Thurston Meadows Recreation Site (Map 4/G6)
Located 3.5 km east of the bridge over the Chilliwack River, Thurston Meadows is another large, open enhanced site that is good for RVs. The site has a

number of day-use picnic sites on the banks of the popular recreational river and space for 50 camping groups. Unlike many of the sites in the Chilliwack Valley, this site is open all year.

Tony Lake Recreation Site (Map 19/C3)
Located off Goat Lake Main, this is a quiet site that sees little use. There is room for 2 units and access to the tiny lake for canoeists.

Twenty Mile Bay Recreation Site (Map 14/E3)
Twenty Mile Bay is an enhanced recreation site and features 25 single sites, 9 double sites, 7 tent only sites, plus 16 overflow sites and a disabled access washroom. The scenic site sits on a sheltered bay and has a boat launch for those people willing to bump their way 35 km up the often busy logging road.

Twin One Creek Recreation Site (Map 31/B2)
This popular enhanced site, located at km 10 on the In-Shuck-Ch Forest Road, is about 6 km south of Strawberry Point. There are 15 vehicle/tent sites here, a nice beach and a boat launch. Perhaps not the quietest getaway, but a good place for boaters to hang out.

Tyaughton Creek Recreation Site (Map 42/E3)
Another small Carpenter Lake site, this location offers room for 3 campers. Set in a semi-open ponderosa forest, there is also a rough cartop boat launch.

Upper Lillooet River Recreation Site (Map 34/F2)
This managed recreation site is located along the banks of the Upper Lillooet River on the way to the Meager Creek Hot Springs. There are 32 campsites here and access to the river.

Vuich Falls Recreation Site (Map 16/F5)
Located about 34 km down the Tulameen River Forest Road, this 3 unit site provides access to a lookout over the cascading waters of Vuich Creek. It is a small forested site that is used primarily by hunters in fall.

Weaver Lake Recreation Site (Map 14/E7)
The short access road to Weaver Lake is accessible by 2wd vehicles. At least, that's what they say, but there is some nasty cross ditching, which will make drivers of smaller vehicles think twice. Weaver Lake is a picturesque lake and the 29 enhanced campsites are set in a lush forest on the lake's shore. There is a separate day-use/picnic area, a gravel boat launch and a great walking trail that circumnavigates the lake. The site is popular with anglers and there is a dock available for boaters with small boats.

Wells Lake Recreation Site (Map 17/B6)
Although it is possible to access Wells Lake by an extreme 4wd road off the Tulameen River Forest Road, most visitors into the area come via trail. There are 4 rustic tenting pads located next to the small fishing lake.

Windsor Lake Recreation Site (Map 46/G6)
This site has one of the most unique pit toilets in the entire province, a hollowed out giant stump of a tree. It's worth the trip just to see it, or, if you like, use it. The portage trail down to Goat Lake crosses the Goat Lake Main (at the 36 km mark), so it is possible to hike in from here.

Wolf Lake Recreation Site (Map 14/E7)
This is a small 3 unit recreation site on the shores of Wolf Lake. Or, at least, one of the campsites is on the shores of this marshy lake; the other two are set back closer to the road.

Wood Lake Recreation Site (Map 14/E5)
This popular, enhanced site is set in an opening next to a small lake. The site has recently been upgraded and now sports 30 campsites spread out between two camping areas on either side of the lake. However, it is gated in the fall and winter. Power boats are not allowed on the lake, which is found 30 km down the West Harrison Forest Road.

Yalakom Recreation Site (Map 43/E2)
Located next to the Yalakom River, this open, 5 unit site is easily accessed by RV. Fishing, hunting and exploring the endless trail system throughout the area are the popular pastimes in this dry, often hot landscape.

Zum Peak Recreation Sites (Map 16/E1)
Although it is possible to camp at the trailhead to Little Douglas Lake, many prefer to camp next to the lake, which is set below the towering Zum Peak. The high elevation lake is a nice summer getaway for anglers or hikers.

BACKCOUNTRY HUTS & CABINS

There are a variety of backcountry huts and shelters scattered across Southwestern BC. Some have been built to provide shelter for climbers in the high alpine. Others were built for other reasons by trappers, miners, geologists, etc. and are now used by backcountry travellers. Here are some of the most popular of these backcountry structures.

Black Tusk Hut (Map 22/D1)
Found along the Black Tusk Trail at Taylor Meadows, this hut is capable of holding 10 people and dozens of mice. The hut is rarely used, except by the aforementioned mice.

Brew Hut (Map 29/C6)
Originally built in 1982, the first Brew Hut was knocked down by snow creep the very first winter. Two years later, it was moved to its present location on a ridge above the lake. It is used extensively in the winter, but can also be accessed by hikers from the Brew Lake Trail. In winter, the Roe Creek Route is the safest way to the hut. It sleeps 12 people comfortably and has a wood stove for winter use only. Contact the Varsity Outdoor Club (VOC) through their website, at www.ubc-voc.com to find out about fees and availability.

Brian Waddington Hut (Map 36/D1)
Located in the Tolkien Group of mountains north of Birkenhead, this hut was built in 1998 for backcountry skiers and mountaineers. There is a rough hiking trail to the hut along Phelix Creek that is closed during grizzly mating season. The hut sleeps 20, but there is no wood stove and a finicky heater. Although the hut is not locked, visitors are asked to contact the VOC to book (www.ubc-voc.com).

Burton [Sphinx Creek] Hut (Map 22/F2)
Located in an ecologically sensitive area of Garibaldi Provincial Park, near where Sphinx Creek runs into Garibaldi Lake, access is difficult in summer. There is no trail and no real reason to go there. In winter it's a fairly easy ski across the frozen lake. The A-frame hut can sleep up to a dozen or so comfortably and has been recently re-insulated. Although the hut is not locked, visitors are asked to contact the VOC to book (www.ubc-voc.com).

Elfin Lakes Hut (Map 22/F5)
The largest hut found in Garibaldi Park is at Elfin Lakes along the Diamond Head Trail. It is a very popular destination, but with no reservations the 34 spaces can fill up quickly on busy weekends. The hut is well equipped with a heater and propane burners for cooking and there is a fee payable when self-registering in the parking lot.

Harrison Hut (Map 34/E3)
Built by the Varsity Outdoor Club in 1983, the Harrison Hut is a popular staging area for backcountry skiers and snowmobilers accessing the Pemberton Icefield. The hut can sleep up to 15 people, but access on foot is difficult. It is a long haul (roughly 20 km along the road, followed by a rustic 4 km trek up a trail that cuts through thick brush). Contact the VOC through their website, at www.ubc-voc.com.

Himmelsbach Hut (Map 30/A7)
Found near Russett Lake in Garibaldi Park, this hut is part of the BC Mountaineering Club network. It holds 12. Contact the BCMC at www.bcmc.ca for more information.

Hollyburn Cabin (Map 11/B7)
Maintained by the Third West Vancouver Scout Troup, this cabin near Cypress Provincial Park is available for rent to large groups, with space for up to thirty people. It is only about a kilometre to hike to the cabin, so access is easy.

Jim Haberl Hut (Map 21/G4)
A new climbers hut in the Tantalus Range replaces the old F.J. Green Shelter (aka Red Tit). The new hut sits on in the Serratus-Dione Column, just outside the boundary of Tantalus Provincial Park, right next to the Serratus Glacier. Access to the hut is by mountaineering routes from Lake Lovely Water or the Squamish River. It holds 12 people, but must be reserved in advance through the Alpine Club of Canada (www.aebc.com/acc/huts.asp).

Keith Flavelle Hut (Map 37/B7)
Located an easy two hour hike from the nearest road, Keith's Hut is a popular spot. It is one of the most popular huts in the Coast Mountains. It rests north of Anniversary Glacier and can hold a dozen people comfortably or twice that amount of real friendly types.

Knuckeheads Cabin (Map 19/F2)
Opened in 2003, this cabin is located about an hour and a half hike from

a gate off the E branch logging road. The cabin is actually a converted ski shack with space for eight, a pellet stove, propane cook stove and white gas lantern. The area is a popular ski destination that can also be accessed by ATV when there is no snow on the ground.

Lake Lovely Water Hut (Map 22/A5)
Open from May to October, this hut is located in Tantalus Provincial Park, at the end of a vigorous climb from the Squamish River. There is space for 20 in the hut and is most often used by mountain climbers. The hut must be reserved in advance through the Alpine Club of Canada (www.aebc.com/acc/huts.asp).

Lizzie Creek Cabin (Map 31/C5)
Originally a private cabin built by David Nickerson, this cabin is small (room for 8), but well decked out. It is located a couple hours hike from Lizzie Lake, which is once again a long haul from Lillooet Lake due to washouts on the Lizzie Forest Road. Set in a sub-alpine basin below the Stein Divide it is a gorgeous location. Unfortunately, mice have claimed the cabin and most people who stay here do so in winter, when the choice between mice and weather favours the rodents.

Mountain Lake Hut (Map 11/D2)
Located in an alpine meadow east of Furry Creek, access to this area is via a long hike along a logging road, which slowly turns into a trail. BC Mountaineering Club members can cut off 10 km or so of this hike by getting the gate key. Others can just walk or take a mountain bike. The area hasn't seen much use in the past and the hut is mostly used by mountaineers heading up Sky Pilot, Mount Sheer or another local peak. Contact the BCMC at www.bcmc.ca for more information.

Mount Steele Cabins (Map 10/B2)
Maintained by the Tetrahedron Outdoor Club, this series of four cabins are located in Tetrahedron Provincial Park. They are located at Batchelor Lake, Edwards Lake, McNair Lake and near the summit of Mount Steele. All the cabins have wood burning stoves and charge a fee. You can pay at the Esso Station is Sechelt or on-line at www.tetoutdoor.ca.

North Creek Cabin (Map 35/A1)
Operated by the BC Mountaineering Club, this hut can sleep up to 18 people and can be reserved with a minimum group size of ten. It sees little use in summer, but is quite popular in winter. Contact the BCMC at www.bcmc.ca for more information.

Pebble Creek Hut (Map 41/A6)
This small hut is located in Ash Pass and is occupied on a reservation system. In summer it is possible to get to the cabin via McParlon Creek Road. In winter, access is usually by helicopter.

Place Glacier Hut (Map 36/E5)
A research hut that is open to the public. It is not very big or well equipped, but it is a place to keep dry and spend the night, if needed.

Snowspider Hut (Map 31/C2)
This hut is primarily used in the winter and has space for four. In the summer, it can be reached by logging roads up Twin One or Van Horlick Creeks.

Sentinel Glacier Huts (Map 22/F2)
Found south of Burton Hut, there is a pair of glaciology research huts near Garibaldi Lake that are open to the public when not occupied by researchers. They are smaller, holding only four people.

Taylor Basin Cabin (Map 42/A1)
There is an old mining cabin near Taylor Pass that is used year round by everyone from mountain bikers to snowmobilers. It is pretty run-down looking, but users have maintained it pretty well.

Tenquille Lake Cabin (Map 35/G3)
A cabin was built at Tenquille Lake in the 1940s and was a popular destination for a few decades. These days, lack of maintenance has left the cabin the worse for wear and a haven for pack rats.

Wendy Thompson Hut (Map 37/A5)
Located in Marriott Basin northeast of Pemberton, this hut sleeps 16 and is mostly used in the winter. The hut is locked and reservations are made through the Alpine Club of Canada, Whistler Section (accwhistler.ca).

Wedgemont Lake Hut (Map 30/B5)
Part of the Garibaldi Park network of backcountry huts, this one isn't far from the trailhead, but the climb is certainly daunting. Regardless, it sees its fair share of visitors since there is no charge. It is a smaller hut holding 6 or so visitors.

refer to indicated pages for more map detail

Park

Steip

Whistler

Singing Pass Trail
Page 29/G7-30/B7

Lillooet
Lake

Black Tusk Trail
Page 29/D1-F2

Nahatlatch
Lake

Skookumchuck

Garibaldi
Provincial
Park

River

Nahatlatch

R

Garibaldi
Lake

99

Brackendale

Port
Douglas

Squamish

Howe
Sound

Britannia
Beach

Pinecone

Burke

Howe Sound Crest Trail
Page 11/A4-B6

Park

Golden
Ears Prov
Park

Harrison
Lake

Cypress
Prov Park

Baden Powell Trail
Page 1, 11

North
Vancouver

Stave
Lake

Bowen
Isl

Pitt
Lake

Harrison
Hot Springs

Vancouver

Maple
Ridge

7

99

Mission

Surrey

Richmond

Abbotsford

Chilliwack

hotspots

The thickly forested Coast Mountains are paradise for outdoors people. Trails lead up, down and around these rugged mountains. Options range from short interpretative trails to epic treks through places that few people have ever visited. Many of the trails are destination oriented, leading to fishing lakes, mountain vistas or waterfalls. Because the mountains often start at or near sea level, much of the hiking happens through lush rainforest before eventually breaking out into sub-alpine and alpine territory. The farther away from the coast you get, the higher your starting point (usually) and the easier it is to break out of the trees (again, usually).

To help you select the trail that best suites your abilities, we have included information on elevation gain, return distance and special features wherever possible. Also included in each description is a symbol to indicate what the trail is used for—hiking, mountain biking, horseback riding, ATV, etc. Unless otherwise noted, distances and times are for round trip hikes.

We rate most of the trails with one of the following descriptors: An easy trail has gentle grades and is suitable for family excursions. A moderate trail can involve a long, steep hill, some technical sections (roots, boulders, etc.) and is probably enough to tax most users. Be careful not to overestimate your ability or underestimate the difficulty of the trail. Only experienced trail users should consider difficult trails or routes. These trails are often rough and/or unmarked.

In this region, finding the trailhead is sometimes the toughest part of the adventure. Although we mark most trails on the appropriate map, the actual trailhead is often not marked and easily missed. In the urban and rural areas, trails often start off small side roads, too small to mark on our maps.

Trail enthusiasts should also note that higher elevation trails and routes (over 1,000 metres/3,000 feet) might have a limited season due to late season snow. These trails should be left for late summer and early fall (July until October). If you are travelling on unmarked trails, we recommend that you have mountaineering knowledge and are equipped with a topographic map and a compass as well as a GPS receiver.

Despite the wealth of trails listed below, it still only represents a fraction of the outdoor opportunities for adventurers. If you are planning on getting off the beaten path, be careful. The Coast Range is very rugged terrain.

A River Runs Through It (Map 29/F5)
This is a short 2.5 km (1.5 mile) technically challenging single-track that loops back up with the Alta Lake Road. This heavily forested trail leads through the swamp between the road and the Valley Trail south of Rainbow Lake Trail. It is often muddy, has lots of roots and a log bridge to cross. There is no elevation gain, but it makes up for it with some serious technical riding.

Agassiz Trails (Map 4/G3)
The Agassiz Dykes provide a series of gated access roads that run along the Fraser River to the south of Agassiz. These routes can be accessed off of Highway 7 below Mount Woodside, south of Maria Slough or from several of the intersecting rural roads. These peaceful trails are bordered by farmland and offer views along the Fraser River.

Alice Lake Route (Map 22/D5)
This park offers good access to several trails in and around the area. The most popular year round trail is the Four Lakes Walk. This well-developed 6.5 km (4 mile) trail leads past four woodland lakes providing a leisurely stroll through a second growth forest. The trail also joins with trails leading to Cat Lake, the highway and Garibaldi Estates.

Alice Ridge Trail (Map 22/E4)

Take the right fork when the road splits at the Alice Lake Provincial Park Headquarters and drive up the rough 4wd road as far as you can. From the end of the road, hike uphill to the Little Diamond Head and the base of Mount Garibaldi. If you can get to the end of the road, you'll only have to walk 8 km (4.8 miles) return hike gaining 700 metres (2,275 feet) along the way. The route, which is best hiked in July to October, provides an alternative route to the Diamond Head Area.

Ambrose Lake Ecological Reserve (Map 20/B6)

To reach the trailhead, follow Timberline Road, found about 500 (1600 feet) from the Earl's Cove Ferry Terminal. The trail leads from the end of the road and follows the powerline to the lake. This is an easy 5 km (3 mile) return hike. The ecological reserve at the lake is home to an abundance of waterfowl.

Ancient Cedars/Showh Lakes (Map 29/F3)

This trail network is located north of Whistler off the Cougar Mountain Road. The poorly signed trail is a 4 km (2.4 mile) loop through some impressive 1000-year-old cedar trees found at the base of Cougar Mountain. This is an easy trail, with 150 metres (488 feet) of elevation gain. However, if you do not have a vehicle that can handle the 4wd access road, you'll have to walk or mountain bike in.

Angus Creek Loop (Map 9/F4)

This mountain bike loop starts on the Sechelt-Crucil Forest Road, which is found south of the Porpoise Bay Park Campsite. The 22 km (13.4 mile) moderate route follows the main roads in a counter-clockwise direction. The steep initial climb is rewarded with panoramic views and then a downhill ride to the hilly Sechelt Inlet Road and the ride home.

Appleton Canyon/Marathon Trails (Map 18/E1)

The trailhead is found only 20 metres (60 feet) north of the Sliammon Lake Trail on the Theodosia Forest Road. It is a well-marked trail that leads along Appleton Creek past some nice waterfalls and through an old growth forest. The **Appleton Canyon Trail** culminates at the Appleton Creek Recreation Site 2 km (1.2 miles) along the way. The **Marathon Trail** continues on and eventually leads to the Southview Road. The trail is 4 km (2.4 miles) one-way and leads past Rieveley's Pond. A side trip leads to the Gibraltar viewpoint, which provides a fantastic view of the Strait of Georgia.

Baden Powell Trail (Map 1, 11)

The main artery to the massive lower elevation trail network of the North Shore Mountains is the Baden Powell Trail. This popular 42 km (25.6 mile) one-way trail leads through the lush second growth forests from Horseshoe Bay all the way to Deep Cove. The trail climbs up and down as it heads east and west. There are a number of dramatic canyons as well as some great views of Vancouver and the surrounding area. The route is well maintained and marked and can be accessed from at least 12 different roads as well as numerous trails. It would take at least 18 hours to do the whole route, so most people break the trail up over a series of day hikes. There are a couple places where backcountry camping is allowed. Most of the route is open to mountain biking but riders should expect a very technical route with lots of ups and downs, tree roots and difficult creek crossings.

Barkley Valley Trail (Map 37/C4)

Better known as an ATV trail (see the end of this section), the old road becomes impassable to even ATVers after the prospector's cabin. People can continue on foot to Twin Lakes.

BC Parkway (Map 1/D2–F3)

A 40 km (25 mile) recreation corridor, stretching from False Creek in Vancouver to Westminster Quay in New Westminster, the BC Parkway follows the Skytrain corridor for the most part. In most places, there are two sets of trails, a paved cycling path and a gravel walking path, although nobody really pays attention to this distinction. This is an urban trail, rarely removed from the hustle and bustle of the city.

Beartooth Mountain Trail (Map 46/F5)

This trailhead is accessed by boat on Powell Lake. The difficult trail begins on the north side of Beartooth Creek and extends 8 km (4.8 miles) from Powell Lake to the summit of Beartooth Mountain gaining 1,720 metres (5,590 feet) along the way. The trail is generally easy to follow and is blazed with flagging tape through an old growth forest.

Belcarra Regional Park Trails (Map 1/G1–2/A1)

Accessed by the Bedwell Bay Road off Ioco Road, this regional park encom-

passes Bedwell Bay and Burns Point, which juts out into Indian Arm. A 5.5 km (3.3 miles) round trip follows the shoreline past Burns Point to Jug Island. There is a pleasant secluded bay at the end of the trail. Views of Mount Seymour and Second Narrows Bridge are provided along the trail. Another pleasant walk circles around Sasamat Lake. This easy, one hour hike offers a cool, refreshing stroll through the heavy forest around the lake. Other trails include the 5 km (3 mile) **Admiralty Point Trail** and the 7 km (4.1 mile) **Cod Rock Trail**.

Ben Lomand Route (Map 11/D2)

If you have the key for the gate on the Britannia Creek Forest Service Road, this trail is a difficult 14.5 km (9 miles) return gaining 884 m (2,900 feet), partially along old logging roads. If you don't have the key, a bike will save you the rather uninspiring 13 km return trip along logging roads. Keeping north from Wind Lake, the cairned route leads to BCMC Mountain Lake Hut. Keeping right at the far end of wind lake reaches a ridge, which you can hike southeast along an undefined route. Some scrambling is required to reach the top of the actual mountain.

Beta Lake/Knuckleheads Trails (Map 19/F2)

Leading from Branch E-100 off the Stillwater Main, a short, 1.5 km (0.9 miles) trail leads from the end of the road to a small sub-alpine lake. The trail is not well marked and often has snow into summer. Black bears are common to the area so take precautions. It is possible to continue on to the Knuckleheads, which is an excellent alpine climbing area with views of the surrounding lakes. The **Knuckleheads Trail** is steep and unmarked and will take 6-8 hours to complete.

Binty's High Trail (Map 29/F4)

A Whistler Mountain Biking Classic, this difficult 7.5 km (4.5 mile) trail climbs 510 metres (1,658 feet) from the top of Alpine Meadows (you start on Rick's Roost Trail). Once you reach the top enjoy the view and then hang on. The trail spills you out on Alta Lake Road but not before crossing several side trails, which offer similar thrills.

Birkenhead Lake Loop (Map 36/D3)

This four hour loop is a popular, moderate ride along gravel roads through a Lodgepole Pine forest to beautiful Birkenhead Lake. From the D'Arcy Road, you start with a tough 3 km (1.8 mile) climb up the Birkenhead Lake Forest Road. Look for the gated road on the east that eventually links up with the access road on the north side of the lake. Continue past the main campsite and back to the highway.

Birkenhead River Trail (Map 36/D5–7)

Starting from the Owl Creek Recreation Site, the Birkenhead River Trail is a scenic 20 km (12.2 mile) trail that makes up part of the Sea to Sky Trail. The easy route follows a rolling road along the powerlines on the west side of the river. From the Birkenhead River crossing, it is a further 15 km (9.2 miles) to Birkenhead Lake.

Blackcomb Mountain (Map 30/A5)

The expansive sub-alpine terrain of Blackcomb Mountain, frequented by skiers throughout the winter months, gives way to some great hiking trails in the summer. For a fee, take the Solar Coaster Chair and walk up to the Rendezvous Restaurant and the start of the trails. Be sure to pick up the complimentary map that highlights the short alpine walks available. The longest trail is only 2.5 km (1.5 miles) and the elevation gains are minimal (although the Overlord Lookout Trail gains 215 metres/699 feet). For mountain bikers, there are guided descents from the top of Solar Coaster, which take about two hours to complete.

Blowdown Lake Trail (Map 37/F6)

Northeast of Duffey Lake, the Blowdown Creek Main extends in a southeasterly direction. This is an old mining road, which leads to the alpine and the Stein Valley Provincial Park. The road passes by the old Silver Queen Mine to provide easy access to the Cottonwood Creek Trail and several ridge walks, which in turn connect to the Stein River Trail. The area offers beautiful alpine meadows with great camping and some classic ridge routes.

Botanie Mountain Trail (Map 39/B6)

The length of the hike really depends on how far you can drive along the old lookout road leading from the Botanie Valley Road. If you do not have a 4wd vehicle then you'll have to hike about 17.5 km (10.7 miles) over 8 hours, climbing 1,425 metres (4,631 feet) to the lookout. Along the way you will pass open meadows with wildflowers (in July) along with great views of the Stein Valley, Thompson River and Fraser River. The hiking season runs from June to October.

Boundary Bay Dyke Trail (Map 1/E7–2/A6)

This dyke trail starts from 17A Ave in Tsawwassen and skirts Boundary Bay all the way to the southern railway tracks (junction of Highway 99 & 91) in Surrey. Along the 25 km (15.3 mile) route, you pass Boundary Bay Airport, Delta Air Park and several access points, which can shorten the route.

Brandywine Meadows Trail (Map 29/C5)

This 6 km (3.7 mile) trail is steep and short with an elevation gain of 1,000 metres (3,280 feet). The trail leads sharply upward from the 6.3 km (3.8 mile) mark of the Branch 10 logging road, through the dense old growth forest to the alpine meadow with spectacular views and a rustic camping spot. From the meadows, it is possible to gain access to Brandywine Mountain and the Metal Dome.

Brett-Hog Creek Trails (Map 42/G3–43/B2)

Accessed off of Marshall Lake Road, you will find 35 km (21.3 miles) of trails taking you around Carol Lake along Hog and Brett Creeks and beyond. There really is no limit to the distance you can travel.

Brew Lake Trail (Map 29/C7)

The signed trailhead begins on the BC Rail tracks just south of the Brandywine Falls Provincial Park. It involves a 10 km (6.1 mile) return hike gaining 1,200 metres (3,900 feet) along the way. At the end of the steep trail–best hiked in July-October–is Brew Lake, where you will find a maintained cabin available on a first come, first serve basis. From the lake, it is possible to explore Mount Brew at 1,740 metres (5,655 feet) in elevation or access the Brew Hut 1,620 metres (5,265 feet). Brew Lake is at 1,430 metres (4,648 feet) in elevation and is a beautiful mountain lake offering reasonably good fishing. In winter, most people head here via Roe Creek.

Bridal Trails (Map 4/G2)

Just east of Harrison Hot Springs, a pair of easy trails can be explored. The Bridal Trail is 3.5 km (2.1 mile) and marked with green markers, while the Mount Streetsidehill Trail is 4 km (2.4 mile) and marked with red markers.

Brodie Trails Loop (Map 10/B5)

Beginning from the Roberts Creek Forest Road, you follow the powerline west to the trail. Follow the markings back to the beginning or explore the many difficult side routes. This moderate 7.5km (4.6 mile) route is home to the Brodie Test of Metal Race.

Brohm Lake Interpretive Trails (Map 22/C4)

From the parking lot off Highway 99, an easy 5 km (3 mile) trail with minimal elevation gain circles the lake. The trail provides access to the picnic area next to Brohm Lake and is used for shore fishing as well as wildlife viewing. Around Brohm Lake, you will also find a network of 11 km (6.7 miles) of interconnecting trails used by mountain bikers and hikers. These trails lead away from the lake and through the bluffs and second growth forest typical of the area. There is a second parking lot 1 km (0.6 miles) south of the main lot.

Brothers Creek Trail (Map 11/C7)

This 7 km (4.3 miles) return hike along Brothers Creek is one of the more popular lower elevation trails in the area. The moderate trail combines longer flat sections with some short, steep grades gaining a total of 435 metres (1,414 feet). This is a good year round hike that follows a fire access road through some older second growth timber dotted by large old growth Douglas-fir and Western Red Cedar. The creek cuts through a scenic canyon that has three sets of waterfalls, while Blue Gentian Lake, which is found on the trail, has picnic tables. Mountain bikers use the road to access some of the steep, difficult trails of the Lower Cypress Area. The trailhead is found on Millstream Road.

Brunswick Mountain Trail (Map 11/B5)

This difficult route that climbs 1,550 metres (5,038 feet) over 15 km (9.1 mile) return. While there is some minor scrambling near the top, the views over Howe Sound are incredible.

Bug Lake Trail (Map 47/F3)

The Bug Lake Trail is a steep, difficult trail that passes through an old growth forest, passing the massive Twin Firs on its way up to a tiny sub-alpine lake. It is possible to hike along the ridge past the lake all the way to Princess Louisa Inlet via the Loquilts Route. The area is protected under the Squamish LRMP as a wild spirit place.

Bunster Hills Loop (Map 18/E2–D1)

From Wilde Road off Highway 101, this moderate bike ride initially climbs 750 metres (2,438 feet) over 12 km (7.2 miles). Enjoy the views of Okeover

Inlet and the Georgia Straight before the descent. The 34 km (20.7 mile) loop is well marked as you follow logging roads back to the highway. Allow four hours.

Buntzen Lake Trails (Map 12/A7)

Lake Beautiful, as it was originally known, is a popular recreation area that is easily accessed by Sunnyside Road to the north of Port Moody. Within the forest next to Buntzen Lake are a series of multi-use trails that range from gentle family strolls to difficult hikes. Most of these trails interconnect, meaning you can create your own adventure. An on site map will help you pick your route.

Academy Trail

This is mostly a horse trail, although it sees a fair number of pedestrians as well. The trail leads from the Alpine Riding Academy at the park entrance all the way to the north end of Buntzen Lake. About halfway along it joins up with the Pumphouse Road. The trail is 8 km (4.8 miles) return with minimal elevation gain.

Buntzen Lake Trail

This popular route is an 8 km (4.8 mile) loop that circles Buntzen Lake. The best place to start is the South Beach Picnic Area and hike in a counter clockwise direction around the lake. At the north end there is suspension bridge, while at the south end there is a floating bridge to cross. Allow 4-5 hours for this easy, well-maintained trail with minimal elevation gain.

Diez Vista Trail

This is a moderate 17 km (10.5 mile) return hike with 455 metres (1,479 feet) elevation gain. The trail goes up and down a lot and is quite steep and challenging in places. Ultimately, you reach the summit at 600 metres (1,950 feet) and will be rewarded with an excellent view of Indian Arm and Buntzen Lake. Or rather, with a series of views, as the name means "ten lookout trail." Although the trail leads from the Pumphouse Road to the north end of the lake, it is recommended to do this trail north to south.

Dilly-Dally Trail

You can't Dilly-Dally if you expect to finish this trail in a day. It is a long, steep, difficult 25 km (15.2 miles) trail leading from the South Beach Parking Lot gaining 1,100 metres (3,575 feet) to the summit of Dilly-Dally Peak. From the summit, you can continue south on to Eagle Peak by following the ridge. The trail is best tackled in July to October.

Eagle Peak Trails

This steep, difficult 15 km (9 mile) hike leads past Eagle Mountain to Lindsay Lake. The 1,020 metres (3,315 feet) in elevation gain is a small payment for the amazing view. From tiny Lindsay Lake, you can continue on to Eagle Peak, which is another 5 km (3.1 miles) return. An alternative route is to traverse down the slope to the north end of Buntzen Lake. The difficult hike is accessed off the gated Powerline Road.

Halvor Lunden [Eagle Ridge] Trail

Call this a route, instead of a trail, as it incorporates parts of the Lindsay Lake Loop, Swan Falls Loop and Dilly Dally. It deserves mention because Halvor Lunden is the father of trail building in the Lower Mainland and he built a number of classic trails (High Falls, Deeks Bluffs and Three Chop) in this book. This route takes you up the ridge and past ten tiny lakes. How far you walk depends on how you string the trails together.

Lakeview Trail

This rough, steep, 5.8 km (3.5 mile) trail extends along the eastern slopes of Buntzen Ridge on the west side of Buntzen Lake. The hiking/biking/equestrian trail is accessed just north of the Pumphouse Road from the south or from the suspension bridge at the north end of the lake.

Lindsay Lake Loop

The trail to Lindsay Lake gains 1,020 metres (3,315 feet) as it makes a 15 km (9.1 mile) loop to Lindsay Lake, as well as to several viewpoints over Vancouver. Take a left at El Paso Junction and up to the small lake. This is where the loop begins and ends some 6-8 hours later.

Nature & Energy Trails

Two short, 1 km trails circle a wooded knoll south of the boat launch. The Nature Trail is a self-guided trail that follows the shores of Buntzen Lake before leading through a forested area to the South Beach Picnic Area. The Energy Trail is another short loop trail with attractive views of Buntzen Lake.

Swan Falls Loop

A difficult 20 km (12.2 mile) loop gaining 1,150 metres (3,738 feet) up through the so-called lakes district (home to ten tarns) of Eagle Ridge. The route continues on to Eagle Peak (Mount Beautiful), then down to Swan Falls and the Powerhouse Road.

Burke Mountain Trails (Map 2/C1–12/D7)

Located at the south end of the new Pinecone Burke Provincial Park, most of the trails are reached by the parking lot near the entrance to the Gun Club off Harper Road.

Burke Ridge Trail

The Burke Ridge trail begins on the gated old road before breaking off onto a well-marked trail, which climbs steadily uphill to the ridge. The trail is 20 km (12.4 miles) return gaining 880 metres (2,860 feet) to the 1,225 metre (3,981 foot) ridge. From the top, you can see into the rarely seen Coquitlam Watershed, as well as the surrounding area.

Galloway Trail

Part of the Burke Mountain maze of trails, the Galloway has the distinction of being one of the best intermediate rides in the area. Which is saying a lot, as most trails around here are either über-hardcore or ultra-easy. This 12 km (7.5 mile) trail is a fast, fun ride with some technical sections.

Munroe-Dennett Loop

See below.

Sawblade

This is the most popular (but misused) mountain biking trail in the area. The trail starts north (left) from the main road. This 11.5 km (7 mile) trail features a difficult crank up 400 metres (1,300 feet) and eventually meets up with the Coquitlam River Trail. An easier option is to continue along the main road past the second gate and follow the trail heading south.

South Slope Trail

This is an 18km (11 mile) trail climbing 880 metres (2,860 feet).

Triple Crown

This is a great moderate ride, which combines three shorter trails into an epic 15 km (9.1 mile) journey, climbing 550 metres (1,787 feet). The trail ultimately takes you down to Galloway Road (south of Harper Road).

Village Lake Trail

A 15 km (9.1 mile) hike gaining 680 metres (2,210 feet). Mountain bikers should expect difficult, rocky trails and a lot of climbing. The trail will take hikers the better part of a day to complete.

Woodland Walk

This easy trail bisects the second growth forest at the base of Burke Ridge. The trail gains only 200 m (650 feet) over 7 km (4.3 miles) as it takes you past some spectacular waterfalls, over a moss covered bridge and through remnants of logging from the turn of the century.

Burkholder Lake Trail (Map 43/A1–C2)

From Lake La Mare Recreation Site off the Yalakom Forest Road, this 10 km (6 mile) trail takes you to Burkholder Lake. From Burkholder, you can continue west to the Shulaps Range, which are over 20 km (12.2 miles) away.

Burnaby Lake Regional Park (Map 1/G2)

You can explore the shores of Burnaby Lake along the 19 km (11.6 miles) of trails that surround the lake. There is an extra 4 km (2.4 miles) of horse trails, but these run close to the freeway and are not the most pleasant to walk on. It is possible to a number of trails together to circumnavigate the lake.

Burnaby Mountain Area (Map 1/G2–2/A2)

The west side of the mountain is now part of an ecological reserve and, outside of the Trans Canada Trail, the trails are only open to hiking. The more popular east side trails are now officially designated as multi-use trails, much to the pleasure of local mountain bikers. Although the trails on top do offer the odd vantage point, most of the trails cut through a thickly forested area. You can access these trails from the SFU Campus, Gaglardi Way or North Road.

Burns Bog [Delta Nature Reserve] (Map 1/G4)

A trio of easy looping trails, ranging from a few hundred metres to 1.3 km (0.9 miles) in length, lead through the ancient Burns Bog. The main trail is a gated service road that can be used by cyclists to join up with the Delta Watershed Trails (see below). Although boardwalks are being added, be prepared for wet trail conditions, especially in winter. Access is from the parking lot of Great Pacific Forum off Nordel Way or from River Road in Delta.

Burrard Thermal Trails (Map 2/A1)

This is a popular mountain biking area. In winter, this area is well drained and usually doesn't see snow; therefore, bikers tend to flock here when the mountain trails are not rideable. The trail network starts near White Pine Beach at Sasamat Lake. Most of the biking trails are accessed off the 3 km (1.8 mile) BC Hydro access road, which climbs a bit, then descends 165 m (531 ft) towards Bedwell Bay. Hikers will enjoy this short, easy trail, with its views over Burrard Inlet, but mountain bikers tend to get off the main road and onto the more challenging motorbike trails, which range from moderate to extreme.

Cabin Lake Trails (Map 27/B1)

To reach Cabin Lake, you can use a 4wd vehicle/ATV or walk along the rough, Cabin Lake Road (7km/4.3 miles) gaining 215 m (700 feet) to the lake. Hiking time is about four hours. Given the elevation (1,860 m/6,045 feet), the best time to sample the area is in June through September. From the lake, it is possible to access the alpine of Stoyoma Mountain by hiking 7 km (4.3 miles) gaining 420 m (1,375 feet). This hike is considered moderate in difficulty and involves hiking through sub-alpine to the open alpine ridge below the summit (at 2,282 m/7415 feet). Another alternative is to access Heather Basin to the west via a 15 km (9.2 mile) hike along an alpine ridge. This difficult route leads past an old aircraft wreck. Another option is to hike to Lightning Lake, which involves a steep 5 km (3 mile) excursion along an old road.

Cal-Cheak Trail (Map 29/D6)

The popular Cal-Cheak or Brandywine Falls Trails lead 4 km (2.4 miles) one-way between Brandywine Falls Provincial Park and the Cal-Cheak Recreation Site. South of the suspension bridge, the trails split with the western trail (under the power lines) being the preferred mountain biking route of the Sea to Sky Trail. Once at the park, be sure to take the side route to look at the spectacular Brandywine Falls.

Campbell Lake Trail (Map 4/F1)

The Campbell Lake Trail is a rugged trail that climbs from the sign on Highway 9 across from Balsam Ave., south of Harrison Hot Springs, to a remote mountain lake. The average grade of the trail is a steep 16%, climbing 630 metres (2,047 feet) over 4.8 km (2.9 miles). Expect to take about three hours to the lake, with good viewpoints of the Harrison Lake and the Cheam Range along the way. It is possible to arrange for a pick up at the top, via the rough 4wd Mount Woodside Forest Road.

Capilano Canyon Trails (Map 1/C1–11/D7)

Several parking lots off the Capilano Park and the Capilano Roads provide access to this network of trails. The Capilano Canyon is a deep, narrow gorge surrounded by sheer granite cliffs. The trails are all well maintained so it makes for easy travel under the large Douglas-fir. Spawning salmon can be seen in the fall. There are 10 named trails in the park, covering a total of 26 km (16 miles) of distance. The longest trail is the Capilano Pacific Trail, at 7.5 km (4.6 miles).

Capilano Mountain Trail (Map 11/C3)

To access this trail, park at Porteau Provincial Park and walk 100 metres (325 feet) north to the end of the concrete wall. From there, a difficult trail leads 26 km (15.9 miles) 10 hours+ return gaining 1,600 metres (5,200 feet) to the summit of Capilano Mountain. The trail initially leads steadily uphill through a second growth forest to a gated logging road. This road leads to Phyllis and Marion Lake if you stay right. From the left branch, the trail eventually takes off to the right and leads past Beth Lake to the summit. An alternative route is to follow the logging road from just north of Furry Creek Golf Course. Mountain bikers can use the road to gain access to the lakes, which offer good fishing.

Caren Range Trails (Map 9/E3)

The Halfmoon Forest Road provides access to an excellent area for hikers and mountain bikers in the summer and cross-country skiers during the winter. The best place to start is at kilometre 12 junction or at kilometre 15, after the road passes though a stand of old-growth timber. The extensive logging road network in the area provides easy backcountry travel with some great views of the ocean and the Sunshine Coast as well as a chance to explore an ancient forest of yellow cedar, hemlock and balsam, believed to be the oldest forest on the coast.

Carlson Lake Loop (Map 9/D2)
Found 6 km (3.6 miles) up the Halfmoon Bay Forest Road (4wd access) this moderate 21 km (12.8 mile) mountain bike loop should take 2.5 hours to ride. The route is marked in a clockwise direction, which begins with a tough initial climb. Most of the route follows old overgrown logging roads as it gains 390 metres (1,268 feet) in elevation. Along the way, you are rewarded with views of Carlson Lake and Sechelt Inlet. The loop eventually brings you back to the Halfmoon Bay Forest Road.

Caswell [Red Mountain] Trail (Map 3/C3)
This is a 9.8 km (6 mile) loop, climbing 310 metres (1,007 feet). This trail heads west from the Mill Pond and combines old roads with single-track trails.

Cat Lake Area (Map 22/D5)
Around Cat Lake, a series of motorbike trails offer very challenging routes for the mountain biker. These trails can be accessed off of the Cheekeye River Forest Road at the old gondola base area or the Cat Lake Recreation Site. It is possible to cross the Cheekeye River and follow the trails down to Alice Lake or Garibaldi Highlands.

Centennial Trail (Map 6/E5–F6)
When it was built in the mid 1960s, the Centennial Trail was one of the most ambitious trail building projects in BC. These days, the trail has fallen out of favour and most of the really interesting sections have been incorporated into other trails, including the most recent mega-trail project, the Trans Canada Trail. In name, the Centennial Trail extends 420 km (256.2 miles) from The Plaza of Nations in Vancouver to Joe Lake near Keremeos, but in truth, the only section that still survives is the section from 26 Mile Bridge to the Skyline Trail along the Skagit River.

Central Valley Greenway (Map 1/D1–2/A3)
The Central Valley Greenway is open to hikers, bikers, wheelchairs and rollerblades. The 24 km (14.6 mile) long trail links Science World on Vancouver's False Creek with the confluence of the Brunette and Fraser Rivers in New Westminster. While the trail is officially open, there are sections that are temporarily routed along roadways. The route basically follows the Millennium Skytrain line. Most of the trail is paved, though there are some sections that are not.

Cerise Creek Trails (Map 37/B7)
Just west of Duffey Lake, turn onto the Cerise Creek Road off the highway and drive approximately 10 minutes to the signed trailhead and the gateway to a popular backcountry hiking and skiing area. From the trailhead, you hike through the forest along Cerise Creek to some alpine meadows where you will find Keith's Hut. It takes about two or three hours to reach the hut although it is a fairly easy hike. From the hut, experienced mountaineers can cross over to the Matier Glacier or Joffre Peaks.

Chapman Falls Trails (Map 9/F4)
A series of trails are found along Lower Chapman Creek. The **Chapman Falls Trail** is reached by parking at the top of Havies Road and walking along the chain link fence. From there, the trail leads 6 km (3.6 miles) return to the falls. The **Hatchery Trail** leads to a viewing platform and a series of spawning channels on Chapman Creek. This is a short (0.5 km/0.3 mile), easy trail. The **Lower Chapman Creek Trail** is considered one of the premier short hikes on the Sunshine Coast. The trail leads through a nice second growth forest with large red cedar stumps next to the creek. The 2.8 km (1.7 mile) one-way trail also leads to several swimming holes and sandy beaches. The trailhead is located at the parking lot of Brookman Park immediately east of Davis Bay beach on Highway 101.

Cheakamus Canyon Trail (Map 22/B3–C2)
Now a part of the Sea to Sky Trail, this trail starts at the end of Paradise Valley Road. It is 3 km (1.8 miles) to the rather unpleasantly named Starvation Lake. Some people turn around here, but the trip doesn't really get interesting until after the lake, as it skirts the edge of the canyon. While you can walk to where the old cattle trail disappears under the new Highway 99, you probably won't want to walk much farther than 1.5 km (0.9 miles) past the lake.

Cheam Wetlands (Map 4/G3)
It was only a few years back that Cheam Lake had been drained to harvest lime. Now, an easy network of trails (totalling about 6 km/3.7 miles) meanders around the eastern edge of Cheam Lake. The highlight here is the abundance of waterfowl and small animals.

Clack Creek Loop (Map 10/A5)
From the junction of Lockyer and Gruman Roads, this 12.3 km (7.5 mile) moderate ride is best done in a counter-clockwise direction. Follow Gruman Road then the Clack Creek Forest Road to its end. Here an old skid road heads down for a wild 2 km (1.2 mile) descent to the East Wilson Forest Road and the ride home. Also found at the end of the Clack Creek Forest Road is the **Three Steps Trails** which will take you down to Highway 101 along a series of three trails.

Confederation Lake Trail (Map 18/G1–46/E6)
The trailhead is found on an old logging road that starts to the east side of Inland Lake. A gate near the Inland Lake Campsite may add an additional 1.5 km (0.9 miles) one-way to the actual trail. From the trailhead, a well-marked trail leads past Confederation Lake and eventually to Powell Lake. A forest service log cabin is located on the east side of Confederation Lake and provides a wood stove and accommodation for six individuals. It is 8 km (4.8 miles) one-way to the cabin. Beyond Confederation Lake, the trail continues 7.5 km (4.6 miles) one-way to the old Fiddlehead Farm site on Powell Lake. The Confederation Lake Trail makes up a portion of the Sunshine Coast Trail.

Coquihalla Summit Recreation Area (Map 16/E1)
Near the tollbooth are several strenuous hikes that allow the experienced mountaineer to reach the peaks for a fantastic view of the Coquihalla River Valley. These high elevation routes are best travelled from July to October.

The Falls Lake Trail
This trail begins off the short road leading from Exit 221 of the Coquihalla Highway. From the parking lot, it is a nice 1.5 km (0.9 mile) return walk to the small mountain lake. The lake provides good fishing for small rainbow trout. East of the main trail is Bridalveil Falls, but accessing the falls requires bushwacking along the creek. (An easier approach is along the old KVR railgrade).

Needle Peak Trail
Beginning across the highway, from the Boston Bar Summit Rest Area, a very strenuous hike climbs 855 m (2,779 feet) up the back side of the Needle. From the top, at 2,105 m (6,841 feet), the reward for this difficult 13 km (7.9 mile) trip is the great view. This hike should only be attempted by experienced hikers.

Thar Peak Route
This trail begins from the Boston Bar Rest Area and follows the gas pipeline before heading upwards along a faint trail to the peak. The trail leads up the back of the mountain and provides a phenomenal view when you reach the summit. Although you only travel 5 km (3 miles), you should allow five hours return as you climb 700 metres (2,275 feet) to the peak, at 1,920 metres (6,240 feet).

Vicuna & Guanaco Peaks
Found at the end of the Upper Coldwater Forest Road, the trails lead virtually straight up to excellent vantage points.

Zoa Peak Trail
Starting from a powerline off of the Falls Lake Trail or from the Upper Coldwater Forest Road, a trail leads 635 metres (2,064 feet) to the 1,875 metre (6,094 foot) summit. The 11 km (6.7 mile) round trip should take about six hours. This is the easiest of the climbs to the alpine.

Zopikos Ridge Trail
The dramatic rock face of Zopikos Ridge is seen on the Coquihalla Highway just south of the tollbooth and a difficult day-long route that is accessed from the Zoa Peak Route climbs to the top. The view from the top is breathtaking.

Coquitlam River Trail (Map 2/B3–C1)
This scenic river trail makes up a good portion of the historic PoCo Trail. From the Mary Hill Bypass to the Orr Creek Falls this trail stretches 13.5 km (8.2 miles) along the Coquitlam River. In fall, spawning salmon can be seen in the waterway. Several roads (Pitt River Road, Lougheed Highway and Shaughnessy Road) provide alternate access points. All levels of mountain bikers and hikers can enjoy this gentle trail. Beyond the falls, the trail narrows and gets more difficult as it climbs to meet up with the Burke Mountain Trails.

Cornell Trail (Map 18/F5)
An easy walk along an old mining trail past Emily Lake on Texada Island. The trail leads from Vananda at Prospect Road and can be extended as long as you like along the gas pipeline.

Cresent Beach (Map 2/A6) 🚶 🅿️
An extremely popular 4 km (2.4 mile) oceanfront walk. This trail system follows a wide, packed trail along the waterfront of Cresent Beach.

Crumpit Woods (Map 22/D6) 🚶 🚴
This is a mountain biking area for people who want to learn how to ride hardcore. There is some seriously technical stuff, but without the 5-metre spills if you happen to slip up. This network of trails is strung together by an easy loop that circumnavigates Mount Crumpit.

Cypress Falls Trail (Map 11/A7) 🚶 🅿️
Despite its natural beauty, Cypress Falls Park is not very well known. A shame. The main trail in the park is an easy 6 km (3.7 mile) trail that loops around Cypress Creek's lower and upper falls. The trail starts out steep, but quickly levels out and becomes easier to hike, but there are a number of other interconnected trails in the park as well.

Cypress Mountain Trails (Map 2/B1–12/B7) 🚶 🎿
While most people think Cypress Mountain is found in Cypress Provincial Park, it is not. It is found in Coquitlam and there is a mess of trails found east of Buntzen Lake offers some challenging hiking and mountain biking. There are 18 named trails, including trails like Fat Bastard and Decapitator. Some of these trails (Buntzen Connector and White Rock) hook up with the Halvor Lunden Trail in Buntzen Park.

Cypress Park Trails (Map 11/B6) 🚶 🎿 🏃 🅿️
The Cypress Parkway provides easy access to the sub-alpine area of the provincial park but for the more adventurous, it is possible to hike or bike up. Within the park are a number of trails as well as the Hollyburn Cross-Country Ski Area and Cypress Bowl Ski Area to explore.

The Black Mountain Loop
Reached by taking the Baden Powell Trail from the downhill ski area, this trail climbs past a few small lakes to the south summit for a view of the ocean and city. This is a 7.5 km (4.6 mile) loop, gaining 300 metres (975 feet) to the summit of Black Mountain. This is the easy way up. A more challenging route is to hike up Black Mountain from Highway 99 at the Whistler/Squamish Exit. From the highway, it's a steep 16 km (9.8 mile) hike gaining 1,140 metres (3,705 feet).

Hollyburn Peak Trail
From the trailhead sign at the cross-country skiing parking lot, this trail leads some 20 km (12.2 miles) return to the top of Hollyburn Mountain. The trail heads east, past the old Hollyburn Lodge next to First Lake before climbing steadily uphill past the powerline and the Fourth and Fifth Lakes. From the summit, there is a great view of the Gulf Islands and Vancouver Island. An alternate and less strenuous option is to follow the Baden Powell Trail from the downhill skiing parking lot.

Howe Sound Crest Trail (B6–A4)
Linking the northern and southern portions of the park, the trail is 29 km (17.7 miles) one-way and is clearly marked with orange markers. It links a number of North Shore Mountain hikes and is best hiked between mid July to the first snowfall. This is a difficult but rewarding hike. From Cypress Bowl, the trail climbs up to St. Marks Summit, drops a few hundred metres before heading up to Unnecessary Ridge, the highest point on the trail at 1,525 metres (4,956 feet). From here, the trail follows an undulating ridge before dropping down to Deeks Creek.

Mount Strachan Trail
From the downhill ski area, this trail climbs 10 km (6.1 miles) return to the double summit of Mount Strachan (pronounced Strawn) at 1,450 metres (4,713 feet). The trail gains 540 metres (1,755 feet).

Upper & Lower Cypress Biking Trails
Speed demons will enjoy cruising the fire access roads from the upper parking lot down to the first switchback on the Cypress Bowl Road. The route is 7.5 km (4.6 miles) and drops 735 metres (2,389 feet). Others like to ride up the scenic road and explore the numerous trails in the area. The side trails, which eventually bring you back to the parkway, should be left to expert mountain bikers who are prepared for some nifty man-made obstacles. On the other side of the Cypress Bowl Road are the Lower Cypress Trails. The Skyline Trail (see below) provides the main corridor through this challenging biking area.

Yew Lake Trail
A 4 km (2.4 mile) wheelchair accessible trail circles Yew Lake. It is a good choice for a family outing as it involves a generally flat walk (145 metres/471 feet in elevation gain) through a sub-alpine forest around

a small lake dotted with lily pads. There is some old growth forest in the area as well as a good view of Snug Cove and Deep Bay. The trail becomes accessible in late June with the season ending in October.

Dakota Creek Loop (Map 10/C4) 🚴 🅿️
This mountain bike ride is found at the junction of Roberts Creek Forest Road and the Dakota Creek Forest Road. It is a moderate 11 km (6.7 mile) ride. Following a counter-clockwise direction you will be rewarded with fine panoramic views.

Daniel Point Trail (Map 9/A1) 🚶 🅿️
Daniel Point is a small spit of land that sticks out into Malaspina Strait. This moderate 2.5 km trail leads to a wonderful viewpoint, while side trails lead to the rocky beach.

Davis Lake Park (Map 3/E1) 🚶 🅿️
Reached by the Lost Creek Forest Road off Sylvester Road, this small provincial park offers a 5 km (3.1 mile) easy, flat walk which circles the pretty lake.

Deeks Bluff Circuit (Map 11/A4) 🚶
Unlike the other trails in the Deeks area, this trail doesn't climb past the 400 metres (1,300 feet) mark, making this a good intermediate trail. Even better, when the higher trails to Deeks Lake and Deeks Peak are snowed under, this trail is still navigable. The trail is 10 km (6 miles) return and should take about 5 hours to hike. This trail hooks up with the Deeks Lake Trail.

Deeks Lake Trail (Map 11/A4) 🚶 🐟 🅿️
There used to be two ways to get to Deeks Lake, but the Sea to Sky improvements have destroyed the more popular (and shorter) trailhead near the Deeks Creek Bridge. Now, the only way up is to start at the north end of the Howe Sound Crest Trail. Watch for the parking lot on the east side of the highway at the new Porteau Overpass. The trail climbs 1,030 m (3,379 ft) as it make its way to the lake. The trail is about 6 km (3.6 mile) to the lake.

Deeks Peak Trail (Map 11/A4) 🚶 🅿️
The general attitude toward this hike is that you do it merely to say you've done it. It is poorly marked, overgrown and hardly worth the effort, save for some outstanding views from the top. It's a 16 km (10 mile) roundtrip gaining 1,615 m (5,300 feet). The trail starts from the new north trailhead for the Howe Sound Trail.

Delta Millennium Trail (Map 1/F5) 🚶 🏃 🅿️
This trail was built to link an existing hiking/biking trail in Ladner with the Deas Island Trails. In 2008, phase 2, a 1 km extension was opened, connecting the trail to Deas Island Regional Park.

Delta Watershed (Map 1/G5–2/A5) 🚶 🏃 🐎
While the city has been developing trails here, to make them more appealing to walkers and horseback riders, creative cyclists have been constructing some impressive structures that rival those found on the famed North Shore. There are several access points including 64th Ave to the north and Highway 10 to the south. As a rule of thumb, the trails to the north of the service road are short and follow well developed trails. To the south, less developed trails offer more of a challenge for cyclists.

Delta-South Surrey Regional Greenway Trail (Map 1/G5) 🚶 🏃 🅿️
Like the other Regional District Greenway Projects, this one is still under construction. When finished, it will run from Mud Bay to Annacis Island along the South Surrey Interceptor sewer corridor. At the time this book went to press, only a 2.3 km section from 64th Avenue to Highway 10 was officially open. The trail will connect to the Boundary Bay Dyke Trail.

Denham's [Weaver Lake] Trail (Map 14/E7) 🚶 🅿️
From the Weaver Lake Recreation Site, a 6.2 km (3.8 mile) trail loops around this picturesque fishing lake. Relatively flat, the trail makes for an easy three hour hike with a number of side trails from which to access the lake.

Dewdney Trail (Map 6/F2–17/F7) ⛺ 🚶 🐎 🅿️
Originally constructed in 1860 by Edgar Dewdney, this was one of the first trade routes linking the coast with the interior. These days, most of the route is either grown over or has been covered by roads, but there are some places where the historic route still survives as a trail. The longest surviving section is found in the Cascade Recreation Area, beginning at the parking lot on Highway 3. The trail extends 36 km (22 miles) to the pass, gaining 1,131 metres (3,676 feet) along the way. It is possible to trek over the divide into the Whipsaw Creek Forest Road. The trail is a popular horseback destination with its panoramic views of the valleys and mountains. There are several side trails and overnight facilities along the well-developed trail system.

Diadem Mountain Trail (Map 20/A1)

This hike is located along a road leading up Lois River Valley. A gate located before the valley may impede travel by vehicle to the trailhead, which is marked by a cairn with flagging tape. The route proceeds through a deep gorge eventually leading up to a ridge. From there, you cross a creek at the end of a box canyon and proceeds up into the sub-alpine past a series of ponds. Eventually, the trail culminates at the summit for a total of 8 km (4.8 miles) return.

Dog Mountain/Landstrom Ridge Trails (Map 15/E7)

A few short trails are found around the Devils Lake area off Highway 7. To the north of the highway, the **Dog Mountain Trail** is a popular mountain biking area. Across the highway and at the end of Landstrom Road, a short, stiff trail climbs to a series of four lookouts on Landstrom Ridge. Although fairly easy, expect to climb 150 metres (488 feet) over the 3 km (1.8 mile) round trip.

Dorman Point Trail (Map 10/G6)

From the picnic grounds at the ferry in Snug Cove on Bowen Island, this trail leads 4 km (2.4 miles) one-way to a small lookout near Dorman Point. The hike involves a steady uphill climb where you will be rewarded with excellent views of Whytecliff Park and Vancouver.

Duck Lake Area (Map 19/A3)

The Duck Lake Forest Road provides access to several hiking/biking trail systems found just east of Powell River. The variety of activities and proximity of all the trails makes this a good area to explore.

Blackwater Trail

Found about 100 metres (325 feet) south of the Y-fork on the Duck Lake Loop, this 7 km (4.3 mile) trail follows an old railgrade, then Blackwater Creek, where it passes by a series of waterfalls. Eventually, the trail climbs over the divide on an old logging road to Washout Creek. Here the trail enters a spectacular gorge and continues in a westward direction back to the start.

Cable Trail

Opposite to the Suicide Creek Loop, this is an easy 8 km (4.8 mile) journey. The trail crosses a footbridge and then meanders through a second growth forest before crossing Sweetwater Creek. From there, the trail follows an old railgrade up a steady incline eventually looping back to Sweetwater Creek and the trailhead. The highlight of the trip is MacGregor Falls.

Duck Lake Loop

Mountain bikers mainly use this 21 km (12.8 mile) moderate trail. It follows logging roads and the powerlines east of Powell River. The route starts at the 3.5 km mark (2.1 miles) on the Duck Lake Forest Road. Follow the road north to the intersection at 7.5 km (4.6 miles) and keep right, following the main roads to the powerlines, which will return you to the parking spot.

Lang Creek Loop

This easy, well-marked trail leads south from the 6 km (3.6 mile) mark of the Duck Lake Forest Road. Mountain bikers can expect a moderate route with some of the best single-track riding in the area. Both the Lang Creek and East Lake Recreation Sites provide picnic sites en route. Spawning salmon can be seen in Lang Creek in September and October.

Mud Lake Trails

A network of generally flat, well marked interconnected trails is found in this area. Although the area can be muddy during wet weather, especially in the spring, they make an ideal family circuit. Wildlife viewing and the beautiful wildflowers around Duck Lake are some highlights as is swimming at Haslam Slough.

Suicide Creek Loop

Located on the opposite side of the road from the Mud Lake Trails, this trail heads in a southeast direction for approximately 8 km (4.8 miles). Highlights of the trail include two sets of waterfalls. The Fern Falls has a picnic table and is below the first bridge, while the Mimulus Falls are found between the two footbridges. Mountain bikers should expect a moderate trail with re-routes around the rougher sections.

Sweetwater Creek Loop

Beginning on an old railgrade leading to Sweetwater Creek, the trail follows the creek draw eventually leading past MacGregor Falls. From there, the trail continues past Donelley Falls before heading south and back to Duck Lake Road. You will cover 7 km (4.2 miles) along a well-marked trail, which is ideal for moderate mountain bikers as well as hikers. The trail also provides access to the Blackwater Trail.

Eagle Ridge (Map 32/F4)

Located just south of Stein Valley Niakapamux Provincial Park, Eagle Ridge towers above the Kwoiek Creek Valley across the valley from the popular Kwoiek Needle. The challenging trail climbs nearly 1 vertical metre for every two travelled. All that elevation means plenty of viewpoints towards Chochiwa Lake, Glacier and the surrounding mountains. From the Eagle Ridge itself, you can see the surrounding tableau of mountains, including Skihist Peak, the highest mountain in Southwestern BC. Note that the trail has recently been re-blazed, but is still quite hard to follow. The old route to Antimony Lake is basically lost to the ravages of time, though that won't stop hardcore route finders from making there way to the lake.

Eaton Lake Trail (Map 5/G2)

This 4.1 km (2.5 mile) trail begins at the Eaton Creek Recreation Site on the Silver Skagit Road, south of Hope. Along the way, you will gain 915 metres (2,974 feet) in elevation, which is a fairly stiff climb. The rewarding trail begins by approaching Eaton Creek before descending rapidly to a log bridge, where there are great views of the falls and rapids. From here, the hike heads upward towards the popular fishing lake. It is possible to camp at the south end of the lake or continue on to Eaton Peak.

Elephant Lake Loop (Map 19/F4)

A long 48 km (29.3 mile) moderate bike ride that follows the main logging roads north of Saltery Bay. The roads lead past several small lakes and offer views of Jervis Inlet, Lois Lake and the surrounding area. You return along Highway 101. Don't be discouraged by the tough 8 km (4.8 mile) initial climb. The riding does get easier and the views are spectacular.

Elk-Thurston Trail (Map 4/F5)

A gruelling 14.6 km (8.9 mile) hike starts on the Chilliwack Bench Forest Road at a small gravel pit. You climb over 1,000 metres/3,280 feet (mostly at the beginning) to the summit of Mount Thurston and breathtaking panoramic views of the Chilliwack Valley and the border peaks. The trail passes through the wildflower carpeted sub-alpine meadows near the base of Elk Mountain. The trail continues onto an exposed ridge, which can be windy. The trail is located in an active logging area and access to the trail (and the surrounding view) may be impacted.

Emerald Estates Trails (Map 29/G4)

There is a network of mountain biking trails in the Emerald Estates area. The most popular trail in this network is the infamous Shit Happens. This 7.5 km (4.6 mile) trail links Emerald Estates to Alpine Meadows to the south.

Emerald Forest (Map 29/F5)

This area is made up of several short trails around the gravel pit, between Alta Lake Road and the Valley Trail. The Forest is located on private property so please respect your surroundings.

Emma Lake Trail (Map 47/A4)

Emma Lake Trail begins off the B-Branch from the Goat Lake Main. The steep trail leads 7 km (4.2 miles) to a forest service cabin set on Emma Lake. That has space for eight, but it is usually full. If you are planning on spending the night at this beautiful blue lake surrounded by sub-alpine meadows expect to tent it. If you stay overnight, you can take day trips to Snowy, Thunder Dome and Crossroads Peaks. Also, the South Powell Divide Route leads southward, including a ridge run from Triple Peaks to Center Lakes.

Evans Lake Area (Map 22/C4)

North of Evans Lake Camp, a series of trails/logging roads link up with Levette Lake. The wooded trails provide challenging single-track riding or enjoyable hiking in and around the park reserve and the wilderness lakes. There is even a Skyline Trail here. You can access these trails where the road branches to the camp.

Flank Trail (Map 29/C5–G4)

Beginning from Alexander Falls (close to the new Olympic Nordic centre), this trail skirts the western side of the Whistler Valley. It begins by dipping down to Function Junction before climbing again along the Rainbow-Sproatt Trail to Twentyone Mile Creek. From here, the trail continues to Alpine Meadows via Nineteen Mile Creek before ending at the Rainbow-Sproatt Trailhead on the Cougar Mountain Forest Road next to Sixteen Mile Creek. It is a fairly challenging trail due to the up and down nature of the terrain and the distance covered.

trailadventures

Flora Lake Trail (Map 5/F5) 🥾🐟👣

It is only a 7 km (4.3 miles) hike to the lake, but because of the stiff climb and rugged trail, it is best done as a two-day trip. The trail climbs 1,130 metres (3,672 feet) in elevation to the ridge before dropping 430 metres (1,397 feet) to the beautiful lake. This is a difficult hike, with two very steep sections, but your reward is breathtaking views of the Chilliwack Valley, old mining trails around the lake and fairly good fishing. It is possible to follow a rough, undeveloped trail past the Flora Creek Falls to Greendrop Lake.

Fool's Gold Route (Map 12/E7–B1) 🥾👣

Heavy lobbying for conservation of the extensive untouched forest to the west of Pitt Lake resulted in the creation of the Pinecone Burke Provincial Park. Within the park is the rugged and nearly impossible to follow Fool's Gold Route. The route runs some 50 km (30.5 miles) and will take most backpackers at least a week to complete. The Boise Creek section, a 12 km (7 mile) return section to Mamquam Pass is still quite popular, though the first section through a clearcut is quite difficult to follow.

Ford Mountain Trail (Map 5/C5) 🥾👣

From the sign at the end of the Ford Mountain Forest Road (4wd access), a short 1.7 km (1 mile) one-way hike follows the treed ridge to an old forestry lookout with panoramic views. The moderate trail gains 400 metres (1,300 feet) in elevation. Experienced hikers can continue along the bare ridge to the base of Williams Peak, which adds an additional 6 km (3.6 miles), climbing 460 metres (1,495 feet) along the way. If you do not have a 4wd vehicle, it is possible to hike the road but this requires an additional climb of 620 metres (2,015 feet) over 4.5 km (2.7 miles) one-way.

Freda Mountain Trails (Map 19/F1–47/A6) 🥾👣

To reach the summit of Freda Mountain, there are three possibilities. The southernmost route is a long trail leading from the Freda Mountain Main just north of the F-Branch. It involves a day+ hike. A more direct route is found on the J-Branch at the south end of Freda Lake. It is 8 km (4.8 mile) return trip that leads through an old growth forest to the sub-alpine. The third trail begins on the Jenna Branch Road at the east end of Freda Lake. This involves a 12 hour hike on a well marked (flagged) trail leading through the old growth timber to the sub-alpine.

Frogpond Lake Trail (Map 46/E5) 🥾👣

This steep, 5 km (3 mile) trail leads from Powell Lake up to Frogpond Lake. The trailhead is accessed by taking a boat to Cassiar Falls where the trail begins on the east side of the creek. Half way along the trail you reach a bench, which overlooks Powell Lake with a good view of Fiddlehead Farm and Tin Hat Mountain to the south.

Galene Lakes Route (Map 6/E7) ⛺🥾👣

This route begins 55 km (33.6 miles) down the Silver Skagit Road, at the Chittenden Bridge parking area. It takes you 32 km (19.5 miles) return to the Galene Lake, climbing 1,250 metres (4,063 feet) along the way. The trail crosses a footbridge and then proceeds through meadows along the Skagit River before following Galene Creek up to the lake. The lake offers a rustic campsite, some decent fishing opportunities and great views. The trail is best hiked from July to October.

Gallagher Hills Trail (Map 18/G3) 🥾👣

The trail begins 100 metres (325 feet) along the Inland Lake Road. The trail leads along an old skid trail up to a rock bluff and then on to a radio tower overlooking Powell Lake and the ocean. The total distance of the hike is 5 km (3 miles) return. It is possible to take a side trip off the bluff and walk down to Mowat Bay.

Gambier Lake Trail (Map 10/E4) 🥾🚶🐟👣

On Gambier Island, this 17 km (10.4 mile) trail leads from the ferry terminal past the general store and continues up the hill. After crossing Mannion Creek, the trail follows an old road eventually leading to Gambier Lake. The trail gains 475 metres (1,544 feet). It is possible to take a side trip to Mount Liddle, which involves a 900 metre (2,925 foot) climb over 14 km (8.5 miles). This second trail follows an overgrown road past Muskeg Lake and along a ridge with some excellent views of the ocean.

Garibaldi Highlands (Map 22/D6) 🥾🚴

The Highlands are the most popular mountain biking area in Squamish. You can access the area from Alice Lake Park in the north or Perth Drive and Glacierview Road in Garibaldi Highlands in the south. The moderate trails offer easier, smoother terrain than others in the Squamish area. To really explore the system, try joining the trails to create a long loop ride.

Garibaldi Provincial Park-Black Tusk (Map 22/D1–F2) ⛺🥾🚴🚶🏠🐟👣

A paved road leads just south of Daisy Lake from Highway 99 to the Rubble Creek parking lot. It is recommended that you either camp at Taylor Meadows or at the Battleship Lakes Camp if you want to explore the surrounding mountains including hiking to the famous Black Tusk. Taylor Meadows is 7.5 km (4.6 mile) from the parking lot.

Garibaldi Lake Trail

Certainly one of the more popular destinations in the park, the main lake is found 9 km (5.5 miles) along a well maintained trail. The trail is best hiked from July to October and provides fantastic views of surrounding glacier and mountains as you climb 940 metres (3,055 feet). Climbing up Panorama Ridge adds an additional 5 km and 630 metres.

Black Tusk Trail

Found an additional 7 km (4.3 mile) hike from Taylor Campground, this trail leads through a sub-alpine meadow and forest to a rocky slope and eventually onto the prominent volcanic pillar (gaining 820 metre/2,665 feet along the way). In the winter, the area turns to a backcountry skiing haven with an expansive trail network including the Garibaldi Neve Traverse, which extends south from Garibaldi Lake all the way to the Diamond Head Trail near Squamish.

Upper Lakes

Continuing on from Taylor Meadows for an additional 4 km (2.4 miles), this extension gains little elevation as it passes through an alpine meadow to a series of smaller lakes to the foot of the Helm Glacier.

Garibaldi Provincial Park-Cheakamus Lake (Map 29/F7–22/F1) ⛺🥾🚶🚴🐟👣

South of Whistler, this popular multi-use trail system begins at the end of the Cheakamus Lake Road, some 8 km (4.8 miles) from Highway 99. Cheakamus Lake is a turquoise coloured lake surrounded by rugged snow-capped peaks that is truly a delight to fish, canoe or just visit. Mountain bikes are allowed on the trail to Singing Creek Camp although hardcore riders may loop back along the south side of the Cheakamus River.

Cheakamus Lake Trail

The lake is only 3.2 km (2 mile) from the parking lot with almost no elevation gain. Don't be surprised to see someone carrying a canoe down the trail that meanders through a boulder field and some slide alders before entering into a forested area next to the river.

Singing Creek Camp

Beyond the first campsite, a trail leads along the north shores of Cheakamus Lake, past some large timber, to the Singing Creek Camp. The easy trail is 14 km (8.5 miles) return to the parking lot with little elevation gain.

Helm Creek Trail

A bridge was built a few years back, bringing this once obscure route new found popularity. The trail is 14.5 km (8.8 miles) one-way, with an elevation gain of 600 metres (1,950 feet). The trail network connects with the Black Tusk system near Upper Lakes as it passes through the extensive sub-alpine terrain of the Garibaldi Provincial Park. The hike is best suited for July to October.

Garibaldi Provincial Park-Diamond Head (Map 22/E6–G4) ⛺🥾🚴🚶🚵🏠

Near Squamish, the Diamond Head parking lot is found at the 16 km (9.8 mile) mark of the Mamquam Road. The road to the parking lot is open year round as the road is usually ploughed to allow backcountry skiers to access Garibaldi Park. This is one of four main access points into the park.

Diamond Head [Elfin Lake] Trail

The main trail into the area, Elfin Lakes require an 11.2 km (6.8 miles) one-way hike. The trail climbs 600 metres (1,970 feet) up an old road before breaking out into the alpine at Red Heather Day Shelter. Mountain bikers looking for a gruelling uphill climb can bike to the hut at Elfin Lake, which sleeps 40 and has a propane heater. Many people set up base camp here and do day hikes deeper into the park. The trail is open from July to October for hikers and then turns into a popular backcountry skiing/snowshoeing area when the snow falls.

Little Diamond Head

From Elfin Lakes, it is 7 km (4.3 miles) return to the Little Diamond Head. The trail leads through some open sub-alpine meadows gaining 625 metres (2,031 feet) along the way.

Opal Cone & Mamquam Lake

Opal Cone is a spectacular volcanic outcrop about 6.4 km (3.9 miles) from Elfin Lakes. It will take four hours return gaining 250 metres (813 feet). Mamquam Lakes requires a bit more work as you climb 570 metres from Elfin Lakes.

Gate Mountain Trail (Map 26/F6)

Also known as the 1858 First Brigade Trail, this steep, difficult trail climbs 1,200 m (3,900 feet) along a 16 km (9.8 mile) old pack trail. The trailhead is found just south of the Coopers Corner Rest Area (watch for a pullout on the west side of the road). The hike follows a mixture of logging roads, old pack trails as well as a newer trail and is best hiked in June-October. Eventually, you will pass through a meadow with wildflowers before reaching the Notch and then finally the summit of Gate Mountain. Both the Notch and the summit both provide excellent views over the Fraser Canyon.

Ghost Pass Trail (Map 6/D2)

This trail begins at the West Gate of Manning Park and leads along an old engineering road to a signed trailhead. You must climb to Ghost Pass, which is 11 km (6.7 miles) one-way from the trailhead, before reaching Ghost Pass Lake. Beyond the lake, the trail disappears.

Goat II Access Trail (Map 47/A5)

At the end of Goat 2 Road is the Goat II Access Trail, a difficult hike to a beautiful alpine area. If you proceed south you will see a trailhead marked by flagging tape. From here, you must do some bushwhacking past two small creeks, across a rockslide before reaching the ridge and ultimately the traverse down to Skwim Lake. If you proceed in a northern direction from the Goat Lake II Road, you will have to walk along the deactivated road to an old trail heading up to the base of Triple Peaks. There are alpine flowers in July and great views of the surrounding mountain peaks. From the alpine area, you can continue on the South Powell Divide Trail leading to Emma Lake and beyond.

Golden Ears Provincial Park Trails (Map 2, 3, 12, 13)

There are a number of trails in this wilderness park, some multi-use, some hiking only. The highlights include an abundance of wildlife, the scenic Alouette Lake and the mountains that glow like golden ears in the sun.

Alouette Mountain Trail (Map 2/G2–13/A7)

This difficult 22 km (13.4 mile) return trip climbs 1,100 metres (3,575 feet) to the summit. Along the way, you will pass some scenic meadows and ponds. There are a couple variations on how to start this trail, either along the Incline Trail, Mike Lake Trail or the old fire access road. The latter is the easiest (but longest) and is open to mountain bikers and equestrians, who are able to follow the fire access road to the hitching post at Lake Beautiful.

East Canyon Trail (Map 3/A1–B7)

A rocky, 11 km (6.7 mile) trail follows the banks of Gold Creek north to the Lower Falls. This trail is open to mountain bikers but expect a difficult trail with rough sections and a 320-metre (1,040 feet) elevation gain. Past here, the Hector Ferguson Trail continues deep into the heart of the park.

Golden Ears Trail (Map 3/A1–13/A7)

This popular 24 km (14.6 mile) trip gains 1,500 metres (4,875 feet) to the popular peak. The hike begins at the West Canyon Parking Lot and follows Gold Creek and the West Canyon Trail to Alder Flats. Most people heading for the peak set up camp here and hike the remaining distance to the peak without a pack. This is a good idea, as most of the elevation gain happens in the last few kilometres. The trail heads steeply up the ridge past a rustic mountain shelter to the summit of Panorama Ridge. You will break out of the trees and into the high, rocky alpine.

Hector Ferguson Trail (Map 13/B6)

A 22 km (13.4 mile) hike along the east side of Gold Creek. The trail leads to a tiny lake that forms the headwaters of the creek, deep in the heart of Golden Ears. This is the farthest north you can hike into the park by land (there are a couple lake access routes that head farther in). Expect to take at least a day to get to the lake and back.

Menzies Trail (Map 3/A1)

More of an equestrian trail than a hiking trail, this is an easy 18 km (11 mile) return trek from the Fern Crescent Trailhead to the West Canyon parking lot.

West Canyon Trail (Map 3/A1–A7)

Beginning at the West Canyon parking lot, this trail heads north, following the western banks of Gold Creek. If you want to loop back along the East Canyon Trail, you will need to ford the creek near Lower Falls. This makes for a nice 9 km (5.5 mile) return hike with minimal elevation gain.

Great Blue Heron Nature Reserve (Map 4/B5)

The Chilliwack Rotary Club has built an Interpretive Centre and trail system next to the Great Blue Heron nesting ground. There are 5 km (3 miles) of easy trails here. As you might expect, most trail users come to see the birds.

Green Lake Route (Map 29/G5–30/A4)

A moderate mountain bike ride that offers a few tough hills as you head south from the Wedgemont Creek Forest Road to the Lost Lake Trail system. The route is 11 km (6.7 miles) and climbs 150 m (490 feet) as you alternate from double track to single-track along the powerlines on the eastern shore of Green Lake.

Green Mountain Trails (Map 4/G3)

This moderate series of mountain biking trails is found off the Agassiz bypass, just north of the railway tracks (on the west side). A tough climb takes you 455 metres (1,479 feet) up the access road to the network of trails at the top of Green Mountain. The access road eventually turns into a single-track trail and will take you down to the farmer's field on the other side.

Green Necklace Greenway (Map 1/E1)

This planned urban green loop will be a 7 km (4.3 mile) loop around the central Lonsdale area. Phase 1 saw 2.2 km (1.3 miles) of trail developed.

Grouse Mountain Trails (Map 11/D7)

Starting at the base of Grouse Mountain at the end of Nancy Green Way are a series of popular trails including the infamous Grouse Grind. Hikers wishing to explore the alpine areas, often prefer to ride the gondola to the top. Those people looking to get a great workout prefer to grunt their way to the top. Either way, the views can be fabulous from the top. Due to snow, hikes up the surrounding mountain are best left until July to early November.

BCMC Trail

The original route up to the top of Grouse Mountain, the steep 3.5 km (2.2 mile) trail is only slightly longer than the much more popular Grind. It climbs the same height, but a ski run has forced the last stretch of the trail to be rerouted. This is one of the oldest hiking trails in BC.

Crown Mountain Route

This route involves making your way along a difficult, exposed route where one misstep could be disastrous. With this in mind, Crown Mountain is best left to folks who know what they're doing. It is 9.6 km (6 miles) from the top of the gondola to the peak, climbing 695 feet (2,278 feet).

Grouse Grind

The Grind isn't a trail; it's a social phenomenon. On evenings after work and on weekends, this trail, which heads straight up the mountainside just east of the gondola, sees hundreds of walkers, looking for a good burn as the trail climbs just about a kilometre (853 metres/2,772 feet) in 2.9 km (1.8 miles). If you do the math, that's about 1 metre up for every 3.4 metres travelled, which makes this a good cardio-workout. This partially explains the high traffic the trail sees. Another important element in the Grind's popularity is the fact that there is a bar at the top and the fact that you don't have to hike back down. Most catch the gondola (for a fee) back down. Besides, who can argue with the chance to hike up a trail with a bunch of young, hard-bodied people wearing really tight clothes? The trail has seen lots of recent improvements and is literally one long wooden and rock staircase. It is also closed in winter.

Goat Mountain Trail

From the top of the gondola, this hike is 8 km (4.9 miles) return gaining 275 metres (894 feet) to the summit at 1,400 metres (4,550 feet). The hike starts on an old road before the trail heads up Goat Ridge. You can include the Dam Mountain Loop in your hike and maybe even a side trip to Little Goat Mountain. The views of the Lower Mainland are great…on days you can actually see Greater Vancouver.

Peak View Trail

An easy walking trail atop Grouse Mountain, this trail runs just 500 metres (1,625 feet) from the top of the Peak Chair to a lookout over Vancouver. The trail is longer and more difficult if you chose to walk up from the chalet along the Dam/Goat Mountain Trail. Head right to access the peak of Grouse.

Halfmoon Creek Loop (Map 9/C4)

Found on an old road on the east side of Homesite Creek just off Highway 101, this easy 8.5 km (5.2 mile) mountain bike loop follows the logging road to the powerline. From the powerline you loop back along the Halfmoon Bay Forest Road and the highway.

Hanging Lake Trail (Map 5/F7)

This is a moderate 8 km (4.9 mile) round trip hike to a gorgeous lake, at the base of Mount Lindeman. Hanging Lake provides good fishing and Lindeman is a fine rock-climbing destination.

Harrison Lookout Trail (Map 14/E4)

Located off the Harrison West Forest Road, this short but steep 4 km (2.4 mile) trail leads to an old forest service lookout on a hill above Harrison Lake. You hike along an old road to a beautifully wooded trail past mossy knolls to the vantage point from the lookout some 350 metres (1,138 feet) later.

Hayward Lake Trails (Map 3/C3)

In and around Hayward Lake are a series of easy trails to explore. The **Pond Interpretative Trail** is a short 1.5 km stroll around a small beaver pond. The **Railway Trail** can be accessed either near Ruskin Dam from Wilson Road or off the parking lot just south of the Dewdney Trunk Road. This easy trail leads 12 km (7.3 miles) return along an old rail bed, which was used in the early part of the century while building Stave Falls Dam. The **Reservoir Trail** follows the east shores of the reservoir for 9 km past Steelhead Falls, a floating bridge and old growth and second growth forests.

Haywire Bay Regional Park Trails (Map 18/G3)

There is a pair of trails here. The Lost Lake Trail is 6 km (3.6 miles) in length and leads through old growth forest past Lost Lake to Inland Lake. There are several steep sections along the trail. Tony's Trail leads along the eastern banks of Powell Lake in a southward direction. This trail is 8 km (4.8 miles) one-way and culminates at Mowat Bay.

High Falls Creek Trail (Map 21/G2—22/A2)

The High Falls Creek Trail was the first trail that local legend Halvor Lunden built, although parts of the trail have been clear cut. From the 24 mile mark on the Squamish Main, the steep trail leads 12 km (6.7 miles) return to a view of the falls and the Squamish River Valley. Past the falls, the trail continues up, climbing 640 metres (2,080 feet) to the vista at 715 metres (2,324 feet). The trail hooks up with a nearby logging road and it is possible to head back along the road. You can also find your way up Cloudburst Mountain or up the road to Tricouni Meadows.

Hillside Demonstration Forest (Map 10/D4)

Located along McNair Creek, this demonstration forest illustrates different silviculture practices of the Sunshine Coast and provides a view of the Port Mellon Mill as well as Howe Sound. The demonstration forest is on the west side of McNair Creek and so it is best to park on the west side of the McNair Creek Bridge and hike up the hill. The demonstration forest trail is 4 km (2.4 miles) return and has a number of interpretative signs along the way.

Hollyburn Heritage Trails (Map 11/C7)

From the west side of Lawson Creek Bridge on Pinecrest Drive, an extensive trail network leads through the second growth forest typical of the North Shore. The main trail leads 6.7 km (4 miles) return to the Hollyburn Fir, an 1100-year-old Douglas-fir that is 3 metres (9.7 feet) in diameter. The trail crosses the Crossover and Baden Powell Trails. Within the area, the remains of logging from the 1920s are seen. Another possible access point is at the junction of Eyremount, Crestwell and Millstream Roads.

Homesite Creek [Gumdrop] Caves (Map 9/C3)

The trailhead is found on the Homesite Forest Road just north of the powerline and is usually signed as long as vandals have not removed the sign. The trail leads half an hour (one-way) in a southeast direction from the road to a series of twelve limestone caverns, the largest one being 10 metres (33 feet) deep.

Homesite Creek Loop (Map 9/C3)

Starting on the Homesite Creek Forest Road, an 8 km (4.8 mile) moderate bike ride follows the logging roads and power lines to the west of Homesite Creek. This one hour loop is best done in a counter-clockwise direction (start left from the Forest Road and follow the markers). This way you end with a fun 5 km (3 mile) downhill, which takes you back to the highway.

Hoover Lake Trail (Map 3/D2)

Give yourself about an hour to reach the lake as you hike through a heavy forest, east of Stave Falls Dam. This trail starts out along an old road, then a trail as it climbs steadily to the lake. The trail is 7.4 km (4.5 miles) return with an elevation gain of 250 metres (812 feet).

Hope Lookout Trail (Map 15/F7)

You have a choice of a short 2 km (1.2 miles) loop around the base of Hope Mountain or a 5 km (3 mile) hike to the lookout. The latter hike involves a 500 m (1,625 feet) climb as you switchback up the talus slopes to the lookout. The trailhead is found off Highway 1 near Exit 173, across from the Rainbow Inn.

Hope Mountain Trail (Map 15/G7)

The trailhead is found opposite Nicolum Park on Highway 3 along a 4wd road. The road climbs 8 km (4.8 miles) over many waterbars to the parking lot. The difficult trail leading to the right (left leads to Wells Peak) will take about 5 hours to climb Hope Mountain. After climbing 800 m (2,600 ft), you will be rewarded with panoramic views (on clear days).

Hope Pass Trail (Map 6/G3—7/C1)

Although this trail begins inside Manning Park, most of this historic trail actually lies in the Cascade Recreation Area. This trail leads from Cayuse Flats on Highway 3, 26 km (15.9 miles) one-way to a branch road off the Whipsaw Creek Forest Road. The first 4 km (2.4 miles) of the trail follow an old fire access road before the trail heads in a northeastern direction along the banks of the Skagit River. At around the two hour mark, watch for the Grainger Creek Trail, which departs to the right. As an alternate, you could loop back along this route and camp at Nicomen Lake. The trail reaches Hope Pass at the 21 km mark (12.8 miles) before descending to the Whipsaw Creek Forest Road. Some people turn around at the pass and hoof it back to Cayuse Flats for a very long (12-14 hour) day hike. From Highway 3 to Hope Pass, there is an elevation gain of 1,050 metres (3,413 feet). There is an interesting side route to Dick's Cabin on top of Skaist Mountain.

Hut Lake Trail (Map 22/C4)

With a 4wd vehicle, you can park at the north end of Levette Lake and follow the overgrown, washed out logging road part way to Hut Lake. It is a 5 km/3 mile (1.5 hour) trek. The lake offers good fishing for small rainbow.

Inland Lake Trail (Map 18/G2)

Inland Lake Trail is a wheelchair accessible area, complete with a cabin, picnic tables and a dock. The trail leads 13 km (7.9 miles) around the lake. From the west side of the lake, it is possible to connect with the Lost Lake Trail, which culminates at the Haywire Bay Regional Park. At the north end of Inland Lake, you may wish to hike 700m (one-way) along the portage route to Powell Lake. This is a well marked and popular family trail enjoyed by both hikers and bikers.

International Ridge Trail (Map 4/D7)

Accessed off the gated Edmesten Road, this 16 km (10 mile) ridge route leads to the 1,525 metre (4,956 foot) high summit of Mount Amadis. You will climb 1,325 metres (4,306 feet) over about eight hours. From the summit, you get a good view of the Fraser Valley and over the border into Washington State.

Joffre Lake Trail (Map 37/A7)

The trailhead is located approximately 23 km (14 miles) east of Mount Currie on Highway 99. The very popular trail is well marked and leads from the parking lot past two smaller lakes on your way to the picturesque Upper Joffre Lake. The upper lake, which offers wilderness camping, is simply spectacular as it lies directly below the icefields of Matier Glacier. The trail is 11 km (6.7 miles) gaining 400 metres (1,300 feet). Some mountaineers hike to the glacier edge or climb Joffre or Matier Peaks (see Twin Goat Ridge Route below).

Keats Island (Map 10/D6)

Keats Island is a small island accessed by foot ferry from Gibsons. From the landing, it is a 2 km (1.2 mile) jaunt to Plumper Cove Marine Park. At the park, a handful of trails weave their way through the woods, taking you to viewpoints and along oceanfront trails.

Killarney Creek/Lake Trail (Map 10/F6)

On Bowen Island, the Killarney Creek Trail follows the north side of Killarney Creek past the small set of falls at the head of the lagoon. You also pass a fish-spawning channel before circling lovely Killarney Lake. The best place to find the trailhead is at the Union Steamship Co. Store in Snug Cove or at St. Gerard's Catholic Church. The trail is about an 8 km (2.5 hour) hike from the ferry landing around the lake.

Kwotlenemo Trails (Map 44/F7)
This popular recreation lake is home to a series of multi-use trails. In winter the 12 km (6.7 miles) system is used by cross-country skiers, while in the spring through fall, mountain bikers and hikers frequent the trails. The lake is accessed by the Fountain Valley Road.

Ladner Creek Trail (Map 16/B4)
This hiking/biking trail leads along a section of the historic Kettle Valley Railway through tunnels and over an abandoned trestle. The 3 km (1.8 mile) hike will take about an hour and makes an excellent side trail from the newly established Trans Canada Trail, which leads south of Highway 5. Alternatively, many visitors simply scramble up the talus slope from the east side of the creek off of the highway. Please be careful as this trail is not maintained and the trestle is in a state of disrepair.

Lake Lovely Water Trail (Map 22/B5)
The hike into this scenic sub-alpine area, now part of the Tantalus Provincial Park, is difficult but rewarding. It involves crossing an Indian Reserve to the Squamish River and then paddling a canoe across the river. From the west banks of the Squamish River, the trail follows the creek draw leading to the lake set in a large glacial bowl. The trail is 15 km (9.2 miles) return gaining over 1,200 metres (3,900 feet). While it is a difficult, sometimes daunting steep climb, the trail is in good condition. The Alpine Club maintains a cabin at the lake, which can be used for a fee ($10-$12). The area also offers good fishing, wilderness camping areas and climbing opportunities.

Lighthouse Park (Map 11/A7)
From the parking lot at Lighthouse Park, an extensive year round trail network leads through old growth forest to the wave washed rocky shoreline of Point Atkinson. If you hike around the perimeter of the park, the 5 km (3 mile) hike should take about two hours. But there are many other trails snaking through the forest. Make sure you visit the eponymous lighthouse, which was erected in 1912.

Lillooet River Dyke Trails (Map 30/C1–B7)
Starting from Highway 99 on the east side of the Lillooet River Bridge, a gentle trail follows the river in a northwest direction for about 5 km (3 miles). At the end of the dyke road, a moderate single-track loops around MacKenzie Lake. From here, it is possible to return along the steep (1,000 metre/3,280 feet) MacKenzie Basin Road. The Dyke Trail also extends for several kilometres in the opposite direction. This easy route cuts through the Indian Reserve, marshland and offers fine views of Mount Currie.

Ling Lake Trail (Map 5/D4)
The trailhead for the Ling Lake Trail is found at the end of Foley Creek Road. Unfortunately, there is a gate located near the Foley Creek Recreation Site so you will have to hike or bike up the logging road before actually starting the trail. From the gate, the trail is about 18 km (11 miles) long. Give yourself at least a day to the alpine lake. The principle users of the trail are fishermen.

Lions Trail (Map 11/B5)
The hike to this popular hike is found at Lions Bay by taking the Oceanside Road exit off Highway 99 and driving to the gate at the end of Mountain Drive (parking is limited). The difficult trail follows an old road upward until there is a fork in the road. The right fork leads to the Lions Trail, while the left fork accesses the Brunswick Mountain Trail. You will climb down to Harvey Creek (a depressing prospect, knowing that you'll just have to climb back up again), then heads up through an old growth forest. The last part of the 15 km (9.1 mile) hike climbs steeply to a small summit to the south of the West Lion, where it is possible to pitch a tent and enjoy the view of the Howe Sound. You will climb 1,280 metres (4,160 feet). The hike is best done in late summer or early fall.

Little Spearhead (Map 29/G5)
From the Upper Village, follow the signs to the Singing Pass Parking Lot. Here you cross Fitzsimmons Creek (be careful, there's no bridge) and descend on Blackcomb Mountain. This 13 km (7.9 mile) round trip climbs 325 metres (1,056 feet) and is a moderate ride.

Liumchen Lake Trail (Map 4/E7)
This is a beautiful alpine hike that starts at the end of the very rough Liumchen East Forest Road (about 9.5 km/5.8 miles along this 4wd road). From the trailhead you climb sharply uphill, through a mix of forest and meadows to a ridge, which offers great views of the Chilliwack Valley. From the ridge, the trail drops 280 metres (910 feet) into the lovely Liumchen Lake bowl. It will take about five hours to hike 9.4 km (5.7 miles) return, but if you're in the

area already, why not set up camp at the lake and spend a day or two exploring the trails to the surrounding peaks. Church Mountain is an additional 1.5 km (0.9 miles) along the ridge. Liumchen Mountain is south from the alpine meadows. You will climb 457 metres (1,485 feet) over 2.5 km (1.5 miles) one-way to this great vantage point that overlooks Washington State. The hike is best done in late summer (for the flowers) or in early autumn.

Lizzie Creek [Stein Divide] Trail (Map 31/C5)
After ascending through a narrow gorge on the Lizzie Creek Main (by foot or 4wd) you will reach beautiful Lizzie Lake. From here, it is a steep 5 km (3 mile) one-way hike gaining 640 metres (2,080 feet) to the Lizzie Creek Cabin. From the cabin, experienced backpackers can make numerous day trips to explore the many alpine lakes and mountains in the area. To reach the Stein Divide requires scrambling up a rockslide, hiking past several small alpine lakes to Cherry Pip Pass and then skirting over to Caltha Lake, which is about a 6-8 hour one-way hike from the cabin. Another two hours or so takes you over the Stein Divide to Tundra Lake. Further along the route are Stein Lake and Elton Lake. This area provides exceptional hiking in the alpine with endless backpacking and backcountry skiing options. The area is quite popular, but is also quite difficult and should be left to experienced hikers.

Loquilts Route (Map 47/F3)
This is, to be frank, a ridiculously tough trip. To get to the trailhead involves taking a boat up Jervis Inlet to the spectacular Princess Louisa Inlet and Chatterbox Falls. From here, a beaten trail runs up to Loquilts Lake, climbing steeply along the creek, through a boulder field. By the time you make it to the lake, you will have climbed 1,300 vertical metres (4,265 feet). From here, there is an unmarked route through the scenic alpine, including crossing some glaciers, before the decent to the trail leading from the Elaho Valley.

Lost Lake Ski Trails (Map 29/G5)
30 km (18.3 miles) of well maintained cross-country ski trails leads from the parking lot adjacent to the municipal hall in Whistler or from the parking lot next to the Chateau Whistler. When the snow is gone, the trail network is heavily used by hikers, joggers and mountain bikers. Periodically, you will find maps and signs to help mark the way. The main trail leads around Lost Lake providing easy access to the north end where you will find a nice wharf and a doggie beach. The trail network connects with the Valley Trail network.

Lower Seymour Conservation Reserve (Map 11/E7–F6)
Formerly known as the Seymour Demonstration Forest, this 5,200 hectare area was created in 1987 to educate the public about forest ecosystems and logging practices. Within the reserve are several well-maintained trails and a few hidden routes to explore. From the parking lot at the end of Lillooet Road, a series of easier routes exist. No dogs are allowed in the reserve.

> **Fisherman Trail & Twin Bridges Trail**
> A popular trail with anglers and mountain bikers, the Fisherman Trail is a moderate 7km route along the scenic Seymour River. Follow the Twin Bridges Trail 2.6 km to the bottom of the hill, then head north (left) before the bridge. Other trails in the area can extend both trails.

> **Poster Child Trail**
> Replacing the bottom half of the old CBC mountain bike trail that used to cross into Mount Seymour Park, the Poster Child is one of the best examples of how mountain biking trails can be built right. It is a difficult trail through a highly sensitive environment, yet the trail has been built to minimize the impact of bikes on the landscape.

> **Rice Lake Trail**
> A gravel road connects the Rice Lake loop trail with the main parking area. In total it is about 4 km (2.4 miles) along an easy grade that is open to mountain biking.

> **Seymour Valley Trailway**
> From the main parking lot, this popular paved route leads 10 km (6.2 miles) one-way to the Seymour Dam. The rolling track is used by walkers, bikers and inline skaters and can be busy. Allow about 3 hours to enjoy the great views en route.

Lower Seymour Trails (Map 1/F1)
A few years back, the rangers at Mount Seymour Provincial Park closed the Lower Seymour Trails that were inside park boundaries, severely limiting mountain biking in this area. Still, some of the classic rides here (Bridal Path, Severed Dick), located below the park boundaries are still open. Compara-

tively speaking, this is one of the easier areas to mountain bike on the North Shore. This large network of trails, which are also enjoyed by hikers and horseback riders, extends between Mt Seymour Parkway and Lynn Canyon Park.

Lucky Four Mine Trail (Map 5/C4)

This moderate trail climbs 650 metres in 4 km (2,113 feet in 2.4 miles) one-way as it makes its way along an old access road to the site of an old mine. From the mine, a difficult route heads up and onto the glacier below Foley Peak, an additional 2.5 km and 400 metres up (1.5 miles and 1287 feet).

Lynn Canyon Park (Map 1/E1–11/E7)

While it's much bigger brother, Lynn Headwaters, gets all the press, Lynn Canyon is arguably a nicer place to be. Its rewards come early. A suspension bridge, just a few steps from the parking lot, is the main feature of the park and few people make it much beyond the bridge. Those that do, usually head north, to a rocky beach and waterfall that is surprisingly busy on a hot summer day. What this means is the short loop trail is usually free of foot traffic, even in the middle of summer. A second bridge, below a series of cascades spans the creek, making an easy loop. More energetic hikers can continue straight and connect up with the Baden Powell Trail, which can be used as the second leg in an 8 km (4.8 mile) loop (the third leg is along the Fisherman/Homestead Trails, back to Lynn Canyon).

Lynn Headwaters Regional Park (Map 11/E7–E5)

This popular park offers a wide variety of trails ranging from easy creek walks to strenuous wilderness treks. The heavily wooded trails make for good wet weather walking. The park is accessed off the Lynn Valley Road past Dempsey Road.

Coliseum Mountain Route

Certainly not one of the easier routes in the area, this difficult hike is best left for the drier weather of late summer and early fall. It is a steep 25 km (15.25 mile) return hike that follows a sometimes indistinct route. The route is marked with orange markers as you pass through the steep forested area and enter the Norvan Meadows on your way to Norvan Pass gaining 1,245 metres (4,046 feet). Although there is no camping allowed in the park, the Coliseum is the type of destination that makes a perfect overnight trip.

Hanes Valley Loop

Linking hikers with Grouse Mountain is a steep 17 km (10.4 mile) hike along Hanes Creek. The trail gains 900 metres (2,995 feet), most of this as you climb up the steep scree slope out of the valley to Crown Pass. The rough trail leaves the Headwaters Trail at Norvan Creek and has some difficult creek crossings. Good route finding skills are a must.

Lynn Loop

Most visitors to the area sample this one. It leads over the bridge near the parking lot (as all trails in Lynn headwaters must) and heads north into the valley along the east bank of Lynn Creek. There is little elevation gain along this trail and you can return the way you came. However, to complete the loop, you must head up (about 350 metres/1,138 feet) into the woods and back along a slightly more challenging path. This trail leads through a vast forest of giant stumps and verdant second growth forest. For some, this trail shows the recovery power of nature. For others, it is a reminder of what this forest once was, before the loggers came. Either way, it is an impressive site. This is a 9.5 km (5.8 mile) trip, with a shortcut trail at about the halfway point, creating a shorter loop.

Norvan Falls

This trail follows the same path as the Lynn Loop, but when the loop doubles back on itself, keep heading north for another 3 km (1.8 miles) to the falls. In total, it is a 13.5 km (8.2 mile) return hike gaining 375 metres (1,230 feet) in elevation to the scenic falls.

Lynn Lake

Since there is no camping allowed, you will really have to leg it to hike the 25 km (15.3 mile) to the lake and back. Even better, the trail is ragged and rough and sometimes not even a trail at all. This route is best left for experienced (and fast) hikers.

Lynn Peak

At 1,000 metres (3,250 feet), the peak is the runt of the North Shore Mountains. But unlike Seymour to the east, which you can drive most of the way up and Grouse to the west, which has its gondola, the only way to the top of Lynn is with your own two feet and that alone is worth a

recommendation. The viewpoint at the top isn't a high alpine clearing, but a rocky outcropping with okay views. It'll take about four hours to hike the 7 km (4.3 mile) moderate return trip. You can continue past Lynn Peak to the Needles.

Lyon Lake Loop (Map 9/D1–C7)

Found on a side road 16 km (9.8 miles) up the Halfmoon Bay Forest Road (4wd access), this difficult 17 km (10.4 mile) mountain bike loop trail should take 2.5 hours to ride. This well marked route is best cycled in a clockwise direction as you follow a series of logging roads that tend to be steep and rocky in places. The loop takes you through some old growth forests to beautiful, panoramic views.

Mackenzie Trails (Map 30/C1–36/C7)

The Mackenzie Trails intertwine with the Mosquito Lake Trails, but are generally rougher, steeper and more challenging. Most of the trails are accessed off the Cell Tower Road, which leads up to the paraglide launch. For people looking for less aggressive riding, it is possible to ride up past the launch (and trails with names like Blood, Sweat and Fear and Cop Killer, named after a local mountain biking policeman who wasn't quite up to the trail) and back down into the valley along the main road, creating the Mackenzie Basin Loop.

Madely Lake Trail (Map 29/D4)

While access is much improved now that the Callaghan Road is paved, the spur road to the lake still calls for a high clearance vehicle. From the trailhead, the trail leads 6 km (3.6 miles) one-way to Rainbow Lake gaining 500 metres (1,625 feet). This is a shorter alternative for hiking to Rainbow Lake, although like the other trail, the approach is through an unremarkable forest. Once you exit the woods, though, the scenery is spectacular, through beautiful meadows with the possibility of scrambling some rocky peaks. Currently, there is a bridge out on the trail and the trail can be hard to follow as it crosses a boulder field. Watch for flagging tape.

Manning Park (Map 6, 7)

Trails cut through all reaches of this fine destination park allowing people to explore the rugged mountains, meadows, lakes and rivers that people cruising the highway or staying in the lodge rarely see. Trail users will find designated areas for backcountry camping, while closer to the core area and highway, there are many short loop trails to explore. Another fine feature of the park is the fact it is equally as popular in the winter as it is in the summer.

Bonnevier Trail (Map 7/D4–F4)

Originally built as a packhorse route in the early 1900s, this is a difficult trail that is best hiked from west to east. You will lose more elevation than you gain in this direction (about 950 metres/3,088 feet). The trail starts 7 km (4.3 miles) along the Heather Trail, head east and follow the trail downhill to McDiarmid Meadows. The total distance hiked is 25 km (15.3 miles) one-way and can be done as a shuttle trip in a long day. Water is available at the 9 km (5.5 mile) mark.

Frosty Mountain Trail (Map 7/C7)

Frosty Mountain is the highest peak in the park. A pair of difficult trails lead to the peak, just below the actual summit. From the Windy Joe Trailhead it is a 29 km (17.7 mile) return trek, while from Lightning Lakes it is a 22.2 km (13.5 mile) route. It is possible to combine the two into a 27.5 km (16.8 mile) loop. The Lightning Lakes route is shorter and has slightly less elevation change (1,150 metres/3,738 feet). Although this trip can be done in a long, strenuous day, there are campsites on either route. The best times to visit Frosty Mountain are in late July/early August when the meadows are full of wildflowers or mid-September when the Larch trees turn a brilliant gold colour. The high elevation and north-facing slope means this is one of the last trails to be free of snow. For folks not wanting to make the entire trip, Larch Plateau at 9 km (5.5 miles) is a worthy destination. Do not be fooled by their size, these trees are estimated to be 2,000 years old.

Grainger Creek Trail (Map 7/A2)

In order to reach the Grainger Creek trailhead, you have to hike 6 km (3.7 miles) along the Hope Pass Trail. At the junction of Grainger Creek and the Skaist River, the Grainger Creek Trail swings east up the valley climbing steadily for 11 km (6.7 miles) to the western end of Nicomen Lake. The trail gains 800 metres (2,600 feet) to the lake, which has a lovely camping area at its northern end. This trail can also be reached by hiking the Heather Trail to Nicomen Lake.

Heather/Three Brothers Trail (Map 7/D5–C2)
This is the main trail through Manning Park's vast sub-alpine meadows. In mid-July to August, the sub-alpine are notorious for their amazing display of colourful wildflowers. To get here, you will have to drive up to the trailhead. Fortunately, the road leads all the way up to the sub-alpine, meaning you will only gain 292 metres (949 feet) to the Nicomen Ridge overlooking Nicomen Lake. The trail is 21 km (12.8 miles) one-way but it is possible to add the steep, 1 km (0.6 mile) side trail up to the top of the First Brother to the venture. Please remember that these sub-alpine meadows are extremely fragile.

Lightning Lakes Chain Trail (Map 7/B7)
This trail begins at the Spruce Bay or the day-use area and leads 12 km (7.3 miles) one-way past a series of good fishing lakes. This is an easy walk through a pleasant forest. Wilderness camping is offered at Stake Lake and fishing can be excellent. Alternately, it is a 9 km loop around Lightning Lake itself.

Monument 78 [Castle Creek] Trail (Map 7/D6–7)
This is one of several trails that offers a chance to hike into Washington State. From the Monument 78/83 parking lot, it's a 12 km (6.7 mile) one-way hike. The trail follows Castle Creek to the USA border and the monument that marks the border between the two countries. Along the trail, you will pass through several meadows climbing about 200 metres (650 feet) along the way. From the monument, it is possible to connect with the Windy Joe Trail via the Pacific Crest Trail. It is also possible to hike to Monument 83, through Washington State. Wilderness camping is available 0.5 km (0.3 miles) south of the monument.

Monument 83 Trail (Map 7/E6–F7)
From the Monument 78/83 parking lot, this is a 16 km (9.8 mile) one-way hike along an old fire access road to the US Forest Service tower. Along the trail, you will pass by an old cabin built in the 1920s by the US Forest Service as well as Pasayten Pete's grave. It is possible to head east out of the park on the Pasayten River Trail, which is part of the historic Centennial Trail. You will gain 850 metres (2,763 feet) to the tower.

North and South Gibson Trails (Map 7/B6)
In the winter, this trail (or pair of trails) is part of the cross-country area. In summer, it is possible to follow the 7.6 km (4.6 mile) trail on foot or mountain bike. There is only 125 metres (650 feet) in elevation change, although most of that comes in one hill. The trail parallels the Gibson Pass Road between Strawberry Flats and the Lightning Lake Campground.

Pacific Crest Trail (Map 7/D6–7)
Dreaming of Mexico? Well if you have 6 months of spare time, the first leg of the famous trail that cuts through the backcountry of USA to Mexico starts from Manning Park. This section is only the first 26 km (15.9 miles) of the 4,000 km (2,440 mile) trail, but think of the bragging rights you will have! This moderate hike will take about 8 hours and you will gain 200 metres (650 feet) in elevation along the way.

Poland Lake Route (Map 7/A5)
This trail is an easy 8 km (4.9 mile) one-way hike from the gate at Strawberry Flats to Poland Lake. Although the climb is gradual, you will still gain 435 metres (1,414 feet) in elevation along the way. The area is a popular cross-country ski area and the backcountry campsite sees a lot of use in the summer. From the lake, it is possible to hike 9 km (5.5 miles) one-way to Allison Pass on Highway 3 rather than return to Strawberry Flats. If you choose this alternate route, the hike will lead you along an unmaintained trail (Memaloose Trail). It is a good idea to have a vehicle waiting for you.

Skagit Bluffs (Map 6/F3)
This is an easy 5.6 km (3.4 mile) one-way trail leading along the bluffs above Highway 3. The trail connects the Dewdney Trail with the Hope Pass Trail at Cayuse Flats.

Skyline Trails (Map 6/F6–7/A6)
Beginning at the Strawberry Flats parking lot, the Skyline Trail leads 12.5 km (7.6 miles) one-way to Mowich Camp. Initially, the trail climbs along the ridge with a good view of Manning Park. Continuing on the trail leads through Despair Pass before reaching the camp, at 475 metres (1,544 feet) in elevation. From the camp, it is possible to hike 13 km (7.9 miles) one-way into the Skagit Valley via the Skyline II Trail.

Another option is to start or return to Lightning Lake via the Skyline I Trail. This option is 16.8 km (10.2 miles) one-way to the camp.

Three Falls/Strawberry Flats Trail (Map 7/A6)
Beginning at the Strawberry Flats parking lot, this is a rather scenic 9km (5.5 miles) return hike. The trail is wide and well used at the beginning as it leads to the downhill ski area. From there, the trail is less used and continues on to Shadow Lake, Nepopekum Falls and eventually Derek Falls. For the most part, the trail follows Nepopekum Creek gaining 125 metres (406 feet) in elevation along the way.

Windy Joe Mountain (Map 7/D6)
Beginning at the Beaver Pond parking lot, this trail leads 15 km (9.2 miles) return along an old fire access road to the summit of Windy Joe Mountain. During the spring, when it is difficult to cross the Similkameen River, an alternative route is to begin at the Canyon parking lot further west. This latter hike is 18km (11 miles) return but not recommended for bikers. Either way, the old fire lookout at the summit offers a great view.

Marion & Phyllis Lakes Route (Map 11/B3)
A long bike ride takes you along the gated access road north of the Furry Creek Golf Course past Marion Lake to Phyllis Lake. The 450 metre (1,463 feet) climb over 16 km (9.8 miles) return brings you to some nice vantage points across Howe Sound as well as good fishing holes. The area beyond Phyllis Lake (the Greater Vancouver Watershed) is closed to the public.

Marriott Basin Trail (Map 37/A6)
From the Duffy Lake Road, this trail heads high into the sub-alpine at the foot of Mount Marriott along an old road. Keep left as you hike up the road and left again where the trail splits (the right trail heads to Rohr Lake). Marriott Basin is an explorer's paradise; once you get up to the basin, you can wander almost anywhere you want to. But please avoid treading on the fragile plant life. You will hike about 16 km (9.8 miles) and climb 370 metres (1,210 feet).

Marshall Lake Trails (Map 42/E2)
The 10 km (6.1 mile) long Marshall Lake Trail takes you up the hill from the east side of Marshall Lake down to Carpenter Lake. From here, you can arrange for a pick up or retrace your path. Also in the area are a variety of other trails that follow old roads and tracks to a variety of vantage points.

Matsqui Trail (Map 3/D5–F5)
Since this dyke system is part of the Trans Canada Trail, you can virtually walk, bike or ride as long as you like. Most visitors start from the picnic area in this popular Regional Park (found at the end of Riverside Road below the Mission Bridge) and walk towards the Page Road trailhead. This portion of the dyke is about 17 km (10.4 miles) return and offers several vantage points of the Fraser River.

McGillivray Pass Trail (Map 37/A1–42/E1)
Best accessed in the winter on skis or a snowmobile, the Kingdom Lake Forest Road beyond Bralorne is washed out and becoming overgrown. It is a better idea to climb to the scenic pass from the Anderson Lake side. Depending on how far you park up the old road, expect at least a 15 km (9.2 miles) one-way trek along McGillivray Creek. Along the way you will pass many historical buildings and mines and other remnants of the area's mining past. The route is challenging and takes you through grizzly bear country.

Melvin Creek Trail (Map 37/E4)
From the Cayoosh Creek Recreation Site on Duffey Lake Road, this 6 km (3.7 mile) one-way trail crosses Cayoosh Creek and accesses a large alpine basin containing several small lakes. The trail was built by hunting guides but hikers and horseback riders can enjoy the route in the spring and summer.

Minnekhada Park Trails (Map 2/D1)
This regional park is located on Quarry Road northeast of Port Coquitlam. Within the park, there are 12 km (7.3 miles) of interconnecting trails through a thick canopy of second growth forest. All the trails are well maintained with little elevation gain. The main trail leads from the large parking lot on the west side of the park past a marshy lake to a picnic site. Eventually, you reach a viewpoint overlooking the Addington Marsh next to Pitt River. Another trail circles the perimeter of the park in a clockwise direction. This trail leads the hiker through some wet, boggy sections and several brooks. A further option is to cross the floating bridge in the middle of the marshy lake and head west to the viewpoint. If you are interested in a dyke walk, then take Oliver Drive off the Quarry Road and park at a convenient point after the gates. From there, you can explore the Addington Marsh for a return distance of up to 14 km (8.5 miles).

Moon Lake Trail (Map 44/B6)
Located off Bridge River Road, this is an 8 km (4.8 mile) 3 hour hike along an old four-wheel drive road/trail to Moon Lake. Extreme cyclists can continue onto Mount McLean.

Mosquito Creek Trails (Map 11/D7)
Mosquito Creek Trail is a great choice if you want to sample the North Shore Mountains without the usual elevation gain. This one only gains 320 metres (1,040 feet). From the bottom of the Grouse Mountain Gondola, head east along the Baden Powell Trail and avoid the steady stream of people climbing the Grouse Grind. The Mosquito Creek Trail departs the Baden Powell only after passing all three (four, if you count the alternate routing of the BCMC Trail) Grouse Mountain Trails. About 25 metres (75 feet) past the Village Chair Trail, the Mosquito Creek Trail finally breaks free of the Baden Powell and heads east to Mosquito Creek. The trail follows the east banks of Mosquito Creek to the Mosquito Creek Cascades (they aren't quite big enough to be called falls). The hike is 8 km (4.8 miles) return.

Mosquito Lake Area (Map 30/C1–36/C7)
A challenging network of mountain bike trails that offer fast, undulating single-track trails with extreme descents. The trails are accessed from Ivey Road (at the crest near the sub-station), the recreation site or along the MacKenzie Basin Road. There are over 80 km (48 miles) of trails here, ranging from intermediate to expert.

Mount Artaban Trail (Map 10/F5)
The trailhead to this Gambier Island hike is accessed by boat to the south end of Halkett Bay Park (near the scout camp). The hike involves a 600 metre (1,950 foot) elevation gain beginning on an old road before passing by a couple of streams and continuing uphill through the forest and some open meadows. As a rule of thumb, stay to your right along the rough trail until you reach the summit, a round trip of 10 km (6 miles).

Mount Cheam Trail (Map 5/A4)
Found at the end of the rough (lots of cross ditching) Chilliwack-Chipmunk Forest Road, the Mount Cheam Trail is a beautiful alpine hike. You climb 632 metres (2,054 feet) over 9.5 km (5.8 miles). Along the way you'll pass Spoon Lake, rolling sub-alpine meadows dotted with wildflowers in July-August and an old trail down to Bridal Falls. The trail is best hiked from July to September since the area is prone to avalanches in the winter. The trail from the Bridal Falls side has all but disappeared and is not recommended.

Mount Crickmer Trail (Map 3/C1)
From the Florence Lake Forest Road, the difficult 20 km (12.2 mile) hike follows an old gated road and then a trail to the top of Mount Crickmer. The route gains 1,190 metres (3,867 feet) as you cross several gullies and creeks on your way to the open meadows below the rocky summit. From the top, there are fantastic views of Stave Lake, Mount Blanshard and Mount Robbie Reid to the north.

Mount Daniel Trail (Map 9/B1)
The parking area for this easy, but steep trail is located 3.4 km down the Garden Bay Road north of Pender Harbour. Follow the old road and take the first left, which eventually turns to a trail. Allow 1.5 hours to climb 2.5 km (1.6 mile) one-way up to the great vantage point. This sacred area also boasts Indian rock formations near the top.

Mount Drew Trail (Map 20/F5)
To reach the 1,885 metre high (6,185 foot) summit of Mount Drew is a difficult trek. Your first obstacle is getting across Sechelt Inlet to the mouth of Earle Creek from Egmont. Boat is the preferred method of travel. From there, hike or mountain bike up the network of logging roads and then scramble to the top of the summit. Given the distance, it is best to make the hike across in two days.

Mount Elphinstone Loop (Map 10/C4–B6)
A long 42 km (25.6 mile) mountain bike route follows the highway and a series of logging roads. Starting from the Langdale Ferry Terminal, you head north, climbing steeply up the Dakota Creek Forest Road. Turn left on the branch road 2011 and follow the signs back down to the Highway and the ride back to the ferry. This difficult route has a few steep sections but the great views of Howe Sound and the islands are worth it. The Lower Elphinstone Area offers more variety as you cycle old roads and trails through old mining remains.

Mount Fromme Trail (Map 11/E7)
A series of trails access Mount Fromme. The main trail is a 15 km (9.1 mile) route that begins off Prospect Road near Mosquito Creek. It is a difficult, steep trail that gains 870 metres (2,828 feet) to the summit. The trail begins on the Baden Powell Trail and shortly turns onto a trail labelled "To the Old Mountain Highway." From there, follow the steep Old Mountain Highway, a popular biking route, past Meech Lake to the summit. Once you reach the top, it is best to descend through Pipeline Pass back to the Old Mountain Highway and walk down the road to St. George's Trail, an alternate trail up. Eventually, you meet up with the Baden Powell Trail and a return to the start. Another alternative is to follow the Per Gynt Trail to the peak of Mount Fromme. This is one of a collection of trails built by legendary trail builder Halvor Lunden.

Mount Gardner Trails (Map 10/F6)
The trailhead to this popular network of multi-trails is found on the road between poles 490 and 491 off the Mount Gardner Road. From the end of the road, a series of trails begins. The main trail climbs 725 metres (2,356 feet) to the summit along paved, gravel and forested paths. From the top, you will be rewarded with a great view of Bowen Island and Howe Sound. The main trail is 10 km (6.1 miles) long, but there are many side trails (mostly old logging roads) to explore. Most of the exploring is by mountain bikers, not hikers. From the ferry landing it is a long 17.5 km (10.7 mile) hike/bike.

Mount Hallowell Trail (Map 20/C7)
From the Halfmoon-Carlson Forest Road, this trail begins at the abandoned red cable spool, about 19.5 km (11.9 miles) from Highway 101. The trail leads through a clearcut and some old growth timber to the summit and a newly restored forest service fire lookout tower. It is about 1 km (0.6 miles) to the summit. From the top, you will get an excellent view of the Sechelt Peninsula and the ocean.

Mount Harvey Trail (Map 11/B5)
The trail up Mount Harvey is quite steep, gaining 1,465 metres (4,761 feet) in 12.5 km (7.6 miles). There are old ropes along the first part of the trail to help with the elevation gain. There are a few points near the top where you may need to use your hands to scramble up, but it isn't too technical. The trail will take most people about 8 hours.

Mount Klaudt Trail (Map 14/E6)
Mount Klaudt is one of the two mountains that frame Hemlock Valley. In summer, a trail climbs to the saddle below Mount Klaudt, before switchbacking its way up to a viewpoint over Harrison Lake. This moderate trail is 11.5 km (7 miles) return. While it doesn't climb to the top, it gets close enough.

Mount Laughington Trail (Map 5/B5)
The spur road from the Chilliwack-Foley Forest Road leading to the base of Mount Laughington is usually gated. This makes the hike fairly strenuous 19 km (11.6 miles) to the summit, gaining 1,340 metres (4,355 feet) in elevation along the way. If the road is not gated, then the hike is reduced to 5 km (3.1 miles) return, gaining 200m (650 feet).

Mount Lincoln Trail (Map 15/F2)
Mount Lincoln towers above Highway 1 just east of Yale. A rough, sometimes sketchy 5 km (3 mile) trail leads up to the 655 metre (2,129 foot) summit, gaining 580 metres (1,885 feet) along the way. This difficult climb sometimes resembles rock climbing more than hiking and indeed, there are a few spots where there are fixed ropes to help you ascend. Although not as tall as other mountains in the area, there are still some great views of the Fraser Canyon.

Mount McLean Trails (Map 44/A6)
Picture yourself descending from a high alpine meadow 2,100 vertical metres (6,825 feet) down to the sagebrush in the valley below. En route you will cover 14 km (8.5 miles) of spectacular single-track trail. Now, keep that image in mind as you grunt 14 km and 2,100 vertical metres up (8.5 miles and 6757 feet) to the top of Mount McLean from Moon Lake. Luckier (and richer) folks have been known to catch a helicopter to the top.

Mount Mulligan Trail (Map 22/E7)
From the spur road along Raffuse Creek, a short climb (4 km/2.4 miles) leads to the summit of Mount Mulligan. Great views of the Stawamus River Valley are provided from the top.

Mount Outram Trail (Map 6/D2)
This trail begins at the West Gate of Manning Park and leads along the old engineering road to a signed trailhead marking the route to Mount Outram.

This moderate trail is 18 km (10.9 miles) return and is best hiked from July to September. The total elevation gain is 1,760 metres (5,720 feet). The trail begins in a forested setting before crossing the creek and then continuing through a series of meadows to a steep, rocky ridge and eventually up to the summit of the mountain. You get a spectacular view of the surrounding mountain peaks from the top.

Mount Rexford Trail (Map 5/D6)
The trail to Mount Rexford is an access trail for climbers and is not well maintained, although a crew went up in 2008 to do some work and it is in much better condition now. There are still places where it is difficult to follow. The trail is only 3 km (1.8 miles) one way, but will take most people about three hours climbing up, as the trail gains nearly a full kilometre (3,248 ft) in that distance. It is relentlessly steep, with no place where the trail levels out for more than a few feet. The views back over Slesse, however, are terrific.

Mount Richardson Trail (Map 9/F2)
The best place to access Mount Richardson is from Richardson Lake, which is 4wd vehicle accessible. From the lake, proceed in a southwestern direction by bushwhacking 2 km (1.2 miles) one-way to the summit along an old road. From the summit at 986 metres (3,205 feet), you will get a great view of the Sechelt Peninsula and Inlet.

Mount Roderick Trail (Map 22/A7–21/G6)
This long day trip requires you to take the ferry to the Woodfibre Pulp Mill before biking or hiking to the trailhead several kilometres up the main logging road. Here you cross a footbridge to join the trail that passes a helipad before narrowing. Continuing north, the trail climbs up the open ridge to the sub-alpine for a great view of Howe Sound. This is a 20 km (12 mile) difficult hike gaining 1,475 metres (4,794 feet). The trail is best hiked in June through October.

Mount Seymour Provincial Park (Map 11/F7–G6)
The 3,508 hectare provincial park is easily reached by way of the Mount Seymour Parkway. The park contains a variety of trails from easy strolls to rough backcountry excursions. All the trails are very popular given their scenic surroundings, views of Vancouver and proximity to the city. The best time to hike in the park is July through November due to snow accumulations at higher levels. In winter, the hills remain busy with snowshoers and backcountry skiers. Please note that the Old Buck Trail is the only trail where horseback riding and mountain biking are allowed:

Dog Mountain Trail
This easy 6 km (3.6 mile) return hike from the north end of the upper parking lot is more popular in winter with snowshoers. There is little elevation gain as it leads through an old growth sub-alpine fir stand to the bluff overlooking the Seymour River and Greater Vancouver. The trail follows the First Lake Trail for 30 minutes, before heading to the west from the lake. On the return trip, complete the First Lake Loop by taking the north branch of the trail at First Lake and connecting with the Mount Seymour Trail. A further option is to hike the short distance (less than a kilometre) to Dinky Peak for another great view.

Elsay Lake Trail
A difficult 20 km (12 mile) hike leads through Canadian Pass and some rugged alpine country. The total elevation gain is 885 metres (2,876 feet), but there are a couple ups and downs along the way. The hike begins at the north end of the upper parking lot, initially following the Mount Seymour Trail. Take the branch trail just before the First Pump that leads northwest to tiny Gopher Lake. Beyond here, the trail narrows and is occasionally marked. A small backcountry shelter marks the end of the trail at the north end of the lake. Most people stay overnight. Be wary, it is a steeper trek on the return trip.

Goldie Lake/Flower Lake Loops
These easy loops are found to the east of the upper parking lot and make fine cross-country skiing and snowshoeing routes. The Goldie Lake Loop is a 2 km (1.2 miles) trail leading past the Goldie Rope Tow area to Goldie Lake, gaining 218 metres (709 feet) along the way. This trail meets with the Flower Lake Loop and the top end of the Perimeter Trail so you can take either of these trails to increase the length of the hike. The Flower Lake Loop is 1.5 km (45 minutes) return with an elevation gain of 150 metres (487 feet). This trail passes through a sub-alpine bog and past a small pond filled with wildlife.

Mount Elsay Trail
Little more than a bushwhack from the Elsay Lake Trail, this is a 16 km (9.8 miles) return trek from the upper parking lot. It involves climbing 1,050 metres (3,413 feet) along a difficult, flagged route with some rock scrambling. From the summit at 1,422 metres (4,665 feet), you are rewarded with an excellent view and most likely, the peak all to yourself (something that can't be said for most other trails in the park). The hike is best left to experienced backpackers.

Mount Seymour Trail
Also known as the Three Pumps Trail, this is the main trail leading from the north end of the upper parking lot. The moderate hike is 9 km (5.5 mile) return, with an elevation gain to 450 metres (1,463 feet) to the Third (and final) Pump. The popular trail climbs steadily through a fairly open sub-alpine forest before breaking out into the alpine meadows. The trail gets more challenging as you dip and climb to the Second Pump and dip and climb again to the Third Pump, which is the actual 1,450 metre (4,713 foot) summit of Mount Seymour. Since great views of Greater Vancouver are offered from any of the three pumps, most people like to shorten the route do not bother climbing beyond the First Pump. Those that make it to the Third Pump will enjoy even better views and peace and solitude as they look back on the crowds at the First Pump.

Mystery Lake Loop
This trail follows the Mystery Ski Lift before connecting with the Mount Seymour Trail and the return to the parking lot. It will take about 1.5 hours to complete this 3 km (1.8 mile) loop, with an elevation gain of 180 metres (585 feet). The beautiful sub-alpine lake is a good spot to swim during a hot summer day.

Old Buck Trail
From the Park Headquarters, this trail climbs steadily uphill connecting with the Baden Powell Trail about 2.3 km (1.4 miles) along the trail. Old Buck also joins the Perimeter Trail near the Deep Cove Lookout about 5.5 km (3.4 miles) later. You will climb 670 metre (2,178 feet) along a sometimes washed out, sometimes rocky old road that parallels the Mount Seymour Parkway. Since this trail does not offer the beauty and views of the other trails in the area, the main users of the trail are mountain bikers, who are usually heading downhill.

Mount Slesse Memorial Trail (Map 5/C7)
This trail climbs about 300 metres (1,000 feet) along the old Nesakwatch Creek Forest Road to a monument built to acknowledge a plane crash. The hike takes about 1.5 hours and has spectacular views of the mountains all around. Beyond the monument at the old logging landing, turn left uphill through the blueberry bushes to a ridge and then follow the trail and ribbons to the old glacier. A propeller in a crevasse indicates the end of the hike, but mountain climbers can continue from this point.

Mount St Benedict Trail (Map 3/F1)
The trail leads from the Davis Lake Provincial Park and is 15 km (9.2 miles) return gaining 1,000 metres (3,250 feet) to the summit. The hike involves traversing a mixture of old road and trails along Mundro Creek past tiny McKay Lake to the summit. Good views of Mount Judge Howay and Robbie Reid are offered from the top, but the hike up is unremarkable (unless you like clear cuts). Snow limits the hiking season to July through October.

Mount Varley Trail (Map 10/D2)
To reach the summit of Mount Varley, you must bushwhack off the end of Rainy Forest Road. It is about 3 km (1.8 miles) one-way to the summit. In order to reach the end of the Rainy Forest Road, it is necessary to use a four-wheel drive vehicle.

Mount Wrottesey Trail (Map 10/F2)
Mount Wrottesey is a prominent land feature overshadowing Howe Sound. To reach the summit, boat to McNab Creek or to Camp Potlatch in Howe Sound. From Camp Potlatch, a well-established trail leads along the creek to the Potlatch Road. Continue up the road to where a small creek drains off the southern side of the mountain. From there, bushwhack through the timber to the sub-alpine and then to the summit. From McNab Creek, your must hike/bike up the main haul road and cross over to the Potlatch Road. It is a full day trip (including the boat crossing) involving an elevation gain of 1,625 metres (5,281 feet).

Mowat Bay Trail (Map 18/F3)
From the Powell Lake Bridge on Highway 101, a 2.3 km (1.4 mile) trail leads to Mowat Bay where you can enjoy a nice swim in Powell Lake. The hike switchbacks (100 metres/325 feet) up the northern side of Valentine Mountain before descending to the bay. From the bay, Tony's Trail (see Haywire Bay above) leads up the eastern shores of Powell Lake.

Munro-Dennett Lake Trail (Map 2/D1–12/D7)
From the signed trailhead on Quarry Road, the hike begins along an old road for a few hundred metres before the trail climbs relentlessly straight up the hillside through a thick, mature Douglas-fir forest. Eventually, the trail levels as you approach the beautiful marshy area around Munro Lake. Since Dennett Lake requires another short but steep grunt up an ill-defined trail, many people stop at Munro Lake. To Dennett, the hike is 10 km (6.1 miles) return gaining 860m (2767 feet) but route finders can join up with the Burke Ridge Trail (see above). Due to snow and wet trail conditions (on top), this hike is best left until late June through October.

Musical Bumps Trail (Map 29/G6)
This fabled 19 km (11.6 mile) hike starts from the top of the Whistler Village Gondola and leads to Singing Pass. The trail is so named, as it crosses Piccolo, Flute and Oboe summits on its way to Singing Pass, where it hooks up with the Singing Pass Trail. Along the way, you get great views of Cheakamus Lake and Glacier.

Myrtle Springs Trail (Map 18/G3)
This 5 km (3 mile) trail begins approximately 200 metres (650 feet) along the Haslam Lake Road. It follows an old road network eventually leading to Duck Lake Road near the Haslam Slough. You can either return along the logging road or the way you came.

Nicomen Island (Map 3/G4–4/A4)
Nicomen is a quiet little island that has a 5 km (3 mile) scenic riverside dyke trail. From December to February, Bald Eagles are common in the area.

North Shore Spirit Trail (Map 1/D1)
This planned 35 km (21.7 mile) waterfront trail will run from Horseshoe Bay to Deep Cove and link with many north shore trails. Construction is expected to be done by 2019 by the latest and the first section, the Squamish Nation Waterfront Greenway is officially open, though it is only 300 m long and is more a symbolic gesture than an actual trailway

Northwest Passage (Map 29/F6)
Found at the top of Nordic Estates off of Whistler Road, a dirt access road climbs under the Quicksilver Chairlift on the bottom of Whistler Mountain. At the crest of this steep climb (420 metres/1,365 feet), you head left for some downhill, roller coaster thrills. The difficult 7 km (4.3 mile) route will spit you out at Whistler Village.

Ogilvie Peak Trails (Map 15/G6)
This trail climbs steeply from the Kawkawa Lake Road for about 4 km (2.4 miles), until it breaks out into the sub-alpine of Ogilvie Peak. From here you can pick your route to a series of peaks and ridges.

Okeover Trail (Map 18/D1–46/C6)
This well marked and scenic trail begins at the south end of Okeover Inlet off the Southview Road. It heads 8 km (4.8 miles) to the Theodosia Forest Road. Rather than proceeding back the way you came, you can follow the forestry road along the eastern shores of the inlet.

One Mile Lake Trails (Map 30/B1)
The popular One Mile Lake picnic area found south of Pemberton offers some enjoyable trails that can be used by mountain bikers or hikers. The **One Mile Loop** is an easy one km (half mile) loop around the lake. The most popular trail is the **Nairn Falls Trail,** which heads 2 km (1.2 miles) south to the provincial campground. This moderate trail has a few sections that require dismounting (if you are on a bike) as you climb over roots and descend along a rocky trail. Side trails also lead to more challenging biking terrain, including Tour de Soo.

Othello Tunnels [Coquihalla Canyon] Trail (Map 15/G6)
This popular trail is part of the Kettle Valley Railway, which is in turn a part of the Trans Canada Trail. Most people only hike though the canyon itself, an easy walk through a dramatic gorge and the equally impressive Othello (Quintette) Tunnels. This short trail is less than a kilometre return but it is possible to stretch this into a 12 km (7.3 mile) trek along the north side of

the Coquihalla River all the way to the Hope Cemetery. Yet another option is to follow the Hope-Nicola Valley Trail from the railgrade up and over the mountain and back to the parking lot. This last option makes a nice 8 km (4.8 miles) loop.

Owl Lake Trail (Map 36/B6)
The trailhead to this hike is found off the Owl Creek Forest Road, which is 4wd accessible. From the trailhead, it is a 7 km (7.4 mile) return trip, gaining 140 metres (455 feet) along the way. The trail leads through the Owl Creek Valley to the lake where you will find a rustic campsite on the western shores.

Pacific Spirit Park [UBC Endowment Lands] (Map 1/B2)
This large urban park offers an enjoyable place to walk, jog, horseback ride or mountain bike. There are over 90 km (54.9 miles) of trails in the park, of which 60 km (36.6 miles) are open to mountain bikers and horseback riders. Please obey the signs. With easy access from a variety of locations (4th Avenue, 16th Avenue or SW Marine Drive), these trails are popular year round as they dissect the lush vegetation and old growth forests of Pacific Spirit Park. Mountain bikers will find the trails north of 4th Avenue more challenging.

Pender Hill Trail (Map 9/A1)
Allow half an hour to climb the steep hill, which offers panoramic views of Pender Harbour. The trail begins about 60 metres (200 feet) east of Lee's Road towards Irvine's Landing Road.

Petgill Lake Trail (Map 11/C1)
The hike begins on the marked trail north of the parking lot of Murrin Provincial Park (on the opposite side of Highway 99). This 11.5 km (7 mile) trail begins by climbing steeply through the bluffs before entering a second growth forest. It soon meets an old logging road and heads south. Eventually, the road becomes completely overgrown at which time the trail departs the road and leads up a ridge to the lake. The trail can be hiked from March through November and gains 640 metres (2,080 feet) in elevation. From the lake, it is possible to access the Goat Ridge Route and several climbing opportunities.

Pierce Lake/Mt McFarlane Trail (Map 5/B7)
A rough, steep trail climbs steadily from the Pierce Creek Recreation Site to the south end of Mount McFarlane. It begins by rising sharply through a second growth forest before breaking out onto a scree slope. From here, the trail crosses Pierce Creek and begins to deteriorate before reaching the lake. On the way, you will pass two lakes, alpine meadows and some spectacular viewpoints. Plan on doing this difficult trail as an overnight trip since you climb 1,780 metres (5,785 feet) on this 7 km (4.3 mile) one-way trail. If you don't want to commit to an overnight trip, a good destination is Pierce Lake, which is a good fishing lake. Pierce Lake is only a 4.3 km (2.6 mile) one-way hike, although you will still climb 1,080 metres (3,510 feet).

Pioneer [Bear Mountain] Trail (Map 3/D3)
Found to the east of the Dewdney Trunk Road, are a series of trails that are best accessed from Saunders Road (off Richards Ave.) to the south. Saunders Trail is a short interpretive 0.6 km (0.3 miles) trail at the foot of Bear Mountain. The Pioneer Trail follows an old forestry road to the top of the hill, where the Bear Mountain Challenge Downhill Mountain Bike Race is held. From the top, you descend along single-track to the Mill Pond, some 3.2 km (2 miles) later. Also in the area is the Carral Loop.

Pitt Polder Wildlife Area (Map 12/F7–2/F1)
The extensive dyke network begins at the end of Rannie Road in Grant Narrows Park. The dykes are flat, wide cart paths perfect for mountain biking, horseback riding and hiking. The distance of the route really depends on how far you want to travel, as there are 20 km (12.2 miles) of interconnected dykes and side trails in the area. Waterfowl is abundant in the marshy wetland.

Pitt River Dyke Trail (Map 2/D2)
As part of the Trans Canada Trail and the historic PoCo Trail, this series of interconnected dyke trails has seen some recent improvements. Still sections remain overgrown, mostly with nasty brambles. The main dyke trail runs from the end of Kingsway north to the Debouville Slough Lookout Trail in Port Coquitlam. This is an 11 km (6.7 mile) trip and leads to a wildlife viewing tower.

Pitt River Regional Greenway (Map 2/D3)
The first phase of the Pitt River Regional Greenway, from Harris Landing at the south end of Harris Road to Ferry Slip Road near the Highway 7 crossing of the Pitt River, is now open. The trail follows a series of dykes along the

Fraser, then Pitt River allowing for good bird watching opportunities. Over the next ten years, additional sections will be added to the route, ultimately stretching about 30 km (18 miles) to Grant Narrows Regional Park. For now, the trail is 10 km (6 miles) long.

Place Creek Trail (Map 36/E5)
Just west of Gates Lake, this steep, rugged 21 km (12.8 mile) hike gains 1,300 metres (4,225 feet) past several waterfalls to the beautiful Place Glacier. Near the foot of the glacier is an A-frame used for camping by both climbers and mountaineers. The hiking season extends from July to October.

Point Grey Foreshore (Map 1/A2)
This is a great place for a hike on a blustery day. The land and ocean have a character that is one part tempest, one part romance. Even better, the beaches, which are usually crawling with people, are yours and yours alone. There are places along here that—if it wasn't for West Vancouver across the water—you could almost fool yourself into thinking you were hundreds of miles away from the nearest human. Access can be found from the steep trail down to Wreck Beach (the famous nude beach) along SW Marine Drive at gate 3 in UBC.

Post-Greendrop Trail (Map 5/F5)
The popular trail starts at the Post Creek Recreation Site and climbs 370 metres (1,202 feet) over 5.2 km (3.2 miles) to the south end of Greendrop Lake, taking you past Lindeman Lake. This moderate trail leads along the steep valley that has some rough rocky sections. There is rustic camping at Greendrop Lake and good fishing in both lakes. The Centennial Trail continues along a logging road, but most people just spend the night at Greendrop Lake, then return. For the more adventurous, an unmarked route runs northeast to Flora Lake.

Powersmart Trails (Map 22/D6)
Located near Crumpit Woods, this trio of trails (it is divided into upper, middle and lower section) is one of the most popular in the Squamish area. Mountain bikers should expect a moderately difficult ride.

Princess Louisa Park (Map 47/E3)
The remote access to this hidden inlet discourages most hikers. However, the spectacular fjord-like setting is certainly worth the visit. Once you are at the provincial park, a short, well-used trail leads to the world famous Chatterbox Falls (a ten minute excursion). From there, the trail continues beyond the falls and is called the Loquilts Creek Trail. The difficult trail passes by an old cabin and through a boulder field to a gorgeous mountain lake. You will climb over 1,300 m (4,265 ft) to the lake or experienced mountaineers can explore the seemingly endless open alpine country with spectacular views of the inlet and nearby rugged snow-capped peaks. Following the route over into the Elaho drainage involves glacier travel.

Radium Lake Trail (Map 5/E6)
BC Parks has closed the trailhead and suspension bridge over the Chilliwack River, but the Trans Canada Trail runs past the new start to this moderate trail. That means the trail is now over 15 km (9.2 mile) return. In addition, it is a stiff climb that gains 880 metres (2,860 feet) to tiny Radium Lake that is nestled below two towering peaks. A forestry cabin can be used as a base to explore nearby peaks, including challenging routes to MacDonald Peak or Mount Webb.

Rainbow Lake Trail (Map 29/E4)
This alpine trail starts from the wooden map located on the west side of Alta Lake Road. The trail to Rainbow Lake is 18 km (11 miles) return, gaining 800 metres (2,600 feet). Once in the area, you can try your luck for wild rainbow trout or explore side trails to Beverly Lake or Gin and Tonic Lakes. No camping is allowed at the lake, but there is a campsite near Hanging Lake just over the ridge on the other side of the lake.

Rainbow Mountain Skywalk Trail (Map 29/E4)
This is a continuation of the Rainbow Lake Trail or at least, you can't start this trail until you hike the 9 km (5.5 mile) to Rainbow Lake. From there, the trail climbs 850 metres (2,790 feet) to the top of Rainbow in just over 3 km (1.2 miles). That's a wickedly steep climb, but people still somehow drag their bikes to the top.

Richmond Dyke Trails (Map 1/B4)
This is an extremely popular place for hikers, bikers, joggers and families looking for an easy walk together. The gravel trails are broad and exposed to the ocean breeze. The open flats along the dyke are a great place to watch the sun set. The most popular section is the West Dyke Path, which runs

10 km (6 miles) from north of Westminster Highway to Steveston. The wide gravel path takes you past radio receivers as you peer out on the Straight of Georgia and there are a couple of really nice fish and chip shops at the end of the trail. The South Dyke is found between Gilbert Road and No. 5 Road.

Ring Creek Rip (Map 22/E6)
This difficult mountain bike trail is found just after the bridge over the Mamquam River on the Mamquam Forest Road. It begins on an old railbed and heads downhill for about half an hour to the Ring Creek crossing and onto the Diamond Head Road. Using our maps you can make a good loop ride along the various logging roads/trails in the area or even hook up with the Powersmart and Crumpit Woods trail systems.

Roberts Bank Dyke Trail (Map 1/C6)
This 9.5 km (5.8 miles) dyke trail leads from River Road and 34th Street to the Ferry Causeway in Tsawwassen.

Roberts Creek Loop (Map 10/B5–C4)
Starting on the Roberts Creek Forest Road, this difficult 30 km (18.3 mile) mountain bike route climbs a stiff 800 metres (2,600 feet) along the B&K logging road. As expected with the elevation gain, the ride has terrific views. It also provides access to a few other trails in the area. For example, the difficult, steep Mexican Jumping Bean Trail heads down to the Brodie Loop Trails. This rough route actually follows an old creek bed.

Rohr Lake Trail (Map 37/A6)
If you hang a right about a kilometre after the old Cayoosh Creek Forest Road turns into a trail, you will climb up and into the Rohr Lake Basin. While the majority of this hike is along the old logging road, the trail climbs quickly into a lovely sub-alpine meadow. You can enjoy a relaxing day at Rohr Lake or make an adventure of it and head for the peak of Mount Rohr. The joy of this area is there are so many options that you will want to spend a few days exploring. The lake is only 9 km (5.5 miles) return from where you parked your car, climbing 430 metres (1,410 feet) along the way.

Rolley Falls Trail (Map 3/C2)
Accessed from the Rolley Lake Provincial Park or the Florence Lake Forest Road, this short, 2 km (1.2 mile) loop leads past two sets of falls providing a great view of Stave Lake along the way. The well-developed trail climbs 130 metres (422 feet) as it meanders through a thick second-growth forest. Allow 1 hour to do the loop or continue around the Lakeside Trail, which circumnavigates Rolley Lake and adds another 1.5 km (.9 miles) and 45 minutes to your trip.

Ross' Rip/Doris Burma Memorial Trail (Map 22/C2)
The Doris Burma Memorial Trail can be found across from the salt sheds south of Daisy Lake on Highway 99. The trail is marked with orange markers as it follows the river to a unique pine tree bridge. A great 7 km (4.3 mile) loop trail can be done when combined with Ross' Rip (part of the Sea to Sky Trail), across the highway.

Ruby Creek Trail (Map 15/B7)
The Deer Lake Forest Road continues past Deer Lake as a four-wheel drive road. This route is a fairly easy 14 km (8.5 mile) return trip to a viewpoint over the Fraser River. While the road connects to Highway 7, it crosses private property, so turn around at the viewpoint, about halfway down into the valley.

Ruby Lake-Klein Lake Traverse (Map 20/C6)
This trail traverses the saddle between Klein and Ruby lakes, a 4 km (2.4 mile) one-way trip. It is easier to start at Klein Lake (if you start from the south end, you must climb a steep stretch of the trail to the saddle). The highlight of the trail is the excellent views from the rocky bluffs along the route. The southern access is found off an old road 50 metres (160 feet) south of Dan Bosch Park.

Salal Creek/Athelney Pass Trail (Map 40/D7)
Mountaineers will find a 15 km (9.2 miles) trail to Athelney Pass, which climbs 800 metres (2,625 feet). Although the trip can be done overnight, allow a few days to explore the surrounding peaks, including Ochre Peak, the "Black Molar", the Icemaker and Guthrum Mountain. The trail leads from the end of the water barred road past an old mining exploration camp, small lakes, pumice meadows and glaciers.

Saltery Bay Park Trails (Map 19/E5)
Saltery Bay Provincial Park has a network of trails worth exploring. The main trail leads 10 km (6 miles) along an overgrown road and then a well-defined trail. There is a steep climb at the beginning of the trail but you get a good

view of Nelson and Hardy Islands from the summit. A much easier option is to walk 2 km (1.2 miles) one-way from the campsite at the provincial park to the beach.

Sargeant Bay/Redroof Trails (Map 9/D4)
A series of trails are found between Sargeant Bay and Redroof. Beginning 100 metres (325 feet) before the Halfmoon Bay Store along Mintie Road, the **Redroofs Loop** is a 2 km (1.2 mile) circuit alongside the estuary of Halfmoon Creek before returning to Mintie Road via Rutherford Road and Redroofs Road. Another trail leads 4 km (2.4 miles) one-way from Sargeant Bay Provincial Park to the bog-like Triangle Lake leading through some old growth timber. The nature trails are designated for hikers only, but mountain bikers have a lot of area to explore. An easy 15 km (9.2 mile) loop starts from Sargeant Bay Park and follows Redroofs Road to the logging workshed where you turn right. Follow the signs back to the park or explore the rat's nest of trails in the woods.

Sasquatch Provincial Park Trails (Map 15/A7)
The roads into and around Sasquatch Park offer enjoyable mountain biking or hiking in a wilderness setting. The **Deer Lake Trail** is an easy route along the north side of Deer Lake. It is possible to continue eat on the **Ruby Creek Trail**. The **Hicks Lake Loop** takes about 3 hours to do the 6 km loop if you take time to enjoy the beach at the south end. It is also possible to follow an old logging road along the **Seabird Island Overlook Trail** at the south end. The **Moss Lake Trail** is the most difficult route in the park as it follows the steep and rocky access road past Moss Lake to several unnamed lakes.

Sea to Sky Trail (Map 22, 29, 30, 36, 37)
This ambitious trail building project, intended to link Squamish to the tiny hamlet of D'Arcy northeast of Pemberton lay dormant for a number of years, before being revived in 2005. Work is ongoing and will take years to complete the entire 180 km (112 mile) trail but the project has a new steering committee, led by the Squamish Lillooet Regional District, a master plan and, more importantly, new funding and the political wherewithal to see the trail formalized. The route from Squamish to Whistler is the newest link in the Trans Canada Trail. There are a number of sections already on the ground (some authorized, others in the process). From Squamish the route follows the Corridor Trail, then the Ray Peters Trail along Squamish Valley Road up to the Paradise Valley Road to the historic PGE Railway road from the Cheakamus River to Highway 99. Follow the highway north for 4.5 km (2.8 miles) to the Chance Creek Bridge over the Cheakamus River. Dirt roads and trails will take you up to the Pinecrest/Black Tusk entrance to Highway 99. Follow Highway 99 again for another 3.5 km (2.2 miles) to Brandywine Provincial Park where 20 km (12 miles) of trail will take you to Whistler Village. North of Whistler the route is still being determined and existing sections lack connections to each other. Until this happens it is mainly along the highway or secondary roads, with existing sections around Pemberton and Birken. For up-to-date information visit the website www.SeaToSkyTrail.ca.

Seaton Highline Road (Map 37/A3–43/D7)
A scenic but gruelling four hour mountain bike ride follows the road next to the hydro lines high above Anderson Lake. The roller coaster route stretches 32 km (18.8 miles) from D'Arcy (and the end of the Sea to Sky Trail) to Seton Portage. The road is open to 4wd vehicles as well.

Serpentine Fen and Dyke Road (Map 2/B6)
Located just north of White Rock, this trail is found on 44th Avenue off of King George Highway. It is an enjoyable trek through a Wildlife Management Area that is home to several species of birds.

Seton Ridge Trail (Map 37/F1)
From a switchback on the Seton Ridge Logging Road, this is an 11 km (6.7 mile) route taking you along the ridge between Cayoosh Creek and Seton Lake. Once you are in the alpine, you can access the surrounding mountains for even better views or explore the endless alpine meadows.

Seven Sisters Trail (Map 4/C6)
This easy 4 km (2.4 mile) trail is found in Cultus Lake Provincial Park near Windfall Creek. It takes you to a group of seven giant Douglas fir trees, some of which have fallen over.

Shadow Lake Interpretive Trails (Map 30/A3)
Shadow Lake Trails are located north of Whistler near the Soo River, right off Highway 99. There are a number of short trails totalling 6 km (3.6 miles) providing examples of the various forest practices. This trail network is a good choice if you want to get away from the crowds of Whistler and enjoy an easy stroll through a forested setting.

Shannon Falls Trail (Map 22/C7)
From the Shannon Falls Park parking lot, this 5 km (3 mile) trail gains 445 metres (1,446 feet) along the creek to a great vantage point overlooking the spectacular 220 metre high (715 foot) waterfall. The trail connects with the Stawamus Chief Trails to the north.

Shelter Point Regional Park (Map 8/A1)
Shelter Point Regional Park is easily accessed off the Texada Island Highway. Within the park is a scenic 2 km (1.2 mile) easy trail that leads along the ocean through some large windswept Douglas-fir.

Sigurd Creek Trail (Map 21/F3)
The trailhead is found at the end of Branch A251 off the Ashlu Road (past the second bridge). The trail climbs 1,322 metres (4,297 feet) over 14 km (8.5 miles) return along the creek to Pelion and Ossa Mountains. Along the trail, you will pass by some waterfalls and some nice vistas. The trail is best hiked in mid-July to October.

Silver Daisy Mountain Trail (Map 6/F3)
It is possible to do this 20 km (12.2 mile) trail up to the summit of Silver Daisy Mountain in about 9 hours. The trail starts at the Sumallo Grove Picnic Area off Highway 3, crosses the Skagit River and switchbacks its way up a steep hill to a saddle, which offers great views of the Skagit Valley. From here, the trail continues through a meadow to the 2,040 metre (6,630 foot) summit, gaining 1,435 metre (4,664 feet) along the way. Part of the trail follows an old mining tram. The trail is best left for late summer/early fall.

Singing Pass Trail (Map 29/G7–30/B7)
The Singing Pass Trail is probably the most popular alpine trail in the Whistler Area. This beautiful hike starts from the end of the well-signed Singing Pass Road and follows Fitzsimmons Creek, then Melody Creek, to the pass. The area offers alpine flowers in late summer along with spectacular glacier and mountain views. Allow 7 hours to complete the moderate 12 km (7.3 mile) hike, which gains 600 metres (1,950 feet). The cabin at Russet Lake is another 2 km (1.2 miles) beyond and 250 metres (813 feet) up. The cabin offers a good base for mountain climbers looking to explore the area's summits.

Skagit River Trail (Map 6/D5–E3)
This trail begins at the Sumallo Grove Picnic Area and leads 13 km (7.9 miles) one-way along the east side of the Skagit River. Along the route, you pass through an ecological reserve, which has a nice grove of old growth cedar, fir and cottonwood. The trail is best hiked in mid-June when the wild Rhododendrons start blooming at Sumallo Grove. The adventurous can hike all the way to the 26 Mile Bridge on the Silver Skagit Road but the last part covers a poor, often indistinct trail. It is 20 km (12.2 miles) one-way to the road.

Skookumchuck Narrows (Map 20/C6)
From Egmont Road, an 8 km (4.8 mile) easy walk leads along a well-maintained trail to the narrows, one of the most popular areas on the coast. You can explore the tidal pools at low tide or watch the tide rip through a narrow, shallow channel during high tide. Consult the tide tables for the best viewing times.

Skyline Trail (Map 11/C7)
Not to be confused with the epic hike in Manning Park, this Skyline Trail is actually an old service road for the powerline that gains 375 metres (1,219 feet) over 7 km (4.3 miles). This trail is an easy, surprisingly scenic hike, but a difficult mountain bike ride that forms part of the Trans Canada Trail hiking route. There are several technically demanding and steep mountain bike trails that depart from this trail.

Skyline Trail [West] (Map 6/F6–7/C6)
The western trailhead to the Skyline Trail is accessed off the Silver Skagit Road at the parking lot north of Ross Lake. The trail leads 26 km (15.9 miles) from the valley bottom to an alpine ridge at Camp Mowich. Along the way, the trail climbs steeply, gaining 1,310 metres (4,258 feet) to the ridge. The hike initially begins in a forest and then crosses several creeks before proceeding into some sub-alpine meadows and then along the ridge. As part of the historic Centennial Trail, it is possible to continue on to Lightening Lake.

Sliammon Lakes Trail (Map 18/F2)
The trail begins at the end of Sutherland Street and proceeds northward eventually leading to the Theodosia Forest Road. The well-marked trail leads through second growth timber and up some steep sections. The hike takes you past Little Sliammon Lake, where there is a nice beach for swimming and

on to Sliammon Lake. The trail connects with Appleton-Marathon Trails so it is possible to walk up to 18 km (11 miles) if you so choose. Other alternatives include a side trail to Three Mile Bay and an old mine site. This trail is 5 km (3 miles) return. It is also possible to hike up Scout Mountain. This trail offers views of Powell Lake and Wildwood Heights before dropping to the Kinsman Park near the Powell Lake Marina.

Smugglers Cove Provincial Park (Map 9/B4)
Smugglers Cove has a fascinating 'history' of illegal Chinese labourer smuggling a century ago. Today, tiny Smugglers Cove is a beautiful marine park and one of the most popular and best summer anchorages on the Sunshine Coast. The park provides easy hiking on a number of short trails totalling about 3.5 km (2.1 miles). A forested trail leads to the secluded anchorage of Smugglers Cove. A little further on, the main trail ends at a small bay off Welcome Pass, with views across to south Thormanby Island and north to Texada Island. This park is accessed by Brooks Road northwest of Sechelt.

Snowcap Lake Route (Map 23/F3–24/A1)
The east side of Garibaldi is far less travelled than the west side. In fact, this route, accessed off logging roads west of Skookumchuck, is about the only viable entry point into this vast wilderness. Even so, you will probably have to bushwhack your way up from the end of the road to the ridge. Don't despair; it is worth the effort. Its 20 km (12.2 miles) from the end of the road to the lake; more, depending on how far you can drive up the logging road, found at km 24.3 of the Lillooet West Forest Road.

Soames Hill Park (Map 10/D6)
This popular trail network is found to the northeast of Gibsons. The trails can be accessed off Bridgeman or Esperanza Roads, which are side streets off Chamberlin Road. From either trailhead, it takes about half an hour to hike several hundred stairs cut out of fallen logs to the top of the hill. The view from the top (at 240 metres/787 feet) is worth the effort. It is also possible to walk the short wooded trails around the southern slope of the hill.

South Eliphinstone Heritage Trails (Map 10/C5)
Mount Eliphinstone has been preserved into a provincial park. The southern slopes of the mountain have a long history of logging and many of the access routes have been turned into fine multi-use trails. There are many different access points from side roads north of Gibsons.

Cablevision Trail
From behind the shed at the top of Gilmour Road, this trail is marked with yellow diamonds for most of its length except towards the top. It takes about 1.5 hours (one-way) to climb to the B&K Logging Road. From there, continue uphill to two abandoned receiver stations which both provide excellent vistas. From the second receiver, it is possible to continue on to the old ski hut and the summit of Mount Elphinstone.

K2 Summit Trail
Marked by pink markers, this trail is accessed by either Stewart Road or Wharf Road. Either way, it is a steady 1.5 hours one-way climb to the K2 summit at 640 metres (2,080 feet) where you get a fantastic view of the ocean and the Sunshine Coast. The trail eventually culminates on a 4wd spur road at the base of the mountain.

Langdale Creek Waterfall Trail
A 2.5 km one-way trail begins 100 metres past the powerline off Stewart Road and leads through a second growth stand of Douglas-fir and along an old road next to the creeks to the falls. It is fairly steep towards the end but is easily followed because of the blue markers that show the way. An option is to walk down the Waterfall Trail to the Wharf Road trailhead.

Mountain Trail
Another short trail, this one is found near the south end of the cemetery off Keith Road. It climbs to the remains of First Camp located next to Chaster Creek. The camp was used by shingle bolt workers in the 1920s. From the First Camp, it is possible to continue uphill to the Second Camp just north of Largo Road or to hike in a northwest direction to the Chinese Camp. In the area, there are remains of an old dam, tramway and wood flume along the trail.

Shaker Trail
From the powerline off Stewart Road orange markers lead steadily uphill for about 35 minutes one-way to the B&K Logging Road. The highlight of this trail is the wooden flume that used to carry shingle bolts to the First Camp.

South Powell Divide Trail (Map 47/A5)
This high ridge route extends 20 km (12 miles) from the Goat Access II Trail north to the B Branch Road. Experienced hikers with the appropriate topographic maps and route finding skills should only consider this route, which usually takes a couple days to complete. Along the way you can enjoy the splendid views of the surrounding lakes and mountain peaks. The popular Emma Lake Cabin makes for a good overnight destination (if it isn't full).

Spirit Caves Trail (Map 15/E2)
The trailhead is located off Highway 1, across from the Pioneer Cemetery at the south end of Yale. This 5 km (3 mile) trail gains 500 metres (1,625 feet) to the caves and several vantage points of the Fraser River and Yale.

Sprockids Mountain Bike Park (Map 10/C5)
A unique community school project created a series of fun, short loops for the young riders of the Sunshine Coast to enjoy. There are about 14 km (8.4 miles) of trails for all skill levels. The trails are accessed off Stewart Road off of North Road in Langdale, near the Langdale Creek Waterfall Trail.

Spruce Lake Trails (Map 41, 42)
The Spruce Lake area offers world-class hiking and backpacking, horse packing, mountaineering, fishing, cross-country skiing and mountain biking. There are 164 km (100 miles) of wilderness trails in the area, which traverse over gentle mountain passes and meander through lush alpine grasslands and flowers to destination trout lakes. The main access points into the area are the Gun Creek Road, Mud Creek-Taylor Creek Forest Road and the Slim Creek Forest Road. Most of the trails have few or no signs and there are a number of rough routes that are only for experienced route finders. Also, due to snow accumulations the trails are best hiked or biked in late summer/early fall.

Eldorado Mountain Routes (Map 41/G1–42/A1)
A combination of old mining roads, trails and alpine ridges give experienced hikers and mountain bikers the opportunity to climb up to some spectacular viewpoints. The trail starts at Taylor Creek, about 0.75 km (0.45 feet) down the trail from the Taylor Basin Cabin and climbs steeply (300 metres in 1 km/965 feet in .6 miles) to a pass overlooking the Upper Eldorado Basin. The trail then drops into the basin and joins the High Trail. From the trailhead to the junction is 4 km (2.4 miles). There are no trail markers or signs.

Gun Creek Trail (Map 41/G2–F1)
From the signed trailhead off Slim Creek Forest Road, this is the main trail into the heart of the Spruce Lake area. The trail crosses a footbridge (Jewel Bridge) and follows the north side of Gun Creek eventually breaking from the pine forest to the open grasslands and aspen trees. The mountain views are tremendous. At the 11.5 km (6.9 mile) mark (at Cowboy Camp), the trail branches. Heading north is the popular trail that climbs 200 metres (650 feet) to Spruce Lake, where campsites and a beach are found. The lake is an excellent fishing lake producing large rainbow trout. Continuing west the Gun Creek Trail passes Hummingbird Lake and Trigger Lake before climbing south to Taylor Pass along the Gun Creek Valley. The northern section beyond Trigger Lake doesn't see a lot of use and is suffering from blow down. Most people heading for the Taseko Lakes area take the Warner Pass Trail.

High Trail (Map 41/G1–42/B2)
The trailhead for this 13 km (7.9 mile) trail is near the south end of Tyaughton Lake. The first 5 km (3 miles) of the trail is an old, 4wd accessible mining road. The trail crosses the Taylor-Pearson Trail, then climbs up and over a steep hill (your highest point is 1,000 metres/3,250 feet higher than the trailhead). Beyond the hill, the trail drops into the Eldorado Basin and climbs 400 metres/1,300 feet up to Windy Pass. Beyond Windy Pass, the trail drops to the Potato Patch Trailhead. The High Trail is 20 km (12 miles) long.

Taylor Basin Trail (Map 42/B1)
This is one of the gentlest mountain routes you will ever encounter. Depending on how far you can drive up the Mud Creek-Taylor Creek Forest Road, it may take you a few hours to walk to the cabin at Taylor Basin. The route follows an old road beyond the footbridge as it slowly climbs through a scenic valley with wildflowers, wildlife and fantastic mountain views. The route is extremely popular with mountain bikers and snowmobilers.

Squamish Estuary Trails (Map 22/C7)
The sea-level dyke trails found in Squamish offer enjoyable year round hiking or biking. Excellent views of the Stawamus Chief, Shannon Falls and Mount Garibaldi combined with the wide variety of birds (including Bald Eagles in the winter) make this area a nice retreat.

Stanley Park (Map 1/C1) 🚶 ⛸ 🚻
We dare you to find another trail in Southwestern BC that sees as much traffic (foot, bike and inline skating) as the Stanley Park Seawall. This 8.8 km (5.5 mile) seawall is part of a much longer (20 km/12.2 mile) seawall system that forms part of the Trans Canada Trail. Besides the Seawall, there are 35 km (22 miles) of trails in the park, although only one other (a combo of Bridle Path, Lake Trail and part of Beaver Lake Trail) is open to bikers. The trails are mostly short, interconnected trails that can be joined together into a number of combinations. The trails on the western side of the park are, in general, longer and wider than the trails on the eastern side of the park.

Statlu Lake Trail (Map 14/B4) 🚶 🚴 🚻
Overgrown beyond the lake and falls, most people stop here to soak in the surroundings. However, determined climbers can bushwhack up the Brotherhood Trail to the Upper Lake or on to the Mount Ratney climbing area. The trail to the falls is about 6 km (3.7 mile) return and gains 610 metres (1,983 feet) along the way.

Stave Dam Interpretive Trails (Map 3/C3) 🚶 ⛸ 🚻
Just east of Stave Falls Dam are a series of short trails. The **Stave Dam Interpretive Trail** is a short (1.7 km/1 mile) trail that cuts through a second growth forest with an elevation gain of 150 metres (488 feet). Further east, the **Steelhead Mountain Trail** is a 2 km (1.2 mile) trail that climbs from the south end of Campbell Street (off Johnson, off Cardinal) along an old forest service road.

Stawamus Chief Trails (Map 22/C7) 🚶 🚻
The dramatic 652 metre (2,140 feet) granite wall is the second largest freestanding granite outcropping in the world (behind the Rock of Gibraltar). There are a series of very popular trails that head from the parking lot north of Shannon Falls Provincial Park up the back of the Stawamus Chief. To hike to the top of the First Peak is 6 km (3.6 miles), to the top of the Second Peak is 9 km (5.5 miles) and to the top of the Third Peak is 11 km (6.7 miles). Regardless of which hike you choose, you should expect a steep uphill climb that is rewarded with great views from the top. The trails are best hiked in March to November. An alternative is to hike the peak behind the Stawamus Chief (formerly known as the Stawamus Squaw) by way of a 14.5 km (8.8 mile) trail gaining 500 metres to the summit at 610 metres (1,983 feet). For rock climbers, there is a choice of over 600 routes between The Chief & the Smoke Bluffs.

Stein Valley Trails (Map 31, 32, 33, 37, 38) 🏕 🚶 🚻
In the late 1980s, environmentalists fought long and hard to see the Stein Valley preserved in a park. This provincial park boasts an array of impressive hiking and backpacking trails, many of which are multi-day treks. It is possible, utilizing a shuttle system, to create some interesting one-way trips, although most of the roads leading to the park are very rough. The main access is from the Westside Road, just north of Lytton.

Blowdown Lake Trail (Map 37/F7)
This is an alternative route into the Stein Valley that requires following an old mining road to the Cottonwood Creek Trail. The area offers beautiful alpine meadows with great camping and some classic ridge routes.

Brimful Lake (Map 38/C6)
Brimful Lake was the spectacular site of the music festivals, back when this area was not a park. From the Texas Creek Trailhead, Brimful Lake is about 6.5 km (4 miles) in. This trail is not marked, but is fairly easy to follow. At last report, the Texas Creek Forest Road had been deactivated and has 103 water bars to cross in the last 14 km (8.5 miles).

Elton Lake Route (Map 31/F4)
This is a route with no defined trail that leads to the spectacular Elton Lake. The route is only 4 km (2.4 miles) long, but climbs steeply to a cobalt-coloured lake at the foot of a glacier.

Stein River Trail (Map 33/B2–31/F4)
This 58 km (35.4 mile) backpacking route leads through the heart of this magnificent wilderness. To reach the trailhead, cross the Fraser River north of Lytton and proceed 4.5 km (2.7 miles) north along the Westside Road to the short side road leading to the trailhead. From here, the trail follows the Stein River through the heart of the park to the park boundary at Tundra Lake. The trail begins as a moderate riverside route that takes you from the dry terrain typical of the Fraser Canyon area to some cool, lush old-growth forests and eventually the spectacular alpine ridges. In addition to 8 campsites, there are cable car crossings and also numerous Indian Pictograph sites along the trail. Beyond Cottonwood Creek (30 km/18.3 miles in) the terrain becomes more difficult and is subject to severe weather changes. The section between Stein Lake and Tundra Lake is a steep, challenging section that climbs about 1,100 m (3,600 ft). Beyond Tundra, it is an additional 12 km (7.3 miles) of alpine travel (losing 700 m/2,200 ft) to make it to Lizzie Lake, where wise travellers have arranged for a shuttle pick up. Many people allow a week to explore the area, but it is possible to do an overnight trip to the first river crossing. This is a wilderness trail; in addition to many fallen trees, bears are common and snow is a definite possibility in the alpine.

Stryen Creek Trails (Map 33/B2–32/G3)
From the main trailhead on West Side Road, there is a 6.5 km (4 mile) access trail to "The Forks." From here, you can head east for 8 km (4.9 miles) or west 5 km (3 miles). The main attraction is the pictographs at the forks. The trail can be difficult to follow at first, but the route gets easier farther along. There is backcountry camping along the eastern fork.

Texas Creek Trail (Map 38/C6)
The Texas Creek Trail is a 10 km (6 mile) long trail (or rather, a pair of trails, one of which swings around Brimful Lake), which provides alternate access into the heart of the Stein. The difficult hike leads through some expansive alpine area providing great views of the surrounding valleys. Getting to the trailhead can be equally as challenging since the road is deactivated and has large waterbars.

Stoltmann Wilderness Route (Map 34/C6–D3) 🏕 🚶 🚻
Also known as the Elaho-Meager Trail since it joins the two valleys, the 29 km (17.7 mile) one-way trail will take at least a couple days to hike. Although marked with orange blazes, the pole and rope bridges are subject to washouts (see our online updates). The chance to encounter moose, cougars and grizzly bears and the remote nature of the trail makes this an area for experienced, well-equipped backpackers. The route takes you past the Elaho Giant near Sundown Creek and the Grizzly Fir, another large Douglas-fir next to Last Chance Creek. After a day and a half, you will reach the Thousand Lakes Plateau, which offers panoramic views of glacier-clad mountains amidst the meadows and ponds. By day three, you will be overlooking the Meager Creek Valley and the half-day journey to the hot springs, the perfect end to a difficult trek. The trailhead is found at kilometre 99 on the E1000 Road (off the Elaho Main). It is best to arrange for a second vehicle to pick you up at the Meager Creek.

Sumas Mountain Trails (Map 3/F5–4/A5) 🚶 🚴 🚻
With the recent development of the Trans Canada Trail, there are a few alternatives up this scenic mountain. From the west the original trail begins off the Sumas Mountain Road (at the tiny sign marked Centennial Trail), while the new trailhead is found at the end of Carlyle Road. Expect to hike through thick underbrush and cross Wades Creek along the way past Chadsey Lake to the summit. From the east side, start at the Sumas Dam beneath a rock bluff off Quadling Road. From there, the trail leads uphill through an old cut block before reaching Chadsey Lake and eventually the summit. Regardless of which route you take, the hike is about 12 km (7.3 miles) return gaining about 700 metres (2,275 feet) in elevation. From the top are great views of Sumas Prairie and Vedder Mountain. Some hikers prefer to forgo the last 280 metre climb to the summit and instead stop at the peaceful Chadsey Lake.

Suncoaster Trail (Map 9–20) 🚶 ⛸ 🐎 🚻
This 33 km (20 mile) multi-use trail starts at Homesite Creek near Halfmoon Bay and passes through the Carin Range to Klein Lake. The trail follows roads in some places, including a stretch along Highway 101. The highlight of the trail is the north end of the trail, with views over Ruby and Sakinaw Lake and a waterfall, viewed from a bridge over Sakinaw Creek. Portions of the route are wheelchair accessible.

Sunset Trail (Map 11/B6) 🚶 🚻
Found opposite the Sunset Marina on Highway 99, the Sunset Trail leads up (up and up) past a gate on the second road (ignore the no trespassing sign), all the way to Yew Lake and Cypress Bowl. You'll have hiked 7 km (14 km/8.5 mile return) and climbed 855 metres (2,779 feet) by the time you're finished. If you still have energy, why not hike to the 1,455 metre (4,728 foot) summit of Mount Strachan. This second alternative is 22 km (13.4 miles), climbing 1,400 metres (4,550 feet) along the way.

Sunshine Coast Trail (Map 19/F5–46/A5) 🏕 🚶 🚻
The Sunshine Coast Trail is located on the Upper Sunshine Coast and stretches 180 km (109 miles) from Saltery Bay in the south to Sarah Point in

Desolation Sound. As a general rule, the closer you get to Sarah Point, the tougher the route gets. Mount Troutbridge is just a few kilometres before the end of the trail and is the highest point on the trail, at 1,263 metres (4,105 feet). One of the interesting aspects of this trail is the fact that there are a couple of Bed and Breakfasts located en route. Along the trail you can find great ocean views, occasional waterfront access, old growth forests, ocean vistas, an oceanfront campsite and a lakeside campsite with swimming and freshwater fishing. If you are planning on beginning (or ending) at Sarah Point, you will have to arrange for a water taxi from Lund, unless you want to hike in. You will also have to arrange for boat transportation to get across Powell Lake. To do the whole trail from end to end will take a week to ten days, but most sections are doable as one or two day hikes.

Teapot Hill Trail (Map 4/C7)
It is only 2.5 km (1.5 miles) and 280 metres (900 feet) to the top of Teapot Hill, but the views are surprisingly good making this a popular trail for locals and visitors to Cultus Lake.

Tenquille Lake Trails (Map 35/F3–36/A3)
Tenquille Lake is a beautiful alpine lake set in meadows surrounded by rugged mountain peaks. At the lake is a cabin together with a recreation site for camping. The area is extremely popular with backpackers, mountaineers, snowmobilers and even extreme mountain bikers. The lake can be accessed four ways. The easiest route (if you have a 4wd vehicle) leads from Branch 12 off the Hurley River Road gaining 450 metres (1,463 feet) over a 12 km (7.3 mile) return route. The trail begins in an old cut block and then crosses a creek before joining with the other trail leading from the Lillooet Valley. An alternative and more challenging route is to climb from the Lillooet Valley some 19 km (11.6 miles) gaining 1,460 metres (4,745 feet) along the way. Although the hike is extremely strenuous, you will be rewarded with excellent vistas of the valley below as well as the opportunity to walk through beautiful meadows filled with wildflowers. The third route is known as the Ronayne Trail. It leads from Owl Creek Forest Road to Tenquille Lake over a rugged mountain route that follows a series of ridges. It should be left to the experienced backpackers. The final trail is an 11 km (6.7 mile) hike from the Tenquille Creek Road gaining 427 metres (1,388 feet).

Tetrahedron Provincial Park Trails (Map 10/B2)
This provincial park is the home of an extensive network of alpine hiking, biking and backcountry ski trails. It also contains a series of small mountain lakes, which provide good fishing opportunities and backcountry huts. The main area is reached off the Sechelt Forest Road.

Chapman Lake
This lake is found off the Five Lake Circuit, approximately 3.5 km (2.1 mile) one-way from Edwards Lake Cabin. The trail leads through some old growth forest and an open meadow. The lake can also be accessed from the McNair Lake Trail.

Five Lake Circuit
One of the more popular trails in the area, this circuit involves a 10.4 km (6.3 mile) hike that passes by the five main lakes in the park. The circuit takes you through old growth forest along an old logging road and a series of trails. One of the highlights is Edwards Lake, a beautiful sub-alpine lake in a bowl surrounded by old growth timber. The four other lakes are Tannis, Bachelor, Mayne and Gilbert Lakes. This hike is not accessible until after June when the snow melts, even then it is quite swampy so it is best to bring some good hiking boots. In winter, this area makes a good cross-country ski circuit with cabins on Edwards and Bachelor Lakes.

McNair Lake Trail
This trail begins at the end of the McNair Forest Road (or as far as you can drive). It leads 3 km (1.8 miles) uphill to the lake and one of the four cabins in the park. The trail parallels McNair Creek on its northeast side and passes through old growth forest and over some rockslides to McNair Cabin. McNair Lake is surrounded by sub-alpine meadows with rugged mountain peaks looming in the background. Wildflowers are a highlight in July and August.

Mount Steele Trail
This popular trail begins by traversing some old growth timber past Edwards and Gilbert Lakes. Eventually, you reach the open sub-alpine terrain and the Mount Steele Cabin. To reach the popular cabin at 1,500 metres (4800 feet), you will climb 540 metre (1,755 feet) across the 9

km (5.5 mile) one-way trail. The trail is well marked and is best hiked in July-October. This trail is also very popular with backcountry skiers.

Panther Peak
This is the prominent southern peak of the park. The best route in begins off the end of the McNair Forest Road (4wd required). From there, follow the McNair Lake Trail to McNair Cabin, located in the sub-alpine. From the cabin, proceed towards No Name Lake and then climb steadily upward through a snow chute to the summit. It takes a minimum of five hours to reach the summit and another three to climb down. The difficult route is well rewarded with panoramic views and the beautiful sub-alpine terrain.

Tetrahedron Peak
Although it is the highest peak on the Sunshine Coast, even the hardcore mountaineers will find it difficult to pick a route up. The easiest route is to travel up the Rainy Forest Road approximately 6.4 km (3.9 miles) and then take the overgrown spur road that crosses Rainy River. You will have to either ford the roaring currents of the river or use a series of ropes. Once across the river, proceed for an additional 2 km (1.2 miles) up the old road and then take a spur road to the valley between Panther and Tetrahedron Peaks. Eventually, an unmarked route leads northward to the open slopes beneath the peak where you can scramble to the summit, climbing a cool 1,600 metres (5,200 feet). It takes a good day just to reach the summit, where spectacular panoramic views are your reward.

Texada Island Loop (Map 8, 18, 19)
From the Blubber Bay Ferry Terminal, this is a long, moderate 73 km (44.5 mile) return bike ride that should take a day to complete. Cycling in a clockwise direction from Vananda, you follow Central (High) Road, to Bell Road and down to the hydro lines. Here a steep downhill will bring you to the Davie Bay Road, where you head north to Gillies Bay and back to Vananda and the ferry. It is possible to take side trips to Bob's Lake Recreation Site or Shingle Beach Recreation Site to camp.

Texas Creek Trail (Map 38/C6)
From the end of the deactivated Texas Creek Road, the trail leads south 10 km (6.1 miles) one-way to the Stein Valley. The difficult hike leads through some expansive alpine areas providing great views of the surrounding valleys. A side trail swings around Brimful Lake.

Thacker Mountain Trail (Map 15/F6)
In the heart of Hope, this trail leads 5 km (3 miles) along an old road to the summit of Thacker. You gain 160 metres (520 feet) and are rewarded with a good view of the Fraser Valley and Hope.

Smoke Bluffs Trails (Map 22/C6)
These multi-use trails are located in Squamish around the Smoke Bluffs Climbing Area. From the parking area on Loggers Lane you wind your way through the Smoke Bluffs to the top of Plateau Drive where a good variety of trails that will suit all levels of mountain bikers can be found. The single-track trails are generally quite technical and twisty. As an added challenge, there is occasionally climbing rope strung across the trail to dodge.

Three-Chop Trail (Map 11/G7)
It is 13 km (7.9 miles) return gaining 550 metres (1,788 feet) to a viewpoint overlooking Deep Cove. The route begins at the 3.2 km (2 mile) mark on the Indian River Road along a hydro access road before the actual trail leads from the road into a second growth forest. From the lookout, you can return to the start via the Old Buck Trail. The hike can be made anytime from May through November. No mountain bikes are allowed.

Thynne Mountain/Mount Henning Trails (Map 16/G1–27/G6)
This area is easily accessed from Coquihalla Lakes. An 8 km (4.9 mile) hike/bike leads along an old road to a viewpoint and then along a faint trail through some alpine meadows to the base of Mount Henning. Overall, the elevation gain is 550 m (1,805 ft) to the summit at 1,818 m (5,965 ft). Most hikers return to the parking lot by way of another faint trail passing by an old mining camp and then leading along the old road. Another option is to hike the 7.5 km (4.6 miles) trail that leads through the sub-alpine between Thynne Mountain and Mount Henning. In the winter, the area becomes an extensive series of snowmobile trails including 55 km (33.5 miles) of trails around Thynne Mountain and 50 km (30.5 miles) of trails around Mount Henning. The trail between Mount Henning and Thynne Mountain links the two trail systems.

Tin Hat Mountain Trail (Map 19/B1)
This trail starts just north of Spring Lake, along an old road. While it is possible to drive part of the way, it is best to park your vehicle and walk the old road northward. Eventually, you will pick up a well maintained but difficult trail that leads to the summit some 13 km (7.9 miles) return gaining 1,600 metres (5,200 feet) along the way. Alpine flowers, bunchberries and great views of the Powell Lake area are offered. The hike is best left for late summer and early fall.

Tommy Creek Trail (Map 42/G4)
This 10km (6.1 mile) hike leads along an old mining exploration road and then along an overgrown trail to the sub-alpine. The trailhead is accessed by boat to the south side of Carpenter Lake. This is grizzly bear country so come prepared.

Toquenatch Trail (Map 18/D1)
This well marked trail begins approximately 3.5 km (2.1 miles) along the Southview Road, from where it leaves Highway 101. The hike extends in a northwest direction 5 km (3 miles) one-way. It leads past two large Douglas-fir trees and follows the creek, where salmon spawn in the fall, to the south end of Okeover Inlet.

Tour de Soo (Map 29/G4–30/B1)
30 km (18 miles) of logging roads and 10 km (6 mile) of single-track make up this difficult ride, which will take good riders about three hours including a few mandatory hike-a-bike sections. From the Cougar Mountain (Soo River 03) Road, you climb over to the Soo River Valley and onto Echo Lakes, Rutherford Creek and eventually out to the Highway. From here, make your way north to Pemberton along trails found around and above the railway.

Tower Roads (Map 29/E6–22/E1, 29\F6)
There are two microwave towers that make for excellent but difficult mountain biking. The Black Tusk Tower requires a 1,270 metre (4,128 foot) climb over 16 km (9.8 miles), while the Whistler Tower is an 8 km (4.9 mile) return route. The steep roads offer great views and fun descents.

Traboulay PoCo Trail (Map 2/C2)
This 25 km (15 mile) trail encircles the City of Port Coquitlam and helps form a portion of the Trans Canada Trail. The PoCo Trail was renamed in 2001 to honour former mayor Len Traboulay who helped establish the easy, sometimes paved, sometimes boardwalked, trail.

Trans Canada Trail (Map 1, 2, 3, 4, 5, 6, 15, 16, 27)
The Trans Canada trail weaves its way from Horseshoe Bay to Hope and into the Okanagan as it ultimately makes its way across the province and the country. While there are a couple extended sections in this region that cannot be easily hiked in less than a day (most notably between Chilliwack and Hope), this section of the TCT is designed for day hiking. In fact, many people have hiked on the TCT without knowing it, as the trail incorporates many pre-existing trails into the route. Included in the TCT are parts of the Centennial Trail, the Baden Powell Trail, Burnaby Mountain Trails, the Pitt River Dykes, the Matsqui Trail, Tamahi Trail, the Kettle Valley Railway and more. Some sections of trail still have yet to be built, but the trail is routed onto interim routes (either roads or trails) in these sections. Visit www.trailsbc.ca for more information.

Trout Lake Loop (Map 9/D3)
From the Trout Lake parking lot on Highway 101, this 15 km (9.2 mile) moderate mountain bike loop will take you clockwise along a series of roads back to the highway. Allow 1.5 hours. Between Trout Lake and Redroofs Road a series of moderate trails can be explored. The powerlines above Trout Lake also offer moderate riding that turns quite difficult the further you head west.

Tuwanek Point Beach Trail (Map 9/F3)
The trailhead to this ocean front walk is found off Upland Road just before the gravel pit. The trail leads 2 km (1.2 miles) to the ocean following the shore of Sechelt Inlet to the point.

Twin Goat Ridge Route (Map 31/A2–37/A7)
This difficult bit of ridge walking traverses 22 km (13.4 miles) one-way from Upper Joffre Lake all the way to Lillooet Lake Road just north of the Twin One Recreation Site. Give yourself a full day to get from one to the other. Initially, you ascend from Upper Joffre Lake at 1,280 metres all the way to 2,380 metres (7,735 feet) at the foot of the Matier Glacier, then you descend steadily to Lillooet Lake, at 200 metres (640 feet) in elevation. It can only be hiked after the snow melts, which is usually July to September.

U.B.C. Research Forest (Map 2/F2–12/G7)
There are a number of trails and old roads in this large research forest, just north of Maple Ridge. The routes range from easy saunters around interpretive trails, to some fairly stiff hikes, with elevation gains of up to 610 metres (1,983 feet). The trails weave their way through a mixed second growth forest and some of the high points offer good views over the Fraser Valley. Take 232nd Street north of Haney and park at the gate near the forestry headquarters. You must register at the office before heading out. No mountain bikes are allowed.

Unnecessary Mountain Trail (Map 11/B5)
Unnecessary Mountain gets it's name from the obstacle it forms on the Howe Sound Crest Trail. As a destination, the mountain does offer a rewarding view. Unfortunately, the trail unmaintained is rough, rugged and steep. From the gate on Oceanview Road (right before the Harvey Creek Bridge in Lions Bay), follow the paved and then gravel road to the trailhead marked by orange markers. In all, it is a difficult 9.5 km (5.8 mile) return hike gaining 1,310 metres (4,258 feet) to the summit at 1,510 metres (4,908 feet).

Upper Chilliwack River Trail (Map 5/G7)
From Depot Creek at the south end of Chilliwack Lake, the trail starts along the shores of the lake to the estuary of the Chilliwack River. Where the trail splits, follow the right branch leading south to the US border along the east side of Chilliwack River. This is a rewarding trail that meanders among an ecological reserve with old growth cedar, majestic Douglas-fir and amabilis fir next to the Upper Chilliwack River. It is also an easy trail covering 5.4 km (3.3 miles) return. The more adventurous can continue on into Washington State, along a difficult two-day trail, which ultimately leads to Mount Baker.

Valley Trail System (Map 29/F5)
Within the Whistler Valley is an extensive 20 km (12 mile) network of well-maintained gravel and paved trails. The trail network extends from Alta Lake along the River of Dreams to Green Lake. At most intersections, there are signs marking the various routes. The trail system is heavily used throughout the summer months by mountain bikers, joggers, hikers and in-line skaters and in the winter, by cross-country skiers. The easy trails will take you through the heart of the Whistler Valley past creeks and lakes, forested areas and golf courses.

Vedder Mountain Trails (Map 4/B6)
An excellent hiking trail is found off an old spur road on the Vedder Mountain Forest Road. This is a well-developed, moderate 11.5 km (7 mile) trail gaining 364 metres/1,194 feet (mostly at the start) to the summit. Once you break out of the dense hemlock forest you will be rewarded with views of Sumas Prairie, Vedder Canal and area. Spring flowers brighten the way. Once on the summit, you can follow an old trail down to return along the road. Alternatively, you can use the old trail from the Yarrow side to access the top.

For mountain bikers, this is one of the best places to ride in the Chilliwack area. The main route follows the forestry road from Parmenter Road, 21.5 km (13.1 miles) around the ridge. This moderate ride offers great views of the surrounding valley while climbing 490 metres (1,592 feet). Several side trails in the area have been developed by motorcyclists and provide experienced mountain bikers with fast and twisty thrills. A popular option follows the Vedder Mountain Classic Route. This route heads south (left) from the main road and follows several trails and old roads back to the main road and the start (some 17 km/10.4 miles and 340 metres/1,105 feet later).

Vedder River Trail (Map 4/A5–C6)
The scenic dyke system along the north side of the Vedder River has benefited from extensive work by the Chilliwack Rotary Club. This trail is open to hikers, bikers and horseback riders and is part of the Trans Canada Trail. The main access points are the Keith Wilson Bridge to the west and Vedder Crossing to the east. While there are many places to access the trail, the longest you can hike here is about 15.5 km (9.6 miles).

Viera Creek Trail (Map 43/E5)
This is an 8 km (4.8 mile) trail along a series of mining exploration tote roads and old hunting trails. The trailhead begins a few kilometres west of Mission Dam off the Carpenter Lake Road.

Walt Lake Ridge Route (Map 19/F2)
A four-wheel drive spur road leads to the Walt Lake Ridge trailhead. From there, a difficult and unmarked route leads to the alpine where you can proceed either to the north or south. Either way, you have miles of beautiful alpine meadows to explore. The north branch leads to Beta Lake whereas the south branch leads to Khartoum Lake.

Wedgemont Lake Trail (Map 30/B4)
A short but steep trail climbs to a beautiful lake set at the foot of a glacier below cascading peaks. From the end of the Wedgemont Creek Forest Road, you climb a gruelling 1,220 metres (3,965 feet) through the heavy forest, past a rockslide with a view of the falls on Wedgemont Creek, to the rocky sub-alpine meadows around the lake. At the lake, it is possible to camp or use the cabin as a base for further exploration. The 12 km (7.3 mile) return trail is best tackled in July to September, after the trail dries.

Wednesday Lake Trail (Map 46/A6)
This 8 km (4.8 mile) hike leads along an old road from Malaspina Forest Road to tiny Wednesday Lake, which drains into Trevenen Bay of Okeover Inlet.

Wells Peak Loop Trail (Map 15/G7–5/G1)
The access road is found opposite Nicomen Park on Highway 3 and is marked by the Hope Mountain Trail sign. Once up the rough waterbared road, the trail to the left leads to Wells Peak some 8 km (4.8 miles) later. Allow 5 hours as the hike is strenuous as it climbs 700 m (2,275 ft) to the summit.

Whatcom Trail (Map 6/F2–17/A7)
From the Cascade Recreation Area parking lot off of Highway 3, this trail follows the Dewdney Trail for 2.5 km (1.5 miles) before splitting off to the right. From there, the trail climbs steeply through second growth forest to the sub-alpine meadows of Whatcom Pass and the Punch Bowl. The trail then descends into the Paradise Valley and the Tulameen River near Wells Lake where a variety of trails continue on. You will gain 650 metres (2,113 feet) over 17 km (10.4 miles) one-way to the ridge. Unless you are on horseback, you will probably want to arrange for a shuttle at the far end. The hike is best done in late summer or early fall.

Whip Me, Snip Me (Map 29/F5)
This difficult trail is found about 100 metres (325 feet) south of the Rainbow Lake Trailhead. This is another challenging system that climbs north to the Rainbow Lake Trailhead and the cruise down.

Whippoorwill Point/Sandy Cove Trail (Map 4/F1)
Most visitors to Harrison Hot Springs enjoy the easy stroll to the source of the hot springs. However, few take in the scenic trail that leads to Whippoorwill Point. This 5 km (2.4 mile) trail climbs quickly from the hot springs to its high point, which is only about 40 metres (130 feet) above the lake. From here it descends to Sandy Cove, which is a great place for a picnic and on to Whippoorwill Point. Although the trail is regarded as easy, there are tricky sections to negotiate.

Whistler Interpretative Forest (Map 29/E6)
The Whistler Interpretative Forest is easily accessed by the Westside Main Cheakamus Lake Roads. It is a total of 3,500 hectare and ranges from the valley bottom all the way to the sub-alpine at 1,600 metres (5,200 feet). Through the interpretative forest are numerous short trails exploring the various silviculture practices and ecosystems of the Cheakamus Valley. There are stands of old growth timber along the western banks of the Cheakamus River, scenic vistas and access to a good fishing lake. The **Ridge Trail, Lower Riverside Trail, Highline Trail** and the **Logger's Lake Access Trail** are open to everyone, while the **Crater Rim Trail, Riverside Interpretative Trail** and **Whistler West Ridge Trail** are closed to mountain bikes. Several signs within the interpretative forest allow you to decide on which route to travel.

Whistler Mountain Trails (Map 29/G6)
After the ski season ends and the snow melts, Whistler Mountain becomes a spectacular hiking and biking destination. The glacier covered peaks and the rugged treeless terrain makes the area a gorgeous place to visit. During the off-season, the Whistler Village Gondola runs to the Roundhouse Lookout for a fee. Be sure to pick up the complimentary map that highlights the routes available. There are four different guided bike routes that lead from the Roundhouse Lodge to the Whistler Village. For hikers, the options include the **Glacier Trail,** the **Harmony Lake Trail,** the **Little Whistler Trail, Musical Bumps** (see above) and the **Ridge Lookout Trail.** Outside of the Musical Bumps Trail, the trails are short (up to 3.5 km long) but do require a bit more climbing than the nearby Blackcomb Mountain Trails. The **Highnote Trail,** which leads to a spectacular viewpoint overlooking Cheakamus Lake, returns to the lodge via the Singing Pass Trail.

Widgeon Bowl Lookout Trail (Map 12/E7)
This is a stiff, stiff climb up 700 metres over a mere 2 km (2,275 feet in 2.4 miles); that's just about one metre up for every two metres you hike. Overall the trail gains just over 900 metres in 5 km (2815 feet in 3 miles). The trailhead is difficult to find from the water accessible Widgeon Lake Recreation Site or from Burke Mountain along a poorly marked trail. Although the views of Pitt Lake from the bowl below Widgeon Peak are spectacular, the stiff climb is only for folks in really good shape.

Widgeon Falls Trail (Map 12/E6)
A popular boat access hike is found across from Grant Narrows Park at the south end of Pitt Lake. From the end of the slough at the Widgeon Lake Recreation Site, it is an easy 2.7 km (1.6 miles) walk along an old logging road (note that the old trail along the creek is now closed). Allow one hour to reach the falls gaining 40 metres (130 feet) along the way.

Widgeon Lake Trail (Map 12/E6)
The first part of this trail from the Widgeon Lake Recreation Site is along an old logging road. It is possible (some would even argue preferable) to bring a mountain bike along in your canoe and cycle the first leg of the trail. The second stretch of this 18.5 km (11.3 mile) trail climbs steeply up into the cirque where Widgeon Lake is located, getting progressively steeper the closer you get. The lake is at found at the 815 metre (2,673 foot) mark and most of that is gained in the last couple kilometres.

Wildwood Hill Trail (Map 18/F2)
The trail begins on the west side of the Powell Lake Bridge off Highway 101. This trail switchbacks twice before it connects with the powerline to the south. It eventually leads back to the Petro Canada Service Station. The trail is easily followed and is wide enough for both mountain bikers and hikers.

Williams Ridge Trail (Map 5/D5)
A gruelling 11 km (6.7 mile) trail is found near the 32 km mark of the Chilliwack Lake Road. Orange markers indicate the steep, undeveloped trail as it rises through a second growth forest past a clearing with a good view of the valley. From here, the trail continues along a forested ridge to connect with the Ford Mountain Trail (see above). This is a tough hike, gaining 1,440 metres (4,680 feet) including a lung-busting 900 metres (2,925 feet) in the first 1.5 km (0.9 miles) to the ridge that runs between the lookout and Williams Peak. It is also possible to scramble up to the prominent Williams Peak.

Williamson Lake Trail (Map 5/C5)
Beginning at the Foley Lake Recreation Site, the trail is a difficult 13 km (7.9 mile) hike gaining 1,200 metres (3,900 feet) to the lake. Not only will you feel like a mountain goat as you scramble up (and up), you might actually see one. The trail begins by crossing Foley Creek and then it rises sharply along the ridge above Williamson Creek to the lake. In spring, runoff makes creek crossings difficult and, if there is snow left, there is a good chance that there will be an avalanche. Leave this one until late summer and early fall.

Wilson Creek Trail (Map 9/G5)
The trail is found by parking on Jack Road and then crossing Highway 101. The scenic trail leads through a second growth forest along Wilson Creek before crossing a bridge. The trail continues on to the powerlines for a 2 km (1.2 mile) round trip. This route can be ridden by experienced mountain bikers.

ATV (OHV) TRAILS

ATVers and dirt bikers have got a bad rap with a lot of outdoorsy types. Irresponsible riding by a very notable minority have made motorized vehicles pariah in many places. Fully half the riding areas still open around Squamish and the Fraser Valley are at risk of being closed. ATVers have enjoyed their independence for many years, but independence comes at a cost, and in this case, it is the loss of riding areas.

What's the solution? A single voice has little clout, but by joining a club like the Fraser Valley Dirt Riders Association (www.fvdra.com), the Squamish Dirt Bike Association (www.squamishdirtbikeassociation.com) or the Lower Mainland ATV club (www.lowermainlandatvclub.ca/) you can be a part of a like-minded organization. But that's just the first step. ATVs and motorbikes can have a dramatic effect on trails, so pitch in and help with trail maintenance. Noise is the number one cause of complaints, so keep your machine running at 96db or less. And for heaven's sake, don't go riding in areas that are not open to motorized vehicles, especially wet areas and in the alpine.

Ashcroft Motorcycle Area (Map 38, 39, 45)
Ashcroft boasts one of the largest motorcycle trail system in the province. Trails range in difficulty from a "Sunday Afternoon Ride with Granny" to "Make Sure Your Will is in Order" difficult. There are pink and blue ribbons marking the trails and arrows to point the riding direction. There are also some signs to mark the most difficult sections, but even the toughest trails usually have an alternate route around the worst of the features. The trails are all interconnected and it is possible to for 400 km (240 miles) in a day and not ride the same trail twice. The trails boast some terrific scenery and plenty of wildlife. Be wary, sections of the trail system are popular with mountain bikers as well.

Barkley Valley Trail (Map 37/C4)
The Barkley Valley Trail is a good ATV trail that begins where the Haylmore Forest Service Road becomes impassable, about 14 km (8.6 miles) from Devine. In the 1950s and 60s, the area was being mined for gold, but despite the road up, the area never produced enough to make it viable and it closed down. However, a counterculture group tried to live in the area, but underestimated the amount of snow one has to deal with when communing with nature in winter. The old road leads up past the prospector's cabin to a point where it becomes impassable to ATVs. People can continue on foot to Twin Lakes.

BC Nickle Mine Road Riding Area (Map 15/E4)
After the closing of the Homestake Mine, the area was opened up to motorcycle riders and ATVers. The tailing ponds are a great place to test your skills, while more difficult roads/trails radiate north to Emory Creek. There are nearly three-dozen named trails in this area, including the difficult Yahoo Hill and Sesame Street. Some of the trails are too narrow for quads.

Bear Lake Trail (Map 4/G1)
Follow a series of old logging roads up Bear Mountain to Bear Lake. The trip is about 20 km (12 miles) return to the tiny lake tucked in a pretty valley. Past the lake, the old roads continue to the top of Bear Mountain. By the time you reach the top, the route has climbed over a thousand metres (3,280 ft). It is an extra 8 km (5 miles) return to get to the top.

Cabin Lake Trails (Map 27/B1)
Cabin Lake Road (7 km/4.3 miles) is a rough 4wd/ATV route, gaining 215 m (700 feet) to the lake. Another option is to hike to Lightning Lake, which involves a steep 5 km (3 mile) excursion along an old road.

Cat Lake Area (Map 22/D5)
Around Cat Lake is a series of challenging motorbike trails. These trails can be accessed off of the Cheekeye River Forest Road at the old gondola base area or the Cat Lake Recreation Site. It is possible to cross the Cheekeye River and follow the trails down to Alice Lake or Garibaldi Highlands.

Chilliwack River Valley (Map 4/E7–5/D7)
The Liumchen East Riding Area is a popular location that is found just past the first bridge over the Chilliwack River near the Tamihi Creek Recreation Site. There is a large parking area off the Chilliwack Lake Road, where you cross the road and continue west on the main road, watching for the main side road to the south. There are a number of old roads here, but the main route follows a steep logging road that switchbacks its way up to Church Mountain for fantastic views over the Chilliwack River Valley. Another popular (and easier) route in the immediate area is the DND Powerline Road. Further up the valley, forest service roads like the Tamihi and Nesakwatch offer easy riding to some very scenic areas.

Chipmunk Creek Area (Map 5/A5)
The parking for this area is in a gravel pit, which doubles as a hill climbing area. There are a number of old roads (and some motorbike trails) that can be ridden in this area. However, the Cheam Peak Area is a hiking trail and is not open to ATVs, no matter how tracked out it looks; the fragile alpine of the Spoon Valley has been heavily damaged in the last few years.

Dakota Ridge Area (Map 10/B4)
The Sechelt-Dakota Forest Service Road is found in the hills above Gibson to the east of Sechelt. The logging road leads to a series of side roads or you could follow the Dakota Creek Loop trail over too the Port Mellon Highway.

Green Mountain Trail (Map 41/G5)
Located near Bralorne, the Green Mountain Trail is a rocky, twisty, difficult route up the mountain. It is found off the infamous Hurley River Road.

Herrling Island Riding Area (Map 5/A2)
Herrling Island is one of the largest and best areas for ATVs in the Lower Mainland. The trail in actually goes through the Fraser River, so riding in this area during high water is a bad idea. There are a number of salmon spawning channels that may look fun to play in. Don't do it. This area is on the brink of being closed to ATVers, so if you ride here, ride responsibly. The ground is very sandy.

Jane Lake Trails (Map 29/D6)
The main access route to the Jane Lakes, a series of three mountain lakes, is blocked by a fence built by BC Rail. Mountain bikers, ATVs and hikers follow an old washed out road from the Whistler Athlete's Village. This is a rugged 18 km (11 mile) return trip along the road to the lakes at 930 metres (3,025 feet) in elevation. The lakes provide good fishing throughout the spring and fall as they are stocked regularly.

Onion Lake/Monkey Wrench Riding Area (Map 39/B4)
This area is considered one of the most challenging (and most fun) motorcycle areas in the province. The trails are rocky, steep and slimy making it better for dirt biking than ATV riding. The popular area offers a series of trails/old roads in the hills around Onion and Turnip Lake. There are dozens of trails here, with some easy riding and some highly technical riding.

Stave Lake Riding Area (Map 3/C2)
From the parking areas along the Florence Lake Forest Service Road, just north of Stave Falls, there are many trails to explore off the main road. This area is muddy in the summer and snowy in the winter which makes for some fun riding. (Winch recommended!)You can venture down to the flats, up to the mountains or through the windy trails.

Truax Creek Forest Road (Map 42/D4)
The Truax Creek Forest Service Road is a deactivated logging road that climbs into the mountains above Carpenter Lake. There are a pair of bridges that are slowly degenerating (and one is partially blocked), so don't be surprised if this route becomes impassable.

Upper Mamquam/Indian Arm Forest Roads (Map 22/D7-12/A5)
Some long road riding routes are found in the Mamquam Valley as well as up and over to Indian Arm. There are a few side routes and the occasional single-track trail tossed in for good measure. Note that the Stawamus-Indian Forest Service Road has been closed to the public as it is part of the watershed area.

Vedder Mountain Trails (Map 4/B6)
Motorcyclists share this area with hikers, bikers and equestrians, which has lead to conflicts in the past; many trails are closed to motorbikes, simply because they are not well constructed. The main route follows the forest service road from Parmenter Road, 21.5 km (13.1 miles) around the ridge. There are several side trails to ride, but these can be difficult to ride when wet.

refer to indicated pages for more map detail

hotspots

O ne of the greatest things about being in the wilderness is spotting the residents in their natural environments. Wildlife watching has always been a popular pursuit, but in the last few decades, the sub-genre of bird watching has gone from the fringe (birdwatchers were usually portrayed in movies as a poorly dressed guy in coke-bottle glasses and a tie stumbling about the bushes with an overly large pair of binoculars) to the mainstream.

Avid birdwatchers are always looking for new and unusual species to add to their lists, and Southwestern BC is a great place to watch birds. In fact, the internationally famous George C. Reifel Bird Sanctuary is one of the best birding locations in the province, if not the country.

Some wildlife is easy to spot. Salmon viewing, for instance, is a matter of getting down to the right stream at the right time. On the other hand, many birds and animals tend to flee when they hear, see or smell humans. In order to improve your chances of spotting these more elusive creatures, wear natural colours and unscented lotions. Bring along binoculars or scopes so you can observe from a distance and move slowly but steadily. Keep pets on a leash, or better yet, leave them at home, as they will only decrease your chances to spot wildlife. Early mornings and late evenings are usually the best time to see most birds and animals.

Never approach an animal directly and for heaven's sake, do not try and bring animals to you by offering them food. Animals can become conditioned to handouts, which may put both of you, into harm's way. Rather, figure out what natural foods they prefer, and situate yourself near where these animals will feed.

This list is certainly far from complete. Black bear are a common site around the berry farms near Minnehkada in fall, for instance, and there are many other rivers and streams where eagles congregate in fall besides the Squamish. It is, however, a fairly good start. Not all wildlife watching sites are created equal. Some of the sites listed cater to birders; others are good places to see salmon spawning. Most wildlife watching is seasonal. Eagles congregate in Squamish in winter, while spring is the time to visit the Reifel Bird Sanctuary. As you discover the joys of watching wildlife, you will learn the rhythms of the seasons.

Another good resource is the books by Anne Murray. Visit natureguidesbc.com for more information on those.

Agassiz Farmlands (Map 4/G2–5/A2)
The farmlands around Agassiz are wintering grounds for waterfowl. During the winter months, the area is home to trumpeter and tundra swans, while large flocks of ducks may be seen on flooded fields. Maria Slough, although surrounded by privately owned land, is an excellent place to see spawning salmon and trumpeter and tundra swans from the water.

Alice Lake Provincial Park (Map 22/D5)
This beautiful provincial park is home to one of the most unique spectacles in the region. In mid-summer, a western toad migration occurs at Fawn Lake. During other times of the year deer and the occasional bear grace the park.

Alouette River Dykes (Map 2/E2)
Great blue heron and hawks are common throughout the year, while in winter there are bald eagles and occasionally, trumpeter swans. A great blue heronry is located on private property across the Alouette River from a small parking lot off 210 Street, where the road turns right. The best viewing time is from March to late July. Bring binoculars.

Bell-Irving Hatchery (Map 3/G3)
Located in Kanaka Creek Regional Park, this hatchery is open to visitors year-round. There are ponds, tanks and troughs which contain Coho and chum, the latter are released with great fanfare in late April every year. There are trails along the creek itself where visitors can watch spawning salmon in the fall.

Birkenhead Lake Provincial Park (Map 36/C3)
Nestled in the Coast Mountains, Birkenhead Provincial Park is home to Phelix Creek. In September and October watch for spawning kokanee. During the rest of the year, deer and even bear can be seen on occasion.

Boundary Bay Regional Park (Map 1/E7)
Boundary Bay is an area of international significance to migrating and wintering birds. There are several trails, a boardwalk and two viewing structures located in the park. Many bird species nest on the ground in the sandy and grassland areas, so please stay on the designated trails. Cresent Beach is home to the Birds on the Bay display from late January to May.

Brackendale Eagles Provincial Park (Map 22/C6)
The Squamish River plays host to thousands of bald eagles every winter. These majestic birds can be seen feasting on the spawned out remains of chum salmon from late November to January. The area on the west side of the Squamish River has been designated as special eagle habitat by BC Parks.

Burnaby Lake Regional Park (Map 1/G2)
Located in the heart of Burnaby, this park is an oasis for wildlife and humans alike. The marshy edges of the lake are an important feeding and nesting habitat for waterfowl, shorebirds and small mammals.

Capilano River Hatchery (Map 11/D7)
The Capilano River Hatchery is located just below Cleveland Dam in North Vancouver. The hatchery is open every day, but the hours of operation change throughout the year. The best viewing time is October and November to see returning adult salmon, and March to May to see juveniles.

Chapman Creek Hatchery (Map 9/G5)
A number of fish species are reared at Chapman Creek Hatchery, including Chinook, Coho, chum and pink salmon as well as cutthroat trout. From August through December adult salmon use Chapman Creek to spawn. pink are present in August and September, while Coho and chum are present beginning in mid October. A viewing platform provides good views of the creek and a trail leads upstream along Chapman Creek.

Cheam Lake Wetlands Regional Park (Map 4/G3)
Located near Bridal Falls, Cheam Lake is a fine example of habitat restoration. The original lake was drained in the 1950s to mine marl, but a water control structure with a fish ladder was installed in 1992 to allow the lake to flood. Changes are occurring as the lake re-establishes and new wildlife species are beginning to visit the park. A wide variety of birds are already present. There are beaver and muskrats, and from late March through August, the park is a good place to look for butterflies.

Chehalis River Hatchery (Map 4/D2)
The Chehalis River Hatchery is responsible for rearing and for releasing a wide range of fish species, including Coho, Chinook and chum salmon as well as steelhead and cutthroat trout. The hatchery compound is open to visitors year round, and there are self-guiding interpretive signs on site. The best viewing time is November when salmon spawn in the hatchery outflow channel and in the small stream near the parking lot.

Chilliwack Lake Provincial Park (Map 5/F6)
There are good salmon viewing opportunities near where the Chilliwack River flows out of the northern end of Chilliwack Lake. October to mid November is the best time to view pink (odd years only), sockeye and Coho salmon. In April look for steelhead trout spawning.

Chilliwack River Hatchery (Map 5/A6)
The Chilliwack River Hatchery is situated just upstream of the junction of Slesse Creek and the Chilliwack River. It is open daily from 8 am to 3:30 pm. A summer run of Chinook begins to arrive at the hatchery in August, and the hatchery is busy through to December with other species of salmon returning. Steelhead trout return in March and April.

Colony Farm Regional Park (Map 2/B3)
Located along the Coquitlam River, this park provides nesting and feeding habitats for a wide range of birds, especially raptors and songbirds. The wooded areas are good places to look for woodpeckers and chickadees, while the old fields are frequented by Short Eared Owls. From Highway 7, turn south onto Colony Farm Road and continue to the parking area at the end of the road.

Copeland Islands Marine Park (Map 46/A6)
The Copeland Islands are a small chain of islands, islets and rocks off the northern corner of the Sunshine Coast. It is an excellent place to explore by kayak or canoe, and is home to marine mammals like seal and sea lion as well as numerous species of waterfowl.

Coquihalla Canyon Provincial Park (Map 15/G5)
Better known for its impressive scenery and equally impressive series of old railway bridges and tunnels, the area is also a great place to watch steelhead spawning up the river. The bridges give a great perspective on the fish as they lay in deep pools of water.

Crabapple Creek (Map 29/F5)
Located in Whistler, a portion of the Valley Trail follows this creek. In early summer, the creek is home to spawning rainbow trout, while in September and October, kokanee spawn here.

Cultus Lake Provincial Park (Map 4/C6)
A popular destination for sun worshippers, Cultus Lake is also home to a wide variety of bird species, such as osprey, Steller's jay and winter wrens. In summer months, bats feed in forest clearings and along the edge of the forest.

Cypress Provincial Park (Map 11/A7–B4)
Established in 1975, this 2,996 hectare park is made up of several types of old growth forests, some mixed second growth forests, sub-alpine wetlands, rocky bluffs and mountaintop plateaus. Black bear and cougars frequent the park and may be encountered on hiking trails and in open areas, and smaller animals and birds are often seen.

Fee Creek Spawning Channel (Map 36/D7)
Located about 11 km (6.6 miles) from Mount Currie along Highway 99, Fee Creek runs into the Birkenhead River. The man-made channels in this area provide important, year-round habitat to young salmon. Watch for fry darting about the channels.

Garibaldi Provincial Park (Map 22, 23, 24, 29, 30)
Garibaldi is a big, spectacular park, containing all kinds of animals and birds. In particular, watch for Hoary Marmots and pika in or near the alpine meadows, or in talus slopes. Access into Garibaldi is mainly on foot.

Gates River Spawning Channel (Map 37/A3)
The spawning channel at Gates River is an excellent place to observe spawning sockeye salmon in late summer and early fall. There is a large fish ladder that provides fish with access from Gates River into the channel. The spawning channel is located in Devine, just south of D'Arcy.

George C. Reifel Migratory Bird Sanctuary (Map 1/B5)
This sanctuary is ground zero for Lower Mainland birders. Located on Westham Island in Delta, it contains habitats important for migrating birds, including tidal saltwater mudflats, freshwater, brackish and salt marshes and upland fields. All types of birds, including raptors, shorebirds and woodpeckers are found here year round. But during the late fall and early winter months the island comes alive with over 25,000 lesser snow geese visiting the area.

Golden Ears Provincial Park (Map 2, 3, 12, 13, 23, 24)
Golden Ears is another big, spectacular park that is home to all sorts of birds and mammals. From chipmunks to black bear and cougars to cowbirds and ospreys you never know what you may encounter next. In the high country, you may even see mountain goats on the rocky mountain cliffs.

Great Blue Heron Nature Reserve (Map 4/B5)
Located in the Wet Bridge training area of the old Chilliwack Armed Forces Base, the Great Blue Heron Nature Reserve is one of the few nesting sites for herons in the Lower Mainland. Look for the colony nests west of the parking area, and along the dyke off Sinclair Road. Things start to happen here in March, when adults begin claiming nests.

Harrison Bay/Chehalis Flats (Map 4/C2)
In winter, bald eagles hang out around the Chehalis Flats in great numbers (some years, there are over 1,000 eagles here). The eagles arrive in November, and stay until January, attracted by dead and dying spawning salmon. As an added bonus, this is also a winter feeding ground for trumpeter swans.

Hayward Lake Reservoir (Map 3/C3)
While wildlife can be seen throughout the Hayward Lake area, the Pond Trail is where you will see more action. Birds (waterfowl, woodpeckers and assorted songbirds) and beavers...or at least, signs of beavers (lodges, felled trees, etc.) are seen from the trail. Nearby Ruskin Dam features a spawning channel where chum salmon may be observed from early October through late November.

Hell's Gate Fishways (Map 26/E5)
More than 31 million sockeye were harvested from the 1913 run on the Fraser River. When the remaining fish reached Hell's Gate, they ran into an almost impenetrable obstacle caused by the construction of what is now the Canadian National Railway. All but the hardiest fish were blocked by a rockslide that shrank the already narrow channel and created a five metre high waterfall. By 1915, the removal of 45,000 cubic metres of rock from the channel had eased the problem; this remains one of the toughest obstacles on the river. There are now specially designed fishways to aid the spawning salmon.

Hope Slough/Camp Slough (Map 4/E3)
While most of these sloughs are on private land, the drive though this area will reveal plenty of great roadside stops to pull over and observe waterfowl and other birds.

Inch Creek Fish Hatchery (Map 3/G4)
Throughout the year, you can see and learn about young salmon in various stages of development in the tanks and troughs. On site, there is a large pond, which is home to several large white sturgeons, the largest of which weighs over 91 kg (200 lb). The hatchery compound is open to visitors every day (except Christmas Day) from 9 am to 3 pm.

Indian Arm Provincial Park (Map 2, 11, 12)
Indian Arm Provincial Park plays host to a number of large mammals, including black bear, blacktail deer, cougar, coyote and red fox. But most visitors are interested in the marine life. The sandy isthmus connecting Twin Islands is home to a variety of clams and other shellfish, while tidal pools along the rocky shoreline abound with sea life.

Inland Lake Provincial Park (Map 18/G2)
Best known for its wheelchair accessible trail that circles the lake, there are a number of places to view wildlife–primarily avian–at the lake. One of the best places is along the marsh boardwalk on the east side of the lake.

Iona Beach Regional Park (Map 1/B3)
This area has long been recognized across North America as one of the best places to study shorebirds. The riverbank, Fraser River tidal flat, marsh, grassland and beach habitats attract over 280 species of birds, including many rare and vagrant species.

John Daly Regional Park (Map 9/B1)
John Daly Regional Park is located on Anderson Creek, an important spawning creek. Chum and Coho spawn here in October and November.

Jones Creek Spawning Channel (Map 5/B1)
This spawning channel is located west of Hope near Laidlaw. Chum, Coho and, on odd-numbered years, pink salmon spawn here during October. Access is from Jones Creek Road east off Highway 1.

Kanaka Creek Regional Park (Map 2/G3–3/B3)
This park stretches along Kanaka Cree. Just off 256 Street, a fish fence was built in conjunction with the Bell-Irving Hatchery. Every October, this location plays host to the annual Return of the Salmon event, during the heart of the chum and Coho spawn. Farther upstream, a hatchery is open to visitors year round. The chum salmon release in late April is worth catching. The riverfront area of the park is located along the estuary and is a great place to watch birds.

Khartoum Lake Recreation Site (Map 19/F3)
The rocky bluffs found around the lake and further up the Lois River Valley are home to mountain goat. They are best seen in the spring and fall.

Kopp Creek (Map 15/F6)
Found near Hope, this small creek is a great place to watch returning kokanee in September and October. Viewing is from the road only.

Lang Creek (Map 19/B4)
Where the fresh water of Lang Creek enters the salt water of Malaspina Strait is a great place to see waterfowl and shorebirds. November to January is the best time to see the eagles, attracted by the salmon carcasses. Also in the area, the Lang Creek Falls and the Lang Creek Hatchery, both of which offer a chance to watch salmon in a spawning channel from mid August to late November.

Langdale Creek (Map 10/D6)
This small creek runs along the southern side of the Langdale Ferry Terminal. Through the fence, Coho and chum salmon can be seen spawning in mid-October through to mid-December.

Mamquam Spawning Channel (Map 22/C6)
This series of spawning channels is located on the north side of the Mamquam River just east of the bridge over the river on Highway 99. Coho and chum salmon can be seen in November and December.

Manning Provincial Park (Map 6, 7)
Manning Park is a big, beautiful park, and more than 200 species of bird have been seen here. In addition to birds the park is a wonderful place to view a wide range of birds, small mammals, and, perhaps some larger mammals, including black bear and mule deer. Be sure to check out the Manning Park Bird Blitz in mid June each year.

Maplewood Flats (Map 1/F1)
Maplewood Flats is about 2 km (1.2 miles) east of the Second Narrows Bridge. This 96 hectare area is made up of mudflats and some salt marsh, which make ideal waterfowl and bird habitat. In addition, several disused log pilings provide perching and nesting habitat for osprey.

Maria Slough (Map 4/G2)
While much of the land surrounding the slough is private, there are several places where the road crosses or approaches the slough. The shallows off Chaplin Road are a great place to watch salmon spawning in the fall, while fall and winter are a good time to watch for birds. Trumpeter and tundra swans can be seen here.

Millar Creek (Map 29/E5)
Miller Creek flows through Whistler. In May and June, rainbow trout spawn in the creek.

Nanton Lake Recreation Site (Map 19/C2)
There is a small herd of Roosevelt elk, which have been transplanted to this area. The best viewing times are in the early morning and before dusk.

Nicomen Slough (Map 3/G5–4/A4)
Nicomen Slough contains habitat that is important to many species, including bald eagles and spawning salmon. Most notably, the slough provides important wintering habitat for between 100 and 200 trumpeter swans, from late November through January.

Noons Creek Hatchery (Map 2/B2)
Started by a handful of area residents who wanted to see salmon reintroduced to Noon Creek, the Noon Creek Hatchery now releases thousands of Coho and chum salmon every year. The best viewing times are in May, when fingerlings are released, and in fall, when salmon return to spawn. The hatchery is located on the west side of the Port Moody Recreation Centre on Ioco Road.

Pitt-Addington Marsh Wildlife Area (Map 2/E1–12/F7)
The Pitt-Addington Marsh Wildlife Management Area encompasses 2,972 hectares (7,344 acres) south of Pitt Lake that includes Grant Narrows Regional Park, Addington Marsh, Pitt Polder, and MacIntyre Creek. The tidal freshwater mudflats, marshes, and wetlands are viewable along a network of dykes, as well as a number of viewing platforms and towers. Viewing highlights include great blue herons, trumpeter swans, ospreys and other raptors, sandhill cranes and a wide variety of songbirds.

Pitt Meadows/Pitt Polder (Map 2/D2–12/F7)
The open farmlands around Pitt Meadows provide great wildlife watching opportunities. During winter, waterfowl can be seen in the flooded fields around Pitt Meadows Airport, as well as hawks. In the summer, short-eared owls are seen hunting, often during the day. Coyote are also frequently seen in the fields.

Pitt River Dykes (Map 2/E2)
To prevent flooding, dykes have been built along the Pitt River. These dykes provide great access along the rivers for birders. Look for osprey who build their nests on top of old pilings along the river.

Porpoise Bay Provincial Park (Map 9/F4)
This 61 hectare park is found on the east side of the Sechelt Inlet. Angus Creek, which flows through the park, is a popular place to watch salmon, but the site is best known as a destination for birders. There are plenty of wa-

terfowl that overwinter here, and in the spring there are migratory songbirds. The estuary is a place to spot bald eagle and other birds.

Rolley Lake Provincial Park (Map 3/C2)
This popular park is home to small mammals, like squirrel and chipmunk, while the forests around the lake are great places to listen for barred owl, as well as a variety of songbirds.

Ruby Creek and Lake (Map 20/B7)
Ruby Creek is a short creek that connects Ruby Lake to Sakinaw Lake. Through habitat enhancement projects, new gravel beds and covers over portions of the creek have been added. These features will help protect the spawning habitat for a rare population of coastal cutthroat trout and for kokanee in fall. Ruby Lake and its lagoon also has 82 species of birds, 150 species of trees and shrubs, painted turtles, Roosevelt elk, deer & bear in a coastal rainforest setting protected by a 99 acre wildlife & bird sanctuary area. Only 1 km from the lake is the Iris Griffith Field Studies and Interpretive Centre, where an innovative nature school program is taught.

Ruskin Dam Recreation Area (Map 3/B3)
Located just south of Hayward Lake, below the Ruskin Dam, a small spawning channel has been built next to the Stave River. Here chum salmon can be seen spawning from early October through late November. Bald eagle and other birds that feed on salmon can also be seen at this time.

Sargeant Bay Provincial Park (Map 9/D4)
This park contains a shingle beach, a small lake with a cattail marsh, and an upland area of second growth forest. The park is noted for its beautiful bay and excellent bird watching.

Sasquatch Provincial Park (Map 15/A7)
There are three main viewing areas in Sasquatch Provincial Park. The most active site is the Beaver Pond area where beaver or signs of beaver, activity can be seen. The best times to observe one of Canada's icons is at dawn or just before sunset. Bird life also abounds in this area. Another place to watch wildlife is at the outlet of Hicks Lake, which features a small dam and fish ladder. A trail leads along the creek and across the dam. In March and April, look for spawning cutthroat trout. They are best seen early in the morning or at sunset. Finally, watch for spawning chum salmon in October and November in the lower reaches of the Trout Lake Creek.

Sechelt Marsh (Map 9/F4)
This marsh is located across the street from the head of Sechelt Inlet. Together the freshwater marsh and the saltwater inlet provide important wildlife habitat, mostly for waterfowl and shorebirds. You will also see woodpeckers and songbirds in the upland areas. Further north, Porpoise Bay Park is also a good birding area.

Serpentine Wildlife Area (Map 2/B6)
The Serpentine Wildlife Area contains 71.3 hectares (176 acres) of extensive marshes, which can be accessed along the many trails in the area. There are three covered viewing towers but please note that many of the dykes are closed to public access. While birds are the big things to see here (from herons to raptors to waterfowls), you will also find small mammals (like muskrats), coyote and harbour seal in the Serpentine River.

Shoreline Park (Map 2/B1)
There is little natural habitat left on Burrard Inlet, so this small park located at the head of Port Moody is a treasure. It is home to a wide variety of habitats and species. Viewing highlights include waterfowl during the winter, including loons, ducks, geese and mergansers. Woodpeckers and chickadees are common year round, and in spring and summer, songbirds. The main access to the Shoreline Park area is from St. Johns Street in Port Moody.

Skagit Valley Provincial Park (Map 6)
The Skagit Valley is home to a diversity of wildlife habitat, and, not surprisingly, a diversity of wildlife. Nearly 200 species of bird have been recorded in the area, and commonly seen mammals include Columbian black-tailed deer, mule deer, snowshoe hare, beaver and common pika. The open meadows near Ross Lake play home to many butterfly species.

Skookumchuk Narrows Provincial Park (Map 20/D6)
Chickadees, nuthatches and woodpeckers are common along the forest trail to the viewpoint over the narrows. At the viewpoint, many diving ducks are visible, including mergansers and grebes. Harbour seal are also common along the inlet.

Sliammon Creek Hatchery (Map 18/E2)
Located alongside Sliammon Creek, the best time to watch spawning chum salmon is during October and November. The hatchery is north of Powell River along Highway 101.

South Arm Marshes Wildlife Area (Map 1/C5)
The Fraser River estuary is the single most important area of aquatic bird and raptor migration and wintering habitat in British Columbia. The 937 hectare (2,316 acre) South Arm Marshes Wildlife Management Area provides critical wintering, migration and breeding habitats for waterfowl, shorebirds, raptors and many passerine species. The management area contains a series of islands surrounded by both freshwater and intertidal marshes, including Ladner Marsh, Ladner Lagoon and seven islands. There are more species of birds here than you could shake a spotting scope at, plus seal, sea lion, beaver, mink and other species of mammals.

Spences Bridge (Map 39/G5)
Large herds of bighorn sheep are visible in and around the community of Spences Bridge throughout the year. Although the sight of the sheep excites visitors, they do cause the local residents grief by eating laundry hanging to dry. A patient wildlife observer in the area surrounding Spences Bridge may also see elk, deer, coyote, black bear, cougar, bobcat, lynx, bald eagles, ospreys and many other wildlife species.

Squamish River and Estuary (Map 22/C7)
The Squamish River and Squamish estuary are home to the largest concentration of wintering bald eagles in the country. They are best seen in December and January, feeding on the rivers late fall run of salmon. But it isn't all eagles. trumpeter swans are seen during the winter, and in spring and summer, the estuary is a great place to see waterfowl and songbirds. On occasion, harbour seal are seen hauling themselves up onto log booms in the area.

Stanley Park (Map 1/C1)
Stanley Park is a well-groomed showcase of the natural wonders that surrounds Vancouver. It is the green heart that beats in a city of concrete and steel. Lost Lagoon teams with waterfowl and small critters.

Sucker [Kawkawa] Creek (Map 15/F6)
Also known as Kawkawa Creek, there is a spawning channel here as well as a boardwalk. Coho and chum return here from early October to mid November.

Sweltzer River (Map 4/C6)
Draining Cultus Lake into the Chilliwack River, this is a popular salmon viewing spot. Chum return from mid-October to mid-December. Other species are seen less frequently, though around the same general timeframe.

Tenderfoot Creek Hatchery (Map 22/C4)
Located off Paradise Valley Road, the hatchery contains tanks and troughs holding young fish most of the year. During November and December spawning Coho and chum salmon may be observed next to the hatchery.

Texada Island (Map 8, 18, 19)
With no natural predators, Texada Island is home to a large population of mule deer. They are visible during most times of the year, especially during dawn and dusk periods. If you get away from the more populated areas, sit along a road or well worn trail and wait. The island is also home to birds, smaller mammals, and harbour seal down on the beach. But the biggest highlight here is the deer.

Weaver Creek Spawning Channel (Map 4/E1)
Weaver Creek spawning channel is one of the biggest in the area. An average of 32,000 sockeye salmon and 2,500 chum salmon use the channel, depositing an estimated 76 million eggs. Next to the Adams River, this is the best site in British Columbia to see sockeye spawning in September. In winter, the channel and surrounding streams are terrific places to look for American Dippers, a small slate-grey songbird that walks under water.

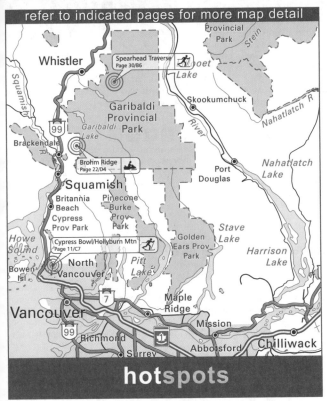

refer to indicated pages for more map detail

(Map labels: Whistler, Provincial Park, Stein, Spearhead Traverse Page 30/B6, Joffre Lake, Skookumchuck, Nahatlatch R, Garibaldi Provincial Park, Garibaldi Lake, Brackendale, Squamish R, Brohm Ridge Page 22/D4, Squamish, Port Douglas, Nahatlatch Lake, Britannia Beach, Pinecone-Burke Prov Park, Cypress Prov Park, Stave Lake, Golden Ears Prov Park, Harrison Lake, Howe Sound, Cypress Bowl/Hollyburn Mtn Page 11/C7, North Vancouver, Pitt Lake, Bowen Isl, Maple Ridge, Vancouver, Richmond, Mission, Surrey, Abbotsford, Chilliwack)

hotspots

SKIING AND SNOWSHOEING

Listed below are some of the more popular trail systems that people prefer to snowshoe or cross-country ski around Southwestern BC. We have also included a few favourite ski touring or backcountry skiing destinations. These are only a fraction of the places the intrepid explorer can get to in winter. If you're looking for more adventurous trips, there are groups out there, like the Federation of Mountain Clubs, who can help.

Atwell Peak (Map 22/E4)
This one is for the ski mountaineers in the crowd. Atwell Peak is one of a bunch of destinations accessed from the Elfin Lakes Hut in Garibaldi Provincial Park. The first few kilometres of the route past the hut are accessed along the Garibaldi Neve Traverse, but just past where the trail heads to Mamquam Lake, turn left (west) instead of right (east) and head up up up to the top. It is a stiff climb to the top with plenty of avalanche slopes to be wary of.

Birkenhead Peak Route (Map 36/E4)
A microwave tower road leaves the Blackwater Lake Road just before it crosses under the power lines. This is the usual access up to Birkenhead Peak, a solitary massive with two officially named peaks—Birkenhead and the secondary Mount McDonald. It is 14.6 km (9 miles) to the actual peak and back, but most people spend a day or two exploring.

Winter storms that bring endless rain to Vancouver in January bring snow, tons of snow to the mountains. While never ending snow might sound like a good thing, it can make touring the mountains dangerous; not just for avalanche hazards, but simply for navigation purposes. Mid-winter trips tend to contain extended periods of time stuck in a tent or at home.

But, come April, the sun comes out and there are a few weeks—and in higher elevation snowfields, months—of perfect touring weather. Sunny, warm and snow everywhere.

Snowshoeing is a sport that has been rapidly gaining popularity for snowbound hikers. Part of its newfound appeal can be attributed to the radical design innovations that have taken place over the last few years. Snowshoes have gone from unwieldy racquets attached to the feet, to devices that are only slightly larger than a pair of boots and are just as easy to walk in.

Whatever the reason, you will now find people snowshoeing all sorts of snow-covered trails in winter. They also tie in well with the few cross-country areas that exist in Southwestern BC. The Coast Mountains are also a paradise for people who like to do ski touring. Routes range from easy (cross-country skiers will find that they don't need special touring skis to do some of these routes) to the extremely precipitous. We could only least a few of the more popular routes, but there are more out there…many more.

Finding places near the Lower Mainland to ride a snowmobile is a challenge, as the lower valleys usually have no snow and the higher mountains are mostly protected behind park boundaries, all of which are snowmobile-free zones. But snowmobiling is actually quite popular once you start to head a bit farther out of the city. Even around Chilliwack, you will start to find areas that are good snowmobiling territory. The heartland of snowmobiling, at least in this mapbook, is the region around Pemberton, Bralorne and Gold Bridge. There are dozens of places to snowmobile that are accessed off (and sometimes on) the Hurley River Forest Road and the Upper Lillooet Forest Road.

It is important to remember that backcountry travel comes with a degree of risk that, while manageable, is never non-existent. If you don't know what you're doing, don't do it! Travel with someone who has more experience, take an avalanche safety training course and always carry an avalanche transceiver.

Image © Walter Bulten

winteradventures

Black Tusk/Garibaldi Lake (Map 22/E2)
This area is an advanced backcountry ski touring area. There are huts on the east side of Garibaldi Lake and people ski across Garibaldi Lake during January and February to spend the night. The day-use shelters at Garibaldi Lake can be used for sleeping in during the winter months only. The road to the parking lot is not ploughed during the winter. Parking is along Highway 99.

Bombtram Mountain (Map 16/B4)
A good spring skiing destination, this mountain is accessed from the Box Canyon parking lot, skinning up through the trees and into alpine bowls that can offer some wonderful late season powder. And, if you come back via the canyon (downhill all the way) it's only about a 1 km traverse back to the vehicle. It is possible to get a couple or three runs on a good day.

Brandywine & Metal Dome (Map 29/B5)
This is a popular summer destination that loses none of its beauty and appeal in winter. The only complaint could be its popularity, both with snowmobilers and heli-skiers. It is still possible to find some areas that are not tracked out. A ridge connects Brandywine Mountain and Metal Dome, although there is a bit of scrambling required to make the traverse. There is a snowmobile warming hut near Metal Dome, maintained by the Powder Mountain Snowmobile Club.

Brohm Ridge (Map 22/E4)
Because it is located outside of Garibaldi Park, anything goes on Brohm Ridge. Depending on when you show up and where you go, you might see ski tourists, snowmobilers and even snowboarders building the biggest darn half pipe you will ever see. There is a warming hut and lots of great skiing that is easily done in a day. The snowmobile trails are maintained by the Black Tusk Snowmobile Club.

Callaghan Country Wilderness Adventure (Map 29/C4)
Located 13 km (8 miles) west of Whistler, this area (formerly Mad River Ski Area) is often used as a staging area for trips to the Callaghan Lake Lodge, 12.5 km (13.4 miles) up trail from Alexander Falls. There are a total of 42 km (26 miles) of groomed trails in the area, plus lots of great backcountry skiing, especially around the lodge found at an elevation of 1,370 metres/4,500 feet. Most people who travel this way stay at the 5-room backcountry lodge, but this is by no means a requirement of using this area. You do have to pay the trail fees, though. In addition to cross-country and backcountry skiing, there is also 15 km (9 miles) of backcountry snowshoeing. In particular, the old growth forests and sub-alpine meadows of the Upper Callaghan Valley make a fine destination on snowshoe.

Callaghan Lake Provincial Park (Map 29/C3)
An average of 275 centimetres (108 inches) of snow falls in the Callaghan Lake area, making it one of the most reliable areas for skiing in the Lower Mainland. While there are no developed trails here, there are many informal trails that can be followed. There are also opportunities for alpine touring on the surrounding mountains.

Cambie Creek Cross-Country Ski Trails (Map 7/C4)
Located in Manning Provincial Park, this series of cross-country ski trails have also become a popular snowshoeing destination. The trails range from the easy Cambie Loop, which is a 2.5 km loop trail through the meadows and over a bridge, to the difficult Fat Dog Trail that climbs all the way up into the sub-alpine. These trails are not groomed, but are usually well tracked.

Cayoosh Range (Map 36/G6–37/B6)
This is a phenomenal ski area. It's so good, in fact, that plans have been underway for about a decade to turn this area into a ski hill. It may take even longer than that to see these plans come to fruition. In fact, the hill may never happen, but that doesn't mean that you can't ski it currently. Without the lifts, plan on spending at least two days here, more if you want to explore the Northern part of this range. Most of the skiing happens on Mount Rohr and Cayoosh Mountain, which are more easily accessed of the Duffey Lake Road (Hwy 99).

Cheam Peak (Map 5/A3)
Cheam is one of the most prominent peaks in the Fraser Valley. How far you have to ski depends on how high you can get a vehicle up the Chipmunk Creek Forest Road to the south. At the base of Cheam Peak is a lovely open meadow and the ascent, while stiff, isn't too difficult. Nearby Knight Peak is another popular ski destination.

Cypress Mountain Ski Area (Map 11/B6)
For cross-country skiers, Cypress Mountain is the closest place to Vancouver for cross-country skiers to get their fix; Cypress Bowl has 19 km (11.6 miles) of trails groomed for skate and classic. 4 km (2.4 miles) of the trails are lit for night skiing. There are some challenging up and down hill sections, but novices will be able to find some interesting loops, too. Cypress is also home to several kilometres of snowshoeing trails. For downhill skiers, the mountain offers nine lifts, servicing 600 skiable acres and 52 named runs, including a number that are lit for night skiing. It is considered the most challenging local ski hill.

Dakota Ridge Area (Map 10/B4)
On the Sunshine Coast, this popular area is a bit challenging to get to in winter but offers a great winter playground. From cross-country and backcountry skiing to snowshoeing and even snowmobiling, there is no shortage of places to explore. It offers one of the most reliable locations for snow in the area and offers great views over the North Shore, Vancouver Island and Mount Baker. Currently, there area about 12 km (7.5 miles) of trails with more planned. Access is 14 km (8.7 miles) along the bumpy Wilson East Forest Road.

Dam Mountain (Map 11/D6)
A popular hiking route in the summer, Dam Mountain is gaining popularity as a winter snowshoeing route. The 3 km (1.5 mile) trail is groomed and patrolled, making it a great place for beginners to practice their snowshoeing chops. The route heads to the left of the lifts from the lodge and climbs stiffly up to the peak of Dam Mountain. On a clear day, stop here and admire the view; on a stormy, foggy, nasty day, continue on the trail, which loops around Dam Mountain, then back to the Grouse Mountain Lodge for a little après-snowshoe.

Diamond Head (Map 22/F4)
Diamond Head is an intermediate backcountry ski touring area that follows the main trail to Elfin Lakes and beyond. In summer, the alpine area is a fragile environment and hikers are bound to the main trail. In winter, the whole area is a playground and some great skiing can be found right near Red Heather Shelter. The Rangers mark the route past the shelter with orange snow poles (below the shelter the trail is fairly obvious through the forest). Snow removal is periodic on the road to the Diamond Head parking lot and you may require a four-wheel drive. This touring area is the most popular ski touring destination in Southwestern BC, with the exception of Hollyburn in Cypress.

Garibaldi Neve Traverse (Map 22/F3)
This moderate route is one of the most popular multi-day skiing trips in the area. The climbs are gentle and there is little in the way of avalanche hazards. The trip crosses a number of glaciers and in times of low snow there are some dangerous crevasses near the Sharkfin. From The Black Tusk Trailhead to the Diamond Head Trailhead is just over 30 km. The trip takes most groups take two or three days.

Grouse Mountain Ski Area (Map 11/E6)
Grouse Mountain is becoming less about the skiing and more about the experience, what with Vancouver's first and only wind turbine (compete in view pod), sleigh rides, ice skating, a sno limo, ziplines, helijets, a wildlife rescue area…oh, yeah, right. And skiing and snowshoeing, too. There are four snowshoeing trails and 26 alpine trails for skiers and snowboarders, serviced by five lifts.

Helm Creek Trail (Map 22/E1–29/F7)
This trail is used to access the alpine meadows east of Black Tusk. Although it is longer than the Black Tusk Trail, it is less crowded. Expect to take at least two days to do a return trip, though a day trip to the Black Tusk Trailhead is possible if you can arrange a shuttle pick-up.

Hemlock Valley Ski Area (Map 14/D6)
Best known for it's small but interesting family downhill area, Hemlock Mountain was closed for a couple years, but has re-opened. The 35 runs are serviced by two chairlifts and two surface lists. There are 7 km (3.6 miles) of cross-country trails here, as well as random snowshoeing. The trails wander around and sometimes through the village at the base of the hill. There are also old logging roads in the area for folks looking to do some easy backcountry exploration. The ski trails are not groomed or track-set, but there still is a trail fee.

Hollyburn Mountain Cross-Country Trails (Map 11/B6)
In the winter, this popular hiking area becomes a popular ski destination for all types of skiers. Cypress maintains a popular cross country ski area (see above), but for folks wanting to learn the basics of ski touring, this is also a popular destination. Trips in this area don't usually last more than a day and there are many routes to choose from.

Knucklehead Recreation Area (Map 19/F2)
This is a popular winter recreation area, accessed beyond the Stillwater Mainline. The area can be accessed in the summer for hiking and bicycling, but has become an extremely popular winter destination in the past few years. It is possible to do this as a day trip, but why not spend the night at the warming hut? From here, you can do a number of day trips into the area.

Lost Lake Cross-Country Area (Map 29/G5)
Nestled amongst the trees at the base of Blackcomb Mountain, this 32 km (19.5 mile) series of trails are some of the best cross-country skiing in the province. The amenities are pure Whistler—water stations, a warming hut, lessons and of course, rentals—the views of the surrounding mountains (at times, the trails break out into flat, wide, open areas, which in summer are golf courses) are breathtaking and the (daily) grooming impeccable. The trails are well signed and rated from novice to expert. There's even 2.5 km (1.5 miles) of trail around Lost Lake lit for night skiing. There are also snowshoe trails located in the same area.

Magnesia Meadows (Map 11/B4)
One of the few open alpine meadows this close to the highway, the route to Magnesia Meadows is mostly along old logging roads. The meadows are tucked in behind Mount Harvey. There is a shelter at the head of Magnesia Creek.

Manning Park Resort (Map 7/C6)
Located between the Manning Park Lodge and the downhill area, the Manning Park Cross-Country Ski Trails are a favourite getaway for many Vancouver cross-country skiers. The trails weave in and out and up and down the rolling forested hills around Lightening Lake. The 30 km (18.3 miles) of groomed trails include 17 km (10.4 miles) groomed for skating. There are also many backcountry routes in the area, from skiing the 3 km (1.8 miles) to the end of Lightening Lake, to some serious climbs up to the ridge of the Three Brothers (to the north of the highway). The family orientated downhill area at Gibson Pass features 140 skiable acres, with two dozen marked trails and four lifts. If you plan to make a weekend trip and stay at the resort, it is best to plan early.

McGillivray Pass/Whitecap Alpine (Map 42/F7)
Whitecap Alpine is now operating out of the classic McGillivray Pass Lodge, one of the most popular ski touring destinations in the mountains south of Gold Bridge. The area started gaining popularity in the 1950s, but really became popular once the lodge was built in 1972. For the past twenty years, the Andrews Family has operated Whitecap Alpine out of the lodge, offering heli-skiing adventures to the local peaks. DIYers can still ski in from Bralorne along the Kingdom Lake Road and stay at the lodge, making trips to Whitecap Mountain, Mount McGillivray, Mount Piebiter and Prospector Ridge, among others. Most people who tour this area, however, do so with Whitecap Alpine.

Meslillooet Mountain (Map 12/B3)
The Meslillooet Icefield is the closest glacier to Vancouver, just north of Indian Arm. However, getting to the icefield is a bit of an adventure, as there is no easy road access. Rather, it is off a long trip north up Highway 99, then backtracking southeast along the Mamquam and Stawamus-Indian Forest Roads. An alternate approach would be via boat up Indian Arm and then hike/ski in along the Hixon Creek Forest Road. Give yourselves at least three days for either option.

Mount Bishop (Map 11/G5)
Mount Elsay and Mount Bishop are the two big summits in behind Mount Seymour. These mountains are accessed from the Mount Seymour Trail at Brocton Point. Many people just stay in the Mount Elsay area, but it is possible, in good snow conditions, to make it to Mount Bishop beyond. There is a cabin near Elsay Lake, but this intermediate trip can be done in a day.

Mount Sedgewick (Map 21/G6)
Mount Sedgewick is located on the west side of Howe Sound, past Mount Roderick on the Mount Roderick Trail. Give yourselves at least two days to explore this moderately difficult area. Access to the area is via the Woodfibre Ferry, just south of Squamish.

Needle Peak Trail (Map 16/D1)
This challenging route climbs over 2 km (6,889 ft) to the summit of this popular route. There are a couple exposed areas near the top, which might prove too much for some, but there is an alternate route to a small lake just below the peak for those not comfortable with the exposure. Much of the climbing happens near the beginning of this 13 km (8 mile) route.

Pemberton Icefield (Map 28, 29, 34, 35)
This huge icefield north of Whistler and east of Pemberton is a backcountry winter sport mecca. The ascents and descents are gentle and a backcountry ski trip here dovetails nicely into the Squamish-Cheakamus Divide (see below), making a good weeklong trip. To ski from the north trailhead to the south trailhead can take as little as three days, but most people take a few more days to explore.

Post Creek Cross-Country Trails (Map 5/E5)
A 7.3km (4.5 mile) cross-country ski trail system with easy and moderate trails, it is recommended to ski these trails in a counter clockwise direction since this is the way the trails are signed. The trails are found adjacent to the Post Creek Recreation Site across from the Chilliwack Lake Road.

Railroad Pass/Icemaker Mountain Area (Map 35/E2–40/F5)
The old fashioned way to do this trip was to ski in and ski out. These days, most people catch a helicopter or bush plane in to Icemaker, stay at the Pebble Hut for a few days and then ski out. Which is not a bad plan as far as things goes. While most people can ski the 40 km (24 miles) down from Icemaker to Railroad Pass in a day, getting up takes most people at least two. The whole area is full of ski touring options, from hardcore mountain skiing to some easy skiing along ungroomed forest service roads.

Roe Creek Ski Route (Map 29/B7)
Roe Creek is the safest and most popular access to the Brew Hut and skiing in the Mount Brew area. The route follows Change Creek and Roe Creek Roads, which can be driven or skied, depending on how much snow there is, to the south. If you have to ski, it adds nearly 10 km (6 miles) to the route. From the actual trailhead, it is 3.6 km (2.1 miles) to Brew Lake. The low, gentle summit of Mount Brew is perfect for ski touring, but most people stay a few days to explore the terrain of the Squamish/Cheakamus Divide.

Seymour Mountain (Map 11/G7)
For alpine skiers and snowboarders, there are 39 named runs and 200 skiable acres, including three terrain parks. The area is serviced by five lifts and considered by many the premier snowboarding area of the three local hills. The official Seymour snowshoeing trails lay to the east of the parking lot, between the Mystery Peak Chairlift and the Goldie Rope Tow. There are ten short trails, ranging from 0.1 km to 1 km (.05 to .5 mile). These add up to 5.5 km (3.4 miles) of trails, mostly in the beginner to intermediate range. But there are other, more challenging, places you can go on snowshoes and backcountry skis. For instance, you can follow a trail from the parking lot along the left-hand edge of the ski area boundary, all the way to the top of the mountain. It is a 10 km (6.1 mile) return trek with a fairly stiff uphill climb all the way to the top. Expect to take about four hours to the top; another two if you want to follow the ridge along the three pump routes. On a clear day, the views are worth the effort. An easier trail runs up the mountain to the right of the ski lifts. This route is also popular with backcountry skiers.

Singing Pass Trail (Map 29/G6–30/A6)
Access to Singing Pass is via Fitzsimmons Creek, which flows between Whistler and Blackcomb Mountains. This is a moderate route, with a good cabin at the north end of Russet Lake, maintained by the BCMC. This trip can easily be done in a day, but the whole joy of this area is exploring the slopes behind Whistler Mountain. Avid skiers spend days on end up here enjoying the wide variety of terrain.

winteradventures

Sky Pilot (Map 11/D1)
At the base of Sky Pilot Mountain (the highest summit in the area) is an area of rolling basins and fine sub alpine skiing. This area is well suited for easy day trips, although the BCMC maintain a locked cabin near Mountain Lake for overnight excursions. This area is reached fairly easily off the Stawamus-Indian Forest Road, although access on this road is currently closed to the public.

Snowcap Lake Route (Map 24/A4–23/E3)
Most of the terrain in Garibaldi Park is accessed from the west side, which means that those people willing to take the extra effort will find more peace and solitude on the east side of the big park. Snowcap Lake is one such location. Allow about three days from logging roads off the Lillooet Lake Road to access the lake. The route isn't as high as some and so it must be done in late winter/early spring. The route does cross over the Icemantle Glacier and the 2,370 metre (7,702 foot) Greenmantle Mountain. From here, longer, more difficult trips can be made to Thunderclap Glacier, Misty Glacier and Stave Glacier, deep in the untrammelled heart of Garibaldi Park.

Snowspider Mountain Area (Map 31/C2–37/B6)
Located in the high mountains above Lillooet Lake, Snowspider Mountain is a great weekend trip. Although the trip can be done in two or three days from the Van Horlick Creek Road, arguably the best approach is to ski up Cerise Creek from the Duffy Lake Road.

Squamish-Ashlu Divide (Map 28/C6–21/E1)
Also known as the Ashlu-Elaho Divide, this area is heavily glaciated and is a great ski touring terrain. The divide is best accessed from the southwest, along an unnamed creek west and slightly south of Porterhouse Peak, though the road is not usually passable until early May. Expect to take about three days to reach the south trailhead on logging roads just off Branch A-700.

Squamish-Cheakamus Divide (Map 29/A3–22/B1)
One of the most popular multi-day trips in the area, the Squamish-Cheakamus Divide was built for ski touring with easy climbs and some great descents. The moderate trip is generally best done from Callaghan Lake south to Tricouni Meadows. The four day route hooks up with other trails, including the Brandywine and Metal Dome Route as well as Brew Mountain and Roe Creek. These other access points allow people to shorten the trip.

Spearhead Traverse (Map 29/G6–30/B7)
This route follows the string of glaciers behind Blackcomb Mountain deep into the heart of Garibaldi Provincial Park. The area is a popular heli-skiing destination and you may even see snowshoers in the area. The traverse is best done clockwise, starting at the Blackcomb Ski Area, along the Blackcomb, Decker, Trorey, Tremor, Platform and Fitzsimmons Glaciers, then south to Overlord Mountain. The loop takes you back to Whistler Mountain, either via the Singing Pass Trail or over the Musical Bumps. This moderate route will take most parties three days, although bad weather can extend the length of this trip.

Stein Divide (Map 31/A3–32/F6)
Give yourself at least a week to ski this route that is as challenging as it is rewarding. The route starts from Lizzie Creek Forest Road, most likely where it meets the In-Shuck-Ch Forest Road. The route follows the road and then the hiking route to Cherry Pip Pass. Once in the alpine, experienced route finders can head farther south, past Figure Eight Lake and onto Mount Skook Jim. From here, the route heads east onto the Rutledge Glacier, past Longslog Mountain, eventually meeting logging roads that head up Log Creek.

Tantalus Range (Map 22/A4)
The Tantalus Range does not offer good winter ski routes, as the mostly up and down construction makes this a place for mountaineers, not ski touring. However, from the ACC hut at Lake Lovely Water, there are a couple of good destinations, including Mount Pelops and Mount Niobe. These trips are fairly strenuous and shouldn't be undertaken by the inexperienced.

Tetrahedron Plateau/Mount Steele Area (Map 10/B2)
At 1,738 metres (5,699 feet), Tetrahedron Peak is the highest on the Sunshine Coast. The surrounding area makes for an easy to moderate ski touring destination with lots of gentle, rolling terrain and some good downhill skiing from either Mount Steele or Panther Peak. The popular area has a well-established trail system and four cabins from which to base camp.

Wedge Mountain (Map 30/B4)
Wedge Mountain is the highest peak in Garibaldi, rising some 2,905 metres (9,441 feet) above sea level. Although the mountain can be scrambled up, the real appeal of this trip is the series of glaciers (Weart, Needle and Chaos) north and east of the peak. Give yourself at least two days to explore. The BCMC maintains a cabin at Wedgemount Lake. It is also possible to access this area from Blackcomb Mountain to the south via Wedge Pass.

Wedge-Currie Traverse (Map 30/B4–D2)
This difficult route follows the Weart Glacier north onto the Hibachi Ridge, which straddle the Garibaldi Park border. From here, experienced route finders can make their way to Mount Currie and out along Gravell Creek.

Whistler Blackcomb Ski Area (Map 29/F6)
With over 8,000 skiable acres, one vertical mile of elevation and more than 200 trails, Whistler Blackcomb is the embodiment of everything that is best and worst in BC skiing. When the snow is right, there is no better place to be anywhere. And when you're out on the mountain, you can ignore the tourist trappings that have built up around the resort. Or you can embrace them, if that's your style. One thing you can't ignore, though, is the people. The 38 lifts shared between the two mountains can move over 65,500 people an hour and there are days when it seems the lifts are at capacity. In addition to downhill skiing and boarding, the resort offers five terrain parks, a super pipe, a snow cross track, 17 on-mountain restaurants and one of the best nightlife scenes in the country.

Whistler Olympic Park (Map 29/C4)
This new Olympic venue opened to the public in 2009 and offers over 95 km (59 miles) of cross-country skiing. Well, not quite. Only 55 km (34 miles) are in the Olympic Park. The rest are located in Callaghan Country Wilderness Adventure located next door, although the trail systems do interlock. The trails are groomed both classic and skate and trails rate from beginner friendly to routes that are designed for Olympic-level athletes. This venue is decked out with all the bells and whistles, including one of the nicest cross-country skiing day lodges around. There are some easy snowshoe trails, but the longer trails are found in Callaghan Country.

Zoe Peak Trail (Map 16/E1)
Zoe Peak is a popular destination in both summer and winter, probably the most popular in the Coquihalla Summit area. It offers a relatively little amount of climbing (635 m/2,083 ft) across its 11 km (6.8 mile) return distance. The trail passes through a gradually thinning forest onto the ridge up to Zoe.

Zupjok-Alpaca Ridge (Map 16/D1)
Offering some gorgeous scenery and the occasional unexploded avalanche control shell, this route is not frequented very often. The trip to Alpaca Peak is 18.2 km (11.3 miles) return, gaining 1,220 m (4,000 feet) as it makes its way up to the top. The route is challenging, and involves a fair bit of climbing, with an average grade of just over 9%. A shorter, easier route would be to turn around at Zupjok Peak, which cuts the distance and elevation gained in half. The route starts along the old Ottormite Mountain Road, but you will have to head off-trail to follow the obvious ridge up the peak. The trail is usually well flagged.

SNOWMOBILING

While it might seem a foreign concept in temperate Vancouver, snowmobiling is quite popular further out in the Fraser Valley and along the Sea to Sky Highway. In fact, places like Pemberton and Gold Bridge have a well deserved reputation for sledding fun. As always, this is not a complete list, but an introduction to some of the most popular snowmobiling areas.

Allen Creek Snowmobile Trails (Map 45/C1)
Off Highway 97 south of Clinton, experienced snowmobilers can ride the popular route into a vast alpine area.

Brandywine Mountain Snowmobile Area (Map 29/B5)
The Brandywine area is the most popular area around Whistler, with an average of 100 people starting from either end of the so-called Around the World Trail. With the upcoming Olympics, entry via the Callaghan (see below) may be restricted, so the local snowmobile club is improving access from the Brandywine area. The main trail is about 40 km (25 miles). There is access to the Pemberton Icefield and the Powder Mountain area. There is a fee to ride here.

Brohm Ridge (Map 22/D4)
Snowmobilers are not allowed into Garibaldi Provincial Park, but this ridge just outside the park is a good approximation of the terrain and scenery inside the boundaries. This is also a busy area for ski touring and in spring, this is a popular backcountry destination for snowboarders, who like to build big half pipes here. The Black Tusk Snowmobile Club leases two chalets in the area and provides a trail maintenance service. There is a fee to ride here.

Burke Mountain (Map 2/C1–12/D7)
When and if snow is available, riding in the Burke Mountain area starts from the first gate on Harper Road. The area consists of various old logging roads that lead up to Dennett and Munro Lakes.

Callaghan Lake Provincial Park (Map 29/C4)
Snowmobiles are allowed on the Callaghan Forest Road through the park to Callaghan Lake. From here, they can make their way across the lake and along a designated trail to a series of bowls outside the park and on to the Pemberton Icefield. Access this way may close soon. Even now, travel through this area is restricted when there is water on the ice of Callaghan Lake. Not just because of safety (although that's a big part of it), but because machines have a habit of stalling and spitting oil into the water.

Chance Creek Snowmobile Area (Map 22/B2–29/B5)
This difficult route follows the Chance Creek Forest Road in behind Tricouni Peak to the Seagram Creek area. The first section is mostly road riding and isn't too difficult. The difficult part is heading up Roe Creek, past Mount Fee to connect up with the Brandywine Mountain Area (see above). There is limited parking here.

Coquihalla Lakes Snowmobile Area (Map 16/G1–17/D3)
The Coquihalla Lakes Lodge is the main access point into this popular area. They even offer special rates for visitors who are members of the Cheam Whiskey Jacks Club of Chilliwack. Trails head north and south (see Thynne Mountain below), but the main trails head southeast from the lakes and can be ridden all the way to Tulameen and beyond.

Cypress Bowl (Map 11/B7)
Although Cypress bowl is best known as a ski area in winter, there are a trio of trails, totalling over 15 km (9.2 miles) for snowmobilers. The riding area is below the ski area, but when ski conditions are good on top, it doesn't necessarily mean good riding below.

Gray Creek Area (Map 10/A2)
Snowmobilers can drive up the Gray Creek Road to the Tetrahedron Provincial Park Parking lot. Snowmobiles aren't allowed in the park itself but heading left takes riders away from the park along the 600 Road and into some good riding that skirts the edge of the park.

Hurley Forest Service Road (Map 35/E3–42/B4)
For the past few years, Backcountry Snowcats has been grooming the Hurley Forest Service Road from Meager Creek to the Hope Creek Turnoff. Picking up on the theme, Bruce, the owner of the Bralorne Bar, has picked up his own groomer and has begun grooming the road all the way to Bralorne. This route has always been used to access some of BC's best snowmobiling areas, including Lone Goat and Noel, but now riders can go to Bralorne without having to go the long way around.

Lodestone Snowmobile Trails (Map 17/D3–C7)
The Lodestone Snowmobile Trails are accessed about a kilometre northeast of Blakeburn near the community of Coalmont. From here, the trails head up to Mount Jackson near Tulameen, Tanglewood Hill or over to Lodestone Lake. There's close to 100 km (60 miles) of trails in the area.

Lone Goat Snowmobile Area (Map 41/F6–C5)
A sprawling area, known for alpine bowls, snow caves and light, fluffy powder, there are about 115 km (70 miles) of trails to explore in this area. The trails are best left to intermediate and expert riders. The Bridge River Snowmobile Club maintains an emergency shelter in the area.

Mount Crucil Snowmobile Area (Map 10/A2)
North of Sechelt, a series of forest service roads head up to Tetrahedron Provincial Park. South of this road is the Mount Crucil Area, about three quarters of the way to the park. This area usually offers the best and most consistent riding on the Sunshine Coast. While it isn't huge, there is enough terrain to keep riders busy for a nice half-day ride.

Noel Snowmobile Area (Map 41/A7–42/B6)
In Upper Noel Creek you will find a rolling alpine country with a beautiful 46 metre (150 foot) high glacier. This terrain is recommended for intermediate and advanced riders. In all, there are about 80 km (50 miles) worth of trails to explore.

North Air Mine Snowmobile Area (Map 29/D5)
This is a small but extremely difficult area around the North Air Mine Road. It's only about 10 km (6 miles) from the road to Sproatt Mountain, but it should be left to expert riders only.

Pemberton Icefield (Map 28, 29, 34, 35)
The Pemberton Icefield is a winter mecca, a seemingly endless area of ice and snow that is popular with snowmobilers and backcountry skiers. A new winter trail up the Rutherford Valley, developed by the Pemberton Valley Snowmobile Club, is the best access to the icefield. Alternatively, riders like to access the area from Meager Creek. Excellent conditions exist between December and April.

Slim Creek Snowmobile Area (Map 41/F2–A2)
The vast, open expanses of the Slim Creek area can be accessed from the north end of Gun Lake. Climbing as high as 2,700 metres (9,000 feet), you can ride all day here without crossing your tracks. You can cover up to 200 km or more in a day, so bring extra gas. Be wary, this is an area for experienced riders only. It is also a terrible place to be in a snowstorm. It is easy to get lost in the wide open terrain, especially if you can't follow your tracks back.

Spipiyus Provincial Park (Map 9/C1)
While snowmobiles aren't allowed in most provincial parks, they are allowed on the road in Spipiyus, which makes a nice loop. It isn't a long ride and you aren't allowed off the road.

Taylor Basin (Map 42/A1)
Taylor Basin is an excellent alpine area to play in. In addition to a warming cabin at the 2,000 metre (6,600 foot) level, there are two mountain slopes that climbing up to 2,460 metres (8,000 feet) in elevation. This area is open to all skill levels, but the higher slopes are best left to intermediate and expert riders. Expect to put on up to 100 km (60 miles) as you play around on these open slopes.

Thynne Mountain Snowmobile Trails (Map 27/G6)
In the winter, the area around Thynne Mountain and Mount Henning becomes an extensive series of snowmobile trails. The Merritt Snowmobile Club maintains the 55 km (33.5 miles) of trails around Thynne Mountain, while the Cheam Whiskey Jacks Club of Chilliwack maintains the 50 km (30.5 miles) of trails around Mount Henning. A 7.5 km (4.6 mile) trail links the two systems.

Upper Lillooet Area (Map 34/F2–40/E7)
When the snow falls and the roads remain unploughed, there are seemingly endless places for sledders. In particular, the 45 km (27.5 mile) trip along Upper Lillooet and Meager Creek Forest Roads north of Pemberton is a popular route for beginners. There are a number of alternate routes in this area for snowmobilers to explore. Avalanche Hazards exist in some areas, especially along Meager Creek.

BCFerries

BC Ferries vessels serve up to 47 ports of call throughout coastal British Columbia including major links between the mainland and Vancouver Island and routes linking coastal island communities.

Mainland – Vancouver Island

F1 Vancouver – Victoria (Tsawwassen – Swartz Bay)
Crossing time: 1 hr 35 minutes
Schedule: Minimum of 8 round trips daily. Summer service provides up to 16 round trips daily. Extra sailings are added during other holiday periods and peak weekends.

F2 Vancouver – Nanaimo (Tsawwassen – Duke Point)
Crossing time: 2 hrs
Schedule: 6 round trips daily

F3 Vancouver – Nanaimo (Horseshoe Bay – Departure Bay)
Crossing time: 1 hr 35 minutes
Schedule: 8 round trips daily, with extra sailings during holiday periods

F4 Powell River – Comox (Westview – Little River)
Crossing time: 1 hr 35 minutes
Schedule: 4 round trips daily

F5 Saanich Peninsula (Brentwood Bay – Mill Bay)
Crossing time: 25 minutes
Schedule: 8 round trips daily

Northern routes

F6 Inside Passage (Port Hardy – Prince Rupert)
Summer schedule: mid-May through September, ship travels northbound from Port Hardy to Prince Rupert one day, returns southbound the following day.
Crossing time: 15 hrs

Other times of the year, the ship also serves the mid-coast communities of Bella Bella, Shearwater, Ocean Falls and Klemtu. Crossing time and schedules vary.

F7 Discovery Coast Passage (Port Hardy, Bella Bella, Klemtu, Ocean Falls, Bella Coola)
This summer service offers direct service between Port Hardy and Bella Coola, as well as extended tours with stops at mid-coast communities. Crossing time and schedules vary.

F8 Queen Charlotte Islands (Prince Rupert – Skidegate)
Crossing time: 8 hrs
Summer schedule: minimum of 4 sailings per week from each port. Other times of the year: 3 sailings per week from each port

Northern Gulf Islands

F9 Vancouver Island – Denman Island (Buckley Bay – Denman Is.)
Crossing time: 10 minutes
Schedule: 16 round trips daily

F10 Denman Island – Hornby Island (Gravelly Bay – Shingle Spit)
Crossing time: 10 minutes
Schedule: minimum 10 round trips daily

F11 Vancouver Island – Quadra Island (Campbell River – Quathiaski Cove)
Crossing time: 10 minutes
Schedule: minimum 16 round trips daily

F12 Quadra Island – Cortes Island (Heriot Bay – Whaletown)
Crossing time: 45 minutes
Schedule: 5 round trips daily

F13 Vancouver Island – Malcolm Island – Cormorant Island (Port McNeill, Sointula, Alert Bay)
Crossing time: varies
Schedule: approximately 6 departures from each port

Sunshine Coast

F14 Vancouver – Sechelt (Horseshoe Bay – Langdale)
Crossing time: 40 minutes
Schedule: 8 round trips daily with extra sailings during holiday periods

F15 Jervis Inlet (Earls Cove – Saltery Bay)
Crossing time: 50 minutes
Schedule: 8 round trips daily

F16 Powell River – Texada Island (Westview – Blubber Bay)
Crossing time: 35 minutes
Schedule: 10 round trips daily

F17 Vancouver – Bowen Island (Horseshoe Bay – Snug Cove)
Crossing time: 20 minutes
Schedule: 14 round trips daily

Southern Gulf Islands

F18 Vancouver – Southern Gulf Islands (Tsawwassen Galiano Island, Mayne Island, Pender Island, Sa Spring Island and Saturna Island)
Routes, schedules and crossing times vary, with t scenic round trips on weekdays and more sailing weekends and during the summer.

F19 Vancouver Island – Southern Gulf Islands (Swar to Pender Island, Saturna Island, Mayne Island, Galiano Island)
Routes, schedules and crossing times vary, with approximately 6 departures from Swartz Bay on weekdays, and more on weekends and during sum

F20 Vancouver Island – Salt Spring Island (Swartz B Fulford Hbr.)
Crossing time: 35 minutes
Schedule: minimum of six round trips daily

F21 Vancouver Island – Salt Spring Island (Crofton – Vesuvius Bay)
Crossing time: 20 minutes
Schedule: minimum of 9 round trips daily

F22 Vancouver Island – Thetis Island – Kuper Island (Chemainus, Thetis, Kuper)
Crossing time: 35 minutes
Schedule: minimum of 10 round trips daily

F23 Vancouver Island – Gabriola Island (Nanaimo Harbour – Descanso Bay)
Crossing time: 20 minutes
Schedule: 15 round trips daily

Check with BC Ferries for current schedule and fare information, travel tips, directions ferry terminals, and for vehicle reservation: available on certain routes:
www.bcferries.com, toll-free within North America at 1-888-223-3779 or 250-386-3431 outside North America.

www.bcferries.com

To the Alaska Highway

37

ALASKA

Smithers

Terrace

Prince Rupert

16

Masset

Kitimat

Yellowhead Highway

Prince George

Skidegate
Sandspit

Alliford Bay

To Jasper 16

*QUEEN
CHARLOTTE
ISLANDS*

FIORDLAND
RECREATION
AREA

Quesnel

Klemtu

97

Ocean Falls

Anahim Lake

20

Bella
Coola

Nimpo
Lake

McLoughlin Bay
Bella Bella

Hagensborg

Shearwater
Denny Island

Puntzi Lake

Williams
Lake

Namu

HAKAI
RECREATION
AREA

Tatla Lake

Alexis Creek

BRITISH COLUMBIA

24

97

Lillooet

1   Banff

Kamloops

Salmon Arm

Duffy Lake Road

Pemberton

Port Hardy   Sointula

Port
McNeill   Alert Bay

VANCOUVER ISLAND

19

Vernon

Merritt

Kelowna

5

99

Whistler

Quadra
Island   Cortes
Island

Campbell
River

19A

Powell
River   Saltery
Bay

Earls
Cove

Princeton

Hope

3

101

Comox

Texada
Island

Langdale

Bowen
Island   Horseshoe Bay

Harrison
Hot Springs

7

Denman
Island

Hornby
Island   19A

Vancouver

1

Port Alberni   4

19A

Tofino

Port Alberni   4

Departure
Bay

19   Nanaimo
Duke Point

Tsawwassen   *CANADA*
U.S.A.

Uncluelet

Chemainus

1

Southern
Gulf Islands
(See inset map)

Bellingham

Port Renfrew

Mill
Bay   Swartz
Bay

5

14

Brentwood
Bay

Sooke   *Victoria*

WASHINGTON

Seattle

Sunshine Coast

Kenay/Comox   Westview

Little River

Powell
River   Saltery Bay

Port
Alberni   Qualicum
Beach   Earls Cove

Texada
Island   Gibsons

Departure Bay   Langdale

NANAIMO   Horseshoe
Bay

Duke Point   Bowen Island

Ladysmith   Gabriola
Island

Chemainus   Thetis Island

VANCOUVER

Crofton   Kuper Island

Duncan   Vesvius

Galiano
Island

Saltspring
Island   Tsawwassen

*VANCOUVER
ISLAND*

Mill Bay   Mayne
Island

Pender
Island

Saturna
Island

SWARTZ BAY

Brentwood
Bay

Port Renfrew

VICTORIA

Railroad ◄••••►
Highways
BC Ferries Routes
Alaska Marine Highway

Index

The index location references consist of a **page number** and a letter, number combination. In the example found below the city **Whistler** is found on page **29/F4**.

The grid lines found in the example below are used for illustrative purposes only, the blue grid lines found on the maps refer to UTM coordinates.

IMPORTANT NUMBERS

Avalanche Awareness .... www.avalanche.ca
Emergencies.. 911
Service BC.............................. 1-800-663-7867
BC Ferries ....www.bcferries.com
.... 1-888-223-3779
Highways Report ....www.drivebc.ca
.... 1-800-550-4997
Tourism BC .... www.hellobc.com
.... 1-800-435-5622
Weather Conditions .... www.weatheroffice.ec.gc.ca
Wildfire Information Line 1-888-336-7378
To Report Forest Fires (Emergency Only)..... 1-800-663-5555
.... *5555 (cellular phones)
Updates .... www.backroadmapbooks.com

B.C. Forest Services (Road & Trail Conditions)

Ministry of Forests .... www.sitesandtrailsbc.ca
Coast Forest Region....................... www.for.gov.bc.ca/rco/
.... 250 751-7001
Southern Interior Forest Region .....www.for.gov.bc.ca/rsi/
.... 250-828-4131
Cascades (Merritt) Forest District 250-378-8400
Chilliwack Forest District 604-702-5700
Road Reports ....
...... www.for.gov.bc.ca/dck/Engineering/fsroadconditions.htm
Squamish Forest District 604-898-2100
Road Reports ....
.....www.for.gov.bc.ca/dsq/Engineering/RoadInformation.htm
Sunshine Coast Forest District 604-485-0700

Fish and Wildlife

BC Wildlife Federation...................................www.bcwf.bc.ca
.... 1-888-881-2293
Conservation Officer Service (Report a Violation)
.... 1-800-663-9453
Fishing Information .... www.BCFishing.com
Freshwater Fisheries Society of BC .... www.gofishbc.com
.... 1-800-601-4200
Department of Fisheries and Oceans ....
.... www.pac.dfo-mpo.gc.ca
.... 1-866-431-3474
Observe, Record and Report.......................www.rapp.bc.ca
.... 1-877-952-7277
Sport Fishing Information ....www.sportfishing.bc.ca

Parks

BC Hydro.........................www.bchydro.bc.ca/environment
BC Parks/Ministry of Environment ....www.bcparks.ca
Garibaldi/Sunshine Coast District 604-898-3678
Lower Mainland District (Surrey)................... 604-582-5200
Park Reservations ....www.discovercamping.ca
.... 604-689-9025 or 1-800-689-9025
Fraser Valley Regional District Parks ....604-702-5000 or
.... 1-800-528-0061
Greater Vancouver Regional District Parks...... www.gvrd.bc.ca/parks
.... 604-432-6352
Sunshine Coast Regional District Parks ....www.scrd.ca

Clubs & Associations

ATV BC.. www.atvbc.ca
Backcountry Horsemen of BC.....................www.bchorsemen.org
BC Snowmobile Federation .... www.bcsf.org
Canoe Kayak BC...........................www.canoekayakbc.ca
Clubtread.. www.clubtread.com
Trails BC.......................................www.trailsbc.ca

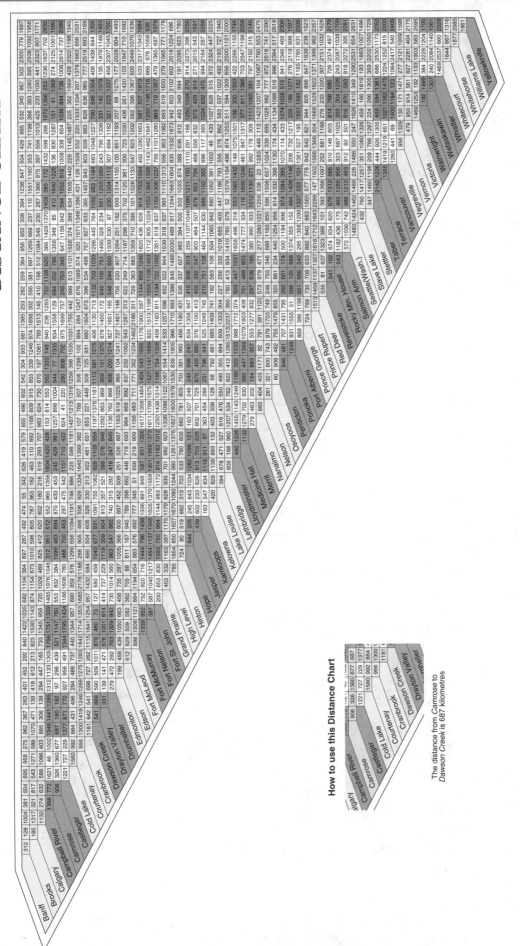

BRITISH COLUMBIA/ALBERTA DISTANCE CHART

How to use this Distance Chart

The distance from *Camrose* to *Dawson Creek* is 687 kilometres

1 Kilometre = 0.621 Mile   1 Mile = 1.6 Kilometres

SPEED CONVERSION CHART

Backroad Mapbooks

...THE START OF EVERY ADVENTURE!!

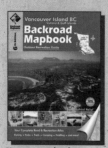

Vancouver Island, Victoria & Gulf Islands BC

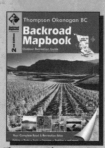

Thompson Okanagan BC

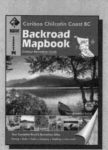

Cariboo Chilcotin BC

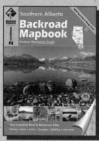

Southern Alberta

Central Alberta

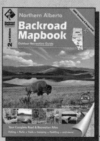

Northern Alberta

Southwestern Ontario

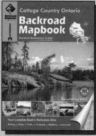

Cottage Country Ontario

Nova Scotia

Testimonials

"One of the most sought after outdoor products in the country."
- *Burnaby Newslead*

"We have found the use of these map books to be invaluable a resource for planning and operating searches."
- **Ken Hruschak**- *Civil Air Search & Rescue Associat*

"These books certainly make our work easier in dealing with pu enquiries when we can refer our clients and the public to this ve reliable mapbook."
- **Teressa McMillan**- *Ministry of Tourism, Culture and the Arts*

The choice for Search and Rescue
When you're counting on them, they're depending on the *Backroad Mapbooks*. Cut out the middle-man, get one for yourself!

Made by users for users
Everyone who works for or with *Backroad Mapbooks* loves to play in the outdoors. Whether you are looking for a popular hike or a seldom-visited fishing hole, we've got you covered.

Accurate & Easy to use maps
You won't find a more up-to-date resource that's easier to use. The maps have the detail needed to get you where you want and don't require a graduate degree in Cartography to understand!

Expert, Local information
Why trust just any book when going outside? Trust the source that uses local writers and researchers to ensure all of our information has that local touch and feel.

Top Selling outdoor guidebook series
Over **800,000** copies of the *Backroad Mapbook* series are found on dashboards across Canada, find out why people just like you have made the *Backroad Mapbook* series the number one guidebook in the country!

A Great way to get outside
Looking for a little motivation to get you out and about, why not pick up the source that shows it all? From local hot spots to remote destinations, we cover more opportunities than you can possibly do in a lifetime.

6 Reasons to love your **Backroad Mapbook**

OTHER PRODUCTS

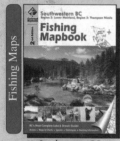

Southwestern BC Fishing Mapbook

Backroad GPS Maps For BC & Alberta

Okanagan Valley British Columbia

British Columbia TOPO Map Series

Published By:

Mussio Ventures Ltd
#106- 1500 Hartley Ave,
Coquitlam, BC, V3K 7A1
P: 604-521-6277
F: 604-521-6260
Toll Free: 1-877-520-5670

...and much more!

For a complete list of titles visit our website or call us toll free **1-877-520-5670**
or visit **www.backroadmapbooks.com**

149